THE SLOW COOK BOOK

THE SLOW COOK  BOOK

HEATHER WHINNEY

LONDON, NEW YORK, MUNICH,
MELBOURNE, and DELHI

Photography Stuart West
Recipe Editor Emma Callery
US Culinary Consultant Wes Martin
US Editors Rebecca Warren, Shannon Beatty

DK UK
Editor Shashwati Tia Sarkar
Senior Art Editor Sara Robin
Managing Editor Dawn Henderson
Managing Art Editor Christine Keilty
Senior Jackets Creative Nicola Powling
Production Editor Tony Phipps
Senior Production Controller Alice Sykes
Creative Technical Support Sonia Charbonnier

DK INDIA
Senior Editor Chitra Subramanyam
Art Editor Heema Sabharwal
Assistant Editor Tina Jindal
Managing Editor Glenda Fernandes
Managing Art Editor Navidita Thapa
DTP Manager Sunil Sharma
DTP Operator Sourabh Challariya

First American Edition, 2011

Published in the United States by

DK Publishing

375 Hudson Street

New York, New York 10014

11 12 13   10 9 8 7 6 5 4 3 2 1
001 – 180673 – September/2011

Published in Great Britain by Dorling Kindersley Limited.

A catalog record for this book is available from the Library
of Congress.

ISBN 978-0-7566-8678-9

DK books are available at special discounts when purchased
in bulk for sales promotions, premiums, fund-raising, or
educational use. For details, contact: DK Publishing Special
Markets, 375 Hudson Street, New York, New York 10014 or
SpecialSales@dk.com.

Printed and bound by Tien Wah Press, Singapore

Discover more at
www.dk.com

Contents

Note:
All the recipes in this book are written for the medium size range of slow cookers, from a minimum of 3.5 quarts (3.5 liters) to 5 quarts (5 liters) capacity. Allowances should be made for the differences within this size range; depending on the internal volume of your slow cooker, liquid quantities may need to be adjusted to ensure the food is covered where necessary.

Foreword

I am generally not a fan of kitchen gadgets, but I have to admit to being a convert to the slow cooker. The thrifty cook in me is thoroughly excited by using the cheaper cuts of meat and beans and pulses that are so suited to slow cooking, while the ease of throwing a collection of ingredients into a pot and letting them do their own thing for hours is enormously attractive—so little effort is needed, but the rewards are great.

Our attitude toward food and cooking is changing. We seem to have a stronger desire to make home-cooked food that nourishes us and our family, as well as reining in our spending. Slow cooking is perfect for meeting this need—it suits every level of cook, especially the novice, as it is a style of cooking that doesn't rely heavily on precision. It's one of the most forgiving cooking techniques, requiring little time or skill from the cook. Moreover, by its very nature, slow cooking isn't an extravagant way to cook. By choosing value cuts and seasonal produce we naturally spend less, and the running costs of a slow cooker are minimal, little more than running a low watt light bulb, consequently conserving energy.

The great benefits of the slow cooker lie in its convenience and versatility. To be able to simply "set and forget" the slow cooker has enormous advantages for our hectic lives—it can sit day or night unattended. It ticks all the boxes for such a wide range of people: those cooking for one, large families, busy moms, and it's ideal for entertaining as it makes dinner party cooking a breeze. It can be used not only for casseroles and stews, but also to cook whole joints of meat, delicate risottos, and delicious soups. It can also be used as a water bath or bain-marie for puddings and desserts, from mousses to steamed cakes.

The practical nature of slow cooking greatly appeals to me. It lends itself to cooking in large batches, and I love being able to cook up something delicious to serve one day and perhaps freeze for another. It is extremely satisfying to know there is the option of leftovers, thus relieving that sometimes niggling pressure of knowing what we are going to cook for dinner the next night. Of course it requires some planning, as does all cooking, but through this it also reduces food waste, which I feel passionately about. Again, the thrifty cook in me rearing its head!

Although we always think of simmering pots of meat and vegetables when slow cooking is mentioned, I think it is fair to say that the slow cooker isn't just for cold winter days. In fact, it is ideal in summer, for maybe a curry or ribs, when you don't want the heat of the stove on all day. I've tried to reflect this throughout the book so you can always find inspiration as you dip in and out throughout the seasons. To me, Creole Fish and Corn Stew or Squid Stew would be just as welcome served up on a warm summer's evening with a hunk of crusty bread and some cold rosé wine as the Stuffed Lamb, Greek Style would be on a fresh spring day.

This book contains more than 200 recipes for slow cooking. It includes a mixture of world cuisines, features many classics, and offers some new adventurous flavor combinations. Chapters cover Soups and Broths; Stews; Casseroles, Cassoulets, and Meatballs; Tagines; Curries; Chilis and Gumbos; Pot Roasts and Ribs; Risottos, Pilafs, and Paellas; and a Desserts chapter that includes favorites such as rice pudding and crème caramel.

Step-by-step photographs take you through the types of slow cooking from stewing to poaching as well as the principles of slow cooking. A comprehensive list is also given for the slow cook's pantry, as a well-stocked pantry is a great asset; once you have this, you need shop for little else but the perishables.

I hope this book inspires you to experiment with slow cooking. Let your imagination conjure up the thought of Beef and Anchovy Stew, the beef nestling in a mixture of heady red wine and robust herbs, cooked to perfection until it melts in your mouth; or a slow-cooked pork dish such as Belly Pork and Prunes cooked with earthy celery root and sage, and simmered slowly in a little wine until the pork falls apart at the touch of your fork. Just the thought of it makes me want to head off into the kitchen and reach for my apron!

Heather Whinney

Techniques

Slow cooking is ideal for many households, from the time-poor cook's to the frugal one's. Food can be left unattended, less expensive ingredients can be used, and it delivers a nutritious meal at the end of the day.

Why slow cook?

Slow cooking is a method of cooking food slowly, as the name suggests, but not all food that is cooked slowly can be defined as "slow cook." To "slow cook" means that ingredients are cooked for a long time at a low heat, in a cooking pot with a fitted lid, and either covered or partially covered in liquid. Stews, casseroles, and pot roasts are all examples of slow cook dishes, and all are satisfyingly simple to make.

Prep and forget

Any cooking involves a certain amount of preparation, but with slow cooking this is kept to a minimum, as practically all the labor takes place early on in the cooking process. Once the food is in the cooking pot, it can be left to its own devices, requiring minimal attention from you. However, planning your meals and organizing your shopping list is essential—it will enable you to assemble a dish effortlessly.

Maximize flavor

When left to slow cook, ingredients "marry" together and the flavors intensify. When meat is slow cooked, the gelatin is extracted from the meat and bones, resulting in a flavorful, concentrated sauce; it is this exchange of flavors between the meat and the sauce that gives slow cooking its wonderful rich but mellow taste. Aromatic vegetables and spices such as cloves, cinnamon, and star anise are great to use as their distinct flavors are not lost when used in slow cooked dishes.

Be thrifty

Slow cooking makes economic sense as it works best using cheaper cuts of meat that have high bone and fat content, and inexpensive staples such as beans and lentils. It is also easy to cook a large quantity of food at once, creating leftovers for another day or food for the freezer. Slow cooking is also an opportunity to be creative and make meals out of very little—long, gentle cooking will turn the remnants of your refrigerator or pantry into a feast.

Tips for success

Choosing the right equipment and using your ingredients with a little know-how will help you achieve great results from slow cooking.

For traditional slow cooking, choose a thick-walled Dutch oven that holds the heat well, such as a cast iron one or an enameled cast-iron one. Ensure it has a well fitting lid and can be used on the stove or in the oven. Cast-iron Dutch ovens can be heavy, so choose one with two easy-to-hold handles. Pick a size to suit your requirements: as a rule of thumb, food should only reduce down to about three-quarters of the pot's volume once cooked from full.

Moroccan tagines, cone-shaped earthenware cooking pots with tall lids, are apt for slow cooking. They are designed to return condensation back into the dish to keep the food moist. Choose one that can be used on the stove (with a diffuser) and in the oven.

For maximum flavor, brown the meat at the start of cooking, and soften aromatic vegetables such as onions and garlic by sautéing.

Be careful not to over season; salty flavors become concentrated with slow cooking. Season lightly initially, then adjust at the end of cooking if needed.

Peppercorns and seeds, such as cumin, coriander, and fennel, are best crushed before adding to the pot so they release their flavor slowly.

Woody herbs, such as rosemary and thyme, are robust enough to add at the beginning of cooking; add delicate herbs, such as parsley, toward the end of cooking or stir into the finished dish.

Always add delicate ingredients that don't need much cooking, such as fish and seafood, toward the end of the cooking time.

If topping up the liquid during cooking, add hot liquid to prevent lowering the cooking temperature.

Clockwise from top left: slow cooking lends itself to soothing soups (Pumpkin and ginger soup p86), fresh and light risottos (Risotto primavera p302), hearty casseroles (Osso bucco p162), and summer ribs (Asian ribs p294).

With so many slow cookers on the market it is important that you choose one to suit your needs. There are certain variables, both in terms of design and price, but slow cookers generally operate on similar principles.

The slow cooker

A slow cooker consists of a sturdy, heatproof outer casing and an inner cooking pot into which the food is placed. The outer casing is made of either stainless steel or aluminum and is where the heating element and controls are housed. The inner cooking pot is usually removable. The lid on a slow cooker fits snugly so that heat cannot escape. The condensation that occurs during the slow, low-heat cooking process gathers around the lip of the pot and creates a water seal. The condensation is then released back into the pot and it is this that keeps the food moist. The combination of a long cooking time and the steam that is created within the pot destroys any bacteria, making it a safe cooking method. It is important to resist the temptation to open the lid to look—this will release heat and break the water seal and you will need to add a further 20 minutes to the cooking time.

Choosing the right shape and size

Slow cookers come in a range of sizes, but small machines start from 1.5 quarts (1.5 liters), which is suitable for 1–2 people; a medium-sized 3.5 quart (3.5-liter) cooker is great for 4 people; for 6 people or more, choose a 5 quart (5-liter) model or larger. However, bigger isn't necessarily better unless you are catering for large numbers or wish to batch cook—you need to half fill a slow cooker for optimum performance, and accommodate it on your kitchen worktop, so choose wisely. Slow cookers can be either round or oval in shape; the choice is down to personal preference. Casseroles, chilis, and curries are all perfect for round cookers but an oval one is preferable if you wish to cook whole joints of meat or chickens and fit in pudding basins or ramekins. The removable inner cooking pots are usually ceramic, but they are also available in cast-aluminum. Ceramic pots are easiest to wash and clean, retain the heat well, and can be served straight to the table. Cast-aluminum pots are lighter and allow you to brown food in them first before cooking. Always choose a slow cooker with recognized safety mark.

Adapting recipes for the slow cooker

You can easily adapt conventional recipes for the slow cooker. Firstly, find a recipe in this book that is similar in style and has similar ingredients, such as the meat cuts, beans, or vegetables. From this you can ascertain the length of cooking time needed. If you are at all worried, leave it to cook for longer—a slow cooker won't boil dry. Secondly, adjust the ingredient quantities to ensure they will all fit in the pot. Finally, as a general guide, halve the liquid in your recipe. This is because the liquid doesn't evaporate in the slow cooker as it does with other methods. You can always top it up if needed, or if you do find yourself with too much, remove the lid and cook on High until the excess liquid has evaporated away. When adapting recipes, bear the following in mind:

The recipe must contain some liquid if going into the slow cooker.

Make sure all frozen ingredients are thawed and meats are thoroughly defrosted before cooking.

If a recipe calls for milk, cream, or sour cream, only add this for the last 30 minutes of cooking. For best results, stir in cream just before serving.

You may need to reduce spices and herbs as their flavor becomes concentrated in the slow cooker.

GENERAL GUIDE TO COOKING TIMES

The table below indicates preferred cooking times, but refer to your manufacturer's instructions.

	Low	High
Meat stews and casseroles	6–8 hours	3–4 hours
Pot roasts	6–8 hours	3–4 hours
Whole chickens	6–8 hours	3–4 hours
Ribs	6–8 hours	n/a
Dried beans	6–8 hours	3–4 hours
Steamed puddings	n/a	3–4 hours

Using the slow cooker

Slow cookers are more efficient than traditional ovens and can help to reduce your fuel bill as they use minimum electricity—often only as much as a low watt light bulb. The vast majority of slow cookers have only 2 or 3 heat settings, making them very easy to use. For best results, the slow cooker should be at least half full but no more than two-thirds full when cooking.

Lid—glass lids allow you to check the food without breaking the water seal.

Inner cooking pot— usually removable to make cleaning easier.

Heat controls—often a simple dial. Some allow you to program the cooking time.

Outer casing—contains the electrical parts. Wipe it with a damp cloth to clean it.

HEAT SETTINGS

The various slow cooker models have different functions for heat settings, but as a rule they all have Low and High. Some also have Auto, Warm, or even Medium settings. Preheating the slow cooker before use raises the temperature of the pot before adding the food. The necessity of doing this differs for each slow cooker so it is advisable to read the manufacturer's instructions for your model.

Low: This is the lowest temperature you can cook at and is ideal for leaving food throughout the day or overnight. It is the best setting for cheaper cuts of meat. Cooking times for Low vary between 6–12 hours. The food will cook at around 200°F (100°C).

High: This setting is around 300°F (150°C), and in general the food cooks between 3–6 hours. As a rule of thumb, the High setting takes half as long as the Low one, so 1 hour on High setting equals 2 hours on Low.

Auto: This setting starts cooking the food on High for 1 hour then reduces it to the Low temperature for the remainder of the cooking time.

Keep warm: This holds the food at a lower temperature than Low to keep it at an ideal heat for serving. Many cookers switch to this setting automatically once the food is cooked. However, do not leave the food standing in the cooker keeping warm for longer than 1–2 hours.

There are various types of slow cooking methods; you can cook dishes traditionally or in a slow cooker. Poaching involves gentle simmering in water, braising is excellent for sealing in flavor before long cooking, stewing produces wonderful sauces where the ingredients have melded together, and pot roasting is ideal for cooking whole joints of meat.

Types of slow cooking

Poaching

The ingredients are immersed in water, then simmered very gently. This is good for both delicate meats, such as fish or chicken breast, and dense or tough meats, such as beef topside; a clean, silky texture is achieved. A fitted lid is essential for keeping moisture in the pot. Never attempt to rush poaching—hard boiling dries out meat. The traditional method (shown with chicken) is described here, but if using a slow cooker, simplify it by adding the meat, water, and any flavorings to the pot at the beginning.

1 Use enough cold water to cover the meat, then bring the water to a boil. Add a pinch of salt and the meat. Reduce the heat and bring back to a gentle simmer, cover the pan, and poach for 30 minutes.

2 Add vegetables to flavor the stock, such as artichokes, carrots, fava beans, and any other green vegetables you want to include—maybe shredded cabbage or runner beans—and cook for 5–10 minutes until they are tender.

3 To test the chicken for doneness, pierce the thigh to the bone—if the juices run clear it is done, if they are red it is not. Tip the bird slightly as you lift it out of the pan so that the hot stock in its cavity runs back into the pan.

Braising

This technique combines both dry heat and moist heat cooking. The meat, poultry, or vegetables are first seared in hot fat and then cooked slowly in a pan with minimal liquid, just enough to cover. Searing helps to keep the meat succulent. The meat is cut into slightly larger pieces than for stewing. Slightly more expensive cuts can be used for braising, although this technique works just as well with cheap cuts. Braising suits cuts such as brisket, shanks, and oxtail very well. The traditional method steps are shown below, but the process is the same for the slow cooker up to step 3; after the alcohol has evaporated, transfer everything to the slow cooker, pour over the stock, and cook on either setting.

1 Heat the oil in a frying pan over medium-high heat and brown the meat. Let the pieces sit for about 5 minutes until brown underneath, then turn them and cook the other side for another 5 minutes. Remove with a slotted spoon and set aside.

2 Add a mixture of aromatic vegetables, such as carrots, onions, celery, and leeks, stir well with a spatula to collect the meat residue, then cook until the vegetables are browned. Add flavorings, such as thyme, bay leaves, and garlic, and continue to cook for a few minutes more.

3 Put the meat and vegetables in a Dutch oven, pour in some wine, and boil over high heat until nearly evaporated. Add enough stock to cover the meat. Bring to a simmer, cover with the lid, and cook in the oven on a low heat until the meat is tender.

Stewing

The food is simmered fully covered in stock or water, and sometimes wine. This is great for tougher cuts because the connective tissue and fat break down while cooking, releasing gelatinous juices and making the meat tender. For a slow cooker, transfer everything to it at the end of step 3 and finish cooking.

1 Cut the meat into large bite-sized pieces and toss in flour, if you wish (this will help to thicken the stew later). Sear the meat in hot fat and cook for about 5–8 minutes until browned on all sides. Remove and set aside.

2 Add a selection of vegetables and cook for 5 minutes until golden. Remove and set aside. Deglaze the pan with a little stock or wine and return the meat and vegetables with any sturdy herbs, such as rosemary.

3 Pour in any remaining wine and enough stock to cover the contents of the pan completely. Raise the heat and bring to a boil.

4 Reduce the heat to bring to a gentle simmer and cover with the lid. Put in the oven or slow cooker to cook on a low heat for a few hours, until the meat is tender.

Pot roasting

This is essentially a braised dish that uses a whole joint of meat, usually of a tougher cut. Liquid is used to barely cover the meat, and vegetables and herbs are added to the pot. A pot roast is cooked in a covered pot on a low heat in the oven or slow cooker for several hours, until the meat is fork tender. The whole joint is usually browned first as this improves the flavor of the finished dish. If using a slow cooker, transfer everything to it at the end of step 2, pour in the stock, and cook on auto/low.

1 Heat 2 tablespoons of oil in a Dutch oven until very hot. Add the meat (it should sizzle) and brown it well on all sides. Remove the pot from the heat, take out the meat, and discard all but 2 tablespoons of fat from the pot.

2 Return the meat to the pot and add vegetables and herbs of your choice. Pour in some wine and cook on the stove for a few minutes so that the alcohol evaporates.

3 Pour in the stock and stir well. Cook for about 3 hours in a low oven, turning the meat 3 or 4 times, and topping up with more stock if too much liquid evaporates.

Keeping a good pantry makes any style of cooking easier, but it can really come into its own if you are slow cooking. It reduces the need to plan too far ahead so you can cook spontaneously and decrease your shopping trips. The pantry shouldn't be just a place to keep half-open packs and half-used jars; when it is organized well with staple ingredients, you can create meals with only a few fresh additions.

The slow cooking pantry

Flavorings

Pastes, seasonings, and oils contribute vital flavor—a spoonful of Thai curry paste or a dab of French mustard can determine the cuisine of your dish in an instant. Use honeys to adjust the sweetness of a marinade. Both olive oil and sunflower oil are versatile enough to be used at high and low temperatures.

- Tomato paste
- Thai curry paste—red and green
- Assorted mustards
- Black peppercorns—whole and crushed
- Sea salt
- Honey
- Olive oil
- Sunflower oil

Canned and jarred ingredients

An assortment of cans and jars is indispensible for slow cooking. Tomatoes form the base of many stews and ragu dishes, while coconut milk is useful for curries and soups. Choose full-fat varieties of coconut milk, though, as low-fat versions can split on cooking. Canned corn and jarred olives are a great way to add vegetables when you have none in the fridge.

- Tomatoes
- Sun-dried tomatoes
- Coconut milk
- Dried mushrooms
- Anchovies
- Corn
- Pulses
- Olives
- Capers

Grains and pasta

Store a range of pasta shapes and sizes so you can add them to soups or casseroles. They are good for late additions to the pot or to serve as accompaniments, as are noodles. Grains such as rice, pearl barley, or farro are good for slow cooking because they will happily simmer slowly on low heat.

- Rice—basmati, white, and brown
- Risotto rice—arborio or carnaroli
- Pearl barley and farro
- Dried pasta
- Dried noodles—rice and egg

Crushed black peppercorns

Dried mushrooms

Dried pasta

Sauces and stocks

A good selection of sauces and stocks gives you countless options. Use sauces for marinades or for adjusting flavor at the end of cooking. Vinegars can be used to deglaze after browning, adding richness and depth to your dish.

While fresh stock is preferable, powered stock, or bouillon, is an essential item to keep in the pantry if you like to cook without planning too far ahead. Be careful with seasoning, however, when you use powdered stocks—they often contain added salt, so taste your dish first before adding any extra seasoning.

- Soy sauce
- Fish sauce
- Tabasco sauce
- Worcestershire sauce
- Flavored vinegars—white wine, red wine, and cider
- Balsamic vinegar
- Rice wine vinegar
- Powdered stock (bouillon)— vegetable, chicken, and beef

Beans and pulses

All beans and pulses are ideal for slow cooking. They retain their shape and texture if cooked for a long time and they are a good way of adding bulk and protein to a dish. They also keep indefinitely, so there is no fear of them spoiling. Plan ahead, as most pulses need soaking overnight, except lentils, which just need rinsing well. The older the pulses, the longer they will need soaking. For general soaking and cooking times, see page 37.

- Kidney beans
- Cannellini beans
- Navy beans
- Butterbeans
- Black beans
- Black-eyed peas
- Adzuki beans
- Borlotti beans
- Flageolet beans
- Pinto beans
- Chickpeas
- Yellow and green split peas
- Red lentils
- Puy lentils

Spices and dried herbs

Herbs and spices play an important role in slow cooking, especially if cooking cheaper cuts of meat because they can transform a simple dish into something special. It is always advisable to taste at the end of cooking and adjust herbs and spices as necessary.

- Allspice
- Cinnamon—ground and sticks
- Coriander seeds
- Cumin—ground and seeds
- Caraway seeds
- Cardamom pods
- Chile flakes
- Cayenne pepper
- Cloves—ground
- Curry powder
- Fennel seeds
- Ginger—ground
- Juniper berries
- Mustard seeds
- Nutmeg—whole
- Paprika
- Saffron threads
- Star anise
- Turmeric
- Dried oregano

Red wine vinegar

Kidney beans

Star anise

As with any cooking, good ingredients will produce good results, but this doesn't necessarily mean choosing expensive ingredients. Slow cooking enables you to make the best possible food with whatever is available, whether it's a collection of humble root vegetables, a cheap meat cut, or some fresh seafood. All it requires is time and care so it can be cooked to perfection.

Choosing and using ingredients

Vegetables

As a rule, the harder, tougher vegetables respond best to slow cooking because it turns them deliciously sweet and tender. The more delicate vegetables should be added to the pot later so they don't fall apart while cooking.

Gem squash
This small squash is sweeter than the rest of the pumpkin family, with orange flesh inside the tough green skin. Peel using a potato peeler and add to stews or curries.

Pumpkin
These are usually more fibrous and watery than other squash. If sold in pieces, use within a few days as the flesh is more perishable once cut.

Butternut squash
A common variety of winter squash with a smooth, dense flesh, which is sweet and nutty. It will keep for a few weeks in a cool place. Good with lentils or coconut milk-based dishes.

Acorn squash
A mild-flavored squash, slightly sweet, with firm, yellow-orange flesh. To prepare, cut in half, scoop out the seeds, then cut into quarters. Peel and cut to the size you require.

Carrot
Use either finely diced and sautéed with celery and onion to form a flavor base, or sliced to add color and sweetness.

Turnip
The familiar top-shaped turnip is usually purple fading to white at the root. When small, the flavor is sweet and delicate.

Parsnip
The flavor of this creamy-beige root has hints of parsley and carrot, but with a slight sweetness and nuttiness. Use the scrubbed peel with other vegetable trimmings to make a winter vegetable stock.

Beets
The firm, juicy flesh of a beet has an earthy, sweet flavor. It is best cooked with other red vegetables, or those that will absorb the seeping crimson juices.

Celery root
Celery root, or celeriac, has a thick, rough skin that conceals a crisp white flesh. It has a refreshing, slightly herbal flavor, combining the tastes of parsley and parsnip with celery.

Shallot
They look like miniature onions, but shallots have a sweet, flowery flavor that does not overwhelm, and forms a rich flavor base for numerous sauces.

Garlic
Sauté garlic briefly at the beginning of a dish to add a layer of flavor; never cook until browned or it will taste bitter.

Sweet red onion
The juicy crimson and white flesh is noticeably sweet, although pungent when raw. Slow cooking caramelizes the juices and mellows the flavor.

Brown onion
The workhorse of the kitchen, the pungent brown onion is used in numerous savory dishes, raw, fried, braised, stewed, boiled, or roasted.

Sweet potato
These have softer flesh than potatoes so will cook far quicker; add them to slow cooked dishes as a late addition. The taste is sweet, rather like squash.

Potato
Choose waxy potatoes if you want them to hold their shape, or floury ones if you want them to dissolve and thicken the sauce.

New potato
Firm, with waxy flesh, these often don't need peeling and can be added to a dish whole. Use in summer casseroles.

Savoy cabbage
The attractively crinkled leaves are more loosely wrapped round the head than those of other cabbages and are more full-bodied in flavor.

Celery
A kitchen staple, celery makes a great base for casseroles and stews, along with carrot and onion. Trim the base and pull away any stringy bits.

Red cabbage
Offering beautiful, vibrant color, red cabbage is sweeter than white, but the leaves are tougher, so they take longer to cook.

Curly kale
Exceptionally nutritious, the leaves have a rich, meaty flavor and robust texture. Kale will hold together quite well when slow cooked, or it can be added at the end.

Fennel
With its sweet, warm licorice flavor and crisp texture, fennel makes a great vegetable for slow cooking. Either chop finely and sauté first with onion, or roughly chop and add to the pot. The flavor is subtler when cooked.

Poultry

The term "poultry" covers domesticated birds, including chicken, turkey, goose, guineafowl, and duck (farmed duck is classified as game). This most versatile of meats works with most flavors and cooking methods. Whole birds or portions with the bone left in are ideal for slow cooking.

Whole chicken leg
Comprises the thigh and drumstick. A leg joint is good for slow cooking as the meat remains tender and juicy. Perfect for classics such as Coq au vin.

Chicken thigh
Sold skin on or off, bone-in, or boneless. Best with bone in for slow cooking as it keeps the meat tender and the taste is superior. When deboned, they are excellent stuffed and rolled up. Thighs are better than breast for slow cooking.

Whole chicken
These are perfect for poaching in flavored liquid. The flesh becomes tender, moist, and silky and falls off the bone effortlessly. The bones can then be used for stock. Choose free range chicken, if you can, for ethical reasons and taste.

Duck leg
These have a superb flavor and rich dark meat. They take longer to cook than breast meat and have a little more sinew, but this makes them an incredibly tasty choice for slow cooking. Pierce or slash the layer of skin and fat before browning in a pan.

Whole duck
It is better to joint these for slow cooking as they can be fatty. Ducks have a rich, dense meat that is best teamed with citrus fruits or spices that will cut through the fattiness of the meat.

Pork

Almost all pork cuts are suitable for slow cooking, but the cheaper, fattier varieties are the best as they provide the tastiest sauce. They go well with acidic-flavored fruits, woody herbs, earthy vegetables, and lentils.

Pork leg
These are very lean so need careful cooking to prevent them from drying out. To cook as an escalope, leg steaks are beaten out very thinly.

Spare ribs
Trimmed ribs are sold as a rack or individually cut. Indivual ribs are easier to fit into a pot.

Rolled leg joint
Cuts from the lower leg, where the muscles are tougher, are suited to slow cooking. Pork leg meat can be bought cut into bite-sized pieces.

Belly slices
This is a fatty cut from the underside of the belly. Buy in whole pieces or slices. Slow cooking transforms it into tender meat. Goes well with Asian spices, hearty vegetables, or pulses.

Hock
The hock is the joint near the foot and is sometimes called pork knuckle. It is a cheap cut with lots of flavor that requires long and slow cooking.

Beef

There are many beef cuts suited to long slow cooking. These come from the forequarters and are less expensive than the leaner cuts. Choose beef that is a good, dark red color, which has preferably been hung for 21 days. Beef responds well to marinating, because it adds depth of flavor to the finished dish and will tenderize the meat.

Ground beef
Ground beef can be quite fatty but has good flavor. Ground shin needs the longest cooking. Ground steak from the back or leg is the leanest and most tender.

Diced braising steak
Usually lean chuck, blade, or flank. Often sold ground. Braise, casserole, or stew.

Beef shin
Cut from the foreleg, it needs careful trimming. Dice and use for stews and casseroles.

Oxtail
The tail is sold in chunks. The bones enrich sauces with their marrow. Stew, braise, or use in soup.

Brisket
Cut from the underside behind the front leg. Brisket needs long slow cooking because it has a lot of connective tissue, but has great flavor.

Lamb

As with all the best meats for slow cooking, the well-exercised parts of the animal make the choicest cuts. The high fat content in lamb meat makes it ideal for the slow cooker or Dutch oven; slow cooking renders the meat meltingly tender and adds lots of flavor. Team lamb with sweet vegetables such as peas or fresh herbs such as mint, because these flavors cut through the fatty richness.

Ground lamb
This can be quite fatty and will add flavor and succulence to a dish. However, too much fat can make it greasy. Leg or shin will yield the leanest ground meat.

Neck filet
Derived from the tender eye of the neck muscles, this cut of lamb is versatile and responds well to both high-heat quick cooking and long slow cooking. Cut into bite-sized pieces, or stuff it and cook it whole.

Shank
Slow, moist cooking is required to turn the sinews in the shank into a succulent jelly. Allow one shank per person. Foreleg shanks are slimmer than those from the back leg.

Half leg
This is a prime cut, but requires long slow cooking. It can be cooked bone in or bone out. It has more flavor when cooked with the bone in, as the meat becomes fork tender and falls away from the bone.

Fish

As a rule, fish is added toward the end of slow cooking because its delicate flesh needs only minimal time to cook. It adds a distinctive flavor to a slowly simmered sauce. Always choose sustainable fish.

Halibut

Noted for its dense, firm, and low-fat white filets, which have a mild taste. It is best served grilled or pan-fried with a flavored butter.

Tuna

Rich and full of flavor, tuna is robust enough to add to a slow cooked dish. Choose steaks that are fairly thick and try searing them first for extra flavor.

Salmon

The flesh is firm, moist, and oily with a rich flavor. Choose chunky pieces and cut to a uniform size to add to the pot. Delicious added to a fish soup or stew.

Monkfish

With its dense texture, this is quite a "meaty" fish. It is a good choice for slow cooking as it won't fall apart easily. Monkfish has mildly flavored, slightly chewy, white flesh.

Swordfish

These meaty steaks have a similar texture to tuna and are ideal for using as a late addition to the pot.

Cod

This fish has white, chunky flakes with a delicate flavor. It needs very little cooking before the flesh is ready and turns opaque. If over-cooked, cod will disintegrate and become chewy.

Haddock

This has a delicate, creamy, sweet flavor, similar to cod, and can be used instead of cod in recipes. Its delicate flesh needs only minimal cooking; add to the pot for a short time once the sauce is cooked.

Seafood

As with fish, seafood needs to be added late because it requires very little cooking. Seafood adds much flavor, texture, and protein to a dish and can transform an everyday sauce into a memorable meal.

Octopus
Slow cooking turns the meat tender and moist; undercooked, it can be chewy. You can buy it prepared or frozen, but be sure to defrost it thoroughly before adding to the pot. It is particularly good with a tomato-based sauce.

Squid
This requires either "fast flash" cooking or slow cooking in a simmering sauce to become tender. Like octopus, it is good in a tomato sauce. It has a mellow flavor so can take punchy sauces.

Clams
These have a delicate, sweet flavor with a texture similar to mussels. They need very little cooking and will steam open in minutes when added to a simmering sauce. A hearty, full-flavored sauce makes a good accompaniment. Discard any clams that don't open after cooking.

Mussels
They taste slightly salty, with an intense flavor of the sea. Add them to a dish late to prevent overcooking, which results in a rubbery texture. Once all the shells are open they are ready to eat.

Shrimp
Add shrimp at the end of cooking because they will become tough and chewy if overcooked. The cooking time is dependent on their size. The shells make a tasty stock.

Most vegetables are suited to slow cooking, although some need longer cooking than others. Knowing how to prepare vegetables correctly saves time and is key to a successful dish.

Preparing vegetables

Peeling and chopping garlic

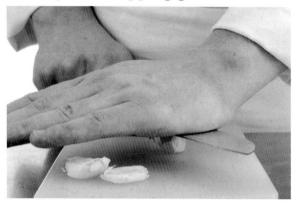

1 Place each garlic clove flat on a chopping board. Place the flat of a large knife blade on top and pound it with the heel of your hand.

2 Discard the skin and cut off the ends of each clove. Slice the clove into slivers lengthwise, then cut across into tiny chunks. Collect the pieces into a pile and chop again for finer pieces.

Peeling and dicing onions

1 Cut the onion in half and peel it, leaving the root to hold the layers together. Make a few slices into the onion, but not through the root.

2 With the tip of your knife, slice down through the layers of onion vertically, cutting as close to the root as possible.

3 Cut across the vertical slices to produce an even dice. Use the root to hold the onion steady, then discard it when all the onion is diced.

Skinning and seeding tomatoes

1 Remove the green stem, score an "X" in the skin of each tomato at the base, then immerse it in a pan of boiling water for 20 seconds, or until the skin loosens.

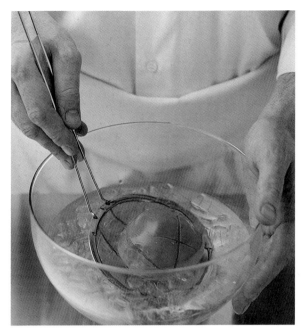

2 Using a slotted spoon, remove the tomato from the pan of boiling water and place it into a bowl of ice water to cool.

3 When cool enough to handle, use a paring knife to peel away the loosened skin.

4 Cut each tomato in half and gently squeeze out the seeds over a bowl. Discard the seeds.

Roasting and peeling peppers

1 Using tongs, hold each pepper over an open flame to char the skin. Rotate the pepper to char it evenly.

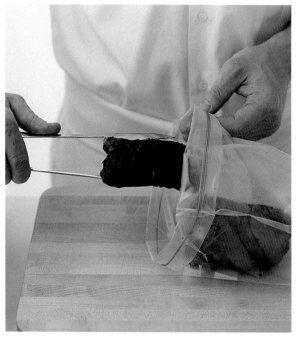

2 Put the peppers into a plastic bag and seal tightly. Set the bag aside and allow the skins to loosen.

3 When the peppers have cooled completely, use your fingers to peel away the charred skin.

4 Pull off the stalk, keeping the core attached. Discard seeds and slice the flesh into strips, or roughly chop.

Coring and shredding cabbage

1 Hold the head of cabbage firmly on the chopping board and use a sharp knife to cut it in half, straight through the stalk end.

2 Cut the halves again through the stalk lengthwise and slice out the core from each quarter.

3 Working with each quarter at a time, place the wedge cut-side down. Cut across the cabbage to shred it finely.

Trimming greens

1 Discard all limp and discolored leaves. Slice each leaf along both sides of the center rib, then remove it and discard.

2 Working with a few leaves at a time, roll them loosely into a bunch. Cut across the roll to the desired width, making strips.

Peeling squashes

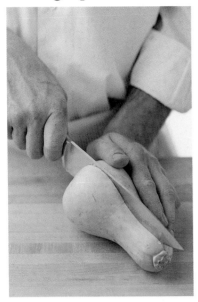

1 Holding the squash firmly, use a chef's knife to cut it lengthwise in half, working from the stalk to the core.

2 Using a spoon, remove the seeds and fibers from each squash half and discard them.

3 Use a vegetable peeler or knife to remove the skin. Cut into pieces, then into chunks, or slice as required.

Rehydrating mushrooms

1 To rehydrate dried mushrooms, place the mushrooms—either wild or cultivated—into a bowl of hot water. Allow them to soak for at least 15 minutes.

2 Remove the mushrooms from the soaking liquid using a slotted spoon. If you plan to use the soaking liquid in your recipe, strain the liquid through a fine sieve, coffee filter, or cheesecloth to remove any sand or grit.

Herbs and spices are essential for adding aroma and flavor to a slow-cooked dish. Experience will teach you which spices to use with which foods, so use them sparingly at first. Add woody herbs, such as thyme and bay, at the beginning of slow cooking, but delicate ones, such as parsley and mint, are best added at the end as they can lose their potency. Chilies, on the other hand, can intensify on slow cooking.

Using herbs and spices

Making a bouquet garni

This is a bundle of herbs used to flavor a sauce. For a classic combination, tie sprigs of thyme and parsley and a bay leaf together. You could also include sage or rosemary.

Seeding and cutting chilies

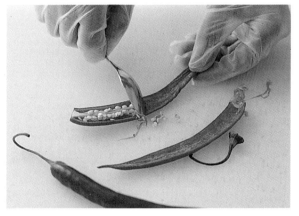

Slice chilies in half lengthwise then scrape out the seeds (this will reduce their heat, so leave if you wish). Slice or chop finely; wearing plastic gloves is a good idea.

Dry-roasting spices

To dry-roast spices such as cloves, cinnamon, and star anise, place them in an oven preheated to 325°F (160°C), or fry them in a dry pan until lightly browned.

Frying spices in oil

When spices are fried until lightly colored, their flavor gets trapped in the oil. This is called tempering. The oil is used along with the spices at the start or end of cooking.

The hard exteriors of dried pulses need long simmering to soften, making them a natural choice for slow cooking. The basic preparation of pulses is simple—sort, rinse, soak if needed, and simmer. They can then be used for different dishes, including favorites from around the world such as Boston baked beans from the US, the fragrant dahls of the Indian subcontinent, or Spain's grand meat and vegetable stew *Cocido*.

Preparing pulses

Sorting and rinsing

Whatever kind of pulse you're using, whether beans, lentils, whole peas, or split peas, start by sorting and rinsing them. Place the pulses in a colander and carefully pick out any damaged or broken ones, and any foreign material such as husks, pieces of grit, or tiny pebbles. Then rinse the pulses well under cold running water. Rinsing is essential for removing excess dust and dirt from the pulses.

Soaking

Apart from lentils and split peas, all pulses need to be soaked for at least 8 hours, and preferably overnight (you will find that old pulses need soaking for longer, so it is best to plan to leave them overnight). Soaking enables pulses to cook more quickly and evenly. Place them in a bowl, add three times their volume of cold water, then cover and place in the refrigerator. When you are ready to cook, drain the pulses and discard the soaking water.

Boiling

Drain the soaked pulses, then place them in a large pan along with any flavorings. Pour in four times their volume of cold water and add 1 tablespoon of vegetable oil to stop them sticking. Bring rapidly to a boil, and boil hard for 10 minutes, skimming away any foam with a slotted spoon. (Some pulses, such as kidney beans, contain toxins that are destroyed by this initial 10 minutes of hard boiling.) Lower the heat, part-cover with a lid, and simmer until tender, or transfer to the slow cooker to cook.

Adding flavor

The flavor of pulses can be rather bland, so it's usually a good idea to add some aromatics. A bouquet garni or a sprig of herbs will do the trick: bay leaf, parsley, rosemary, or thyme all work well. A pinch of cumin, cilantro, chile, or caraway is another option, but you can also pop a carrot into the pan, or an onion studded with cloves. Alternatively, you can cook pulses in a well-flavored stock, but never season it with salt—it will prevent them from softening.

SOAKING AND COOKING TIMES

Use the following soaking times to prepare pulses for both the slow cooker and for traditional cooking. The cooking times given are general guides for the stove; for the slow cooker, allow 6–8 hours on Low or 3–4 hours on High.

Type of pulse	Soaking time	Approximate cooking time
Adzuki beans	overnight	40–45 mins
Black beans	overnight	1 hr
Black-eyed peas	overnight	1–1½ hrs
Borlotti beans	overnight	1–1½ hrs
Butter beans	overnight	1–1½ hrs
Cannellini beans	overnight	1–1½ hrs
Chickpeas	overnight	2–3 hrs
Flageolet beans	overnight	1½ hrs
Navy beans	overnight	1–1½ hrs
Lentils (split)	not required	25 mins
Lentils (whole)	not required	45 mins
Pinto beans	overnight	1–1½ hrs
Kidney beans	boil hard for 10 mins, then soak for 4 hrs	1–1½ hrs
Split peas	not required	45 mins

Versatile poultry works well with all types of slow cooking. The following techniques show you how to truss a bird for pot roasting, debone it, and portion it for stews and casseroles.

Preparing poultry

Trussing

This technique can appear quite fiddly but once mastered, it only takes minutes to do. Trussing a bird before cooking allows it to hold its shape perfectly. It also helps cook it evenly, without overcooking any of the bony parts first. A poussin is shown here, but this works on other birds, too.

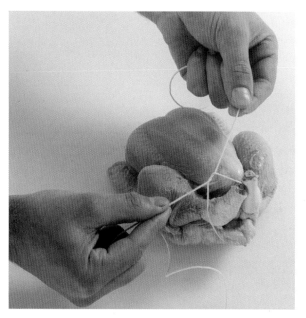

1 Season the insides of the bird with salt and pepper. Holding the bird breast-side down on a clean work surface, tuck the neck skin under the bird, and fold the wings over it.

2 Turn the bird over and pass a length of string under the tail end of the bird; tie a secure knot over the leg joints. Bring the strings along the sides of the body, between the breast and the legs, and loop them around the legs.

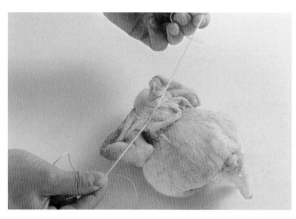

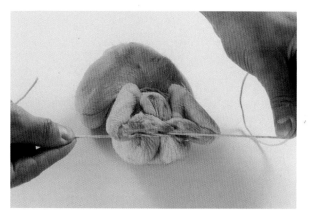

3 Turn the bird over so it is breast-side down again and tie the strings tightly under the body. Bring both ends of the string down between the sides of the body and the insides of the wings.

4 Tie the wing bones at the neck opening so they are tucked securely under the body. After cooking, cut the string to remove it.

Deboning poultry

If you prefer boneless meat, leg pieces (shown here) are better for slow cooking than the leaner breast meat. You may also wish to remove the bone to stuff the meat. Use a good, sharp knife and a series of shallow cuts to free the bone while preserving all the flesh. You can save the bones for stock.

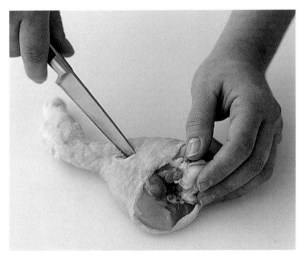

1 To debone a drumstick, start in the middle and insert the tip of your knife until you locate the bone. Slice along the bone in both directions to expose it fully.

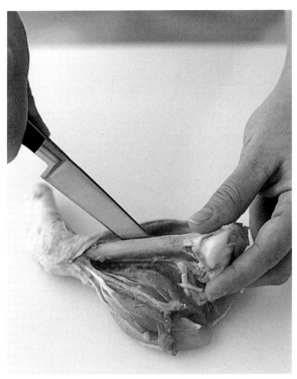

2 Open the flesh and cut neatly around the bone using short strokes to free it completely from the flesh. Discard the bone, or use it to flavor stock.

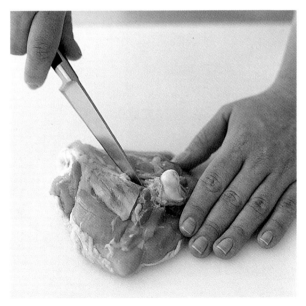

3 To debone a thigh, place the thigh skin-side down on a chopping board. Using a small, sharp knife, cut away the flesh to expose the thigh bone.

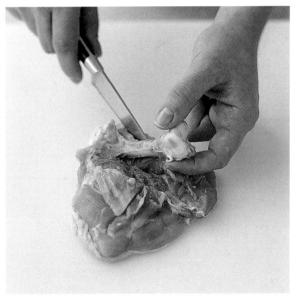

4 Cut an incision through the flesh, following the contour of the exposed bone. Cut around the bone to free it from the flesh. Discard the bone or use it for stock.

Jointing a chicken

This is a good skill to learn as it is often more economical to buy a whole chicken and joint it yourself than to buy expensive chicken pieces. The leftover bones and carcass can be used to make stock or soup. This jointing technique can be used for all poultry.

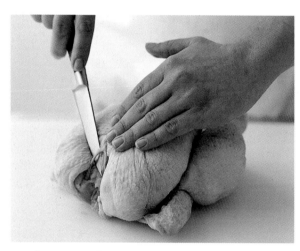

1 First, remove the wishbone. Using a sharp knife, scrape the flesh away from the wishbone, then use your fingers to twist and lift it free.

2 Place the bird breast-side up onto a chopping board. Cut down and through the thigh joint to separate the leg from the rest of the body.

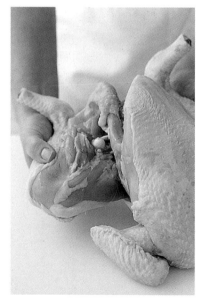

3 Bend the leg back to dislodge the leg joint. When the ball is free from the socket, you will hear a pop.

4 Cut any meat or skin still attached to the body. Repeat to remove the other leg. Each leg can be divided into a thigh and a drumstick.

5 Fully extend one wing, then use sharp poultry shears to cut off the winglet at the middle joint. Repeat to remove the other winglet.

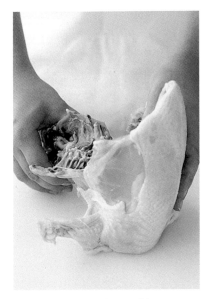

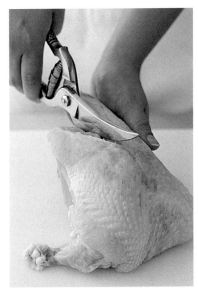

6 Grasp the backbone with your hands and break it from the crown (the 2 breasts and wings on the bone).

7 Using poultry shears, cut the lower end of the backbone from the remaining body.

8 Starting at the neck, cut all the way through the backbone to separate the breasts. The bird is now in 4 pieces.

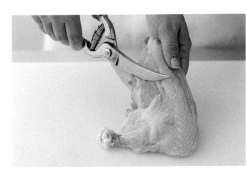

9 Use the poultry shears to cut each breast in half diagonally, producing one breast and one wing. Repeat to separate the other breast.

10 Cut each leg through the knee joint, above the drumstick that connects to the thigh, to separate. Now, there is one drumstick and one thigh. Repeat to separate the other leg.

11 The chicken is now cut into 8 pieces. Leg and thigh pieces are the choicest cuts for slow cooking, although breast pieces can work well when left on the bone for stewing. The wings contain juicy meat that is excellent for pot roasting.

Many cooks lack confidence when it comes to preparing fish, but all you need is the correct tools and a little know-how. An essential tool is a fileting knife, which is slightly flexible with a long blade. This makes it easy to remove the skin from fish and cut through the bones. Always buy good quality fresh fish and buy seafood on the day you will cook it. Clean seafood carefully so that nothing unwanted goes into the pot.

Preparing fish and seafood

Scaling and trimming fish

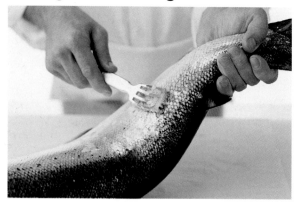

1 Lay the fish on top of a clean work surface. Holding the fish by the tail, scrape the scales off with a fish scaler or the blade of a chef's knife, using strokes toward the head.

2 Once the fish is descaled, use kitchen scissors to remove the dorsal (back) fin, the belly fins, and the two fins on either side of the head.

Fileting and skinning a fish

1 Don't scale a fish if you plan to skin it. To filet, gut the fish through the stomach, then cut into the head at an angle, just behind the gills, until you reach the backbone. Move to the top side of the backbone and, starting near the gills, cut down the length of one side of the backbone.

2 Turn over, and repeat the cut on the other side of the backbone. Place the filet skin-side down onto a clean work surface. Insert a fileting knife into the flesh of the fish near the tail end. Turn the blade at an angle almost parallel to the skin and cut off the flesh, while holding the skin taut.

Preparing mussels

1 Discard any mussels that are broken or wide open. In the sink, scrub the mussels under cold, running water. Rinse away grit or sand and remove any barnacles with a small, sharp knife.

2 To remove the "beard," pinch the dark, stringy piece between your fingers, pull it away from the mussel, and discard. If a mussel is not tightly closed, tap it to check it is fresh; if it doesn't close when you tap it, discard it.

Peeling and deveining shrimp

1 Remove the head and legs by pulling them off with your fingers, then peel away the shells. Save the shells for stock, if you like.

2 Using the tip of a paring knife or toothpick, hook the vein where the head was and gently pull it away from the body.

Slow cooking provides a convenient one-pot cooking method, but with most dishes there are a few stages of cooking that are needed first, such as marinating, browning the meat, or sautéing vegetables. Each of these techniques adds depth of flavor to the finished dish. Deglazing during cooking is vital for enhancing the taste of your sauce, while reducing and thickening are great troubleshooting techniques for thin sauces.

Essential recipe techniques

Marinating

A marinade is a mixture that meat or fish is steeped in before cooking, and should be made up of acidic ingredients such as wine, citrus juice or vinegar, and salt. Soaking the meat is called marinating, a process that tenderizes and enhances flavor in tougher, cheaper cuts. Trim the meat before marinating and cut it to the required size. Natural yogurt can also be used as a marinade and is a common tenderizer for chicken, turkey, or seafood, although it can be used for red meat as well. Spices, herbs, and aromatic vegetables such as garlic, onion, and ginger are often included in marinades to add extra flavor. Make sure the meat is immersed in the marinade, then leave it in the refrigerator to marinate for 4–12 hours.

Browning

This technique caramelizes the natural sugars that are in meat and turns it a rich golden color. Browning adds flavor and depth to your dish, so it is well worth doing at the beginning of the recipe before adding the meat to the other ingredients. Season the meat and add it to a little hot oil or butter in a pan and cook at a medium-high heat. Leave the meat to cook undisturbed for a few minutes. You will know it is ready when it comes away from the bottom of the pan easily. When the underside is golden, turn and cook the other side. Remove the meat and set it aside while you prepare the rest of the ingredients. You could dust the meat in seasoned flour before browning, as it is a good way to help thicken the consistency of the sauce.

Sautéing

This requires high heat and a good heavy-based saucepan. Sautéing vegetables enables their natural water content to evaporate, thus concentrating their flavor. Heat some oil or butter, add the vegetables to the pan, and cook until they start to caramelize and soften. This takes no longer than around 5–8 minutes, depending on the vegetables you are cooking. Move them around the pan to prevent burning. Always cook the hardest vegetables first as these will take longer. Don't overcrowd the pan or the vegetables will sweat rather than sauté.

Deglazing

The sauce is all-important as it can make or break the finished dish. Pan sauces and gravies are made from deglazed caramelized juices released from roasted or fried meat, poultry, and vegetables. In slow cooking, this technique is used often after browning and sautéing. Remove the food from the pan and spoon off excess fat, then deglaze the caramelized juices by adding stock, water, or wine. Stir to loosen the particles and incorporate them into the liquid. Reduce and finish as required. Making a sauce like this gives a richness and depth of flavor that cannot be achieved just by simmering ingredients.

Reducing and thickening

When a sauce is too thin, it can be either reduced or thickened to improve its flavor and texture. Reducing decreases the sauce's volume through evaporation and intensifies its flavor. To reduce, cook in an uncovered pan over high heat, stirring occasionally. Add stock and bring back to boil, then boil, uncovered, for about 20 minutes to reduce again by half, regularly skimming off any impurities. Thickening gives sauces extra body and consistency. There are different ways to do this. A simple method is to dissolve cornstarch in water and add the mixture to the simmering dish. You could also add a roux—a mixture of flour and water—stirring it into the simmering sauce and cooking to prevent it from turning the sauce lumpy.

Using your slow cooker is a simple and efficient way to make stock—the liquid won't evaporate and boil dry, so you can leave it unattended. Save the carcass or bones from poultry, meat, or fish when preparing a dish, then add them to the slow cooker with water and flavorings and leave it to simmer overnight. Stock freezes well, so if you are not using it immediately, let it cool and freeze it for up to 1 month.

Making stock in the slow cooker

Vegetable stock

1 Save scraps, peelings, stalks, tops, and ends from vegetables such as onion, carrot, celery, leek, and fennel to use as the base of your stock.

2 Add the vegetable scraps to the slow cooker. You can also add any herbs you may have, such as parsley sprigs and a bay leaf, along with a few black peppercorns and a pinch of salt.

3 Boil enough water to cover all the ingredients, then pour this into the slow cooker. Cover with the lid, and cook on auto/low for 6–8 hours. Skim the stock halfway through the cooking time, if needed. Strain the stock and allow to cool before storing in the refrigerator or freezer.

Meat stock

1 Add a chicken carcass or beef bones to the slow cooker with a handful of raw vegetables such as carrot tops, celery, and onion.

2 Add some black peppercorns and a pinch of salt to the slow cooker, along with herbs such as parsley or a bay leaf, if you wish.

3 Boil enough water to cover all the ingredients, then pour this into the slow cooker. Cover with the lid, and cook on auto/low for 6–8 hours. Skim the stock halfway through the cooking time, if needed. Strain the stock and allow to cool before storing in the refrigerator or freezer.

Fish stock

1 Ask your fish seller for some fish heads, or use leftovers from another dish. Choose white fish such as sea bass or haddock, but avoid oily fish because their stonger flavor will taint the stock.

2 Add the fish scraps to the slow cooker along with some fresh herbs, such as thyme, and some fennel scraps or onion.

3 Pour over enough boiling water to cover all the ingredients, cover with the lid, and cook on auto/low for 6–8 hours. Skim the stock halfway through the cooking time, if needed. Strain the stock and allow to cool before storing in the refrigerator or freezer.

Fish stock

Skimming stock

When making stock, quite often a layer of frothy "scum" will appear on the surface. To skim it off, use a ladle or a metal spoon to scoop it away and then discard it. You may find you need to do this a few times during cooking. Meat and fish stocks are most likely to need skimming.

Straining stock

Once the stock has finished cooking, strain it immediately; don't leave it sitting. To strain the stock, turn the slow cooker off then lift out the inner pot. Carefully strain the stock liquid into a pitcher or bowl through a fine nylon mesh sieve, or you could line a sieve with cheesecloth. It is easiest to do this a ladleful at a time. Discard any bones, carcass, and vegetables used and leave the stock to cool.

Adding dumplings, a cobbler topping, or bread crumbs to a stew or casserole can make a dish inviting, more filling, and substantial. All are easy to prepare while your dish is simmering; simply add them to the pot to get a complete one-pot meal without any additional cooking.

Extras and toppings

Dumplings

1 The secret to light and fluffy dumplings lies in handling the dough as little as possible. Add 5½oz (150g) vegetable shortening and 5½oz (150g) self-rising flour to a bowl and mix together with your hands. Season well with salt and pepper.

2 If you wish, some extra flavorings could be added to the mixture at this point, such as 1oz (30g) freshly grated Parmesan cheese, a teaspoon of horseradish or mustard, or 1–2 teaspoons of fresh chopped herbs like parsley, thyme, and rosemary. Mix any flavorings into the dry ingredients.

3 Make a well in the middle of the flour mixture and slowly drizzle in cold water a little at a time. Mix with your hands until the mixture starts to come together and leaves the sides of the bowl easily.

4 Turn out onto a lightly floured board and roll into a sausage shape. Form into 6 large or 12 small dumplings (they will double in size as they cook). For the slow cooker, add the dumplings in for the last 45–60 minutes of cooking. For the traditional method, add them to the pot for the last 30 minutes of cooking. They should be just immersed in the liquid and covered with a lid.

Vegetable casserole (p168) with herby dumplings

Butter dumplings

1 This recipe uses butter instead of shortening to make a light, moist version of the dumpling. Add 3½oz (100g) white bread crumbs, 3½oz (100g) self-rising flour, and 5oz (140g) butter to a food processor and blend into a crumb mixture. You could also add some extra flavorings to the food processor, if you like, such as freshly grated Parmesan cheese, horseradish or mustard, or fresh chopped herbs like parsley, thyme, and rosemary.

2 Add 2 eggs to the food processor and season with salt and pepper. Blend again until the mixture comes together as a moist dough.

3 Turn the dough out onto a lightly floured board and roll into 6 large or 12 small balls (keep in mind that the dumplings will double in size as they cook). For the slow cooker, add the dumplings to the pot for the last 45–60 minutes of cooking. For the traditional method, add them to the pot for the last 30 minutes of cooking. They should be just immersed in the liquid and covered with a lid.

Artichokes, beans, and peas (p298) with bread crumbs stirred in

Bread crumbs

1 Using a food processor, pulse 2 slices of torn bread into coarse crumbs. Add any flavorings of your choice, such as herbs or grated cheese, and pulse again. If your recipe calls for fresh bread crumbs, then they can be used at this stage. For the slow cooker, lightly toast the bread crumbs in a dry frying pan; sprinkle over, or carefully fold into, the finished dish. For the traditional method, sprinkle into the pot and cook in the oven for the last 30 minutes of cooking; remove the lid for the last 10 minutes, or until the topping is golden.

2 For fine, golden bread crumbs, spread them onto a baking tray and put in the oven at 400°F (200°C) for about 10 minutes until golden. Remove, add back into the food processor, and pulse again until fine. You can add any flavorings at this time, if you wish, such as fresh herbs or grated cheese. Use to top the dish for the last hour of cooking for both the slow cooker and for the traditional method.

3 If you are not using the bread crumbs immediately, they can be frozen for up to 3 months. They don't require defrosting before use.

Cobblers

1 A cobbler topping is a savory biscuit that makes a wholesome and filling dish. Use them to top chicken, beef, lamb, or vegetable stews and casseroles. Put 7oz (200g) sifted self-rising flour and salt and pepper in a bowl and mix together. Add any flavorings, such as grated cheese, sun-dried tomatoes, olives, or ground walnuts to the mixture, if you wish.

2 Cut 3½oz (100g) butter into cubes and rub it into the ingredients in the bowl with your fingertips until the mixture resembles bread crumbs. Add 2 lightly beaten eggs and mix until the dough comes together, then add ¼ cup milk, a little at a time, mixing until it becomes a soft dough.

3 Turn the dough out onto a lightly floured board and roll out so it is fairly thick. Using a 1in (2.5cm) metal cutter, cut out 6 rounds. For the slow cooker, add the cobblers to the top of the dish for the last hour of cooking. For the traditional method, add the cobblers to the top of the pot, brush the tops with the milk, and cook in the oven, uncovered, for the last 30–45 minutes of cooking.

Recipe
choosers

Vegetarian

Provençal vegetable soup p68
🕐 Slow cooker 8 hrs or 4 hrs; Traditional method 1 hr

SOUPS

Ribollita p80
🕐 Slow cooker 5–6 hrs or 3–4 hrs;
Traditional method 1¼ hrs

Borscht p81
🕐 Slow cooker 6–8 hrs or 3–4 hrs;
Traditional method 1½ hrs

Minestrone p89
🕐 Slow cooker 6–8 hrs;
Traditional method 1¾ hrs

Cannellini bean, garlic, and mushroom soup p98
🕐 Slow cooker 4 hrs;
Traditional method 50 mins

Spanish pepper and tomato soup p99
🕐 Slow cooker 8 hrs or 3 hrs;
Traditional method 1¼–1½ hrs

MAINS

Sweet and sour pumpkin stew p129
🕐 Slow cooker 8 hrs or 4 hrs;
Traditional method 1 hr

Ratatouille p166
🕐 Slow cooker 4–5 hrs or 2–3 hrs;
Traditional method 1¼ hrs

Pumpkin and ginger soup p86
🕐 Slow cooker 8 hrs or 4 hrs;
Traditional method 1 hr

Risotto primavera p302
🕐 Slow cooker 1½–2 hrs;
Traditional method 1 hr

Eggplant massaman curry p228
🕐 Slow cooker 8 hrs or 3–4 hrs;
Traditional method 1 hr

Jamaican corn stew p126
🕐 Slow cooker 6–8 hrs or 3–4 hrs; Traditional method 1½–2 hrs

Vegetable casserole with dumplings p168
🕐 Slow cooker 6–8 hrs or 4 hrs; Traditional method 1¼ hrs

Zucchini, herb, and lemon tagine p199
🕐 Slow cooker 2–3 hrs;
Traditional method 45–55 mins

Chickpea, tomato, and herb tagine p219
🕐 Slow cooker 6–8 hrs or 3–4 hrs;
Traditional method 1¼ hrs

Sri Lankan coconut pumpkin curry p226
🕐 Slow cooker 3–4 hrs;
Traditional method 1¼ hrs

Malaysian mango curry p227
🕐 Slow cooker 3–4 hrs;
Traditional method 1 hr

Cauliflower curry p238
🕐 Slow cooker 8 hrs or 4 hrs;
Traditional method 1 hr

Paneer and sweet pepper curry p243
🕐 Slow cooker 5–6 hrs or 3–4 hrs;
Traditional method 1 hr

Asparagus and Taleggio risotto p322
🕐 Slow cooker 1–1¼ hrs;
Traditional method 45–55 mins

Vegetable biryani p325
🕐 Slow cooker 2–3 hrs;
Traditional method 1¼ hrs

SIDES
Red cabbage with cider p138
🕐 Slow cooker 8 hrs or 4 hrs;
Traditional method 1–1½ hrs

Red lentil dahl p244
🕐 Slow cooker 8 hrs or 4 hrs;
Traditional method 1¼ hrs

Rice and peas p326
🕐 Slow cooker 2–3 hrs;
Traditional method 45 mins

Thai coconut rice p327
🕐 Slow cooker 2½–3 hrs;
Traditional method 40 mins

Fish and seafood

Prawn laksa p100
🕐 Slow cooker 6–8 hrs; Traditional method 1½ hrs

SOUPS
Japanese-style fish broth p84
🕐 Slow cooker 3 hrs;
Traditional method 1 hr

New England chowder p90
🕐 Slow cooker 2–3 hrs;
Traditional method 55–60 mins

Shellfish soup p91
🕐 Slow cooker 6–8 hrs or 3–4 hrs;
Traditional method 1¼ hrs

MAINS
Pork and clam cataplana p106
🕐 Slow cooker 6–8 hrs or 3–4 hrs;
Traditional method 2¼–2½ hrs

Salt cod braised with vegetables p111
🕐 Slow cooker 6–8 hrs or 3–4 hrs;
Traditional method 40 mins

Rich fish soup p82
🕐 Slow cooker 8 hrs or 4 hrs; Traditional method 1 hr

Red mullet with Middle Eastern spices p212
🕐 Slow cooker 3–4 hrs;
Traditional method 1½ hrs

Creole fish and corn stew p270
🕐 Slow cooker 3–4 hrs; Traditional method 1¼ hrs

Seafood stew p130
🕐 Slow cooker 3–4 hrs; Traditional method 1½ hrs

Monkfish and green chile stew p132
🕐 Slow cooker 6–8 hrs or 3–4 hrs; Traditional method 1¼ hrs

Squid stew p133
🕐 Slow cooker 6–8 hrs or 3–4 hrs; Traditional method 1¼–1¾ hrs

Bouillabaise p134
🕐 Slow cooker 2–3 hrs; Traditional method 45 mins

Monkfish and white wine stew p140
🕐 Slow cooker 2–3 hrs; Traditional method 40–45 mins

Fish tagine p211
🕐 Slow cooker 4–5 hrs; Traditional method 1¼–1½ hrs

Shrimp makhani p230
🕐 Slow cooker 4–5 hrs or 3–4 hrs; Traditional method 40 mins

Kenyan fish curry p237
🕐 Slow cooker 6–8 hrs or 3–4 hrs; Traditional method 45 mins

Shrimp dhansak p242
🕐 Slow cooker 6–8 hrs or 3–4 hrs; Traditional method 50 mins

Shrimp and okra gumbo p253
🕐 Slow cooker 6–8 hrs or 3–4 hrs; Traditional method 1¼ hrs

Paella p316
🕐 Slow cooker 2¾ hrs; Traditional method 1 hr

Risotto with mussels p323
🕐 Slow cooker 1 hr; Traditional method 45–55 mins

Shrimp risotto p324
🕐 Slow cooker 2–3 hrs; Traditional method 50 mins

Poultry

Mustard chicken casserole p190
🕐 Slow cooker 6–8 hrs or 3–4 hrs; Traditional method 1¾ hrs

SOUPS

Chunky chicken soup p75
🕐 Slow cooker 6–8 hrs or 4 hrs;
Traditional method 1½ hrs

Malaysian chicken soup p92
🕐 Slow cooker 6–8 hrs or 3–4 hrs;
Traditional method 40–50 mins

Chicken broth with celery root and orange p95
🕐 Slow cooker 8 hrs or 4 hrs;
Traditional method 1 hr

MAINS

Chicken and beer stew p116
🕐 Slow cooker 6–8 hrs or 3–4 hrs;
Traditional method 1 hr

American Brunswick stew p125
🕐 Slow cooker 6–8 hrs;
Traditional method 2–2½ hrs

Coq au vin p161
🕐 Slow cooker 6–8 hrs or 3–4 hrs;
Traditional method 1½–1¾ hrs

Chicken fricassée p165
🕐 Slow cooker 5–6 hrs or 3–4 hrs;
Traditional method 1 hr

French-style duck and lentils p176
🕐 Slow cooker 4½–5 hrs;
Traditional method 3¾ hrs

Duck legs with cabbage, pine nuts, and raisins p136
🕐 Slow cooker 6 hrs or 3–4 hrs;
Traditional method 2½ hrs

Hunter's chicken stew p114
🕐 Slow cooker 5–6 hrs or 3–4 hrs;
Traditional method 45–60 mins

Chicken and green olive tagine p196
🕐 Slow cooker 6–8 hrs or 3–4 hrs;
Traditional method 2 hrs

Turkey mole p250
🕐 Slow cooker 6–8 hrs or 3–4 hrs; Traditional method 1¼–1¾ hrs

Chicken cobbler p177
🕐 Slow cooker 6–8 hrs or 4 hrs;
Traditional method 2¼ hrs

Turkey and cranberry casserole p182
🕐 Slow cooker 6–8 hrs or 4 hrs;
Traditional method 1¼–1¾ hrs

Duck with turnips and apricots p186
🕐 Slow cooker 6–8 hrs or 3–4 hrs;
Traditional method 1½–2 hrs

Chicken paprika with dumplings p193
🕐 Slow cooker 6–8 hrs or 3–4 hrs;
Traditional method 1½ hrs

Chicken with olives and peppers p198
🕐 Slow cooker 6–8 hrs or 3–4 hrs;
Traditional method 1½ hrs

Chicken and orange tagine p206
🕐 Slow cooker 6–8 hrs or 3–4 hrs;
Traditional method 1¾ hrs

Chicken, eggplant, and tomato tagine p215
🕐 Slow cooker 6–8 hrs or 3–4 hrs;
Traditional method 1¼ hrs

Chicken tikka masala p233
🕐 Slow cooker 4–5 hrs or 2–3 hrs;
Traditional method 50 mins

Pot roast chicken with turnips and fennel p284
🕐 Slow cooker 8 hrs or 4 hrs;
Traditional method 2–2½ hrs

Poussins with plums and cabbage p286
🕐 Slow cooker 6–8 hrs;
Traditional method 1¾ hrs

Arroz con pollo p317
🕐 Slow cooker 3–3½ hrs;
Traditional method 45 mins

Duck curry p240
🕐 Slow cooker 8 hrs;
Traditional method 2 hrs

Chicken jambalaya p264
🕐 Slow cooker 2–3 hrs;
Traditional method 1½ hrs

Pork

Pea, ham, and potato soup p78
🕐 Slow cooker 16 hrs or 8 hrs; Traditional method 2 hrs

SOUPS
Pistou soup p88
🕐 Slow cooker 6–8 hrs or 3–4 hrs; Traditional method 1¾ hrs

MAINS
Pork and clam cataplana p106
🕐 Slow cooker 6–8 hrs or 3–4 hrs; Traditional method 2¼–2½ hrs

Pork goulash p135
🕐 Slow cooker 6–8 hrs or 3–4 hrs; Traditional method 1 hr

Stuffed pork noisettes p150
🕐 Slow cooker 6–8 hrs or 3–4 hrs; Traditional method 2 hrs

Feijoada p174
🕐 Slow cooker 6–8 hrs or 3–4 hrs; Traditional method 1¾ hrs

Spanish lentils p175
🕐 Slow cooker 5–6 hrs or 3–4 hrs; Traditional method 1 hr

Pork with red cabbage, pears, and ginger p183
🕐 Slow cooker 8 hrs or 4 hrs; Traditional method 1¾ hrs

Lentil and sausage casserole p156
🕐 Slow cooker 6–8 hrs; Traditional method 1¾ hrs

Pot roast smoked ham p282
🕐 Slow cooker 16 hrs or 8 hrs; Traditional method 3¼ hrs

Belly pork and prunes p178
🕐 Slow cooker 8 hrs; Traditional method 3–3½ hrs

Asian pork ribs p294
🕐 Slow cooker 8 hrs; Traditional method 2–2½ hrs

Red lentil and spicy sausage hotpot p189
🕐 Slow cooker 6–8 hrs or 4 hrs;
Traditional method 1¾ hrs

Pork vindaloo p232
🕐 Slow cooker 6–8 hrs or 3–4 hrs;
Traditional method 1 hr

Chilean pork and beans p263
🕐 Slow cooker 6–8 hrs;
Traditional method 3–3½ hrs

Sausage chili pot p266
🕐 Slow cooker 6–8 hrs or 3–4 hrs;
Traditional method 1¾ hrs

Ribs in a chile and ginger tomato sauce p285
🕐 Slow cooker 6–8 hrs;
Traditional method 2–3 hrs

Spicy pork with cabbage and caraway seeds p291
🕐 Slow cooker 6–8 hrs;
Traditional method 2½ hrs

Belly pork and squash p292
🕐 Slow cooker 8 hrs;
Traditional method 2¼–2¾ hrs

Spicy deviled pork ribs p296
🕐 Slow cooker 6–8 hrs;
Traditional method 2–2½ hrs

Pork with rice and tomatoes p306
🕐 Slow cooker 1–1½ hrs;
Traditional method 1 hr

Hoppin' John p310
🕐 Slow cooker 6–8 hrs;
Traditional method 3–3½ hrs

Sausage and mixed pepper savory rice p312
🕐 Slow cooker 2–3 hrs;
Traditional method 1 hr

Squash, sausage, and pecorino risotto p318
🕐 Slow cooker 1½–2 hrs;
Traditional method 50–60 mins

Beef

Vietnamese beef soup p96
🕓 Slow cooker 8 hrs or 4 hrs; Traditional method 1¼ hrs

SOUPS
Oxtail soup with nutmeg and star anise p74
🕓 Slow cooker 8 hrs;
Traditional method 2¾–3¼ hrs

Beef mulligatawny soup p94
🕓 Slow cooker 8 hrs or 4 hrs;
Traditional method 1½ hrs

MAINS
Beef with barley and mushrooms p110
🕓 Slow cooker 6–8 hrs or 3–4 hrs;
Traditional method 2¼–2½ hrs

Asian beef and bok choy p113
🕓 Slow cooker 6–8 hrs;
Traditional method 2¼–2¾ hrs

Italian beef braised in red wine p117
🕓 Slow cooker 6–8 hrs;
Traditional method 2¼–3¼ hrs

Peppery Tuscan beef p118
🕓 Slow cooker 8 hrs;
Traditional method 2–2½ hrs

Greek stifado p122
🕓 Slow cooker 8 hrs;
Traditional method 2¼ hrs

Shredded beef in barbecue sauce p274
🕓 Slow cooker 8 hrs;
Traditional method 3¼ hrs

Beef and greens p142
🕓 Slow cooker 6–8 hrs;
Traditional method 1¾ hrs

Beef pot roast p278
🕓 Slow cooker 8 hrs;
Traditional method 2½ hrs

Osso bucco p162
🕐 Slow cooker 6–8 hrs or 4 hrs; Traditional method 1¾–2¼ hrs

Braised oxtail with star anise p146
🕐 Slow cooker 8 hrs; Traditional method 3¼ hrs

Beef and anchovy stew p145
🕐 Slow cooker 6–8 hrs;
Traditional method 2¼–2¾ hrs

Provençal daube of beef p149
🕐 Slow cooker 6–8 hrs or 3–4 hrs;
Traditional method 3½–4 hrs

Beef stew with Stilton dumplings p151
🕐 Slow cooker 8 hrs or 4 hrs;
Traditional method 2¾ hrs

Boeuf bourguignon p160
🕐 Slow cooker 6–8 hrs;
Traditional method 2½ hrs

Beef carbonnade p170
🕐 Slow cooker 8 hrs or 4 hrs;
Traditional method 3¼ hrs

Mexican meatballs p180
🕐 Slow cooker 6–8 hrs;
Traditional method 1¾–2¼ hrs

Cumin beef tagine p210
🕐 Slow cooker 6–8 hrs or 3–4 hrs;
Traditional method 2½ hrs

Cardamom and ginger beef curry p224
🕐 Slow cooker 5–6 hrs or 3–4 hrs;
Traditional method 2–2¼ hrs

Beef rendang p225
🕐 Slow cooker 6–8 hrs;
Traditional method 3¾–4¼ hrs

Hot and fiery chili with beer p256
🕐 Slow cooker 6–8 hrs or 3–4 hrs;
Traditional method 1¾ hrs

Beef chili mole p262
🕐 Slow cooker 6–8 hrs;
Traditional method 2¼–2¾ hrs

Slow-cooked beef p272
🕐 Slow cooker 6–8 hrs;
Traditional method 2¼ hrs

Pot au feu p281
🕐 Slow cooker 6–8 hrs;
Traditional method 3½–4 hrs

Lamb

Lamb and squash with green chilies p258
🕐 Slow cooker 8 hrs;
Traditional method 1½–2 hrs

Lamb with artichokes, fava beans, and dill p152
🕐 Slow cooker 6–8 hrs or 3–4 hrs;
Traditional method 1¾ hrs

Slow-cooked lamb with orange and chestnuts p208
🕐 Slow cooker 6–8 hrs; Traditional method 2¼ hrs

SOUPS
Moroccan harira soup p72
🕐 Slow cooker 8 hrs;
Traditional method 2 hrs

MAINS
Fruity lamb shanks p123
🕐 Slow cooker 8 hrs;
Traditional method 3¼–3¾ hrs

Lamb ratatouille p141
🕐 Slow cooker 6–8 hrs or 3–4 hrs;
Traditional method 2–2¼ hrs

Smoky eggplant and lamb stew p144
🕐 Slow cooker 6–8 hrs;
Traditional method 1¾ hrs

French braised lamb p148
🕐 Slow cooker 6–8 hrs or 3–4 hrs;
Traditional method 2–2½ hrs

Navarin of lamb p164
🕐 Slow cooker 6–8 hrs or 3–4 hrs;
Traditional method 2 hrs

Lamb shanks with harissa and shallots p171
🕐 Slow cooker 6–8 hrs or 4–5 hrs;
Traditional method 2¼–2¾ hrs

Lamb chops champvallon p181
🕐 Slow cooker 6–8 hrs;
Traditional method 2¼ hrs

Lebanese meatballs p187
🕐 Slow cooker 6–8 hrs or 3–4 hrs;
Traditional method 1 hr

Lamb meatballs in a tomato sauce p188
🕐 Slow cooker 6–8 hrs or 3 hrs;
Traditional method 2½ hrs

Fiery lamb and chutney tagine p203
🕐 Slow cooker 6–8 hrs or 3–4 hrs;
Traditional method 1½ hrs

Lamb tagine with walnuts and figs p207
🕐 Slow cooker 6–8 hrs or 3–4 hrs;
Traditional method 1¾–2¼ hrs

Braised lamb with lemon and peas p214
🕐 Slow cooker 6–8 hrs or 3–4 hrs;
Traditional method 1¼ hrs

Turkish lamb and lemon p218
🕐 Slow cooker 6–8 hrs or 3–4 hrs;
Traditional method 1¼–1¾ hrs

Lamb dhansak p231
🕐 Slow cooker 6–8 hrs or 3–4 hrs;
Traditional method 2 hrs

Lamb korma p247
🕐 Slow cooker 5–6 hrs or 3–4 hrs;
Traditional method 2½–3 hrs

Sweet and sour lamb p297
🕐 Slow cooker 6–8 hrs;
Traditional method 2 hrs

Saffron and lamb biryani p305
🕐 Slow cooker 6–8 hrs or 3–4 hrs;
Traditional method 1¾ hrs

Provençal lamb daube with olives p184
🕐 Slow cooker 6–8 hrs; Traditional method 3¾–4¼ hrs

Stuffed lamb, Greek style p120
🕐 Slow cooker 8 hrs;
Traditional method 2¼–2¾ hrs

Turkish lamb and pomegranate pilaf p308
🕐 Slow cooker 2–3 hrs;
Traditional method 1 hr

Lamb with parsley, tomato, and bread crumbs p288
🕐 Slow cooker 8 hrs;
Traditional method 3¼ hrs

Healthy

Malaysian chicken soup p92
🕐 Slow cooker 6–8 hrs or 3–4 hrs; **Traditional method** 40–50 mins

SOUPS

Asian chicken and shrimp broth with ginger and cilantro p70
🕐 Slow cooker 2–2½ hrs;
Traditional method 1 hr

Chunky chicken soup p75
🕐 Slow cooker 6–8 hrs or 4 hrs;
Traditional method 1½ hrs

Beef broth with Parmesan dumplings p76
🕐 Slow cooker 6–8 hrs;
Traditional method 2½ hrs

MAINS

Braised pork in soy and cinnamon p112
🕐 Slow cooker 6–8 hrs or 4 hrs;
Traditional method 2¼–2½ hrs

Mixed mushroom stew p128
🕐 Slow cooker 3–4 hrs;
Traditional method 1 hr

Sweet and sour pumpkin stew p129
🕐 Slow cooker 8 hrs or 4 hrs;
Traditional method 1 hr

Middle Eastern chickpea stew p216
🕐 Slow cooker 6–8 hrs or 3–4 hrs;
Traditional method 1¼ hrs

Ham hock with red cabbage p108
🕐 Slow cooker 12–16 hrs;
Traditional method 3 hrs

Pumpkin and parsnip cassoulet p172
🕐 Slow cooker 8 hrs or 4 hrs;
Traditional method 1¾ hrs

Brazilian black bean and pumpkin stew p104
🕒 Slow cooker 6–8 hrs;
Traditional method 2½–3 hrs

Mixed vegetable tagine p204
🕒 Slow cooker 3 hrs;
Traditional method 50 mins

Karahi chicken p222
🕒 Slow cooker 6 hrs or 3 hrs;
Traditional method 1 hr

Ginger and okra curry p245
🕒 Slow cooker 8 hrs or 4 hrs;
Traditional method 1¼ hrs

Spicy turkey and corn p268
🕒 Slow cooker 6–8 hrs;
Traditional method 1¼ hrs

Hot chili and beans p269
🕒 Slow cooker 8 hrs or 4 hrs;
Traditional method 1 hr

SIDES
Red cabbage with cider p138
🕒 Slow cooker 8 hrs or 4 hrs;
Traditional method 1–1½ hrs

Middle Eastern lentils and peppers p200
🕒 Slow cooker 1½–2 hrs;
Traditional method 45 mins

Vegetable sambar p234
🕒 Slow cooker 4–6 hrs or 2–3 hrs;
Traditional method 50 mins

Red lentil dahl p244
🕒 Slow cooker 8 hrs or 4 hrs;
Traditional method 1¼ hrs

Cashew and zucchini rice p320
🕒 Slow cooker 2–2½ hrs; Traditional method 40 mins

Soups & broths

This soup is just as good in summer made with fresh tomatoes and basil pesto stirred through it, as it is in winter with added canned beans to bulk it out. It is excellent for freezing.

Provençal vegetable soup

SERVES 4–6 **FREEZE** UP TO 3 MONTHS

1 tbsp olive oil
1 onion, finely chopped
salt and freshly ground black pepper
3 garlic cloves, finely chopped
2 celery stalks, finely chopped
2 carrots, peeled and roughly chopped
sprig of tarragon, leaves finely chopped
2 sprigs of rosemary

14oz (400g) can tomatoes, blended until smooth
3 cups hot vegetable stock, for
 both methods
3 potatoes, peeled and chopped
 into bite-sized pieces
11oz (325g) baby green beans or French or fine green
 beans, trimmed and chopped into bite-sized pieces
1oz (30g) grated Parmesan cheese, grated (optional)

in the slow cooker   PREP 15 MINS   COOK 10 MINS PRECOOKING; AUTO/LOW 8 HRS OR HIGH 4 HRS

1 Preheat the slow cooker, if required. Heat the oil in a large heavy-based pan over medium heat, add the onion, and cook for 3–4 minutes until soft. Season with salt and pepper, then stir in the garlic and celery and cook for a further 5 minutes or until the celery is soft.

2 Stir in the carrots, tarragon, and rosemary and cook for a minute before transferring everything to the slow cooker. Stir in the puréed tomatoes and stock and cook on auto/low for 8 hours or on high for 4 hours. Add the potatoes for the last 15 minutes of cooking.

3 When the potatoes are soft, add the beans and cook for 10 minutes, or until they are cooked but retain a bite. Taste and season, remove the rosemary, and ladle into warmed large shallow bowls. Sprinkle over the Parmesan, if using, and serve with some crusty French bread.

traditional method   PREP 15 MINS   COOK 1 HR

1 Heat the oil in a large heavy-based pan over medium heat, add the onion, and cook for 3–4 minutes until soft. Season with salt and pepper, then stir in the garlic and celery and cook for a further 5 minutes or until the celery is soft.

2 Stir in the carrots, tarragon, and rosemary and cook for a minute, then add in the puréed tomatoes and a little stock, and bring to a boil. Add the remaining stock and return to a boil, then reduce to a simmer, partially cover with the lid, and cook gently for about 45 minutes. If more liquid is needed, top up with a little hot water. Add the potatoes for the last 15 minutes of cooking.

3 When the potatoes are soft, add the beans and cook for a further 10 minutes, or until they are cooked but retain a bite. Taste and season, remove the rosemary, and ladle into warmed large shallow bowls. Sprinkle over the Parmesan, if using, and serve with some crusty French bread.

Lots of complex flavors make up this warming broth. The water chestnuts add an unexpected texture, and the chicken and shrimp add plenty of protein, making it a substantial dish.

Asian chicken and shrimp broth with ginger and cilantro

SERVES 4–6   **HEALTHY**

1 quart hot chicken stock, for
  both methods
salt and freshly ground black pepper
1 tbsp dark soy sauce
3 tbsp fish sauce (nam pla)
3 tbsp mirin
1 tsp tahini
2 garlic cloves, finely chopped
2in (5cm) piece of fresh ginger, peeled
  and sliced into fine strips

½ tsp dried chile flakes
7oz (225g) can bamboo shoots, drained and rinsed
7oz (225g) water chestnuts, drained and rinsed
4½oz (125g) button mushrooms, whole or larger
  ones halved
2 skinless chicken breasts, finely sliced
bunch of scallions, finely chopped
bunch of cilantro leaves
8oz (250g) pack of ready-cooked small shrimp

in the slow cooker   **PREP** 15 MINS   **COOK** HIGH 2–2½ HRS

1 Preheat the slow cooker, if required. Put everything into the slow cooker except the scallions, cilantro, and shrimp, and add 1 cup of hot water.

2 Cover with the lid and cook on high for 2–2½ hours, stirring in the scallions, cilantro, and shrimp for the last 20 minutes of cooking. Taste and season with salt and pepper as required, and ladle into warmed bowls while piping hot.

traditional method   **PREP** 15 MINS   **COOK** 1 HR

1 Put the stock into a large stock pot, season with salt and pepper, and add a further 2 cups of hot water. Add the soy sauce, fish sauce, mirin, and tahini and bring to a boil.

2 Reduce to a simmer and add the garlic, ginger, and chile flakes together with the bamboo shoots, water chestnuts, and mushrooms. Stir, then add the chicken, cover with the lid, and cook gently for 40 minutes. Top up with hot water if necessary.

3 Taste and adjust seasoning as required, then stir in the scallions and cilantro leaves, and simmer on low heat for a further 10 minutes. Finally, add the shrimp and simmer for 5 minutes. Ladle into warmed bowls while piping hot.

The secret of a good French onion soup is to let the onions caramelize slowly so they become wonderfully sweet. If you like, you could use a dry cider instead of the wine.

French onion soup

SERVES 4 ❄ **FREEZE** UP TO 1 MONTH, WITHOUT THE BREAD OR CHEESE

2 tbsp butter
1 tbsp sunflower oil
1½lb (675g) onions, thinly sliced
1 tsp superfine sugar
salt and freshly ground black pepper
½ cup dry white wine
2 tbsp all-purpose flour

3½ cups hot beef stock for the slow cooker
  (5½ cups for the traditional method)
¼ cup brandy
1 garlic clove, chopped in half
4 slices of baguette, about ¾in (2cm) thick, toasted
1 cup Gruyère or Emmental cheese, grated

in the slow cooker 🕐 **PREP** 20 MINS **COOK** 45 MINS PRECOOKING;
AUTO/LOW 4–6 HRS OR **HIGH** 2–3 HRS

1 Melt the butter with the oil in a large Dutch oven over low heat. Stir in the onions and sugar, and season with salt and pepper. Press a piece of wet parchment paper over the surface and cook, stirring occasionally, uncovered, for 40 minutes, or until the onions are rich and dark golden brown. Take care that they do not stick and burn at the bottom.

2 Preheat the slow cooker, if required. Remove the paper and stir in the wine. Increase the heat to medium and stir for 5 minutes, or until the onions are glazed. Sprinkle with the flour and stir for 2 minutes. Stir in the stock and bring to a boil. Transfer everything to the slow cooker, cover with the lid, and cook on auto/low for 4–6 hours or on high for 2–3 hours. Taste and adjust the seasoning, if necessary.

3 Preheat the broiler on its highest setting. Divide the soup between 4 flameproof bowls and stir 1 tablespoon of brandy into each. Rub the garlic over the toast and place a slice in each bowl. Sprinkle with cheese and broil for 2–3 minutes, or until the cheese is bubbling. Serve at once.

traditional method 🕐 **PREP** 10 MINS **COOK** 1½ HRS

1 Melt the butter with the oil in a large Dutch oven over low heat. Stir in the onions and sugar, and season with salt and pepper. Press a piece of wet parchment paper over the surface and cook, stirring occasionally, uncovered, for 40 minutes, or until the onions are rich and dark golden brown. Take care that they do not stick and burn at the bottom.

2 Remove the paper and stir in the wine. Increase the heat to medium and stir for 5 minutes, or until the onions are glazed. Sprinkle with the flour and stir for 2 minutes. Stir in the stock and bring to a boil. Reduce the heat to low, cover with the lid, and leave the soup to simmer for 30 minutes. Taste and adjust the seasoning, if necessary.

3 Meanwhile, preheat the broiler on its highest setting. Divide the soup between 4 flameproof bowls and stir 1 tablespoon of brandy into each. Rub the garlic clove over the toast and place a slice in each bowl. Sprinkle with the cheese and broil for 2–3 minutes, or until the cheese is bubbling and golden. Serve at once.

This is a substantial meal-in-one that is full of complex flavors. It's also one of those dishes that tastes better when reheated, so if you have the time, make it a day ahead and reheat to eat.

Moroccan harira soup

SERVES 4–6 ❄ **FREEZE** UP TO 1 MONTH

1 tbsp olive oil
1 red onion, finely chopped
salt and freshly ground black pepper
3 garlic cloves, finely chopped
1 celery stalk, chopped
1½lb (675g) boneless shoulder or
  shank of lamb, cut into bite-sized pieces
1 tsp ground turmeric
1 tsp ground cinnamon
2in (5cm) piece of fresh ginger, peeled
  and finely chopped

3 cups hot vegetable stock for the slow cooker
  (5 cups for the traditional method)
heaping ½ cup green or brown lentils, rinsed
  well and picked over for any stones
14oz (400g) can chickpeas, drained and rinsed
1 tsp harissa paste
few sprigs of cilantro, leaves only, to serve

in the slow cooker
PREP 25 MINS **COOK** 25–30 MINS PRECOOKING; **AUTO/LOW** 8 HRS

1 Preheat the slow cooker, if required. Heat the oil in a large Dutch oven over medium heat, add the onion, and cook for 3–4 minutes until soft. Season with salt and pepper, then stir in the garlic and celery and cook for a further 6–10 minutes until the celery is soft.

2 Add the lamb, turmeric, cinnamon, and ginger. Increase the heat a little, stir until the lamb is coated, and cook for 6–10 minutes until the lamb is no longer pink. Add a ladleful of stock and bring to a boil. Stir in the lentils and chickpeas, turning them to coat evenly, add the remaining stock, and bring back to a boil.

3 Transfer everything to the slow cooker. Stir in the harissa paste, cover with the lid, and cook on auto/low for 8 hours. Ladle into warmed bowls, top with cilantro leaves, and serve with lemon wedges on the side.

traditional method
PREP 25 MINS **COOK** 2 HRS

1 Heat the oil in a large Dutch oven over medium heat, add the onion, and cook for 3–4 minutes until soft. Season with salt and pepper, then stir in the garlic and celery and cook for a further 6–10 minutes until the celery is soft.

2 Add the lamb, turmeric, cinnamon, and ginger. Increase the heat a little, stir until the lamb is coated, and cook for 6–10 minutes until the lamb is no longer pink. Add a ladleful of stock and bring to a boil. Stir in the lentils and chickpeas, turning them to coat evenly, add the remaining stock, and bring back to a boil.

3 Reduce to a gentle simmer and cook for 1–1½ hours until the lamb is meltingly tender. Check occasionally that it's not drying out, topping up with a little hot water if needed. Stir in the harissa paste and cook for a few more minutes. Ladle into warmed bowls, top with cilantro leaves, and serve with lemon wedges on the side.

Oxtail has a distinctive flavor and is perfectly suited to slow cooking. You may have to get the meat from your butcher, as not all supermarkets have it. You could use stewing beef if you prefer.

Oxtail soup with nutmeg and star anise

SERVES 4–6 **FREEZE** UP TO 3 MONTHS

2 tbsp olive oil
1lb 5oz (600g) oxtails
1 red onion, finely chopped
salt and freshly ground black pepper
3 garlic cloves, finely chopped

2 star anise
pinch of grated nutmeg
3 cups hot vegetable stock,
  for both methods
2 x 14oz (400g) cans whole tomatoes

in the slow cooker   PREP 15 MINS   COOK 15 MINS PRECOOKING; AUTO/LOW 8 HRS

1 Preheat the slow cooker, if required. Heat half the oil in a Dutch oven over medium-high heat, add the oxtails, and cook them for about 10 minutes or until beginning to color on all sides. Remove them and leave to cool, then remove the bones from the oxtails and set aside.

2 Meanwhile, reduce the heat a little, heat the rest of the oil, add the onion, and cook for 3–4 minutes until soft. Season with salt and pepper, then stir in the garlic, star anise, and nutmeg, and cook for 1–2 minutes more. Add a little stock and stir to scrape up the bits from the bottom of the pan. Transfer everything to the slow cooker, including the oxtails, add in the tomatoes and remaining stock, and stir. Cover with the lid and cook on auto/low for 8 hours.

3 Discard the star anise, then remove the oxtails with a slotted spoon. Shred the meat with a fork, and return it to the slow cooker. Use an immersion blender to blend the soup until smooth, or transfer in batches to a liquidizer and blend. Transfer the soup to a clean pan to heat through, adding a little hot water if you need to thin it down. Taste and adjust seasoning as needed, and serve piping hot with crusty white bread.

traditional method   PREP 15 MINS   COOK 2¾–3¼ HRS

1 Heat half the oil in a Dutch oven over medium-high heat, add the oxtails, and cook them for about 10 minutes or until beginning to color on all sides. Remove them and set aside. Reduce the heat a little, heat the rest of the oil, add the onion, and cook for 3–4 minutes until soft. Season with salt and pepper, then stir in the garlic, star anise, and nutmeg, and cook for 1–2 minutes more. Add a little stock and stir to scrape up the bits from the bottom of the pot.

2 Return the meat to the pan, add in the tomatoes and the remaining stock, and bring to a boil. Reduce to a simmer, and cook on a gentle heat, partially covered, for 2½–3 hours or until the meat falls off the bone, topping up with a further cup of hot water (or more if needed) as required. Discard the star anise, then remove the oxtails with a slotted spoon. Shred the meat with a fork, and return it to the pot. Use an immersion blender to blend the soup until smooth or transfer in batches to a liquidizer and blend. Transfer the soup to a clean pan to heat through, adding a little hot water if you need to thin it down. Taste and adjust seasoning as needed, and serve piping hot with crusty white bread.

A cure-all soup to which you can add vegetables or some ready-cooked noodles. The key to successful soups is the stock—use the leftover bones in this recipe to make your own.

Chunky chicken soup

SERVES 6   **FREEZE** UP TO 3 MONTHS   **HEALTHY**

1 whole chicken, weighing about 3lb (1.35kg)
1 tbsp olive oil
1 onion, finely chopped
salt and freshly ground black pepper
3 garlic cloves, finely chopped
2 celery stalks, roughly chopped

4 carrots, peeled and chopped into chunky pieces
12oz (350g) can corn niblets, drained
3 potatoes, peeled and roughly chopped
2 leeks, chopped into chunky pieces
few sprigs of curly parsley, finely chopped

in the slow cooker   **PREP** 15 MINS   **COOK** AUTO/LOW 8 HRS, THEN
AUTO/LOW 6–8 HRS OR **HIGH** 4 HRS

1 Put the chicken, upside down, in the slow cooker. Pour in 3 cups of water, cover, and cook on auto/low for 8 hours. Remove the chicken, cover it, and set aside. Strain and reserve the stock. When cold, store the chicken in the fridge.

2 Preheat the slow cooker, if required. Heat the oil in a large Dutch oven over medium heat, add the onions, and cook for 3–4 minutes until soft. Season with salt and pepper, then add the garlic and celery, and cook for a further 5 minutes until the celery softens. Stir in the carrots, add the corn, and transfer everything to the slow cooker. Measure the reserved stock and add hot water to make 3 cups and pour this over the casserole. Add the potatoes and leeks and stir, then cover with the lid and cook on auto/low for 6–8 hours or on high for 4 hours.

3 Meanwhile, remove the skin from the chicken and pull away the meat. Stir this into the soup for the last 20 minutes of cooking. Taste and season as required. Ladle into wide bowls, sprinkle with a little parsley, and serve with crusty white bread.

traditional method   **PREP** 15 MINS   **COOK** 1½ HRS

1 Put the chicken in a large stock pot and pour in enough water to just cover it. Season with salt and pepper, then bring to a boil. Reduce to a simmer, cover with the lid, and cook for about 20 minutes until the chicken is cooked and the juices run clear when pierced with a sharp knife. Remove the chicken from the stock, set aside, and cover with foil; strain the stock and also set aside.

2 Heat the oil in a large Dutch oven over medium heat, add the onions, and cook for 3–4 minutes until soft. Season with salt and pepper, then add the garlic and celery, and cook for a further 5 minutes until the celery softens. Stir in the carrots and add the corn. Measure the reserved stock and add hot water to make 3 cups and pour this in. Bring the soup to a boil, then reduce to a simmer and cook on very low heat with the lid partially covering the pan for about 30 minutes, topping up with hot water, if needed. Add the potatoes and leeks and cook for a further 20 minutes, partially covered with the lid.

3 Remove the skin from the chicken and pull away the meat. Stir this into the soup, taste, and season as required. Ladle into wide bowls, sprinkle with a little parsley, and serve with crusty white bread.

The broth in this recipe has a rich beef flavor with the barley and dumplings adding plenty of texture and variety. They also turn the soup into a hearty, warming meal.

Beef broth with Parmesan dumplings

SERVES 6 **FREEZE** UP TO 3 MONTHS, WITHOUT THE DUMPLINGS **HEALTHY**

2½lb (1.1kg) brisket on the bone, cut into small
 pieces (ask your butcher to do this for you)
salt and freshly ground black pepper
¼ cup pearl barley
1 onion, roughly chopped
3 celery stalks, finely chopped
3 garlic cloves, finely chopped
4 carrots, peeled and sliced
3 small turnips, peeled and diced
4 tomatoes

few sprigs of flat-leaf parsley, leaves only,
 finely chopped

FOR THE PARMESAN DUMPLINGS
¼ cup breadcrumbs
¼ cup Parmesan cheese, grated,
 plus extra, to serve
pinch of grated nutmeg
1 egg

in the slow cooker **PREP** 15 MINS **COOK** AUTO/LOW 6–8 HRS

1 Preheat the slow cooker, if required. Put the beef bones, with enough water to cover them (about 3 cups), and all the other soup ingredients, into the slow cooker, including seasoning. Cover with the lid and cook on auto/low for 6–8 hours. Remove the beef bones and then remove the meat, chop if needed, and return it to the slow cooker.

2 Meanwhile, prepare the dumplings. Mix together the breadcrumbs, Parmesan cheese, and nutmeg, season well with salt and pepper, and then mix in the egg. Turn the mixture out onto a floured board and knead for a couple of minutes, then form into tiny balls. Add them to the slow cooker for the last 10 minutes of cooking. Ladle the soup into warmed shallow bowls and sprinkle with Parmesan cheese and parsley. Serve with crusty bread rolls.

traditional method **PREP** 15 MINS **COOK** 2½ HRS

1 Put the beef bones into a large Dutch oven and cover with 5 cups of water. Season well with salt and pepper, and bring to a boil. Skim off any scum that builds up, reduce the heat, cover with the lid, and let the broth simmer gently for about 1½ hours. Add the pearl barley, onion, celery, garlic, carrots, turnips, and tomatoes, partially cover with the lid, and cook for a further 45 minutes, or until the pearl barley is tender. Top up with a little hot water, if needed.

2 Meanwhile, prepare the dumplings. Mix together the breadcrumbs, Parmesan cheese, and nutmeg, season well with salt and pepper, and then mix in the egg. Turn the mixture out onto a floured board and knead for a couple of minutes, then form into tiny balls.

3 When the meat is cooked, use a slotted spoon to take the beef bones out of the pan. Remove the meat, chop if needed, and return it to the pan. Add the dumplings to the soup and cook gently for about 5 minutes, then ladle it into warmed shallow bowls and sprinkle with Parmesan cheese and parsley. Serve with crusty bread rolls.

This soup will make a really substantial meal on its own. Make it without the chorizo if you are feeding vegetarians, but add a little smoked paprika to replace the smoky flavor.

Cajun mixed bean soup

SERVES 4–6 ❄ **FREEZE** UP TO 3 MONTHS

1 tbsp olive oil
1 onion, finely chopped
salt and freshly ground black pepper
3 garlic cloves, finely chopped
2 celery stalks, finely chopped
7oz (200g) chorizo, cubed
pinch of dried chile flakes

few sprigs of thyme
2 sweet potatoes, peeled and cubed
2 yellow bell peppers, seeded and roughly chopped
2 x 14oz (400g) cans black beans, drained and rinsed
14oz (400g) can kidney beans, drained and rinsed
1¾ cups hot vegetable stock for the slow cooker
    (3 cups for the traditional method)

in the slow cooker   ⏱ **PREP** 10 MINS   **COOK** 25 MINS PRECOOKING;
AUTO/LOW 8 HRS OR **HIGH** 3 HRS

1 Preheat the slow cooker, if required. Heat the oil in a large Dutch oven over medium heat, add the onion, and cook for 3–4 minutes until soft. Season with salt and pepper, then stir in the garlic and celery, and cook for a further 10 minutes until the celery is soft. Stir in the chorizo, chile, and thyme, and cook for a minute. Add the sweet potatoes and cook for a few minutes, then add the peppers and let this cook gently for about 5 minutes, stirring so it doesn't stick.

2 Transfer everything to the slow cooker. Add in the black and kidney beans and the stock, stir, then cover with the lid and cook on auto/low for 8 hours or on high for 3 hours. Use an immersion blender, or transfer in batches to a food processor, to blend until it is well combined but still retains some texture. Add a ladleful of hot water if it is too thick. Transfer the soup to a clean pan and heat through. Taste and season as needed, then ladle into warmed bowls and serve with tortillas, sour cream, Cheddar cheese, and a sprinkling of finely chopped parsley.

traditional method   ⏱ **PREP** 10 MINS   **COOK** 1–1½ HRS

1 Heat the oil in a large Dutch oven over medium heat, add the onion, and cook for 3–4 minutes until soft. Season with salt and pepper, then stir in the garlic and celery, and cook for a further 10 minutes until the celery is soft. Stir in the chorizo, chile, and thyme, and cook for a minute. Add the sweet potatoes and cook for a few minutes, then add the bell peppers and let this cook gently for about 5 minutes, stirring so it doesn't stick.

2 Add in the black and kidney beans, add a little of the stock, increase the heat, and let the mixture simmer. Add the remaining stock, bring to a boil, then reduce to a simmer, partially cover with a lid, and cook for 45–60 minutes on low heat. Check occasionally that it's not drying out, topping up with a little hot water if needed.

3 Use an immersion blender, or transfer in batches to a food processor, to blend until it is well combined but still retains some texture. Add a ladleful of hot water if it is too thick. Transfer the soup to a clean pan and heat through. Taste and season as needed, then ladle into warmed bowls and serve with tortillas, sour cream, grated Cheddar cheese, and a sprinkling of finely chopped parsley.

A firm favorite with everyone, this soup tastes even better served the next day. Go easy on the salt when adding seasoning because the ham may be salty enough for most people's taste.

Pea, ham, and potato soup

SERVES 4–6 **FREEZE** UP TO 3 MONTHS

2½lb (1.1kg) fresh uncured ham
1 bay leaf
1 tbsp olive oil
1 onion, finely chopped
salt and freshly ground black pepper
1 tbsp Dijon mustard
3 garlic cloves, finely chopped

2 sprigs of rosemary
handful of thyme, leaves only
3 cups hot beef stock for the slow cooker
  (1 quart for the traditional method)
about 4 cups frozen peas
3 potatoes, peeled and chopped into
  bite-sized pieces

in the slow cooker **PREP** 15 MINS **COOK AUTO/LOW** 8 HRS OR **HIGH** 4 HRS, THEN **AUTO/LOW** 8 HRS OR **HIGH** 4 HRS

1 Preheat the slow cooker, if required. Sit the ham and bay leaf in the slow cooker and cover with 3 cups of water. Cover and cook on auto/low for 8 hours or on high for 4 hours, then remove the ham and set aside. Discard the stock, or strain and reserve a little to add to the soup.

2 Heat the oil in a large heavy-based pan over medium heat, add the onion, and cook for 3–4 minutes until soft. Season with salt and pepper, then stir in the mustard, garlic, and herbs (reserve some thyme leaves for garnish). Add a little stock and bring to a boil, then add in the peas (if you prefer them puréed, pulse them gently in a food processor or use an immersion blender). Transfer to the slow cooker, add the remaining stock and the potatoes, cover, and cook on auto/low for 8 hours or on high for 4 hours. Remove any fat from the ham, chop into bite-sized pieces, and stir into the soup. Taste and season as needed. Garnish with the reserved thyme leaves and serve with whole grain bread.

traditional method **PREP** 15 MINS **COOK** 2 HRS

1 Add the ham and bay leaf to a large pan, cover with 1 quart of water, and bring to a boil. Partially cover, reduce to a simmer, and cook for about 1 hour or until the ham is cooked. Skim away any scum that comes to the surface of the pan as you go. Discard the stock, or strain and reserve a little to add to the soup. Set the ham aside until cool enough to handle.

2 Heat the oil in a large heavy-based pan over medium heat, add the onion, and cook for 3–4 minutes until soft. Season with salt and pepper, then stir in the mustard, garlic, and herbs (reserve some thyme leaves for garnish). Add a little stock and bring to a boil, then add in the peas and remaining stock. Bring to a boil, reduce to a simmer, and cook for 45 minutes, topping up with hot water as needed.

3 About 20 minutes before the end of the cooking time, bring a separate pot of water to a boil. Add the potatoes, bring back up to a boil, and then simmer for 12–15 minutes until soft. Drain and set aside. Remove the rosemary from the soup, then use an immersion blender to gently purée the peas, or ladle them into a food processor and pulse a couple of times. Return them to the pot and stir in the potatoes. Remove any fat from the ham, chop into bite-sized pieces, and stir into the soup. Taste and adjust seasoning as needed. Garnish with the reserved thyme leaves and serve with whole grain bread.

This classic Tuscan bean soup is named after the traditional method of reboiling soup from the day before. You can keep adding to it and re-cooking it, and it's ideal for using leftovers.

Ribollita

SERVES 4–6　**FREEZE** UP TO 3 MONTHS, WITHOUT THE CIABATTA　**HEALTHY**

¼ cup extra virgin olive oil, plus extra for drizzling
1 onion, chopped
2 carrots, peeled and sliced
1 leek, trimmed and sliced
salt and freshly ground black pepper
2 garlic cloves, chopped
14oz (400g) can chopped tomatoes
1 tbsp tomato paste

3 cups hot chicken stock, for both methods
14oz (400g) can borlotti beans, flageolet beans, or cannellini beans, drained and rinsed
about 8 cups baby spinach leaves or spring greens, shredded
8 slices ciabatta bread
grated Parmesan cheese, to serve

in the slow cooker　**PREP** 15 MINS　**COOK** 15 MINS PRECOOKING; **AUTO/LOW** 5–6 HRS OR **HIGH** 3–4 HRS

1 Preheat the slow cooker, if required. Heat the oil in a large heavy-based saucepan over low heat, add the onions, carrots, and leeks, and cook for 10 minutes until softened but not colored. Season with salt and pepper, stir in the garlic, and cook for 1 minute. Add the tomatoes, tomato paste, and stock and bring to a boil.

2 Transfer everything to the slow cooker and season. Mash half the beans with a fork and stir these in together with the remaining whole ones. Cover with the lid and cook on auto/low for 5–6 hours or on high for 3–4 hours. Add the spinach for the last 20 minutes of cooking.

3 Toast the bread until golden, place 2 pieces in each soup bowl, and drizzle with olive oil. To serve, spoon the soup into the bowls, top with a sprinkling of Parmesan cheese, and drizzle with a little more olive oil.

traditional method　**PREP** 15 MINS　**COOK** 1¼ HRS

1 Heat the oil in a large heavy-based saucepan over low heat, add the onions, carrots, and leeks, and cook for 10 minutes until softened but not colored. Season with salt and pepper, then stir in the garlic and cook for 1 minute. Add the tomatoes, tomato paste, and stock, and season with salt and pepper once more to taste.

2 Mash half the beans with a fork and add to the pan. Bring to a boil, lower the heat, and simmer for 30 minutes. Add the remaining beans and spinach and leave to simmer for a further 30 minutes.

3 Toast the bread, place 2 pieces in each soup bowl, and drizzle with olive oil. To serve, spoon the soup into the bowls, top with a sprinkling of Parmesan cheese, and drizzle with olive oil.

Choose smaller beets for this recipe, if you can, because they have a more intense flavor than the larger ones. The beets will flavor and thicken the soup, resulting in a wonderful color.

Borscht

🌀 **SERVES** 4   ❄️ **FREEZE** UP TO 3 MONTHS   🤍 **HEALTHY**

3 tbsp butter or goose fat
2½ lb (1.1kg) raw red beets, grated
1 onion, grated
1 carrot, peeled and grated, plus extra to serve
1 celery stalk, grated
14oz (400g) can chopped tomatoes
1 garlic clove, crushed

3 cups hot vegetable stock for the slow cooker
  (6 cups for the traditional method)
2 bay leaves
4 cloves
2 tbsp lemon juice
salt and freshly ground black pepper
¾ cup sour cream

in the slow cooker   🕐 **PREP** 20 MINS   **COOK** 15 MINS PRECOOKING;
AUTO/LOW 6–8 HRS OR **HIGH** 3–4 HRS

1 Preheat the slow cooker, if required. Melt the butter or goose fat in a large heavy-based saucepan over medium heat. Add the beets, onion, carrot, and celery and cook, stirring, for 5 minutes or until just softened. Add the tomatoes and garlic and cook for 2–3 minutes, stirring frequently. Then stir in the stock and bring to a boil. Reduce to a simmer, then transfer everything to the slow cooker.

2 Tie the bay leaves and cloves together in a small piece of cheesecloth and add to the slow cooker. Cover with the lid and cook on auto/low for 6–8 hours or on high for 3–4 hours.

3 Discard the cheesecloth bag. Stir in the lemon juice and season with salt and pepper. Blend the soup with an immersion blender, or in batches in a food processor, if you wish. Ladle the soup into warmed bowls and add a swirl of sour cream to each. Serve with grated carrot and dark rye bread.

traditional method   🕐 **PREP** 15 MINS   **COOK** 1½ HRS

1 Melt the butter or goose fat in a large heavy-based saucepan over medium heat. Add the beets, onion, carrot, and celery and cook, stirring, for 5 minutes or until just softened. Add the tomatoes and garlic and cook for 2–3 minutes, stirring frequently. Then stir in the stock.

2 Tie the bay leaves and cloves together in a small piece of cheesecloth and add to the pan. Bring the soup to a boil, reduce the heat, cover with the lid, and simmer for 1 hour 20 minutes.

3 Discard the cheesecloth bag. Stir in the lemon juice and season with salt and pepper. Blend the soup with an immersion blender or in batches in a food processor, if you wish. Ladle the soup into warmed bowls and add a swirl of sour cream to each. Serve with grated carrot and dark rye bread.

The subtle combinations of meaty monkfish, delicate haddock, aniseed fennel, and the light scent of saffron marry well. You could add some mussels or shrimp, if you like.

Rich fish soup

SERVES 4–6   **FREEZE** UP TO 1 MONTH

1 tbsp olive oil
1 onion, finely chopped
salt and freshly ground black pepper
1 sprig of thyme
3 garlic cloves, finely chopped
1 fennel bulb, trimmed and finely chopped
1 red chile, seeded and finely chopped

1 cup dry white wine
2 x 14oz (400g) cans chopped tomatoes
2 cups hot light vegetable stock for the slow cooker
  (3 cups for the traditional method)
pinch of saffron threads
7oz (200g) monkfish, cut into bite-sized pieces
7oz (200g) haddock loin, cut into bite-sized pieces

in the slow cooker   **PREP** 15 MINS   **COOK** 10 MINS PRECOOKING; **AUTO/LOW** 8 HRS OR **HIGH** 4 HRS

1 Preheat the slow cooker, if required. Heat the oil in a large heavy-based pan over medium heat, add the onion, and cook for 3–4 minutes until soft. Season with salt and pepper and throw in the thyme. Add the garlic and fennel, and cook gently for a further 5 minutes until the fennel begins to soften.

2 Stir in the chile and cook for 1 minute, then increase the heat, add the wine, and let it bubble for a minute. Transfer everything to the hot slow cooker, add in the tomatoes and stock, and stir in the saffron. Cover with the lid and cook on auto/low for 8 hours or on high for 4 hours.

3 Use an immersion blender to blend the soup until smooth, or transfer in batches to a liquidizer and blend until smooth. Return to the slow cooker. Taste and season as needed, then add the fish, put the lid back on, and leave for about 10 minutes or until the fish is opaque and cooked through. Ladle into warmed bowls and serve with white crusty bread. Garnish with chopped fennel fronds, if you like.

traditional method   **PREP** 15 MINS   **COOK** 1 HR

1 Heat the oil in a large heavy-based pan over medium heat, add the onion, and cook for 3–4 minutes until soft. Season with salt and pepper and throw in the thyme. Add the garlic and fennel, and cook gently for a further 5 minutes until the fennel begins to soften.

2 Stir in the chile and cook for 1 minute, then increase the heat, add the wine, let it bubble for a minute, and then add in the canned tomatoes and stock. Add the saffron, bring to a boil, then reduce to a simmer and cook gently, partially covered with the lid, for about 45 minutes. Take care that the sauce doesn't dry out, topping it up with a little hot water if needed.

3 Use an immersion blender to blend the soup until smooth, or transfer in batches to a liquidizer and blend until smooth and return to a clean pan. Top up with a little hot water—you will probably need about 1½ cups in total—and simmer gently. Taste and season as needed, then add the fish, put the lid back on, and cook on a low heat for 6–10 minutes or until the fish is opaque and cooked through. Ladle into warmed bowls and serve with white crusty bread. Garnish with chopped fennel fronds, if you like.

The hot and fragrant broth in this recipe is a perfect foil for the delicate white fish. You could add some noodles to the soup, if you wish, or some soy beans for a little more bulk.

Japanese-style fish broth

SERVES 4–6

¾ cup dried shiitake mushrooms
3 carrots, peeled and sliced finely on the diagonal
1 tbsp dark soy sauce
2in (5cm) piece of fresh ginger, peeled and finely sliced
bunch of cilantro
1 leek, finely sliced on the diagonal
9oz (250g) white fish
1 tsp pickled sushi ginger, drained (optional)

FOR THE BROTH
2 sheets of kombu (dried kelp seaweed), wiped clean and soaked for 30 minutes (optional)
2 tbsp bonito dried fish flakes (optional)
OR
6 cups hot light vegetable stock, for both methods
1 tsp fish sauce (nam pla)
1 tbsp rice vinegar

in the slow cooker   **PREP** 15 MINS   **COOK** 20 MINS PRECOOKING; **HIGH** 3 HRS

1 Preheat the slow cooker, if required. Put 4 cups of water in a large stock pot and add the kombu and bonito flakes, if using. Almost bring to a boil, then drain through a sieve and return the water to the pan (reserve the kombu and bonito flakes for another use). If not using kombu and bonito, put the vegetable stock into a stock pot, add the fish sauce and rice vinegar, and simmer very gently for 20 minutes.

2 Meanwhile, soak the shiitake mushrooms in warm water for 20 minutes. Drain and add to the broth, then transfer everything to the slow cooker and add the carrots, soy sauce, fresh ginger, cilantro, and leeks. Cover with the lid and cook on high for 3 hours.

3 Add the fish and re-cover. The fish will cook in minutes in the hot broth. Stir in the sushi ginger, if using, then taste and adjust the flavor with soy sauce and fish sauce. Serve immediately while piping hot.

traditional method   **PREP** 15 MINS   **COOK** 1 HR

1 Put 4 cups of water in a large stock pot and add the kombu and bonito flakes, if using. Almost bring to a boil, then drain through a sieve and return the water to the pan (reserve the kombu and bonito flakes for another use). If not using kombu and bonito, put the vegetable stock into a stock pot, add the fish sauce and rice vinegar, and simmer very gently for 20 minutes.

2 Meanwhile, soak the shiitake mushrooms in warm water for 20 minutes. Drain and add to the broth along with the carrots, soy sauce, fresh ginger, and cilantro. Partially cover with the lid and simmer gently for 20 minutes or until the carrots are cooked, then stir in the leek and cook for a further 10 minutes.

3 Add the fish, cover with the lid, and cook for a few minutes until the fish is opaque and cooked through. Stir in the sushi ginger, if using, then taste and adjust the flavor with soy sauce and fish sauce. Serve immediately while piping hot.

Dried mushrooms and lardons add plenty of flavor to the lentils. This is a great soup for a crowd because you can make it in advance and it tastes even better when reheated.

Lentil, mushroom, and bacon soup

🌀 **SERVES** 4   ❄️ **FREEZE** UP TO 1 MONTH

1 tbsp olive oil
1 red onion, finely chopped
freshly ground black pepper
3 garlic cloves, finely chopped
2 celery stalks, finely chopped
2 sage leaves
9oz (250g) smoked lardons, chopped smoked
  bacon, or pancetta cubes
pinch of dried chile flakes

1 cup Puy lentils, rinsed and picked
  over for any stones
¾oz (20g) dried mushrooms, soaked in
  1 cup warm water for 20 minutes,
  strained, and liquid reserved
1 tbsp dry sherry
4 cups hot vegetable stock for
  the slow cooker (5 cups for
  the traditional method)

in the slow cooker   🕐 **PREP** 15 MINS, PLUS SOAKING   **COOK** 25 MINS PRECOOKING; **AUTO/LOW** 8 HRS OR **HIGH** 2 HRS

1 Preheat the slow cooker, if required. Heat the oil in a large Dutch oven over medium heat, add the onions, and cook for 3–4 minutes until soft. Season with pepper, then stir in the garlic and celery and cook for a further 6–10 minutes until the celery is soft. Increase the heat, add the sage and lardons, and cook for about 5 minutes, until the lardons begin to color a little and release some juice.

2 Stir in the chile flakes, lentils, and the drained soaked mushrooms. Add the sherry, increase the heat, and stir to scrape up the bits from the bottom of the pan. Transfer everything to the slow cooker and pour in the reserved mushroom liquid and the stock. Stir and cover with the lid, and cook on auto/low for 8 hours or on high for 2 hours. Taste and season, as required, and adjust the consistency with some hot water, if needed. Ladle into warmed bowls and serve with crusty bread.

traditional method   🕐 **PREP** 15 MINS   **COOK** 1¾–2 HRS

1 Heat the oil in a large Dutch oven over medium heat, add the onions, and cook for 3–4 minutes until soft. Season with pepper, then stir in the garlic and celery and cook for a further 6–10 minutes until the celery is soft. Increase the heat, add the sage and lardons, and cook for about 5 minutes, until the lardons begin to color a little and release some juice.

2 Stir in the chile flakes, lentils, and the drained soaked mushrooms. Add the sherry, increase the heat, and stir to scrape up the bits from the bottom of the pan. Then pour in half the stock and all the reserved mushroom liquid and bring to a boil. Partially cover with the lid, reduce to a simmer, and cook on a low heat for about 1¼ hours, topping up with the reserved stock (and more if needed) as you go. Taste and season, as required, and adjust the consistency with some hot water, if needed. Ladle into warmed bowls and serve with crusty bread.

This velvety smooth soup can be made using pumpkin or butternut squash, depending on what is in season. The dried chile flakes give it just the right kick to cut through the richness.

Pumpkin and ginger soup

SERVES 4–6 **FREEZE** UP TO 3 MONTHS

1 tbsp olive oil
1 onion, finely chopped
salt and freshly ground black pepper
3 garlic cloves, finely chopped
2in (5cm) piece of fresh ginger,
  peeled and finely chopped
pinch of dried chile flakes

1 small cinnamon stick
2lb (900g) pumpkin or butternut squash, peeled,
  seeded, and diced
2 cups hot vegetable stock for the slow cooker
  (3 cups for the traditional method)

in the slow cooker **PREP** 15 MINS **COOK** 15 MINS PRECOOKING;
AUTO/LOW 8 HRS OR **HIGH** 4 HRS

1 Preheat the slow cooker, if required. Heat the oil in a large heavy-based pan over medium heat, add the onion, and cook for 3–4 minutes until soft. Season with salt and pepper, then add the garlic, ginger, chile flakes, and cinnamon stick, and cook for a few seconds before adding the pumpkin or squash (and a little more olive oil if needed) and stir to coat.

2 Pour in a little of the stock, increase the heat, and scrape up the bits from the bottom of the pan. Transfer everything to the slow cooker. Add the remaining stock, cover with the lid, and cook on auto/low for 8 hours or on high for 4 hours.

3 Remove the cinnamon stick and use an immersion blender to blend the soup until smooth, or transfer in batches to a food processor and blend until smooth. Transfer to a clean pan to heat through, taste, and season as required. Serve with some chunky whole grain bread or some rye bread.

traditional method **PREP** 15 MINS **COOK** 1 HR

1 Heat the oil over medium heat in a large heavy-based pan, add the onion, and cook for 3–4 minutes until soft. Season with salt and pepper, then add the garlic, ginger, chile flakes, and cinnamon stick, and cook for a few seconds before adding the pumpkin or squash (and a little more olive oil if needed) and stir to coat.

2 Pour in a little of the stock, increase the heat, and scrape up the bits from the bottom of the pan. Add the remaining stock, boil for 1 minute, then reduce the heat to barely a simmer, cover with the lid, and cook for about 45 minutes until the pumpkin is soft and the flavors have developed.

3 Remove the cinnamon stick and use an immersion blender to blend the soup until smooth, or transfer in batches to a food processor and blend until smooth. Add a ladleful of hot water as you go if it is too thick. Transfer to a clean pan to heat through, taste, and season as required. Serve with some chunky whole grain bread or some rye bread.

This rustic soup owes its substance to navy beans, which can be canned, fresh,or dried. Canned ones are easiest to use, while fresh beans are quicker to cook and easier to digest than dried ones.

Pistou soup

SERVES 6 ❄ **FREEZE** UP TO 3 MONTHS, WITHOUT THE MACARONI AND PISTOU

1 ham hock, or a thick piece of smoked bacon,
  about 5½oz (150g)
14oz (400g) can cannellini beans, drained and rinsed
14oz (400g) can borlotti beans, drained and rinsed
2 Russet potatoes, peeled and diced
3 tomatoes, skinned, seeded, and chopped
2 zucchini, trimmed and chopped
salt and freshly ground black pepper
5½oz (150g) green beans, sliced
1 cup small macaroni

FOR THE PISTOU
3 garlic cloves, peeled
sea salt and freshly ground black pepper
large handful of basil leaves
2 small tomatoes, skinned, seeded,
  and chopped
¼ cup grated mimolette cheese
  or Parmesan cheese, grated
3 tbsp olive oil

in the slow cooker ⏱ **PREP** 30 MINS **COOK** AUTO/LOW 6–8 HRS OR **HIGH** 3–4 HRS

1 Preheat the slow cooker, if required. To make the pistou, pound the garlic in a mortar with a pestle, then add a little sea salt and the basil, and pound to a paste. Add the tomatoes and continue pounding and mixing until you have a thick sauce. Add some pepper and then the cheese and oil. Mix well, taste, add salt and pepper if needed, and set aside.

2 Put the ham in the slow cooker and pour in 2½ cups water. Add the canned beans and the potatoes, tomatoes, and zucchini, and top up with more water to cover, if needed. Season lightly, if you wish, then cover with the lid and cook on auto/low for 6–8 hours or on high for 3–4 hours. Skim halfway through if needed. For the last 30 minutes of cooking, add the green beans and macaroni.

3 Remove the ham hock from the slow cooker and, when cool enough to handle, remove the skin and any fat, and shred the meat off the bone. Lift half of the ingredients out of the slow cooker and mash with a fork, then return to the soup together with the ham. Stir in the pistou and serve.

traditional method ⏱ **PREP** 30 MINS **COOK** 1¾ HRS

1 To make the pistou, pound the garlic in a mortar with a pestle, then add a little sea salt and the basil, and pound to a paste. Add the tomatoes and continue pounding and mixing until you have a thick sauce. Add some pepper and then the cheese and oil. Mix well, adjust the seasoning, and set aside.

2 For the soup, put 7 cups cold water in a large heavy-based saucepan. Add the ham hock, bring to a simmer, then partly cover and leave to simmer gently for 30 minutes, skimming occasionally. Add all the vegetables to the pan and season lightly with salt and pepper. Return the pan to a simmer, partly cover, and let it cook gently for 1 hour, skimming occasionally.

3 Remove the ham hock and, when cool enough to handle, remove the skin and any fat, and shred the meat off the bone. Lift half of the ingredients out of the pan, mash with a fork, then return to the soup together with the ham. Add the macaroni and cook until just tender. Stir in the pistou and serve.

You can add whatever vegetables are in season to this substantial soup—zucchini or yellow squash would be nice. Spaghetti or linguine are good pastas to use—break them into small pieces.

Minestrone

SERVES 4–6   **FREEZE** UP TO 1 MONTH, WITHOUT THE PASTA   **HEALTHY**

1 cup dried cannellini beans, soaked
  in cold water overnight, and drained
2 tbsp olive oil
2 celery stalks, finely chopped
2 carrots, peeled and finely chopped
1 onion, finely chopped
14oz (400g) can chopped tomatoes

salt and freshly ground black pepper
2½ cups hot chicken or vegetable stock,
  for both methods
¾ cup small short-cut pasta
¼ cup chopped flat-leaf parsley
⅓ cup Parmesan cheese, finely grated

in the slow cooker   **PREP** 15 MINS, PLUS SOAKING   **COOK** 15 MINS PRECOOKING; AUTO/LOW 6–8 HRS

1 Preheat the slow cooker, if required. Put the beans in a large heavy-based saucepan, cover with cold water, and bring to a boil over high heat, skimming the surface as necessary. Boil for 10 minutes, then reduce the heat to low, drain, and set aside.

2 Heat the oil in the rinsed-out pan over medium heat. Add the celery, carrots, and onion, and cook for 5 minutes until softened. Stir in the tomatoes with their juice and let it bubble. Transfer everything to the slow cooker, including the beans, season with salt and pepper, and stir in the stock. Cover with the lid and cook on auto/low for 6–8 hours.

3 Add the pasta for the last 15 minutes of cooking until just tender. Stir in the parsley and half the Parmesan cheese, then taste and add salt and pepper if needed. Serve hot in warmed bowls, sprinkled with the remaining Parmesan.

traditional method   **PREP** 15 MINS, PLUS SOAKING   **COOK** 1¾ HRS

1 Put the beans in a large heavy-based saucepan, cover with cold water, and bring to a boil over high heat, skimming the surface as necessary. Boil for 10 minutes, then reduce the heat to low, partially cover with the lid, and leave to simmer for 1 hour or until just tender. Drain well and set aside.

2 Heat the oil in the rinsed-out pan over medium heat. Add the celery, carrots, and onion, and cook for 5 minutes until softened. Stir in the beans, the tomatoes with their juice, and the stock, and season with salt and pepper. Bring to a boil, stirring, then cover with the lid and leave to simmer for 20 minutes.

3 Add the pasta and simmer for a further 10–15 minutes, or until cooked but still tender. Stir in the parsley and half the Parmesan cheese, then taste and add salt and pepper if needed. Serve hot in warmed bowls, sprinkled with the remaining Parmesan.

A hearty dish laden with chunks of cod, potatoes, and mussels to add color and flavor. The traditional New England accompaniment is oyster crackers, crumbled into the bowls.

New England chowder

SERVES 6

1 quart hot fish stock, for both methods
2 bay leaves
½ cup white wine
5oz (140g) smoked sliced bacon, diced
1 onion, finely chopped
2 celery stalks, finely chopped
1 carrot, peeled and finely chopped
2 tsp dried thyme
⅓ cup all-purpose flour

2 potatoes, total weight about 12oz (350g), peeled and finely diced
1 cup heavy cream
2lb (900g) skinned sustainable cod filets, cut into bite-sized pieces
about 1lb (500g) mussels, scrubbed and debearded (discard any that do not close when tapped)
salt and freshly ground black pepper
5–7 sprigs of dill, leaves finely chopped, to serve

in the slow cooker   ⏱ PREP 15 MINS   COOK 20 MINS PRECOOKING; HIGH 2–3 HRS

1 Preheat the slow cooker, if required. Put the fish stock and bay leaves into a saucepan and pour in the wine. Bring to a boil and simmer for 10 minutes. Put the bacon in a large Dutch oven over medium-high heat and cook, stirring occasionally, for 3–5 minutes until crisp and the fat has rendered. Reduce the heat to low, add the onion, celery, carrot, and thyme and cook for 15 minutes, stirring, until soft. Sprinkle the flour over and cook, stirring, for a minute. Add the hot stock mixture and bring to a boil, stirring, until the liquid thickens slightly. Transfer everything to the slow cooker, add the potatoes, cover with the lid, and cook on high for 2–3 hours.

2 For the last 20 minutes of cooking, crush about a third of the potatoes with a fork, and stir in the cream and cod. Cover and cook for 10 minutes. Add the mussels, cover, and cook for 10 minutes or until the mussels have opened (discard any that do not open). Taste and season if needed. Discard the bay leaves. Ladle the chowder into warmed soup bowls and sprinkle dill over each bowl. Serve very hot.

traditional method   ⏱ PREP 45–50 MINS   COOK 55–60 MINS

1 Put the fish stock and bay leaves into a saucepan and pour in the wine. Bring to a boil and simmer for 10 minutes. Put the bacon in a large Dutch oven over medium-high heat and cook, stirring occasionally, for 3–5 minutes until crisp and the fat has rendered. Reduce the heat to low, add the onions, celery, carrot, and thyme and cook for 15 minutes, stirring, until soft. Sprinkle the flour over and cook, stirring, for a minute. Add the hot stock mixture and bring to a boil, stirring, until the liquid thickens slightly. Add the potatoes and simmer for about 20 minutes, stirring occasionally, until the potatoes are very tender. Remove the pot from the heat. With a fork, crush about a third of the potatoes against the side of the pot, then stir to combine.

2 Return the pot to the heat and stir in the cod and simmer for 1–2 minutes. Add in the mussels and simmer for a further 2–3 minutes until the shells have opened and the fish is opaque and cooked through. Pour in the cream and bring just to a boil. Taste and season with salt and pepper if needed. Discard the bay leaves and any mussels that have not opened. Ladle the chowder into warmed soup bowls and sprinkle dill over each bowl.

This is a delicious tomato-based soup. Mix and match the shellfish to suit whatever is available; add pre-cooked lobster and use fresh shellfish stock if you can get hold of it.

Shellfish soup

 SERVES 6

1 tbsp olive oil
2 celery stalks, finely chopped
2 carrots, peeled and finely diced
2 onions, finely diced
6oz (175g) sliced bacon, cut into bite-sized pieces
14oz (400g) can chopped tomatoes
1 star anise

1¾ cups hot fish stock for the slow cooker
  (2 cups for the traditional method)
about 1¾lb (800g) fresh shellfish, such as clams,
  mussels, scallops, and shrimp, scrubbed and
  debearded where necessary (discard any clams
  and mussels that do not close when tapped)
bunch of flat-leaf parsley, finely chopped

in the slow cooker **PREP** 20 MINS **COOK** 15 MINS PRECOOKING;
                                        AUTO/LOW 6–8 HRS OR **HIGH** 3–4 HRS

1 Preheat the slow cooker, if required. Heat the oil in a large Dutch oven, add the celery, carrots, and onions and cook for about 10 minutes until soft. Add the bacon and cook for about 5 minutes, then stir in the tomatoes and add the star anise. Pour in the stock and bring to a boil. Transfer everything to the slow cooker and cook on auto/low for 6–8 hours or on high for 3–4 hours.

2 Add the shellfish for the last 10 minutes of cooking, or until the clams and mussels have opened (discard any that do not open). Sprinkle the parsley over and stir it in. Ladle into warmed bowls and serve with crusty bread and some spicy mayonnaise.

traditional method **PREP** 20 MINS **COOK** 1¼ HRS

1 Heat the oil in a large Dutch oven, add the celery, carrots, and onion and cook for about 10 minutes until soft. Add the bacon and cook for about 5 minutes, then stir in the tomatoes and add the star anise. Pour in the stock and bring to a boil. Reduce the heat and simmer gently for about 45 minutes, topping up with hot water if it starts to reduce too much.

2 Add the shellfish and cook for 5–10 minutes until the clams and mussels have opened (discard any that do not open). Sprinkle the parsley over and stir it in. Ladle into warmed bowls and serve with crusty bread and some spicy mayonnaise.

The poached chicken in this recipe has an incredibly silky texture and is very tender. You can add extras to the soup at the end, such as Asian greens, noodles, shrimp, or crunchy bean sprouts.

Malaysian chicken soup

 SERVES 4–6 **FREEZE** UP TO 1 MONTH **HEALTHY**

3lb (1.35kg) whole free-range chicken
1 onion, quartered
2in (5cm) piece of fresh ginger, peeled and sliced
6 garlic cloves, crushed
salt and freshly ground black pepper

splash of soy sauce
splash of fish sauce (nam pla)
1 cup hot vegetable stock (optional)
bunch of scallions, finely sliced, to serve

in the slow cooker **PREP** 15 MINS **COOK** AUTO/LOW 6–8 HRS OR **HIGH** 3–4 HRS

1 Preheat the slow cooker, if required. Put the chicken, upside down, into the slow cooker, add the onion, ginger, and garlic, and season with salt and pepper. Pour in enough water to cover the chicken. Cover with the lid and cook on auto/low for 6–8 hours or on high for 3–4 hours. Remove the chicken from the broth and set aside until it is cool enough to handle.

2 Remove the skin from the chicken and discard, then remove all the meat from the bones. Strain the broth from the slow cooker into a clean heavy-based pan, add the chicken meat, and stir in the soy sauce and fish sauce. Top up with some stock, if necessary, then simmer gently to warm through, taste, and season as required. Ladle into warmed Asian soup bowls and garnish with scallions.

traditional method **PREP** 15 MINS **COOK** 40–50 MINS

1 Put the chicken, onion, ginger, and garlic in a large pan and cover with water. Season with salt and pepper and bring to a boil. Reduce to a simmer, cover with the lid, and cook on a low heat for 30–40 minutes or until the chicken is cooked and the juices flow clear when pierced with a sharp knife. Remove the chicken from the broth and set aside until it is cool enough to handle.

2 Remove the skin from the chicken and discard, then remove all the meat from the bones. Strain the broth from the pan into a clean heavy-based pan, add the chicken meat, and stir in the soy sauce and fish sauce. Top up with some stock, if necessary, then simmer gently to warm through, taste, and season as required. Ladle into warmed Asian soup bowls and garnish with scallions.

This is a rich and lightly curried soup with a hint of apple added for sweetness. The lentils give it real substance, making it a perfect main meal soup.

Beef mulligatawny soup

⊚ **SERVES** 4–6   ❄ **FREEZE** UP TO 3 MONTHS

1 tbsp olive oil
1 onion, finely chopped
salt and freshly ground black pepper
1 tbsp coriander seeds
1 red chile, seeded and finely chopped
1–2 tsp garam masala (depending on how
  much spice you like)
1¼lb (550g) beef skirt steak or chuck roast,
  cut into bite-sized pieces

3 garlic cloves, finely chopped
3 carrots, peeled and diced
1 crisp apple, such as Gala, peeled,
  cored, and diced
heaping ½ cup red lentils, rinsed well
  and picked over for any stones
3 cups hot beef stock for the slow cooker
  (4 cups for the traditional method)
cilantro leaves, chopped, to serve

in the slow cooker   🕓 **PREP** 35 MINS   **COOK** 25 MINS PRECOOKING;
                                                AUTO/LOW 8 HRS OR **HIGH** 4 HRS

1 Preheat the slow cooker, if required. Heat the oil in a large Dutch oven over medium heat, add the onion, and cook for 3–4 minutes until soft. Season with salt and pepper, then stir in the coriander seeds, chile, and garam masala. Cook for a few minutes, increase the heat a little, add the beef (adding a little more oil, if necessary), and cook for about 6 minutes until the beef is no longer pink.

2 Reduce the heat, add the garlic, carrots, and apple, and cook for about 5 minutes until the carrots begin to soften. Add in the lentils and stir to coat. Transfer everything to the slow cooker and stir in the beef stock. Cover with the lid and cook on auto/low for 8 hours or on high for 4 hours. Taste and adjust the seasoning, then blend with an immersion blender, or transfer to a food processor and pulse very briefly. Don't purée the soup too much because it still needs plenty of texture. Add a little hot water as you go, if needed. Return to a clean pan, taste and adjust seasoning as needed, and heat through. Ladle into warmed bowls and garnish with the cilantro.

traditional method   🕓 **PREP** 35 MINS   **COOK** 1½ HRS

1 Heat the oil in a large Dutch oven over medium heat, add the onion, and cook for 3–4 minutes until soft. Season with salt and pepper, then stir in the coriander seeds, chile, and garam masala. Cook for a few minutes, increase the heat a little, add the beef (adding a little more oil, if necessary), and cook for about 6 minutes until the beef is no longer pink.

2 Reduce the heat, add the garlic, carrots, and apple, and cook for about 5 minutes until the carrots begin to soften. Add in the lentils and stir to coat, then pour in the stock. Bring to a boil, reduce to a simmer, and cook gently, covered, for about 1 hour. Check occasionally that it's not drying out, topping up with hot water if needed. You will probably need to add at least 1½ cups. Don't worry if it is a little thick, you can dilute it when you blend it. Taste and adjust the seasoning, then blend with an immersion blender, or transfer to a food processor and pulse very briefly. Don't purée it too much as it still needs plenty of texture. Add a little hot water as you go, if needed. Return to a clean pan, taste and adjust seasoning as needed, and heat through. Ladle into warmed bowls and garnish with the cilantro.

This main meal soup has a great balance of flavors with the aromatic orange zest and juice giving it an extra tang that really lifts the poached chicken and earthy celery root.

Chicken broth with celery root and orange

SERVES 4–6 **FREEZE** UP TO 3 MONTHS

1 tbsp olive oil
1 onion, finely chopped
1 bay leaf
salt and freshly ground black pepper
2 garlic cloves, finely chopped
zest of 1 orange and juice of ½ orange

few sprigs of oregano, leaves only
1 celery root peeled and chopped into small chunks
2 cups hot chicken stock, for both methods
4 skinless chicken breasts
4 sprigs of flat-leaf parsley, finely chopped, to serve

in the slow cooker **PREP** 15 MINS **COOK** 10 MINS PRECOOKING; **AUTO/LOW** 8 HRS OR **HIGH** 4 HRS

1 Preheat the slow cooker, if required. Heat the oil in a large Dutch oven over medium heat, add the onion and bay leaf, and cook for 3–4 minutes until the onion is just beginning to soften. Season with salt and pepper, then add the garlic, orange zest, and oregano and cook for a few seconds.

2 Stir in the celery root and orange juice, scraping up the bits from the bottom of the pot. Transfer everything to the slow cooker, pour in the stock, and stir in the chicken breasts. Cover with the lid and cook on auto/low for 8 hours or on high for 4 hours.

3 Remove the chicken breasts with a slotted spoon and set aside until cool enough to handle, then shred into chunky pieces using your hands or two forks, and return the meat to the slow cooker. Taste and adjust the seasoning, if needed, and remove the bay leaf. Serve in warmed bowls, garnished with parsley.

traditional method **PREP** 15 MINS **COOK** 1 HR

1 Heat the oil in a large Dutch oven over medium heat, add the onion and bay leaf, and cook for 3–4 minutes until the onion is just beginning to soften. Season with salt and pepper, then add the garlic, orange zest, and oregano and cook for a few seconds.

2 Stir in the celery root and orange juice, scraping up the bits from the bottom of the pot. Then pour in the stock, add the chicken breasts, and bring to a boil. Reduce to a simmer and cook gently for 20–30 minutes or until the chicken breasts are cooked. Remove the chicken breasts with a slotted spoon and set aside until cool enough to handle, then shred into chunky pieces using your hands or two forks.

3 Continue simmering the stock for a further 15 minutes or so, topping up with a little hot water if needed. Taste and adjust the seasoning, if needed, and remove the bay leaf. Return the shredded chicken to the pan and stir. Serve in warmed bowls, garnished with parsley.

It's the slow-cooked beef stock, flavored with gentle spices, that really makes this dish. Use glass noodles, if you can find them, for a traditional Vietnamese touch.

Vietnamese beef soup

SERVES 4–6 ❄ **FREEZE** STOCK UP TO 1 MONTH

about 1½lb (675g) beef bones, rinsed and dried
1 tbsp dark soy sauce
1 tbsp olive oil
1 star anise
1 tsp black peppercorns
cinnamon stick
1½ tbsp fish sauce (nam pla)
1 onion, finely chopped
3 garlic cloves, finely chopped
1 chile, seeded and finely chopped

1 lemongrass stalk, trimmed, woody outer leaves removed and very finely chopped
1in (2.5cm) piece of fresh ginger, peeled and finely sliced
salt and freshly ground black pepper
12oz (350g) beef filet, very finely sliced across the grain
2oz (60g) vermicelli noodles, soaked in hot water for 5 minutes (or as per pack instructions) and drained
bunch of scallions, finely sliced

in the slow cooker 🕐 **PREP** 15 MINS **COOK** 20 MINS PRECOOKING;
AUTO/LOW 8 HRS OR **HIGH** 4 HRS

1 First make the beef stock. Preheat the slow cooker, if required. In a bowl, toss the beef bones with the soy sauce. Heat a little of the oil in a large heavy-based pan over medium-high heat, add the bones and cook, stirring, for about 15 minutes until the meat is no longer pink. Transfer them to the slow cooker together with the star anise, peppercorns, cinnamon stick, and fish sauce. Pour in 3 cups (1½ pints) of water, cover with the lid, and cook on auto/low for 8 hours or on high for 4 hours.

2 Halfway through the cooking time, heat the remaining oil in a large heavy-based pan over medium heat, add the onion, and cook for 3–4 minutes until soft. Stir in the garlic, chile, and lemongrass and cook for a minute. Strain the stock from the slow cooker through a sieve and return to the slow cooker with the onion mixture. Add the ginger and taste, adding seasoning if needed.

3 Just before serving, add the beef to the stock and put the lid on. The beef will cook in the hot stock in minutes. Stir in the noodles and scallions and ladle into warmed bowls.

traditional method 🕐 **PREP** 15 MINS **COOK** 1¼ HRS

1 First make the beef stock. In a bowl, toss the beef bones with the soy sauce. Heat a little of the oil in a large heavy-based pan over medium-high heat, add the bones and cook, stirring, for about 15 minutes until the meat is no longer pink. Transfer them to a large stock pot, pour in 4 cups of water and add the star anise, peppercorns, cinnamon stick, and fish sauce. Bring to a boil, then partially cover with the lid, reduce to a simmer and cook for 1 hour. Strain the stock through a sieve into a clean pan, topping up with water to 3 cups, if necessary, and reserve.

2 Heat the remaining oil in a large heavy-based pan, add the onion, and cook for 3–4 minutes until soft. Do not brown. Stir in the garlic, chile, and lemongrass and cook for a minute. Then pour in the beef stock, add the ginger, and taste, adding seasoning if needed. Gently simmer for a few minutes, then add the sliced steak to the stock and cook for 2–3 minutes. Stir in the noodles and scallions and ladle into warmed bowls.

To change this recipe up a bit, you could swap the cannellini beans for butter beans if you wish. Butter beans can be used, like potatoes, as a thickener.

Cannellini bean, garlic, and mushroom soup

SERVES 4–6 ❄ **FREEZE** UP TO 3 MONTHS

1 tbsp olive oil
1 onion, finely chopped
salt and freshly ground pepper
3 garlic cloves, finely chopped
few sprigs of oregano, leaves only
7oz (200g) mushrooms, finely chopped

¾oz (20g) porcini mushrooms
3 cups hot vegetable stock,
   for both methods
2 x 14oz (400g) cans cannellini beans
handful of basil leaves
drizzle of basil oil, to serve (optional)

in the slow cooker   🕐 PREP 15 MINS   COOK 15 MINS PRECOOKING; HIGH 4 HRS

1 Preheat the slow cooker, if required. Heat the oil in a large Dutch oven over medium heat, add the onion, and cook for 3–4 minutes until soft. Then season with salt and pepper, add the garlic and oregano, and cook for a few seconds.

2 Add all the mushrooms and cook for about 5 minutes until they begin to release their juices, then increase the heat, add a little stock, and let it simmer. Transfer everything to the slow cooker, add the remaining stock and the beans, cover with the lid, and cook on high for 4 hours.

3 Add the basil leaves to the soup and use an immersion blender to blend until smooth, or transfer in batches to a food processor and blend. Add a ladleful of hot water if it is too thick. Pour the soup into a clean pan, taste and season as needed, and heat through. Garnish with a drizzle of basil oil and serve with some crusty bread.

traditional method   🕐 PREP 15 MINS   COOK 50 MINS

1 Heat the oil in a large Dutch oven over medium heat, add the onion, and cook for 3–4 minutes until soft. Then season with salt and pepper, add the garlic and oregano, and cook for a few seconds.

2 Add all the mushrooms and cook for about 5 minutes until they begin to release their juices, then increase the heat, add a little stock, and let it simmer. Add the remaining stock and bring to a boil, then reduce to a simmer, add the beans and cook gently, partially covered with a lid, for about 40 minutes, topping up with more hot water if needed.

3 Add the basil leaves to the soup and use an immersion blender to blend until smooth, or transfer in batches to a food processor and blend. Add a ladleful of hot water if it is too thick. Pour the soup into a clean pan, taste and season as needed, and heat through. Garnish with a drizzle of basil oil and serve with some crusty bread.

Just a touch of chile and paprika enlivens this soup and the slow cooking of the peppers enhances their sweet flavor. You could add canned chickpeas for a more substantial soup.

Spanish pepper and tomato soup

SERVES 4–6   **FREEZE** UP TO 3 MONTHS

1 tbsp olive oil
1 onion, finely chopped
salt and freshly ground black pepper
2 celery stalks, roughly chopped
3 garlic cloves, finely chopped
1 large carrot, peeled and chopped
pinch of dried chile flakes

pinch of paprika
6 red bell peppers, seeded and roughly chopped
3 tomatoes, roughly chopped
3 cups hot vegetable stock for the slow cooker
  (5 cups for the traditional method)
3oz (85g) feta cheese, crumbled, to serve (optional)

in the slow cooker   **PREP** 20 MINS   **COOK** 35 MINS PRECOOKING;
AUTO/LOW 8 HRS OR **HIGH** 3 HRS

1 Preheat the slow cooker, if required. Heat the oil in a large Dutch oven over medium heat, add the onion, and cook for 3–4 minutes until soft. Season with salt and pepper, then add the celery, garlic, and carrot, and cook for 5–10 minutes until soft, stirring occasionally.

2 Stir in the chile flakes and paprika and cook for a minute, then add the peppers and tomatoes. Cook on very low heat for about 20 minutes, stirring so they don't stick. Transfer everything to the slow cooker. Pour in the stock, stir, then cover with the lid and cook on auto/low for 8 hours or on high for 3 hours.

3 Use an immersion blender to blend the soup until smooth, or transfer in batches to a food processor and blend. Add a ladleful of hot water if it is too thick. Pour the soup into a clean pan, taste and season as needed, and heat through. Serve with a little feta cheese on top, if using, together with some crusty bread on the side.

traditional method   **PREP** 20 MINS   **COOK** 1¼–1½ HRS

1 Heat the oil in a large Dutch oven over medium heat, add the onion, and cook for 3–4 minutes until soft. Season with salt and pepper, then add the celery, garlic, and carrot, and cook for 5–10 minutes until soft, stirring occasionally.

2 Stir in the chile flakes and paprika and cook for a minute, then add the peppers and tomatoes. Cook on very low heat for about 20 minutes, stirring so they don't stick. Pour in half of the stock and bring to a boil, then reduce to a simmer, partially cover with the lid, and cook on low heat for 45–60 minutes, topping up with the reserved stock as the cooking liquid reduces.

3 Use an immersion blender to blend the soup until smooth, or transfer in batches to a food processor and blend. Add a ladleful of hot water if it is too thick. Pour the soup into a clean pan, taste and season as needed, and heat through. Serve with a little feta cheese on top, if using, together with some crusty bread on the side.

The two main ingredients of a laksa are noodles and coconut milk, and it is often served with the addition of shellfish, in this case king prawns. You could replace the noodles with rice vermicelli.

Prawn laksa

SERVES 4–6

1¼lb (550g) raw king prawns with shells on, peeled (but keep the tails on) and shells reserved
2 tbsp sunflower oil
2–3 tbsp fish sauce (nam pla)
6 shallots, peeled
2in (5cm) piece of fresh ginger, peeled and finely chopped
3 garlic cloves, peeled

2 red chilies, seeded
salt and freshly ground black pepper
14oz (400ml) can coconut milk
6oz (175g) medium rice noodles, soaked in hot water for 10 minutes
pinch of sugar (optional)
handful of mint leaves, finely chopped
handful of cilantro leaves, finely chopped

in the slow cooker   **PREP** 15 MINS   **COOK** 10 MINS PRECOOKING; **HIGH** 3–4 HRS, THEN 3–4 HRS

1 Preheat the slow cooker, if required. To make the soup base, put the prawn shells into a heavy-based pan with a sprinkling of oil and cook for a few minutes, stirring, until they turn pink. Transfer to the slow cooker, then pour over 1 quart of water and add the fish sauce, to taste. Cover with the lid, and cook on high for 3–4 hours. Strain the stock and reserve.

2 Keep the slow cooker heated, if required. Put the shallots, ginger, garlic, chilies, and 1 tablespoon of the oil in a food processor and blend to a paste. Season with salt and pepper. Heat the remaining oil in a small heavy-based pan over medium heat, stir in the paste, and cook for a couple of minutes. Ladle in a little of the stock, stir, and transfer everything to the slow cooker. Pour in the coconut milk and the remaining stock, cover with the lid, and cook on high for another 3–4 hours.

3 Taste and adjust seasoning as required, adding a little more fish sauce, if you like, or you may wish to sweeten it with a little sugar. Stir in the noodles and the prawns to cook for 10 minutes more. To serve, stir in the mint and cilantro and ladle into warmed shallow bowls.

traditional method   **PREP** 15 MINS   **COOK** 1½ HRS

1 To make the soup base, put the prawn shells into a large heavy-based pan with a sprinkling of oil and cook for a few minutes, stirring, until they turn pink. Pour over 1 quart of water and add the fish sauce, to taste. Bring to a boil, then reduce to a simmer, partially cover with the lid, and cook gently for 30–45 minutes. Strain the stock and reserve.

2 Put the shallots, ginger, garlic, chilies, and 1 tablespoon of the oil in a food processor and blend to a paste. Season with salt and pepper. Heat the remaining oil in a large heavy-based pan over medium heat, stir in the paste, and cook for a couple of minutes. Ladle in a little of the stock and bring to a boil, then pour in the coconut milk and the remaining stock, and let it bubble for a few minutes. Reduce to a gentle simmer, partially cover, and cook for 30–40 minutes topping up with a little hot water if needed.

3 Taste and adjust seasoning as required, adding a little more fish sauce, if you like, or you may wish to sweeten it with a little sugar. Stir in the noodles and the prawns, and simmer for a couple of minutes. To serve, stir in the mint and cilantro and ladle into warmed shallow bowls.

Stews

A colorful and gutsy dish, you could always add some spicy sausage or chorizo if you prefer a meaty meal. Black beans are also called turtle beans and need soaking overnight.

Brazilian black bean and pumpkin stew

SERVES 4–6 ✳ **FREEZE** UP TO 3 MONTHS ♡ **HEALTHY**

11oz (325g) dried black beans, soaked
 overnight and drained
1 tbsp olive oil
1 onion, finely chopped
salt and freshly ground black pepper
3 garlic cloves, finely chopped
1 small Sugar Pie pumpkin or butternut squash,
 peeled, seeded, and diced

2 red peppers, seeded and diced
2 x 14oz (400g) cans chopped tomatoes
1 small green chile, seeded and diced
2 cups hot vegetable stock for the slow cooker
 (3 cups for the traditional method)
1 mango, peeled, pitted, and diced
bunch of cilantro, chopped

in the slow cooker 🕐 **PREP** 25 MINS, PLUS SOAKING **COOK** 10 MINS PRECOOKING; AUTO/LOW 6–8 HRS

1 Preheat the slow cooker, if required. Put the beans in a large heavy-based pan and cover with water. Bring to a boil, and then drain the beans and set aside.

2 Dry the pan and heat the oil in it over medium heat, add the onion, and cook for 3–4 minutes until soft. Season with salt and pepper, then stir in the garlic, and cook for 1–2 minutes until soft. Stir in the pumpkin or butternut squash and also cook for about a minute.

3 Transfer everything to the slow cooker and add the beans, red peppers, tomatoes, and chile together with the stock. Season well, cover with the lid, and cook on auto/low for 6–8 hours. Taste and season, if necessary, then stir in the mango and cilantro. Serve with some sour cream and rice on the side.

traditional method 🕐 **PREP** 25 MINS, PLUS SOAKING **COOK** 2½–3 HRS

1 Preheat the oven to 325°F (160°C). Put the beans in a large heavy-based pan and cover with water. Bring to a boil, then reduce to a simmer, partially cover with the lid, and cook on low heat for 1 hour. Drain and set aside.

2 Heat the oil in a large heavy-based pan over medium heat, add the onion, and cook for 3–4 minutes until soft. Season with salt and pepper, then stir in the garlic, and cook for 1–2 minutes until soft. Stir in the pumpkin or butternut squash, red peppers, tomatoes, and chile.

3 Add the beans, pour in the stock, and bring to a boil. Then reduce to a simmer, cover with the lid and put in the oven for 1½–2 hours. Taste and season, if necessary, then stir in the mango and cilantro. Serve with some sour cream and rice on the side.

This combination of rich pork and salty clams—and, indeed, any pork with shellfish—has been enjoyed for centuries in Portugal. A squeeze of lemon at the end brings out the flavors.

Pork and clam cataplana

⊚ **SERVES** 4 ❄ **FREEZE** UP TO 1 MONTH, WITHOUT THE CLAMS ♡ **HEALTHY**

2lb (900g) pork tenderloin, cut into 1in (2.5cm) cubes
2 tbsp olive oil
1 large onion, thinly sliced
2 garlic cloves, finely chopped
14oz (400g) can whole tomatoes
1 tbsp tomato paste
dash of Tabasco sauce (or more to taste)
2¼lb (1kg) clams, such as Littlenecks, scrubbed
 (discard any that do not close when tapped)
bunch of parsley, leaves chopped

FOR THE MARINADE
2 garlic cloves, finely chopped
1 bay leaf
1½ tbsp paprika
1 tbsp olive oil
1½ cups dry white wine
pinch of freshly ground black pepper

in the slow cooker ⏱ PREP 20 MINS, PLUS MARINATING COOK 30 MINS PRECOOKING; AUTO/LOW 6–8 HRS OR HIGH 3–4 HRS

1 To make the marinade, put all the ingredients into a bowl and whisk to combine. Add the pork and mix well. Cover and refrigerate for 2 hours, or 12 hours if time permits, stirring occasionally. Preheat the slow cooker, if required. Lift the meat from the marinade with a slotted spoon and pat dry with paper towels. Reserve the marinade. Heat the oil in a large Dutch oven over medium-high heat. Add the pork, in batches, and brown well on all sides. Transfer to a bowl and set aside.

2 Reduce the heat and add the onion and garlic to the pot. Cover and cook very gently for about 15 minutes, until the onion is very soft and brown. Add the tomatoes, tomato paste, Tabasco, and pork. Pour in the marinade and stir. Transfer everything to the slow cooker, cover with the lid, and cook on auto/low for 6–8 hours or on high for 3–4 hours. Add the clams for the last 20 minutes of cooking, or until all the clams are open (discard any that do not open). Transfer to a warmed serving bowl, remove the bay leaf, sprinkle with the parsley, and serve with lemon wedges on the side.

traditional method ⏱ PREP 20 MINS, PLUS MARINATING COOK 2¼–2½ HRS

1 To make the marinade, put all the ingredients into a bowl and whisk to combine. Add the pork and mix well. Cover and refrigerate for 2 hours, or 12 hours if time permits, stirring occasionally. Preheat the oven to 350°F (180°C). Lift the meat from the marinade with a slotted spoon and pat dry with paper towels. Reserve the marinade. Heat the oil in a large Dutch oven over medium-high heat. Add the pork, in batches, and brown well on all sides. Transfer to a bowl and set aside.

2 Reduce the heat and add the onion and garlic to the pot. Cover and cook very gently for about 15 minutes, until the onion is very soft and brown. Add the tomatoes, tomato paste, Tabasco, and pork. Pour in the marinade and stir. Cover with the lid and cook in the oven for 1½–1¾ hours, until tender when pierced. Check occasionally that it's not drying out, topping up with a little hot water if needed. Arrange the clams on top of the pork, cover with the lid, and cook in the oven for 15–20 minutes longer until the clams open (discard any that do not open). Transfer to a warmed serving bowl, remove the bay leaf, sprinkle with the parsley, and serve with lemon wedges on the side.

This is a filling one-pot meal, known as *Cocido* in Spain. Vary the vegetables, if you wish—turnip, green beans, or even pumpkin are all delicious. Chickpeas are a must for this dish.

Spanish stew

SERVES 6

3 tbsp olive oil
2 small onions, quartered
2 garlic cloves, sliced
2 slices pork belly, about 1¼lb (550g), cut into
   large chunks
4 bone-in, skin on chicken thighs, about 1lb 5oz
   (600g) total weight
4oz (115g) beef chuck, cut into bite-sized pieces
4oz (115g) smoked bacon, cut into bite-sized pieces
4 small pork spare ribs, 5½oz (150g) total weight
½ cup white wine
4oz (115g) dried chorizo, chopped into 4 pieces

1 bay leaf
salt and freshly ground black pepper
6 small waxy potatoes, such as Yukon Golds,
   chopped into large chunks
3 carrots, peeled and chopped into large chunks
14oz (400g) can chickpeas, drained
½ Savoy cabbage or green cabbage heart, cored
   and quartered
3 tbsp chopped parsley, to serve

in the slow cooker   **PREP** 35 MINS   **COOK** 30 MINS PRECOOKING; **AUTO/LOW** 6–8 HRS

1 Preheat the slow cooker, if required. Heat 1 tablespoon of the oil in a large Dutch oven over medium heat, add the onions and garlic, and cook for 10 minutes, stirring occasionally. Transfer to the slow cooker. Heat the remaining oil in the pot and cook the pork, chicken, beef, bacon, and spare ribs, in batches, until lightly browned on all sides. Also transfer to the slow cooker.

2 Pour the wine into the pot and reduce by half over high heat. Add to the slow cooker along with the chorizo and bay leaf, season with salt and pepper, then pour in enough hot water to cover. Cover with the lid and cook on auto/low for 6–8 hours, adding the potatoes, carrots, chickpeas, and cabbage for the last hour of cooking. Remove the bay leaf, bones, and chicken skin from the stew. Divide the meat and vegetables between warmed serving plates. Add a few spoonfuls of the hot broth and garnish with parsley. Serve with crusty bread.

traditional method   **PREP** 35 MINS   **COOK** 2¾ HRS

1 Heat 1 tablespoon of the oil in a large Dutch oven over medium heat, add the onions and garlic, and cook for 10 minutes, stirring occasionally. Remove and set aside in a bowl. Heat the remaining oil in the pot and cook the pork, chicken, beef, bacon, and spare ribs, in batches, until lightly browned on all sides. Transfer to the bowl with the onions.

2 Pour the wine into the pot and reduce by half over high heat. Add the chorizo and bay leaf together with the onions and browned meat. Season with salt and pepper, then pour in enough cold water to cover. Bring to a boil, then reduce the heat and simmer, covered, for 1½ hours. Add the potatoes and carrots to the pot, continue to cook for 15 minutes, then add the chickpeas and cabbage and cook for a further 15 minutes. Remove the bay leaf, bones, and chicken skin from the stew. Divide the meat and vegetables between warmed serving plates. Add a few spoonfuls of the hot broth and garnish with parsley. Serve with crusty bread.

Slow-cooked sweet cabbage is the perfect complement to ham, and with the addition of spices and dried fruit, the humble piece of meat is transformed. Ham hocks are also known as knuckles.

Ham hock with red cabbage

SERVES 4–6 **HEALTHY**

2 ham hocks, about 3lb (1.35kg) each
1 red cabbage, cored and finely shredded
2 onions, sliced
4 garlic cloves, finely chopped
few sprigs of thyme
2oz (60g) raisins

pinch of freshly grated nutmeg
pinch of ground cinnamon
½ cup white wine vinegar for the slow cooker
 (1 cup for the traditional method)
2 cups hot vegetable stock, for both methods
salt and freshly ground black pepper

in the slow cooker **PREP** 20 MINS **COOK** AUTO/LOW 6–8 HRS, THEN **AUTO/LOW** 6–8 HRS

1 Preheat the slow cooker, if required. Put the ham hocks in the pot and cover with water so that the cooker is three-quarters full. Cover with the lid and cook on auto/low for 6–8 hours.

2 Remove the hams and reserve the cooking liquid, if you wish to use it instead of the vegetable stock (it can be salty). When the hams are cool enough to handle, remove the skin and discard, then sit the hams back in the slow cooker. Add all the other ingredients, using either the stock or the cooking liquid, and season with salt and pepper. Cover with the lid and cook on auto/low for 6–8 hours. Remove the hams, shred the meat, and stir it into the slow cooker. Serve with baked or roast potatoes.

traditional method **PREP** 20 MINS **COOK** 3 HRS

1 Preheat the oven to 325°F (160°C). Sit the ham hocks in a large heavy-based pan and cover with water. Bring to a boil, then reduce to a simmer, partially cover, and cook gently for 1 hour. Remove the hams and reserve the stock, if you wish to use it instead of the vegetable stock (it can be salty). When the hams are cool enough to handle, remove the skin and discard, then sit the hams in a large Dutch oven.

2 Add all the other ingredients to the pot, using either the stock or the cooking liquid, and tuck the hams in neatly. Season with salt and pepper, then cover and put in the oven for 2 hours. Check occasionally that it's not drying out, topping up with a little hot water if necessary. Remove the hams, shred the meat, and stir it into the pot. Serve with baked or roast potatoes.

Barley is a grain that used to be overlooked, but it has made a well-deserved comeback due to its ability to add body and earthy flavor to all sorts of dishes. For a treat, use wild mushrooms, too.

Beef with barley and mushrooms

SERVES 4–6 ❄ **FREEZE** UP TO 3 MONTHS

3 tbsp vegetable oil
2¼lb (1kg) chuck steak, cut into 2in (5cm) pieces
1lb (450g) onions, thinly sliced
salt and freshly ground black pepper
1 bouquet garni, made with 5–6 parsley sprigs,
  2–3 thyme sprigs, and 1 bay leaf
2½ cups hot beef stock for the slow cooker
  (3½ cups for the traditional method)

4 carrots, sliced
2 celery stalks, sliced
¾ cup pearl barley
about 1lb (500g) mushrooms, trimmed and sliced
2–3 sprigs of parsley, leaves finely chopped, to serve

in the slow cooker 🕐 **PREP** 30 MINS **COOK** 20 MINS PRECOOKING; AUTO/LOW 6–8 HRS OR **HIGH** 3–4 HRS

1 Preheat the slow cooker, if required. Heat the oil in a large Dutch oven over medium-high heat, add the beef (in batches, if necessary) and cook for about 5 minutes until well browned. Remove and set aside.

2 Reduce the heat to medium, add the onions and a little salt and pepper, and cook for 5–7 minutes until lightly browned. Return the beef and add the bouquet garni and more seasoning. Pour in the stock, stir, and then add the carrots, celery, and barley. Transfer everything to the slow cooker, cover, and cook on auto/low for 6–8 hours or on high for 3–4 hours. Add the mushrooms for the last 20 minutes of cooking.

3 Discard the bouquet garni and taste the stew for seasoning, adding more salt and pepper if needed. Serve in warmed bowls, garnished with the parsley and with crusty bread on the side.

traditional method 🕐 **PREP** 30 MINS **COOK** 2¼–2½ HRS

1 Preheat the oven to 350°F (180°C). Heat the oil in a large Dutch oven over medium-high heat, add the beef (in batches, if necessary) and cook for about 5 minutes until well browned. Remove and set aside.

2 Reduce the heat to medium, add the onions and a little salt and pepper, and cook for 5–7 minutes until lightly browned. Return the beef and add the bouquet garni and more seasoning. Pour in the stock and stir. Cover with the lid and put in the oven for 1½ hours, stirring occasionally. Then add the carrots, celery, and barley, together with more hot water, if necessary, to keep the stew moist. Cover, and continue to cook for a further 40–45 minutes until the meat and vegetables are tender when pierced. The barley should be tender but still slightly chewy. About 20 minutes before the end of cooking, stir in the mushrooms.

3 Discard the bouquet garni and taste the stew for seasoning, adding more salt and pepper if needed. Serve in warmed bowls, garnished with the parsley and with crusty bread on the side.

In this dish, salt cod is tender and fragrant with the classic Spanish aromas of garlic, bay leaves, and saffron. If you can't get salt cod, use a white fish and add it in for the last 15 minutes of cooking.

Salt cod braised with vegetables

🕑 **SERVES** 4 ❤ **HEALTHY**

1¾lb (800g) thick-cut salt cod, or fresh white fish
  such as sustainable cod, haddock, or halibut
3 tbsp olive oil
1 onion, finely diced
2 leeks, trimmed and white parts finely sliced
3 garlic cloves, finely chopped
3 tomatoes, skinned and chopped

about 1lb (500g) potatoes, diced
salt and freshly ground black pepper
2 bay leaves
large pinch of saffron threads
½ cup dry white wine
2 tbsp chopped parsley, to serve

in the slow cooker 🕑 PREP 20 MINS, PLUS SOAKING   COOK 10 MINS PRECOOKING; AUTO/LOW 6–8 HRS OR HIGH 3–4 HRS

1 If using the salt cod, soak the pieces of cod in enough cold water to cover them for at least 24 hours, changing the water 2–3 times to remove the saltiness of the brine. Drain and cut the fish into 4 pieces, then pat dry with paper towels. If using the fresh fish, simply cut the fish into 4 pieces.

2 Preheat the slow cooker, if required. Heat the oil in a large heavy-based skillet over medium heat, add the onion and leeks, and cook for about 5 minutes until soft. Add the garlic and tomatoes and cook for a further 2 minutes, stirring. Add the potatoes, salt and pepper, bay leaves, and saffron.

3 Transfer everything to the slow cooker, then pour in the wine and ½ cup of water. Cover with the lid and cook on auto/low for 6–8 hours or on high for 3–4 hours. Sit the salt cod, skin-side up, on top of the vegetables for the last hour of cooking. Ladle into warmed bowls, garnish with the parsley, and serve with a crisp mixed salad and some crusty bread.

traditional method 🕑 PREP 20 MINS, PLUS SOAKING   COOK 40 MINS

1 If using the salt cod, soak the pieces of cod in enough cold water to cover them for at least 24 hours, changing the water 2–3 times to remove the saltiness of the brine. Drain and cut the fish into 4 pieces, then pat dry with paper towels. If using the fresh fish, simply cut the fish into 4 pieces.

2 Heat the oil in a large heavy-based Dutch oven over medium heat, add the onion and leeks, and cook for about 5 minutes until soft. Add the garlic and tomatoes and cook for a further 2 minutes, stirring. Add the potatoes, salt and pepper, bay leaves, and saffron.

3 Pour in the wine and 1 cup water and sit the cod, skin-side up, on top of the vegetables. Bring gently to a simmer and cook for 25–30 minutes until the fish is opaque and cooked through. Shake the pot once or twice every 5 minutes to help release gelatin from the fish, to thicken the sauce. Ladle into warmed bowls, garnish with the parsley, and serve with a crisp mixed salad and some crusty bread.

Asian flavors perk up the pork in this stew. Five-spice powder is a favorite ingredient in Asian dishes, and is made from Szechuan pepper, star anise, fennel seeds, cloves, and cinnamon.

Braised pork in soy and cinnamon

◉ SERVES 4–6　**✳ FREEZE** UP TO 3 MONTHS　**♡ HEALTHY**

2½lb (1.1kg) boneless pork shoulder
　or leg, cut into bite-sized pieces
2 tsp five-spice powder
2–3 tbsp olive oil
2 bunches of scallions, white and green
　parts separated and finely chopped
3 garlic cloves, sliced
2in (5cm) piece of fresh ginger, peeled
　and sliced

⅓ cup dark soy sauce
2 cinnamon sticks, broken in half
9oz (250g) small button mushrooms,
　any large ones halved
about 1 cup hot chicken stock for
　the slow cooker (3 cups for the
　traditional method)
freshly ground black pepper

in the slow cooker　🕐 **PREP** 15 MINS　**COOK** 15 MINS PRECOOKING;
AUTO/LOW 6–8 HRS OR **HIGH** 4 HRS

1 Preheat the slow cooker, if required, and toss the pork in the five-spice powder. Heat half the oil in a large Dutch oven over medium-high heat, and cook the pork in batches for 5–6 minutes until it turns golden. Remove and set aside.

2 Heat the remaining oil in the pot over medium heat. Add the scallion whites and cook for a minute, then stir in the garlic and ginger until coated. Add the soy sauce and bring to a boil, then reduce to a simmer, and transfer everything to the slow cooker, including the pork.

3 Stir in the cinnamon and mushrooms, and then pour in the stock just to cover. Season with pepper, cover with the lid, and cook on auto/low for 6–8 hours or on high for 4 hours. Taste and season some more with soy sauce, if needed, remove the cinnamon sticks, and top with the scallion greens. Ladle into warmed bowls and serve with noodles or rice.

traditional method　🕐 **PREP** 15 MINS　**COOK** 2¼–2½ HRS

1 Preheat the oven to 325°F (160°C) and toss the pork in the five-spice powder. Heat half the oil in a large Dutch oven over medium-high heat, and cook the pork in batches for 5–6 minutes until it turns golden. Remove and set aside.

2 Heat the remaining oil in the pot over medium heat. Add the scallion whites and cook for a minute, then stir in the garlic and ginger until coated. Stir in the soy sauce, add the cinnamon and mushrooms, and return the pork to the pot. Finally, add the stock, bring to a boil, then reduce to a simmer and season with pepper. Cover with the lid and put in the oven for 2 hours.

3 If the sauce is too thin, remove the meat with a slotted spoon and set aside, then sit the pot on the stove and let it simmer for about 10 minutes, to reduce a little and intensify the flavors. Return the meat, remove the cinnamon sticks, and top with the scallion greens. Ladle into warmed bowls and serve with noodles or rice.

Bok choy is a versatile vegetable used frequently in Chinese stir-fries, appetizers, and main dishes. Also known as pak choi, it cooks quickly, so it is added toward the end of the cooking time.

Asian beef and bok choy

🕐 **SERVES** 4–6 ❄ **FREEZE** UP TO 3 MONTHS

2 tbsp olive oil
1 onion, roughly chopped
freshly ground black pepper
4 garlic cloves, peeled and left whole
2in (5cm) piece of fresh ginger,
  peeled and sliced
2 dried chilies, left whole
2 star anise

⅔ cup Chinese rice wine or dry pale sherry
2 tbsp demerara sugar
2 tbsp oyster sauce
1 tbsp dark soy sauce
1 tsp toasted sesame oil
2½lb (1.1kg) beef shank, cut into bite-sized pieces
9oz (250g) bok choy, sliced lengthwise

in the slow cooker   🕐 **PREP** 15 MINS   **COOK** 15 MINS PRECOOKING; **AUTO/LOW** 6–8 HRS

1 Preheat the slow cooker, if required. Heat the oil in a large Dutch oven over medium heat, add the onion, and cook for 3–4 minutes until soft. Season with pepper, then stir in the garlic, ginger, chilies, and star anise.

2 Increase the heat, pour in the Chinese wine or sherry, and let it simmer for a few minutes. Stir in the sugar, oyster sauce, soy sauce, and sesame oil. Boil for a minute, then reduce to a simmer, add the beef, and stir to coat.

3 Transfer everything to the slow cooker and pour in just enough water to cover. Cover with the lid and cook on auto/low for 6–8 hours. Add the bok choy for the last hour of cooking, pushing it under the liquid slightly so it doesn't go dry at the edges. Remove the whole dried chilies and serve with white rice.

traditional method   🕐 **PREP** 15 MINS   **COOK** 2¼–2¾ HRS

1 Preheat the oven to 325°F (160°C). Heat the oil in a large Dutch oven over medium heat, add the onion, and cook for 3–4 minutes until soft. Season with pepper, then stir in the garlic, ginger, chilies, and star anise.

2 Increase the heat, pour in the Chinese wine or sherry, and let it simmer for a few minutes. Stir in the sugar, oyster sauce, soy sauce, and sesame oil. Boil for a minute, then reduce to a simmer, add the beef, and stir to coat.

3 Pour over just enough water to cover, cover with the lid, and put in the oven for 2–2½ hours, until the meat is tender. Check occasionally that it's not drying out, topping up with a little hot water if needed. Add the bok choy for the last 15 minutes of cooking, pushing it under the liquid slightly so it doesn't go dry at the edges. Remove the whole dried chilies and serve with white rice.

In Italy, this dish is called *alla cacciatora*, meaning "hunter's style." Chicory, with its slight bitterness, makes a flavorful addition and must be added toward the end of cooking.

Hunter's chicken stew

SERVES 4 · **FREEZE** UP TO 3 MONTHS, WITHOUT THE CHICORY

about 3lb (1.5kg) chicken, cut into 8 pieces
salt and freshly ground black pepper
¼ cup olive oil
1 onion, chopped
4 garlic cloves, finely chopped
1 sprig of rosemary

1 bay leaf
¼ cup dry white wine
½ cup hot chicken stock, for both methods
2 heads of chicory (also known as Belgian endive), trimmed, leaves separated, and roughly chopped

in the slow cooker · **PREP** 15 MINS · **COOK** 30 MINS PRECOOKING; **AUTO/LOW** 5–6 HRS OR **HIGH** 3–4 HRS

1 Preheat the slow cooker, if required. Season the chicken all over with salt and pepper. Heat half the oil in a large Dutch oven over medium heat, add the thighs and drumsticks, skin-side down, and cook for about 5 minutes until they begin to brown. Add the breast pieces, skin-side down, and cook gently for 10–15 minutes until very brown. Turn and brown the other side. Lower the heat.

2 Add the onion and garlic, stir, and continue cooking gently for 3–4 minutes until they are soft. Season with salt and pepper, then stir in the rosemary, bay leaf, wine, and stock, and bring to a boil. Transfer everything to the slow cooker, cover with the lid, and cook on auto/low for 5–6 hours or on high for 3–4 hours.

3 Add the chicory for the last 15 minutes of cooking. Discard the bay leaf and rosemary from the sauce, taste, and add salt and pepper if needed. Spoon into bowls and serve with crusty bread.

traditional method · **PREP** 20–25 MINS · **COOK** 45–60 MINS

1 Season the chicken all over with salt and pepper. Heat half the oil in a large Dutch oven over medium heat, add the thighs and drumsticks, skin-side down, and cook for about 5 minutes until they begin to brown. Add the breast pieces, skin-side down, and cook gently for 10–15 minutes until very brown. Turn and brown the other side. Lower the heat.

2 Add the onion and garlic, stir, and continue cooking gently for 3–4 minutes until they are soft. Season with salt and pepper, then stir in the rosemary, bay leaf, wine, and stock. Cover and simmer for 15–20 minutes until tender.

3 Add the chicory for the last 5 minutes of cooking, return the lid, and cook gently until it has just softened. Discard the bay leaf and rosemary from the sauce, taste, and add salt and pepper if needed. Spoon out into warmed bowls and serve with crusty bread.

The darker the beer, the richer this dish will be. Cognac is also added, to add depth of flavor. Mashed potatoes would be good with it and, naturally, you can guess what is the best drink to serve.

Chicken and beer stew

SERVES 4–6   **FREEZE** UP TO 3 MONTHS

4 chicken breasts on the bone
salt and freshly ground black pepper
2 tbsp butter
2 tbsp vegetable oil
1lb 10oz (750g) onions, thinly sliced
¼ cup all-purpose flour
3–4 tbsp Cognac
about 1lb (500g) mushrooms, quartered

1 bouquet garni, made with 5–6 parsley sprigs,
  2–3 thyme sprigs, and 1 bay leaf
2 tsp juniper berries, gently crushed
2 cups beer
1 cup hot chicken stock, for both methods
¼ cup heavy cream
small bunch of flat-leaf parsley, leaves
  finely chopped

in the slow cooker   **PREP** 15 MINS   **COOK** 20 MINS PRECOOKING; AUTO/LOW 6–8 HRS OR **HIGH** 3–4 HRS

1 Preheat the slow cooker, if required. Season the chicken pieces. Heat the butter and oil in a large Dutch oven over medium-high heat until foaming. Add the chicken, skin-side down (in batches, if necessary) and cook for about 5 minutes on each side until browned. Remove and set aside.

2 Reduce the heat to medium, add the onions, and cook for about 10 minutes until soft and well browned. Sprinkle with the flour and cook, stirring, for 1–2 minutes until the flour is just lightly browned. Return the chicken to the pot in a single layer. Add the Cognac and bring to a boil for a few minutes, basting the chicken with the Cognac. Add the mushrooms, bouquet garni, and crushed juniper berries. Pour in the beer and stock, bring to a boil, and transfer everything to the slow cooker. Cover with the lid and cook on auto/low for 6–8 hours or on high for 3–4 hours.

3 Discard the bouquet garni and skim off excess fat from the surface. Stir in the cream for the last 15 minutes of cooking. Taste, add salt and pepper if needed. Garnish with the parsley and serve.

traditional method   **PREP** 15 MINS   **COOK** 1 HR

1 Season the chicken pieces. Heat the butter and oil in a large Dutch oven over medium-high heat until foaming. Add the chicken, skin-side down (in batches, if necessary) and cook for about 5 minutes on each side until browned. Remove and set aside.

2 Reduce the heat to medium, add the onions, and cook for about 10 minutes until soft and well browned. Sprinkle with the flour and cook, stirring, for 1–2 minutes until the flour is just lightly browned. Return the chicken to the pot in a single layer. Add the Cognac and bring to a boil for a few minutes, basting the chicken with the Cognac. Add the mushrooms, bouquet garni, and crushed juniper berries. Pour in the beer and stock, bring to a boil, cover with the lid, and simmer for 40–50 minutes until the chicken is tender when pierced and the juices run clear.

3 Discard the bouquet garni and skim off excess fat from the surface. Stir in the cream for the last 15 minutes of cooking. Taste, add salt and pepper if needed. Garnish with the parsley and serve.

This stew is a favorite dish in northern Italy. Barbera is the preferred wine, but substitute any good-quality dry red; you will taste a bad wine if you use it in a dish.

Italian beef braised in red wine

SERVES 6

2 tbsp olive oil
2¼lb (1kg) stewing beef, cut into bite-sized pieces
1 small onion, finely chopped
1 small carrot, peeled and finely chopped
1 celery stalk, finely chopped
2 cups dry red wine

2 tbsp tomato paste
about 1¼ cups hot beef stock for the slow cooker
(about 2 cups for the traditional method)
2–3 thyme sprigs
salt and freshly ground black pepper

in the slow cooker **PREP** 15 MINS **COOK** 15 MINS PRECOOKING; **AUTO/LOW** 6–8 HRS

1 Preheat the slow cooker, if required. Heat the oil in a large Dutch oven over medium-high heat, add the beef (in batches, if necessary) and cook for about 5 minutes until browned on all sides. Remove from the pot and set aside. Add the onion, carrot, and celery, and cook, stirring, for 3–5 minutes until the vegetables are soft.

2 Add the red wine, stir to dissolve the casserole juices, and bring to a boil. Stir in the tomato paste, then transfer everything to the slow cooker, including the meat. Add enough stock to cover the meat and add thyme and salt and pepper. Cover with the lid and cook on auto/low for 6–8 hours. Discard the thyme, taste, and add seasoning if needed. Ladle into shallow bowls and serve with some crusty bread.

traditional method **PREP** 15 MINS **COOK** 2¼–3¼ HRS

1 Preheat the oven to 300°F (150°C). Heat the oil in a large Dutch oven over medium-high heat, add the beef (in batches, if necessary) and cook for about 10 minutes until browned on all sides. Remove from the pot and set aside. Add the onion, carrot, and celery, and cook, stirring, for 3–5 minutes until the vegetables are soft.

2 Add the red wine, stir to dissolve the casserole juices, and bring to a boil. Stir in the tomato paste and return the beef. Add enough stock to cover the meat, then add the thyme and salt and pepper and bring to a boil. Cover with the lid and put in the oven to cook for 2–3 hours or until the meat is very tender when pierced with a fork. Check occasionally that it's not drying out, topping up with a little hot water if needed. Discard the thyme, taste, and add salt and pepper if needed. Ladle into shallow bowls and serve with some crusty bread.

Chianti is the wine of Tuscany, but you can use any good-quality, full-bodied red wine. The beef benefits from being prepared ahead and kept in the refrigerator; its flavors will mellow.

Peppery Tuscan beef

SERVES 4–6 ❄ **FREEZE** UP TO 3 MONTHS

2 tbsp freshly ground black pepper
¾ cup olive oil, plus 3 tbsp for cooking
2½lb (1.1kg) chuck steak, cut into 2in (5cm) cubes
4½oz (125g) pancetta, diced
1 large onion, chopped
5 garlic cloves, finely chopped

14oz (400g) can chopped tomatoes
2 bay leaves
3–4 sprigs of sage, leaves chopped
1 cup hot beef stock, for both methods
1¼ cups red wine for the slow cooker
  (2 cups for the traditional method)

in the slow cooker ⏱ PREP 20 MINS, PLUS MARINATING COOK 20 MINS PRECOOKING; AUTO/LOW 8 HRS

1 In a large bowl, combine 1 tablespoon of the black pepper with ¾ cup of oil. Add the beef and stir until well coated. Cover with plastic wrap and refrigerate, stirring occasionally, for 8–12 hours.

2 Preheat the slow cooker, if required. Remove the beef from the marinade and pat dry with paper towels. Heat the cooking oil in a large Dutch oven over high heat, add the meat (in batches, if necessary), and cook for 3–5 minutes until browned on all sides. Remove and set aside. Reduce the heat to medium, add the pancetta, and cook, stirring occasionally, for 2–3 minutes, until the fat has rendered. Add the onion and cook for 3–4 minutes until soft. Return the beef and add the garlic, tomatoes, bay leaves, sage, stock, and wine, together with the remaining pepper. Bring to a boil, then transfer everything to the slow cooker, cover with the lid, and cook on auto/low for 8 hours.

3 Discard the bay leaves, taste, and add salt and pepper if needed. Serve with some greens, such as Savoy cabbage or broccoli, and Italian-style cubed roasted potatoes and rosemary.

traditional method ⏱ PREP 20 MINS, PLUS MARINATING COOK 2–2½ HRS

1 In a large bowl, combine 1 tablespoon of the black pepper with ¾ cup of oil. Add the beef and stir until well coated. Cover with plastic wrap and refrigerate, stirring occasionally, for 8–12 hours.

2 Remove the beef from the marinade and pat dry with paper towels. Heat the cooking oil in a large Dutch oven over high heat, add the meat (in batches, if necessary), and cook for 3–5 minutes until browned on all sides. Remove and set aside. Reduce the heat to medium, add the pancetta, and cook, stirring occasionally, for 2–3 minutes, until the fat has rendered. Add the onion and cook for 3–4 minutes until soft. Return the beef and add the garlic, tomatoes, bay leaves, sage, stock, and wine, together with the remaining pepper. Bring to a boil, cover, reduce the heat, and leave to simmer for 1¾–2 hours until very tender, stirring occasionally. During cooking, add more hot water if the stew seems dry. The beef is ready when it is tender enough to crush in your fingers.

3 Discard the bay leaves, taste, and add salt and pepper if needed. Serve with some greens, such as Savoy cabbage or broccoli, and Italian-style cubed roasted potatoes and rosemary.

In Mexico, chorizo is made with fresh pork, but in Spain, the pork is smoked first for even more flavor. Chorizo works its magic as it cooks and gives the sauce a rich, deep flavor.

Chicken with chorizo

⊚ **SERVES** 4 ❄ **FREEZE** UP TO 1 MONTH

2 tbsp olive oil
4 skinless chicken leg quarters
9oz (250g) dried chorizo, chopped in bite-sized pieces
1 red onion, thinly sliced
1 tsp ground coriander
1 tsp chopped thyme leaves
1 red bell pepper, seeded and chopped
1 yellow bell pepper, seeded and chopped

1 zucchini, trimmed and sliced
2 garlic cloves, crushed
14oz (400g) can chopped tomatoes
½ cup hot chicken stock for the slow cooker
  (1 cup for the traditional method)
½ cup dry sherry
freshly ground black pepper

in the slow cooker 🕒 **PREP** 10 MINS   **COOK** 20 MINS PRECOOKING;
                                        AUTO/LOW 6–8 HRS OR **HIGH** 3–4 HRS

1 Preheat the slow cooker, if required. Heat the oil in a large Dutch oven over medium-high heat, add the chicken, and fry for 5–8 minutes, turning frequently, until evenly browned. Remove and set aside. Then add the chorizo to the pot and cook for 2–3 minutes until lightly browned, stirring frequently. Also remove and set aside.

2 Reduce the heat to medium, add the onion to the pot, and cook for 3–4 minutes until soft. Add the coriander, cook for 1 minute, and then add the thyme, peppers, zucchini, and garlic and cook for 5 minutes. Add the tomatoes, stock, and sherry. Season with black pepper, if needed, and bring to a boil. Transfer everything to the slow cooker, including the chicken and chorizo. Cover with the lid and cook on auto/low for 6–8 hours or on high for 3–4 hours. Serve with mashed sweet potatoes and peas.

traditional method 🕒 **PREP** 10 MINS   **COOK** 1 HR

1 Preheat the oven to 350°F (180°C). Heat the oil in a large Dutch oven over medium-high heat, add the chicken, and fry for 5–8 minutes, turning frequently, until evenly browned. Remove and set aside. Then add the chorizo to the pot and cook for 2–3 minutes until lightly browned, stirring frequently. Also remove and set aside.

2 Reduce the heat to medium, add the onion to the pot, and cook for 3–4 minutes until soft. Add the coriander, cook for 1 minute, and then add the thyme, peppers, zucchini, and garlic and cook for 5 minutes. Add the tomatoes, stock, and sherry. Season with black pepper, if needed, and bring to a boil. Return the chicken and chorizo, and cook in the oven for about 40 minutes until the chicken is tender when pierced with a fork. Serve with mashed sweet potatoes and peas.

Olives, feta cheese, and thyme are all synonymous with Greek cuisine, and here they are combined with a succulent leg of lamb. The feta adds a fabulous saltiness to the finished dish.

Stuffed lamb, Greek style

SERVES 4–6

1 leg of lamb, boned and butterflied
 (about 4lb/1.8kg after boning—ask your butcher
 to do this), or use a boneless shoulder
salt and freshly ground black pepper
2 tbsp olive oil
1 tbsp dried oregano
2 red peppers, seeded and roughly chopped

⅓ cup black olives, pitted and finely chopped
6oz (175g) feta cheese, finely chopped
3 red onions, roughly chopped
4–6 tomatoes, roughly chopped
2 cups red wine
few sprigs of thyme

in the slow cooker   **PREP** 30 MINS   **COOK** 10 MINS PRECOOKING; **AUTO/LOW** 8 HRS

1 Preheat the slow cooker, if required. Lay the lamb out flat and season well with salt and pepper. Rub both sides all over with the oil and oregano. Cover one side of the lamb with the red peppers, then the olives, and then the feta. Starting from one end, roll up the lamb, tucking in any loose pieces to neaten it. Tie it up with butcher's string so it is secure.

2 Heat a large Dutch oven over medium heat, add the lamb, and cook for 4–6 minutes on each side until it begins to color. Transfer the lamb to the slow cooker and add the onions, tomatoes, and wine. Season and add the thyme, cover with the lid, and cook on auto/low for 8 hours.

3 Remove the meat from the slow cooker, cover loosely with foil, and leave to rest for 15 minutes. Remove the string and carve into slices. Serve with some of the sauce, together with baby roasted potatoes with rosemary, and some wilted spinach.

traditional method   **PREP** 30 MINS   **COOK** 2¼–2¾ HRS

1 Preheat the oven to 325°F (160°C). Lay the lamb out flat and season well with salt and pepper. Rub both sides all over with the oil and oregano. Cover one side of the lamb with the red peppers, then the olives, and then the feta. Starting from one end, roll up the lamb, tucking in any loose pieces to neaten it. Tie it up with butcher's string so it is secure.

2 Heat a large Dutch oven over medium heat, add the lamb, and cook for 4–6 minutes on each side until it begins to color. Throw in the red onions and tomatoes and cook for a minute more, then pour in the wine. Bring to a boil, then reduce to a simmer and add some seasoning and the thyme. Cover with the lid and put in the oven for 2–2½ hours or until cooked to your liking. Check occasionally that it's not drying out, topping up with a little hot water if needed.

3 Remove from the oven, cover the meat loosely with foil, and leave to rest for 15 minutes. Remove the string and carve into slices. Serve with some of the sauce, together with baby roasted potatoes with rosemary, and some wilted spinach.

Stifado is a rich mix of beef and onions, but the onions are added later in the recipe as this helps them to keep their shape. This is a good "make-ahead" stew, as it tastes great reheated the next day.

Greek stifado

SERVES 4–6 **FREEZE** UP TO 3 MONTHS

3 tbsp olive oil
2½lb (1.1kg) chuck roast, cut into bite-sized pieces
salt and freshly ground black pepper
¾ cup red wine
2 tbsp red wine vinegar
1 cinnamon stick
1 tsp ground cloves
½ tsp grated nutmeg

3 garlic cloves, finely chopped
4 tomatoes, roughly chopped
1 tbsp tomato paste
1¾ cups hot vegetable stock for the slow cooker
  (2 cups for the traditional method)
few sprigs of thyme
pat of butter
1lb 2oz (500g) shallots, peeled and left whole

in the slow cooker **PREP** 30 MINS **COOK** 20 MINS PRECOOKING; **AUTO/LOW** 8 HRS

1 Preheat the slow cooker, if required. Heat 2 tablespoons of the oil in a large Dutch oven over medium-high heat. Add the meat, season with salt and pepper, and cook for about 6 minutes until lightly browned. Increase the heat and add the wine and vinegar. Cook for a couple of minutes, then stir in the cinnamon stick, cloves, nutmeg, and garlic and cook for a further minute.

2 Add the tomatoes and tomato paste and cook for a few minutes. Transfer everything to the slow cooker, pour in the stock, and add the thyme. Cover with the lid and cook on auto/low for 8 hours.

3 About halfway through the cooking time, heat the remaining oil together with the butter in a Dutch oven over medium heat. Add the shallots and cook for 6–8 minutes until golden, then add them to the slow cooker. Taste and season, remove the cinnamon stick and thyme, and serve with creamy mashed potatoes or baby roasted potatoes with rosemary.

traditional method **PREP** 30 MINS **COOK** 2¼ HRS

1 Preheat the oven to 350°F (180°C). Heat 2 tablespoons of the oil in a Dutch oven over medium-high heat. Add the meat, season with salt and pepper, and cook for about 6 minutes until lightly browned. Increase the heat and add the wine and vinegar. Cook for a couple of minutes, then stir in the cinnamon stick, cloves, nutmeg, and garlic and cook for a further minute.

2 Add the tomatoes and tomato paste and then add the stock. Bring the sauce to a boil, then throw in the thyme, cover with the lid, and put in the oven for about 1 hour. Check occasionally that it's not drying out, topping up with a little hot water if needed.

3 Heat the remaining oil together with the butter in a Dutch oven over medium heat, add the shallots and cook for 6–8 minutes until golden, then spoon these into the stew and stir carefully. Cover and return to the oven. Reduce the temperature to 325°F (160°C) and cook for a further hour. Check occasionally that it's not drying out, topping up with a little hot water if needed. Taste and season, remove the cinnamon stick and thyme, and serve with creamy mashed potatoes or baby roasted potatoes with rosemary.

Lamb works very well with fruit, and the prunes and apple in this recipe are no exception. If you're not a fan of prunes, use dried apricots or dates instead. They add a piquant flavor.

Fruity lamb shanks

⊚ **SERVES** 4 ❄ **FREEZE** UP TO 3 MONTHS

4 tbsp olive oil
4 lamb shanks
1 tbsp all-purpose flour
1 cup white wine
1 large onion, sliced
salt and freshly ground black pepper
3 garlic cloves, finely chopped
1 tsp fennel seeds

few sprigs of thyme
2 bay leaves
1 celery root, peeled and chopped into small pieces
1 cooking apple, peeled, cored, and diced
7oz (200g) soft prunes, pitted and left whole
¾ cup fresh orange juice
⅔ cup hot vegetable stock for the slow cooker
   (3 cups for the traditional method)

in the slow cooker 🕐 PREP 15 MINS COOK 20 MINS PRECOOKING; AUTO/LOW 8 HRS

1 Preheat the slow cooker, if required. Heat half the oil in a large Dutch oven over medium-high heat, and toss the lamb shanks in the flour. Add the shanks to the pot, one or two at a time, and cook for about 10 minutes until golden on all sides. Remove and set aside in a bowl. Pour the wine into the pot, increase the heat, and let it simmer while stirring to remove the bits from the bottom of the pot. Pour this over the lamb and wipe the pan with paper towels.

2 Heat a little more oil over medium heat, add the onion, and cook for 3–4 minutes until soft. Season with salt and pepper, then stir in the garlic, fennel seeds, thyme, bay leaves, and celery root, and cook for about 5 minutes, adding more oil if necessary, until just beginning to turn golden.

3 Add the apple and prunes, season, and cook for 1–2 minutes. Return the lamb and sauce to the pot, add the orange juice and stock, and bring to a boil. Transfer everything to the slow cooker, cover with the lid, and cook on auto/low for 8 hours. Serve with creamy mashed potatoes.

traditional method 🕐 PREP 15 MINS COOK 3¼–3¾ HRS

1 Preheat the oven to 300°C (150°C). Heat half the oil in a large Dutch oven over medium-high heat, and toss the lamb shanks in the flour. Add the shanks to the pot, one or two at a time, and cook for about 10 minutes until golden on all sides. Remove and set aside in a bowl. Pour the wine into the pot, increase the heat, and let it simmer while stirring to remove the bits from the bottom of the pot. Pour this over the lamb and wipe the pan with paper towels.

2 Heat a little more oil over medium heat, add the onion, and cook for 3–4 minutes until soft. Season with salt and pepper, then stir in the garlic, fennel seeds, thyme, bay leaves, and celery root, and cook for about 5 minutes, adding more oil if necessary, until just beginning to turn golden.

3 Add the apple and prunes, season, and cook for 1–2 minutes. Return the lamb and sauce to the pot, add the orange juice and stock, and bring to a boil. Reduce to a simmer, cover with the lid, and put in the oven for 3–3½ hours until the lamb is falling off the bone. Check occasionally that it's not drying out, topping up with a little hot water if needed. Serve with creamy mashed potatoes.

Pear makes the perfect partner to venison and is tasty served with steamed Savoy cabbage with butter and black pepper. You could use beef instead of venison, cooking it for the same length of time.

Venison stew with pears

⊘ **SERVES** 6 ❄ **FREEZE** UP TO 3 MONTHS ♡ **HEALTHY**

2 tsp black peppercorns, crushed
2 tsp juniper berries, crushed
4 shallots, roughly chopped
2 garlic cloves, peeled and left whole
2 onions, quartered
2 carrots, peeled and roughly sliced
1 bouquet garni
2 tbsp red wine vinegar
1¾ cups dry red wine for the slow cooker
  (2½ cups for the traditional method)

2¼lb (1kg) stewing venison (leg or shoulder),
  fat trimmed and cut into 1½in (4cm) cubes
3 tbsp vegetable oil
¼ cup all-purpose flour
1¾ cups hot beef stock for the slow cooker
  (2½ cups for the traditional method)
salt and freshly ground black pepper
4 ripe pears, peeled, cored, and chopped
3 tbsp red currant jelly

in the slow cooker
🕐 **PREP** 30 MINS, PLUS MARINATING   **COOK** 20 MINS PRECOOKING; **AUTO/LOW** 6–8 HRS OR **HIGH** 3–4 HRS

1 To make the marinade, put the spices, vegetables, bouquet garni, vinegar, and wine in a pan and bring to a boil, then simmer for about 2 minutes. Transfer to a shallow dish and leave to cool. Add the venison, stir to coat evenly, cover, and refrigerate for 6–8 hours, turning occasionally.

2 Preheat the slow cooker, if required. Remove the venison and pat dry. Strain the marinade, reserving the bouquet garni, vegetables, and marinade separately. Heat half the oil in a large Dutch oven over high heat, add the venison (in batches and with extra oil, if necessary) and cook for 3–5 minutes until brown all over. Transfer to a bowl. Heat the remaining oil over medium heat, add the reserved vegetables, and cook, stirring, for 5–7 minutes until they start to brown. Add the flour and cook, stirring, for 3–5 minutes until it has been absorbed. Stir in the marinade, venison, bouquet garni, stock, and seasoning. Transfer to the slow cooker, cover, and cook on auto/low for 6–8 hours or on high for 3–4 hours. Stir in the pears and red currant jelly for the last 20 minutes of cooking.

traditional method
🕐 **PREP** 30 MINS, PLUS MARINATING   **COOK** 1½–1¾ HRS

1 To make the marinade, put the spices, vegetables, bouquet garni, vinegar, and wine in a pan and bring to a boil, then simmer for about 2 minutes. Transfer to a shallow dish and leave to cool. Add the venison, stir to coat evenly, cover, and refrigerate for 6–8 hours, turning occasionally.

2 Preheat the oven to 350°F (180°C). Remove the venison and pat dry. Strain the marinade, reserving the bouquet garni, vegetables, and marinade separately. Heat half the oil in a large Dutch oven over high heat, add the venison (in batches and with extra oil, if necessary) and cook for 3–5 minutes until brown all over. Transfer to a bowl. Heat the remaining oil over medium heat, add the reserved vegetables, and cook, stirring, for 5–7 minutes until they start to brown. Add the flour and cook, stirring, for 3–5 minutes until it has been absorbed. Stir in the marinade, venison, bouquet garni, stock, and seasoning. Cover and cook in the oven for 1¼–1½ hours until tender. Stir in the pears and red currant jelly and cook for 6–8 minutes until the pears are tender.

This colonial American dish uses lots of Southern ingredients, such as smoked ham, beans, corn, and chile—although it was originally made with squirrel!

American Brunswick stew

◎ **SERVES** 4–6 ❄ **FREEZE** UP TO 3 MONTHS

4 chicken thighs with bones in
2¼lb (1kg) ham hock
1 tbsp dark soft brown sugar
1 bouquet garni
1 onion, chopped
3 celery stalks, trimmed and thinly sliced
14oz (400g) can chopped tomatoes

7oz (200g) thawed frozen or canned corn
salt and freshly ground black pepper
1 cup fresh or thawed frozen lima or fava beans
13oz (375g) potatoes, peeled and chopped
  into chunks
1 tsp dried chile flakes

in the slow cooker   🕑 **PREP** 25 MINS   **COOK** AUTO/LOW 6–8 HRS

1 Preheat the slow cooker, if required. Put the chicken and ham hock in the slow cooker and add the sugar, bouquet garni, onion, celery, tomatoes, corn, and salt and pepper. Pour in water to cover. Cover with the lid and cook on auto/low for 6–8 hours. Add the lima beans for the last hour of cooking.

2 Meanwhile, put the potatoes in a saucepan of salted water. Bring to a boil, cover, and simmer for 15–20 minutes until tender. Drain, mash until very smooth, and set aside.

3 Stir in the chile flakes into the slow cooker for the last 10 minutes of cooking. Lift out the ham and chicken and pull the meat from the bones of both, in large pieces, using a knife and fork. Discard the skin and fat, shred the meat into chunky bits, and stir it back into the stew. Stir the mashed potatoes into the stew. Discard the bouquet garni and taste, adding salt and pepper if needed.

traditional method   🕑 **PREP** 10 MINS   **COOK** 2–2½ HRS

1 Put the chicken in a large Dutch oven with the ham hock and pour in enough water to cover. Add the sugar and bouquet garni. Bring to a boil and skim well with a slotted spoon. Cover and simmer gently until the chicken joints are almost tender when pierced; it will take about 1 hour. Lift out the chicken with a slotted spoon and reserve. Remove the pot from the heat and set aside. Bring the cooking liquid in the pot back to a boil. Add the onion, celery, and tomatoes and simmer, stirring often, for 20–30 minutes. Make sure the heat is gentle; the liquid should be barely bubbling. Add the corn and simmer for 10 minutes longer.

2 Put the potatoes in a saucepan of salted water. Bring to a boil, cover, and simmer for 15–20 minutes, until tender. Drain and mash until smooth (an old-fashioned potato ricer can make potatoes really smooth). Stir the potatoes, chile flakes, and beans into the stew and season to taste. The heat of the chile will mellow, if you are cooking this dish in advance. Return the chicken to the stew and simmer, stirring often, for about 15 minutes more, or until the meats and vegetables are tender.

3 Lift out the ham. Using a fork and knife, pull the meat from the bones in large pieces, discarding the skin and fat. Shred the meat into chunky bits and stir it back into the stew. The sauce should be thick, but if it is too sticky (which it may be, depending on the potatoes you used), add a little more water to thin it out. Discard the bouquet garni and taste, adding salt and pepper if needed.

There is plenty of vibrant color and a lot of heat in this vegetable dish. This is good on its own or with plain boiled rice and, to change it up, you may wish to add some chorizo or chicken.

Jamaican corn stew

SERVES 4–6

2 tbsp olive oil
2 onions, finely chopped
salt and freshly ground black pepper
3 garlic cloves, finely chopped
1 tsp cayenne pepper
3 corn cobs, cut into slices about
 ½in (1cm) thick
2 red bell peppers, seeded and roughly chopped

3 sweet potatoes, peeled and diced
¾ cup yellow split peas
½ cup hot vegetable stock for the slow cooker
 (1 cup for the traditional method)
14oz (400ml) can coconut milk
small handful of thyme
1 Scotch bonnet chile, left whole

in the slow cooker
PREP 20 MINS   **COOK** 10 MINS PRECOOKING;
AUTO/LOW 6–8 HRS OR **HIGH** 3–4 HRS

1 Preheat the slow cooker, if required. Heat the oil in a large, heavy Dutch oven over medium heat, add the onions, and cook for 3–4 minutes until soft. Season with salt and pepper, then stir in the garlic and cayenne pepper, and cook for 1 minute. Add the corn, peppers, and sweet potatoes and turn so it is all coated evenly. Then stir in the split peas and a little of the stock.

2 Transfer the mixture to the slow cooker. Pour in the coconut milk and the remaining stock. Add seasoning, the thyme, and the Scotch bonnet, then stir, cover with the lid, and cook on auto/low for 6–8 hours or on high for 3–4 hours.

3 Remove the Scotch bonnet, taste, and season as required. Ladle into warmed bowls and serve with rice and some lime wedges on the side.

traditional method
PREP 20 MINS   **COOK** 1½–2 HRS

1 Preheat the oven to 325°F (160°C). Heat the oil in a large Dutch oven over medium heat, add the onions, and cook for 3–4 minutes until soft. Season with salt and pepper, then stir in the garlic and cayenne pepper, and cook for 1 minute. Add the corn, peppers, and sweet potatoes and turn so it is all coated evenly. Then stir in the split peas and a little of the stock.

2 Bring to a boil, then add the remaining stock and coconut milk. Bring back to a boil, reduce to a simmer, season, and add the thyme and the Scotch bonnet. Cover and put in the oven to cook for 1½–2 hours. Check occasionally that it's not drying out, topping up with a little hot water if needed.

3 Remove the Scotch bonnet, taste, and season as required. Ladle into warmed bowls and serve with rice and some lime wedges on the side.

A medley of earthy mushrooms and potatoes makes this vegetarian dish a really hearty supper. Portabella mushrooms are especially meaty in texture so cut them into substantial chunks.

Mixed mushroom stew

⊚ **SERVES** 4–6 ❋ **FREEZE** UP TO 3 MONTHS ◌ **HEALTHY**

1 tbsp olive oil
1 onion, finely chopped
salt and freshly ground black pepper
6oz (175g) cremini mushrooms, grated
1lb (450g) white mushrooms, thickly sliced
1 sprig of rosemary
3 garlic cloves, finely chopped
4 portabella mushrooms, roughly chopped
1 tbsp sherry vinegar

6 tomatoes, roughly chopped
1 tbsp tomato paste
1 cup hot vegetable stock for the slow cooker
   (1¾ cups for the traditional method)
3 potatoes, peeled and chopped into
   bite-sized pieces
pinch of dried chile flakes
small bunch of curly parsley, finely chopped
2 tbsp Parmesan cheese, grated (optional)

in the slow cooker 🕐 **PREP** 30 MINS **COOK** 20 MINS PRECOOKING; **HIGH** 3–4 HRS

1 Preheat the slow cooker, if required. Heat the oil in a large heavy-based pan over medium heat, add the onion, and cook for 3–4 minutes until soft. Season with salt and pepper, then add the grated cremini mushrooms and cook for 5 minutes until they start to release their juices.

2 Throw in the white mushrooms, rosemary, garlic, and portabella mushrooms, and stir. Add the sherry vinegar and allow the sauce to bubble for 1 minute, then add the tomatoes and tomato paste. Cook on a gentle heat for 5 minutes, stirring occasionally, then transfer everything to the slow cooker. Add the stock and potatoes, season and cover with the lid, and then cook on high for 3–4 hours.

3 Taste and season as needed, remove the rosemary, then stir in the chile flakes and parsley. Ladle into warmed bowls and serve with the grated Parmesan cheese, if using, and some chunky bread.

traditional method 🕐 **PREP** 30 MINS **COOK** 1 HR

1 Heat the oil in a large heavy-based pan over medium heat, add the onion, and cook for 3–4 minutes until soft. Season with salt and pepper, then add the grated cremini mushrooms and cook for 5 minutes until they start to release their juices.

2 Throw in the white mushrooms, rosemary, garlic, and portabella mushrooms, and stir. Add the sherry vinegar and allow the sauce to bubble for 1 minute, then add the tomatoes and tomato paste. Cook on a gentle heat for 5 minutes, stirring occasionally, then add the stock and bring to a boil. Reduce the heat to a simmer and cook, uncovered, on a low heat for 40–45 minutes.

3 Stir in the potatoes for the last 20 minutes of cooking, and cook until tender. Taste and season as needed, remove the rosemary, then stir in the chile flakes and parsley. Ladle into warmed bowls and serve with the grated Parmesan cheese, if using, and some chunky bread.

Puy lentils add texture to this dish as they hold their shape well when cooked. Add a little chili powder, if you wish, and use butternut squash if pumpkin isn't available or out of season.

Sweet and sour pumpkin stew

SERVES 4 **FREEZE** UP TO 3 MONTHS **HEALTHY**

2 tbsp olive oil
1 onion, finely chopped
salt and freshly ground black pepper
3 garlic cloves, finely chopped
1 carrot, peeled and finely diced
2 celery stalks, finely diced
2 bay leaves
¼ cup red wine vinegar
pinch of demerara sugar

1 pumpkin or large butternut squash, peeled, seeded, and chopped into chunky pieces (about 1lb 2oz/500g prepared weight)
1¾ cups hot vegetable stock for the slow cooker (3 cups for the traditional method)
¾ cup Puy lentils, rinsed and picked over for any stones
bunch of mint leaves, roughly chopped
pumpkin seeds, to serve

in the slow cooker **PREP** 15 MINS **COOK** 15 MINS PRECOOKING; **AUTO/LOW** 8 HRS OR **HIGH** 4 HRS

1 Preheat the slow cooker, if required. Heat the oil in a large Dutch oven over medium heat, add the onion, and cook for 3–4 minutes until soft. Season well with salt and pepper, then stir in the garlic, carrot, celery, and bay leaves, and cook for a further 5 minutes until soft.

2 Increase the heat, add the vinegar, and let it bubble for a minute, then stir in the sugar and pumpkin. Turn to coat well and add a little stock before cooking on high for a minute. Then stir in the lentils.

3 Transfer everything to the slow cooker, stir in the stock, cover with the lid, and cook on auto/low for 8 hours or on high for 4 hours. Taste and season, if needed, and remove the bay leaf. Stir in the mint, then serve on a bed of rice with some pumpkin seeds scattered over.

traditional method **PREP** 15 MINS **COOK** 1 HR

1 Heat the oil in a large Dutch oven over medium heat, add the onion, and cook for 3–4 minutes until soft. Season well with salt and pepper, then stir in the garlic, carrot, celery, and bay leaves, and cook for a further 5 minutes until soft.

2 Increase the heat, add the vinegar, and let it bubble for a minute, then stir in the sugar and pumpkin. Turn to coat well and add a little stock before cooking on high for a minute. Stir in the lentils, add the remaining stock, and bring to a boil.

3 Partially cover with the lid, reduce the heat, and simmer gently for about 45 minutes or until the lentils are soft. Top up with hot water if the stew is becoming too dry. Taste and season, if needed, and remove the bay leaf. Stir in the mint, then serve on a bed of rice with some pumpkin seeds.

Except for squid, seafood doesn't take kindly to slow cooking, so make the stew base first and add the fish at the last minute. For ease of preparation, you could always make this the day before.

Seafood stew

◎ **SERVES** 4–6   ♡ **HEALTHY**

2 tbsp olive oil, plus extra for drizzling
1 onion, finely chopped
2 celery stalks, finely chopped
salt and freshly ground black pepper
1 tbsp dried oregano
1 fennel bulb, trimmed and roughly chopped
1lb (450g) cleaned squid, sliced into ½in (1cm) rings
1½ cups dry white wine
2 lemons, zest peeled into strips using a
   vegetable peeler

1 tbsp tomato paste
14oz (400g) can chopped tomatoes
2 cups hot fish stock for the slow cooker
   (3 cups for the traditional method)
2¼lb (1kg) mussels, scrubbed and debearded
   (discard any that do not close when tapped)
9oz (250g) raw shelled king prawns
12oz (350g) sea bass filet (or other white fish such
   as haddock), skinned and cut into chunky pieces
few sprigs of flat-leaf parsley, finely chopped

in the slow cooker   ⏱ **PREP** 20–30 MINS   **COOK** 15 MINS PRECOOKING; **HIGH** 3–4 HRS

1 Preheat the slow cooker, if required. Heat the oil in a large heavy-based pan over medium heat, add the onion and celery, and cook for about 5 minutes until soft. Season with salt and pepper, then stir in the oregano and fennel and cook for a further 5 minutes.

2 Add the squid and cook over low heat for a few minutes, stirring occasionally, then stir in the wine, and bring to a boil for 5 minutes. Stir in the strips of lemon zest and tomato paste, season well, and then add the canned tomatoes and stock. Transfer everything to the slow cooker, cover with the lid, and cook on high for 3–4 hours.

3 For the last 10 minutes of cooking, add the mussels, prawns, and sea bass, cover, and cook until the mussels have opened (discard any that do not open) and the fish is opaque and cooked through. Taste and season as needed. Ladle into deep, warmed bowls and serve with rice, couscous, or quinoa, a drizzle of olive oil, and a sprinkling of parsley.

traditional method   ⏱ **PREP** 20–30 MINS   **COOK** 1½ HRS

1 Preheat the oven to 325°F (160°C). Heat the oil in a large Dutch oven over medium heat, add the onion and celery, and cook for about 5 minutes until soft. Season with salt and pepper, then stir in the oregano and fennel and cook for a further 5 minutes.

2 Add the squid and cook over low heat for a few minutes, stirring occasionally, then stir in the wine, and bring to a boil for 5 minutes. Stir in the strips of lemon zest and tomato paste, season well, and then add the canned tomatoes and stock. Bring back to a boil, reduce to a simmer, cover, and put in the oven for 1 hour, topping up with hot stock if needed.

3 Add the mussels, prawns, and sea bass to the pot, cover with the lid once more, and put back in the oven for 5 minutes or until the mussels have opened (discard any that do not open) and the fish is opaque and cooked through. Taste and season as needed. Ladle into deep, warmed bowls and serve with rice, couscous, or quinoa, a drizzle of olive oil, and a sprinkling of parsley.

Monkfish is the ideal fish to use in this robust stew as it holds its texture well. Its firm flesh also makes it good to serve to meat lovers as it has a particularly "meaty" quality about it.

Monkfish and green chile stew

SERVES 6 ⚙ **FREEZE** UP TO 1 MONTH 💗 **HEALTHY**

1 tbsp olive oil
1 onion, finely chopped
salt and freshly ground black pepper
3 garlic cloves, finely chopped
2 green chilies, seeded and finely chopped
3 celery stalks, finely chopped
pinch of paprika
½ cup red wine
14oz (400g) can chopped tomatoes

1 cup hot vegetable stock for the slow cooker
    (2 cups for the traditional method)
about 1lb 2oz (500g) potatoes, peeled and
    chopped into bite-sized cubes
6oz (175g) green beans, trimmed and chopped
about 2lb (900g) monkfish tails, cut into
    chunky pieces
about 4 packed cups spinach leaves,
    roughly chopped

in the slow cooker 🕐 **PREP** 15 MINS **COOK** 15 MINS PRECOOKING;
AUTO/LOW 6–8 HRS OR **HIGH** 3–4 HRS

1 Preheat the slow cooker, if required. Heat the oil in a large heavy-based pan over medium heat, add the onion, and cook for 3–4 minutes until soft. Season with salt and pepper, then stir in the garlic, chilies, and celery and cook for 5 more minutes until the celery softens.

2 Add the paprika and toss everything together, then increase the heat, add the wine, and let it bubble for a minute. Add in the tomatoes and stir. Transfer everything to the slow cooker, add salt and pepper, and pour in the stock. Then stir in the potatoes and beans.

3 Cover with the lid and cook on auto/low for 6–8 hours or on high for 3–4 hours. Add the fish and spinach for the last 15 minutes of cooking and cook until the fish is opaque and cooked through. Taste and season as needed, then ladle into warmed bowls. Serve with crusty bread and a squeeze of lemon juice.

traditional method 🕐 **PREP** 15 MINS **COOK** 1¼ HRS

1 Heat the oil in a large heavy-based pan over medium heat, add the onion, and cook for 3–4 minutes until soft. Season with salt and pepper, then stir in the garlic, chilies, and celery and cook for 5 more minutes until the celery softens.

2 Add the paprika and toss everything together, then increase the heat, add the wine, and let it bubble for a minute. Add in the tomatoes and stock and bring to a boil. Reduce to a simmer and cook, partially covered with the lid, for about 45 minutes, stirring occasionally, and topping up with a little hot water if needed.

3 Add the potatoes, beans, and monkfish, pushing them all down so they are covered in the sauce, and simmer, uncovered, for a further 15 minutes until the potatoes are soft and the fish is opaque and cooked through. Stir in the spinach and cook for 1–2 minutes until it wilts. Taste and season as needed, then ladle into warmed bowls. Serve with crusty bread and a squeeze of lemon juice.

Squid transforms when it is cooked slowly. It defies all rubbery associations and becomes wonderfully tender. This tomato-based stew is richly spiced with smoky chorizo.

Squid stew

SERVES 4–6 **FREEZE** UP TO 3 MONTHS **HEALTHY**

1 tbsp olive oil
1 onion, finely chopped
salt and freshly ground black pepper
1 bay leaf
few sprigs of thyme
3 garlic cloves, sliced
2 red chilies, seeded and sliced into thin strips
7oz (200g) dried chorizo, sliced
2½lb (1.1kg) squid (about 1lb 10oz/750g
   prepared weight), cleaned and cut into rings
   (and tentacles, if you wish)

1 cup red wine
14oz (400g) can chopped tomatoes
1½ cups hot vegetable stock for the slow cooker
   (2 cups for the traditional method)
14oz (400g) can butter beans, drained
handful of curly parsley, very finely chopped

in the slow cooker
PREP 30 MINS **COOK** 15 MINS PRECOOKING;
AUTO/LOW 6–8 HRS OR **HIGH** 3–4 HRS

1 Preheat the slow cooker, if required. Heat the oil in a large Dutch oven over medium heat, add the onion, and season with salt and pepper. Add the bay leaf and thyme, and cook gently for about 6 minutes until the onions are soft.

2 Stir in the garlic, chilies, and chorizo and cook for a few minutes. Then add the squid (in batches, if necessary) and cook for a few more minutes until the squid starts to color slightly. Increase the heat and pour in the wine. Let it bubble for 1–2 minutes, then transfer everything to the slow cooker. Stir in the tomatoes, stock, butter beans, and seasoning. Cover with the lid and cook on auto/low for 6–8 hours or on high for 3–4 hours.

3 Taste and season if needed, remove the bay leaf and thyme, and stir in the parsley. Ladle into warmed bowls and serve with crusty bread.

traditional method
PREP 30 MINS **COOK** 1¼–1¾ HRS

1 Preheat the oven to 325°F (160°C). Heat the oil in a large Dutch oven over medium heat, add the onion, and season with salt and pepper. Add the bay leaf and thyme, and cook gently for about 6 minutes until the onions are soft.

2 Stir in the garlic, chilies, and chorizo and cook for a few minutes. Then add the squid (in batches, if necessary) and cook for a few more minutes until the squid starts to color slightly. Increase the heat and pour in the wine. Let it bubble for 1–2 minutes, then add the tomatoes and stock, and bring to a boil.

3 Add in the butter beans and stir, then add the seasoning, cover with the lid, and put in the oven for 1–1½ hours. Check occasionally that it's not drying out, topping up with a little hot water if needed. Taste and season if needed, remove the bay leaf and thyme, and stir in the parsley. Ladle into warmed bowls and serve with crusty bread.

Originally nothing more than a humble fisherman's stew using the remains of the day's catch, bouillabaisse has evolved into one of the great Provençal dishes. The rouille has a fine garlic kick to it.

Bouillabaisse

SERVES 4

¼ cup olive oil
1 onion, thinly sliced
2 leeks, trimmed and thinly sliced
1 small fennel bulb, thinly sliced
2–3 garlic cloves, finely chopped
4 tomatoes, skinned, seeded, and chopped
1 tbsp tomato paste
1 cup dry white wine
2 cups hot fish stock for the slow cooker
  (5½ cups for the traditional method)
pinch of saffron threads
strip of orange zest
1 bouquet garni

salt and freshly ground black pepper
2½lb (1.1kg) mixed white and oily fish and
  shellfish, heads and bones removed, and cut,
  if needed, into bite-sized pieces
2 tbsp Pernod
8 thin slices day-old French bread, toasted, to serve

FOR THE ROUILLE
1 cup mayonnaise
1 bird's-eye chile, seeded and roughly chopped
4 garlic cloves, roughly chopped
1 tbsp tomato paste
pinch of salt

in the slow cooker   **PREP** 30 MINS   **COOK** 20 MINS PRECOOKING; **HIGH** 2–3 HRS

1 To make the rouille, put all the ingredients in a food processor and blend until smooth. Transfer to a bowl, cover with plastic wrap, and chill until required.

2 Preheat the slow cooker, if required. Heat the oil in a large heavy-based saucepan over medium heat. Add the onion, leeks, fennel, and garlic and cook, stirring, for 5–8 minutes until the vegetables are softened. Stir in the tomatoes, tomato paste, and wine and bring to a boil. Transfer everything to the slow cooker, add the stock, saffron, orange zest, and bouquet garni and season with salt and pepper. Cover with the lid and cook on high for 2–3 hours. Add the fish for the last 10 minutes of cooking. Remove the orange zest and bouquet garni. Stir in the Pernod and season, if needed. To serve, spread each piece of toast with rouille and put 2 slices in the bottom of each bowl. Ladle the stew on top and serve.

traditional method   **PREP** 30 MINS   **COOK** 45 MINS

1 To make the rouille, put all the ingredients in a food processor and blend until smooth. Transfer to a bowl, cover with plastic wrap, and chill until required.

2 Heat the oil in a large heavy-based saucepan over medium heat. Add the onion, leeks, fennel, and garlic, and cook, stirring, for 5–8 minutes until the vegetables are softened. Stir in the tomatoes, tomato paste, and wine. Add the stock, saffron, orange zest, and bouquet garni, season with salt and pepper, and bring to a boil. Reduce the heat, partially cover the pan, and simmer for 30 minutes, or until the stew is reduced slightly, stirring occasionally. Remove the orange zest and bouquet garni from the soup and add the firm fish. Reduce the heat to low and let the soup simmer for 5 minutes, then add the delicate fish and simmer for a further 2–3 minutes, or until all the fish is opaque, cooked through, and flakes easily. Stir in the Pernod, and season if needed. To serve, spread each piece of toast with rouille and put 2 slices in the bottom of each bowl. Ladle the soup on top and serve.

Often made with beef and the addition of peppers, goulash should have a fairly thick consistency. Caraway seeds give goulash its distinctive taste, but be restrained as they can be overpowering.

Pork goulash

 **SERVES** 6 ❄ **FREEZE** UP TO 3 MONTHS

2lb (900g) stewing pork, cut into bite-sized pieces
1 tbsp all-purpose flour
2 tsp paprika
2 tsp caraway seeds, crushed
salt and freshly ground black pepper
2 tbsp olive oil
1 tbsp cider vinegar

2 tbsp tomato paste
2 cups hot vegetable stock for the slow cooker
 (4 cups for the traditional method)
4 tomatoes, skinned and roughly chopped
1 onion, sliced into rings
handful of curly parsley, finely chopped

in the slow cooker 🕐 **PREP** 25 MINS **COOK** 15 MINS PRECOOKING;
AUTO/LOW 6–8 HRS OR **HIGH** 3–4 HRS

1 Preheat the slow cooker, if required. Toss the meat with the flour, paprika, and caraway seeds, and season well with salt and pepper. Heat the oil in a large Dutch oven over high heat, add the meat and cook, stirring occasionally, for 8–10 minutes or until it begins to brown. Add the vinegar and stir well for a couple of minutes, scraping up all the sticky bits from the bottom of the pot.

2 Add the tomato paste, followed by the stock, and bring to a boil. Transfer everything to the slow cooker, cover with the lid, and cook on auto/low for 6–8 hours or on high for 3–4 hours.

3 Stir in the tomatoes, taste, and season again if needed. Top with the onion rings and parsley, and serve with rice.

traditional method 🕐 **PREP** 25 MINS **COOK** 1 HR

1 Toss the meat with the flour, paprika, and caraway seeds, and season well with salt and pepper. Heat the oil in a large Dutch oven over high heat, add the meat and cook, stirring occasionally, for 8–10 minutes or until it begins to brown. Add the vinegar and stir well for a couple of minutes, scraping up all the sticky bits from the bottom of the pot.

2 Add the tomato paste, followed by the stock, and bring to a boil. Reduce to a simmer, cover with the lid, and cook gently for 1 hour. Check occasionally that it's not drying out, topping up with a little hot water if needed—the goulash should be fairly thick though.

3 Stir in the tomatoes, taste, and season with salt and pepper again if needed. Top with the onion rings and parsley, and serve with rice.

Duck legs are very succulent with lots of tasty meat on them. They can, however, be fatty so the addition of red currant jelly and raisins helps to balance this. Pine nuts give an added twist.

Duck legs with cabbage, pine nuts, and raisins

SERVES 4–6

6 duck legs
2 red onions, roughly chopped
2 garlic cloves, finely chopped
few sprigs of thyme
1 bay leaf
1 tbsp red currant jelly (or cherry preserves)

1½ cups hot chicken stock for the slow cooker
 (2 cups for the traditional method)
salt and freshly ground black pepper
⅓ cup raisins
⅓ cup pine nuts, toasted
1 Savoy cabbage, cored and chopped into eighths

in the slow cooker   **PREP** 15 MINS   **COOK** 30 MINS PRECOOKING; **AUTO/LOW** 6 HRS OR **HIGH** 3–4 HRS

1 Preheat the slow cooker, if required. Heat a large Dutch oven over medium heat, then add the duck legs and cook for 15–20 minutes, turning them as you go, until they begin to turn golden. Remove them from the pot, set aside, and pour off any fat.

2 Add the onions, garlic, thyme, and bay leaf and cook for 5 minutes, then add the red currant jelly and cook for a few minutes more. Transfer everything to the slow cooker and add the duck legs, nestling them into the onion mixture, skin-side up. Pour over the stock, season with salt and pepper, cover with the lid, and cook on auto/low for 6 hours or on high for 3–4 hours.

3 Add the raisins, pine nuts, and cabbage to the slow cooker for the last 1 hour of cooking. Discard the bay leaf, taste, and adjust the seasoning. Serve with creamy mashed potatoes and some chile jelly on the side.

traditional method   **PREP** 15 MINS   **COOK** 2½ HRS

1 Preheat the oven to 350°F (180°C). Heat a large Dutch oven over medium heat, then add the duck legs and cook for 15–20 minutes, turning them as you go, until they begin to turn golden. Remove them from the pot, set aside, and pour off any fat.

2 Add the onions, garlic, thyme, and bay leaf and cook for 5 minutes, then add the red currant jelly and cook for a few minutes more. Return the duck legs to the pot and nestle them into the onion mixture, skin-side up. Pour in the stock, bring to a boil, and then reduce to a simmer. Season with salt and pepper, cover with the lid, and put in the oven for 2 hours. Check occasionally that it's not drying out, topping up with a little hot water if needed.

3 Add the raisins, pine nuts, and cabbage to the pot for the last 30 minutes of cooking. Discard the bay leaf, taste, and adjust the seasoning. Serve with creamy mashed potatoes and some chile jelly on the side.

Red cabbage is transformed when slow cooked, becoming sweet and tender. Add a handful of golden raisins, if you wish, for extra flavor, and serve with couscous or sausages for a simple supper.

Red cabbage with cider

 SERVES 4   HEALTHY

½ red onion, sliced
1 large red cabbage (weighing about 2¼lb/1kg),
  cored and shredded
1 apple, cored (but not peeled) and finely chopped

1 tsp five-spice powder
salt and freshly ground black pepper
¾ cup dry cider for the slow cooker
  (1 cup for the traditional method)

 in the slow cooker   PREP 15 MINS   COOK AUTO/LOW 8 HRS OR HIGH 4 HRS

1 Preheat the slow cooker, if required. Put the onion, cabbage, apple, and five-spice powder into the slow cooker and season well with salt and pepper. Mix everything together.

2 Pour in the cider and stir, then cover with the lid and cook on auto/low for 8 hours or on high for 4 hours. Taste and season as needed.

 traditional method   PREP 15 MINS   COOK 1–1½ HRS

1 Put the onion, cabbage, apple, and five-spice powder into a large Dutch oven, and season well with salt and pepper. Mix everything together.

2 Pour in the cider and stir, then cover with the lid and cook on a low heat for 1–1½ hours, stirring occasionally. Taste and season as needed.

The venison is marinated in red wine to tenderize the meat—the longer you can leave it to marinate, the better. You could switch the venison to beef if you prefer.

Venison stew

◎ **SERVES** 4–6 ✲ **FREEZE** UP TO 3 MONTHS

2 cups red wine
3 tbsp olive oil
1 tbsp crushed juniper berries
2 sprigs of rosemary
2½lb (1.1kg) boneless venison, chopped small
2 tbsp flour, seasoned with salt and pepper
1 onion, roughly chopped
7oz (200g) pancetta cubes

1oz (30g) dried porcini mushrooms, soaked in warm water for 30 minutes
coarsely chopped zest of 1 orange
1¾ cups hot vegetable stock for the slow cooker (3 cups for the traditional method)
pat of butter
9oz (250g) cremini mushrooms, halved
salt and freshly ground black pepper

in the slow cooker   ◷ **PREP** 15 MINS, PLUS MARINATING   **COOK** 15 MINS PRECOOKING; AUTO/LOW 8 HRS

1 Preheat the slow cooker, if required. Put the wine, 2 tablespoons of the oil, the juniper berries, 1 sprig of rosemary, and the venison in a large bowl. Ensure the meat is immersed in the wine, cover, and marinate for 1 hour or overnight, if possible. Drain the meat, reserve the liquid and rosemary.

2 Heat the remaining oil in a large Dutch oven over medium-high heat, and toss the venison in the flour. Cook in batches for about 5 minutes until golden on all sides. Remove and set aside. Reduce the heat to medium, add the onion and pancetta, and cook for about 5 minutes until the pancetta begins to color. Drain the porcini and strain the juice. Add the mushrooms and a little of the juice to the pot with the orange zest, wine marinade, and rosemary. Bring to a boil.

3 Transfer everything, including the venison, to the slow cooker and pour in the stock. Heat the butter in a frying pan, add the cremini mushrooms, and cook for a few minutes until golden, then stir into the slow cooker. Cover with the lid, and cook on auto/low for 8 hours. Taste and season as needed. Ladle into shallow bowls and serve with polenta.

traditional method   ◷ **PREP** 15 MINS, PLUS MARINATING   **COOK** 1¾–2¼ HRS

1 Put the wine, 2 tablespoons of the oil, the juniper berries, 1 sprig of rosemary, and the venison in a large bowl. Ensure the meat is immersed in the wine, cover, and leave to marinate for 1 hour or overnight, if possible. Drain the meat, reserving the liquid and rosemary.

2 Heat the remaining olive oil in a large Dutch oven over medium-high heat, and toss the venison in the flour. Cook in batches for about 5 minutes until golden on all sides. Remove and set aside. Reduce the heat to medium, add the onion and pancetta, and cook for about 5 minutes until the pancetta begins to color. Drain the porcini and strain the juice. Add the mushrooms and a little of the juice to the pot with the orange zest, wine marinade, and rosemary. Add the stock and boil. Add the meat, reduce to a simmer, cover, and cook on low heat for 1½–2 hours until tender. Top up with the reserved porcini juice or hot water to keep the meat covered. For the last 30 minutes, heat the butter in a frying pan and cook the cremini mushrooms for a few minutes until golden, then stir into the stew. Taste and season as needed. Ladle into shallow bowls and serve with polenta.

The delicate flavor of the monkfish is highlighted by white wine, and the sauce is given a velvety consistency by adding a kneaded butter and flour paste, known as beurre manié.

Monkfish and white wine stew

⟳ **SERVES** 4–6 ❄ **FREEZE** UP TO 1 MONTH

5 tbsp butter, at room temperature
2 shallots, diced
2 garlic cloves, finely chopped
2 leeks, trimmed, cut lengthwise, and chopped
  into bite-sized diagonal pieces
about 1lb (500g) small zucchini, trimmed and
  chopped into bite-sized pieces
salt and freshly ground black pepper
9oz (250g) mushrooms, trimmed and quartered
3–5 thyme sprigs, leaves only

1 bay leaf
1 cup dry white wine
1¼ cups hot fish stock for the slow cooker
  (2 cups for the traditional method)
1lb 10oz (750g) skinned monkfish filets, membrane
  removed and cut into bite-sized diagonal pieces
3 tbsp flour
small bunch of parsley, leaves chopped

in the slow cooker ⏱ **PREP** 30 MINS **COOK** 5 MINS PRECOOKING; **AUTO/LOW** 2–3 HRS

1 Preheat the slow cooker, if required. Melt 2 tablespoons of the butter in a large heavy-based saucepan over medium heat, add the shallots, garlic, leeks, and zucchini, and cook for 3–5 minutes until soft. Season with salt and pepper, then add the mushrooms, thyme, bay, wine, and stock and bring to a boil. Transfer everything to the slow cooker, cover with the lid, and cook on auto/low for 2–3 hours.

2 Add the monkfish for the last 15 minutes of cooking and stir very gently to combine. Do not stir too vigorously or the fish may fall apart.

3 Fork together the remaining butter with the flour to form a smooth paste. Add to the slow cooker for the last 5 minutes of cooking and stir to combine. Discard the bay leaf, stir in half the parsley, and add salt and pepper, if needed. Serve sprinkled with the remaining parsley.

traditional method ⏱ **PREP** 30 MINS **COOK** 40–45 MINS

1 Melt 2 tablespoons of the butter in a large heavy-based saucepan over medium heat, add the shallots, garlic, leeks, and zucchini, and cook for 3–5 minutes until soft. Season, then add the mushrooms, thyme, bay, wine, and stock, cover with the lid, and simmer gently for 25–30 minutes.

2 Add the monkfish and stir very gently to combine. Do not stir too vigorously or the fish may fall apart. Cover the pan, bring back to a boil, and simmer for 3–5 minutes until the fish is opaque and cooked through.

3 Fork together the remaining butter with the flour to form a smooth paste. Add to the pan, stir to combine, and simmer for 2 minutes. Discard the bay leaf, stir in half the parsley. Serve sprinkled with the remaining parsley.

The lamb is tossed in cumin and chile, which lends a gentle touch of spice to the mixture and the wine adds depth to the sauce. The trick with this dish is to cook the vegetables separately.

Lamb ratatouille

SERVES 6 ❄ **FREEZE** UP TO 3 MONTHS

2 tbsp vegetable oil
1lb 10oz (750g) boneless lamb shoulder,
   cut into 1–1½in (2.5–4cm) cubes
2 tbsp all-purpose flour
salt and freshly ground black pepper
1 tsp ground cumin
1 tsp dried chile flakes
1 cup red wine
14oz (400g) can chopped tomatoes

1½ cups hot chicken or lamb stock for the slow
   cooker (2 cups for the traditional method)
3 tbsp olive oil
1 large onion, sliced
3 garlic cloves, finely chopped
1 red bell pepper, seeded and sliced
1 green bell pepper, seeded and sliced
1 eggplant, chopped into 1in (2.5cm) chunks

in the slow cooker ⏱ **PREP** 20 MINS **COOK** 15 MINS PRECOOKING;
AUTO/LOW 6–8 HRS OR **HIGH** 3–4 HRS

1 Preheat the slow cooker, if required. Heat the vegetable oil in a large Dutch oven over high heat. In a bowl, toss the lamb with the flour, seasoning, cumin, and chile flakes. Add the meat to the pot (in batches, if necessary) and cook for 3–5 minutes, stirring occasionally, until evenly browned.

2 Pour in the wine, increase the heat, and let it bubble for a minute, then add the tomatoes and the stock and bring to a boil. Transfer everything to the slow cooker, cover with the lid, and cook on auto/low for 6–8 hours or on high for 3–4 hours.

3 Meanwhile, heat the olive oil in a large heavy-based saucepan over medium heat, add the onion and garlic, and cook for 3–5 minutes until soft. Stir in the bell peppers and cook for 2–3 minutes, then add the eggplant and cook for about 10 minutes, stirring, until just tender. Stir these into the slow cooker for the last hour of cooking. Serve with rice.

traditional method ⏱ **PREP** 20 MINS **COOK** 2–2¼ HRS

1 Heat the vegetable oil in a large Dutch oven over high heat. In a bowl, toss the lamb with the flour, seasoning, cumin, and chile flakes. Add the meat to the pot (in batches, if necessary) and cook for 3–5 minutes, stirring occasionally, until evenly browned.

2 Pour in the wine, increase the heat, and let it bubble for a minute, then add the tomatoes and the stock and bring to a boil. Reduce the heat and simmer, partially covered, for 1¼ hours.

3 Meanwhile, heat the olive oil in a large heavy-based saucepan over medium heat, add the onion and garlic, and cook for 3–5 minutes until soft. Stir in the bell peppers and cook for 2–3 minutes, then add the eggplant and cook for about 10 minutes, stirring, until just tender. Stir these into the pot, top up with a little hot water if too dry, and cook, uncovered, for a further 15 minutes. Serve with rice.

Tender beef with robust kale is a great combination. The chile hint is subtle, but just enough to add interest to the dish, while the anchovies are added to enrich the sauce.

Beef and greens

SERVES 4–6 **FREEZE** UP TO 3 MONTHS

3–4 tbsp olive oil
2¾lb (1.25kg) beef chuck roast, cut into
  bite-sized pieces
salt and freshly ground black pepper
1 tsp paprika
1 tbsp all-purpose flour
2 onions, roughly chopped
3 garlic cloves, finely chopped
1 green chile, seeded and finely chopped

8 salted anchovies
4 large carrots, peeled and roughly chopped
1 cup red wine
2 cups hot beef or vegetable stock for
  the slow cooker (3 cups for the
  traditional method)
4 large potatoes, peeled and roughly chopped
7oz (200g) curly kale, stems trimmed and
  leaves roughly chopped

in the slow cooker **PREP** 15 MINS **COOK** 20 MINS PRECOOKING; **AUTO/LOW** 6–8 HRS

1 Preheat the slow cooker, if required. Heat 1 tbsp of the oil in a large Dutch oven over medium heat. Season the meat with salt, pepper, and paprika, then toss in the flour. Add the beef to the pot (in batches and with extra oil, if necessary), and cook for 5–8 minutes until browned all over. Remove with a slotted spoon and set aside.

2 Add the remaining oil to the pot, add the onions, and cook for 3–4 minutes until soft. Then stir in the garlic, chile, and anchovies and cook for a minute. Add the carrots and cook for a further 2–3 minutes. Pour in the wine and bring to a boil, stirring and scraping up the bits from the bottom of the pot.

3 Transfer everything to the slow cooker, add the stock, and then the meat and potatoes. Cover with the lid and cook on auto/low for 6–8 hours. Add the kale for the last 1 hour of cooking. Serve while piping hot with some crusty bread.

traditional method **PREP** 15 MINS **COOK** 1¾ HRS

1 Preheat the oven to 325°F (160°C). Heat 1 tbsp of the oil in a large Dutch oven over medium heat. Season the meat with salt, pepper, and paprika, then toss in the flour. Add the beef to the pot (in batches and with extra oil, if necessary), and cook for 5–8 minutes until browned all over. Remove with a slotted spoon and set aside.

2 Add the remaining oil to the pot, add the onions, and cook for 3–4 minutes until soft. Then stir in the garlic, chile, and anchovies and cook for a minute. Add the carrots and cook for a further 2–3 minutes.

3 Pour in the wine and bring to a boil, stirring and scraping up the bits from the bottom of the pot. Pour in the stock and bring back to a boil, then add the meat and potatoes, cover, and put in the oven for 1½ hours. Check occasionally that it's not drying out, topping up with a little hot water if needed. Add the kale and cook for a further hour, again checking that it doesn't dry out too much. Serve while piping hot with some crusty bread.

Eggplant and lamb and are a classic combination from the Middle East, and the paprika adds a fine smoky flavor. The eggplant can sop up the oil, so keep topping it up.

Smoky eggplant and lamb stew

SERVES 6–8 **FREEZE** UP TO 3 MONTHS

3–4 tbsp olive oil
2 eggplants, cubed
1–2 tsp smoked paprika
1lb 10oz (750g) middle neck of lamb,
  chopped into large chunks
1 onion, roughly chopped
7oz (200g) dried chorizo, diced
1 tbsp sherry vinegar

3 garlic cloves, finely chopped
1 tsp ground cumin
14oz (400g) can chickpeas, drained and rinsed
1¾ cups hot vegetable stock for the slow cooker |
  (3 cups for the traditional method)
few sprigs of thyme, leaves only
bunch of mint, leaves roughly chopped

in the slow cooker **PREP** 15 MINS **COOK** 20 MINS PRECOOKING; **AUTO/LOW** 6–8 HRS

1 Preheat the slow cooker, if required. Heat 2 tablespoons of the oil in a large Dutch oven over medium-high heat, add the eggplant and smoked paprika, and toss to coat. Cook, stirring, and adding more oil as needed, for 6–8 minutes until the eggplant begins to color. Remove with a slotted spoon and set aside.

2 Add a drizzle of oil and cook the lamb (in batches, if necessary) for 4–6 minutes until it browns on all sides. Remove and set aside. Add the onion and chorizo (again, with a little oil, if needed), and cook for 2 minutes, then add the vinegar. Increase the heat and cook for 2 minutes until the vinegar has evaporated. Stir to scrape up the bits from the bottom of the pot, then add the garlic and cumin.

3 Return the lamb to the pot, add the chickpeas, and transfer everything to the slow cooker. Pour in the stock and throw in the thyme, cover with the lid, and cook on auto/low for 6–8 hours. Taste and season as needed, then remove the thyme, and stir in the mint. Serve with couscous and crusty bread.

traditional method **PREP** 15 MINS **COOK** 1¾ HRS

1 Heat 2 tablespoons of the oil in a large Dutch oven over medium-high heat, add the eggplant and smoked paprika, and toss to coat. Cook, stirring, and adding more oil as needed, for 6–8 minutes until the eggplant begins to color. Remove with a slotted spoon and set aside.

2 Add a drizzle of oil and cook the lamb (in batches, if necessary) for 4–6 minutes until it browns on all sides. Remove and set aside. Add the onion and chorizo (again, with a little oil, if needed), and cook for 2 minutes, then add the vinegar. Increase the heat and cook for 2 minutes until the vinegar has evaporated. Stir to scrape up the bits from the bottom of the pot, then add the garlic and cumin.

3 Return the lamb to the pot, add the chickpeas, and pour in the stock. Throw in the thyme and bring to a boil, then partially cover and cook for 1 hour, checking the liquid level and topping up with hot water if needed. Stir in the eggplant and cook for a further 30 minutes, then remove the thyme, and stir in the mint. Serve with couscous and crusty bread.

This is a deep-flavored stew to be served up on cold days. The anchovies melt into it and the red currant jelly adds a distinctive sweetness. It is delicious spooned over mashed or baked potatoes.

Beef and anchovy stew

⊚ **SERVES** 4–6 ❄ **FREEZE** UP TO 3 MONTHS

¼ cup olive oil, plus extra if necessary
pat of butter
12 baby onions, peeled
few sprigs of thyme
salt and freshly ground black pepper
2½lb (1.1kg) beef chuck roast, cut into chunky cubes
1 tbsp flour, seasoned with salt and pepper
2 leeks, trimmed and sliced

pinch of ground allspice
1 cup red wine
6 anchovy filets in oil, drained and chopped
1 tbsp small capers
1 cup hot beef stock for the slow cooker
  (3 cups for the traditional method)
1–2 tbsp red currant or cranberry jelly

in the slow cooker 🕑 **PREP** 20 MINS **COOK** 20 MINS PRECOOKING; **AUTO/LOW** 6–8 HRS

1 Preheat the slow cooker, if required. Heat half the oil and the butter in a large Dutch oven over medium heat, then add the onions, thyme, and salt and pepper. Cook for about 10 minutes until the onions start to take on some color. Remove with a slotted spoon and set aside. Toss the beef in the flour. Add the remaining oil to the pot, increase the heat to medium-high, and cook the beef in batches for a few minutes on each side until browned all over. Remove and set aside. Add a little more oil, stir in the leeks and allspice, and cook for about 5 minutes. Also remove and set aside.

2 Add the wine and bring to a boil, scraping up the bits from the bottom of the pot. Let it bubble for a few minutes, then stir in the anchovies, capers, stock, and red currant jelly. Bring to a boil, then reduce to a simmer and transfer everything to the slow cooker along with the meat, leeks, and onions. Taste and season if needed, then pour in just enough of the hot stock to cover. Put the lid on and cook on auto/low for 6–8 hours. Serve while piping hot.

traditional method 🕑 **PREP** 20 MINS **COOK** 2¼–2¾ HRS

1 Preheat the oven to 325°F (160°C). Heat half the oil and the butter in a large Dutch oven over medium heat, then add the onions, thyme, and salt and pepper. Cook for about 10 minutes until the onions start to take on some color. Remove with a slotted spoon and set aside.

2 Toss the beef in the flour. Add the remaining oil to the pot, increase the heat to medium-high, and cook the beef in batches for a few minutes on each side until browned all over. Remove and set aside. Add a little more oil, stir in the leeks and allspice, and cook for about 5 minutes. Also remove and set aside.

3 Add the wine and bring to a boil, scraping up the bits from the bottom of the pot. Let it bubble for a few minutes, then stir in the anchovies, capers, stock, and red currant jelly. Bring to a boil, then reduce to a simmer, return the meat, leeks, and onions to the pot, and season again if you wish. Cover with the lid and cook in the oven for 2–2½ hours until the beef is tender. Check occasionally that it's not drying out, topping up with a little hot water, if needed. Serve while piping hot.

Rich and robust, oxtail becomes tender after braising it very slowly. Prunes are always a tasty addition to a stew because their sweetness and texture complement the meat.

Braised oxtail with star anise

⊙ SERVES 4–6 **❄ FREEZE** UP TO 3 MONTHS

2 oxtails, about 3lb (1.35kg) each, cut
  into bite-sized pieces
salt and freshly ground black pepper
2 tbsp olive oil
2 red onions, sliced
3 garlic cloves, finely chopped
pinch of dried chile flakes
1½ cups red wine
4 star anise

handful of black peppercorns
1 bay leaf
8 soft prunes, pitted and chopped
2 cups hot beef stock for the slow cooker
  (3 cups for the traditional method)
4 clementines or 2 oranges, peeled and
  sliced into rings
small bunch of curly parsley leaves,
  finely chopped

in the slow cooker ⏱ PREP 20 MINS COOK 15 MINS PRECOOKING; AUTO/LOW 8 HRS

1 Preheat the slow cooker, if required. Season the oxtail with salt and pepper. Heat half the oil in a large Dutch oven over medium heat, then add the meat in batches, and fry for 8–10 minutes until browned on all sides. Remove from the pot and set aside.

2 Heat the remaining oil in the pot over medium heat, add the onions, and cook for 3–4 minutes to soften. Stir through the garlic and chile flakes, then pour in the wine and let it simmer before adding it to the slow cooker together with the meat, star anise, peppercorns, bay leaf, prunes, and stock. Cover with the lid and cook on auto/low for 8 hours. Add the clementines for the last 30 minutes of cooking.

3 Shred the meat from the bone into the slow cooker, and discard the bone, bay leaf, and star anise. Serve on a bed of pasta with the parsley sprinkled over.

traditional method ⏱ PREP 20 MINS COOK 3¼ HRS

1 Preheat the oven to 300°F (150°C). Season the oxtail with salt and pepper. Heat half the oil in a large Dutch oven over medium heat, then add the meat in batches, and fry for 8–10 minutes until browned on all sides. Remove with a slotted spoon and set aside.

2 Heat the remaining oil in the pot over medium heat, add the onions, and cook for 3–4 minutes to soften. Stir in the garlic and chile flakes, then pour in the wine and let it simmer for about 5 minutes until slightly reduced. Return the meat to the pot and add the star anise, peppercorns, bay leaf, and prunes, and pour in just enough stock to cover the meat.

3 Bring to a boil, then reduce to a simmer, add the remaining stock, cover, and put in the oven for about 3 hours. Check occasionally that it's not drying out, topping up with a little hot water if needed. Add the clementines or oranges for the last 30 minutes of cooking and leave the pot uncovered to allow the liquid to thicken slightly. Stir it occasionally to keep the oxtail moist and coated with the gravy. When ready, the meat will fall away from the bone. Remove the bone and discard it together with the bay leaf and star anise. Serve on a bed of pasta with the parsley sprinkled over.

The traditional name for this recipe is *Jarret d'agneau*, or braised lamb shanks, and it is the perfect way to cook cheap cuts of meat—here, lamb shanks are slow cooked in a white wine sauce.

French braised lamb

SERVES 4–6

6–8 lamb shanks, weighing about
   12oz (375g) each, fat trimmed
¼ cup all-purpose flour, seasoned
   with salt and pepper
2 tbsp vegetable oil
2 tbsp butter
1 carrot, peeled and finely sliced
2 onions, finely chopped

1 cup white wine
1 garlic clove, finely chopped, plus 2 extra to serve
grated zest of 1 orange
salt and freshly ground black pepper
½ cup hot chicken stock, for both methods
4 plum tomatoes, skinned, seeded, and chopped
3–5 sprigs of rosemary, leaves chopped

in the slow cooker   ● **PREP** 20 MINS   **COOK** 15 MINS PRECOOKING; AUTO/LOW 6–8 HRS OR **HIGH** 3–4 HRS

1 Preheat the slow cooker, if required. Toss the lamb in the flour, coating it well. Heat the oil and butter in a large Dutch oven over medium-high heat. Add the lamb shanks (in batches, if necessary) and cook for 6–8 minutes until browned thoroughly on all sides. Remove and set aside. Discard all but 2 tbsp of fat from the pot and reduce the temperature to medium. Add the carrot and onions and cook for about 5 minutes until soft. Add the wine and boil until it has reduced by half, then stir in the garlic, orange zest, and salt and pepper.

2 Transfer everything to the slow cooker and lay the lamb on top. Pour in the stock, cover with the lid, and cook on auto/low for 6–8 hours or on high for 3–4 hours. Finely chop 2 cloves of garlic and mix with the tomatoes and rosemary. Sprinkle this mixture over the lamb just before serving. Serve with sautéed potatoes and vegetables of your choice.

traditional method   ● **PREP** 20 MINS   **COOK** 2–2½ HRS

1 Heat the oven to 350°F (180°C). Toss the lamb in the flour, coating it well. Heat the oil and butter in a large Dutch oven over medium-high heat. Add the lamb shanks (in batches, if necessary) and cook for 6–8 minutes until browned thoroughly on all sides. Remove and set aside. Discard all but 2 tbsp of fat from the pot and reduce the temperature to medium. Add the carrot and onions, and cook for about 5 minutes until soft. Add the wine and boil until it has reduced by half, then stir in the garlic, orange zest, and salt and pepper. Lay the lamb on top.

2 Pour in the stock, cover with the lid, and cook in the oven for about 2–2½ hours until the meat is very tender when pierced with a fork. Check occasionally that it's not drying out, topping up with a little hot water if needed, but at the end of cooking, the sauce should be thick and rich. Finely chop 2 cloves of garlic and mix with the tomatoes and rosemary. Sprinkle this mixture over the lamb just before serving. Serve with sautéed potatoes and vegetables of your choice.

This is a truly delicious classic. The beef is marinated in all the aromas of the Mediterranean—oranges, red wine, and herbs—before being very slowly braised with lots of black olives.

Provençal daube of beef

SERVES 6   **FREEZE** UP TO 3 MONTHS

2¼lb (1kg) braising steak, cut into 1½in (4cm) cubes
12oz (350g) smoked bacon, cut into lardons
14oz (400g) can whole tomatoes
2 onions, sliced
2 carrots, peeled and sliced
6oz (175g) mushrooms, trimmed and sliced
7oz (200g) pitted black olives
1 cup hot beef stock, for both methods
freshly ground black pepper

FOR THE MARINADE
zest of 1 orange, cut in wide strips
2 garlic cloves, finely chopped
2 cups red wine
2 bay leaves
3–4 sprigs each of rosemary, thyme, and parsley
10 peppercorns

in the slow cooker   **PREP** 15 MINS, PLUS MARINATING   **COOK AUTO/LOW** 6–8 HRS OR **HIGH** 3–4 HRS

1 For the marinade, combine all the ingredients in a non-metallic bowl. Add the beef and mix well, cover with plastic wrap and refrigerate, turning occasionally, for 8–12 hours.

2 Preheat the slow cooker, if required. Remove the beef from the marinade, pat dry on paper towels, and set aside. Strain the marinade. Reserve the liquid and tie the flavoring ingredients in a piece of cheesecloth. Spread the bacon on the bottom of the slow cooker and cover with the beef.

3 Layer the tomatoes and onions on top, then the carrots, mushrooms, and olives. Pour in the strained marinade and stock, and season with pepper. Add the bag of flavorings. Cover with the lid and cook on auto/low for 6–8 hours or on high for 3–4 hours. Discard the flavoring bag, taste, and add seasoning, if needed. Serve with sautéed zucchini and mashed potatoes.

traditional method   **PREP** 15 MINS, PLUS MARINATING   **COOK** 3½–4 HRS

1 For the marinade, combine all the ingredients in a non-metallic bowl. Add the beef and mix well, cover with plastic wrap and refrigerate, turning occasionally, for 8–12 hours.

2 Preheat the oven to 300°F (150°C). Remove the beef from the marinade, pat dry on paper towels, and set aside. Strain the marinade. Reserve the liquid and tie the flavoring ingredients in a piece of cheesecloth. Spread the bacon on the bottom of a Dutch oven and cover with the beef.

3 Layer the tomatoes and onions on top, then the carrots, mushrooms, and olives. Pour in the strained marinade and stock, and season with pepper. Add the bag of flavorings. Bring to a boil, then cover with the lid, and cook in the oven for 3½–4 hours until the beef is tender enough to crush in your fingers. Check occasionally that it's not drying out, topping up with a little hot water if needed. Discard the flavoring bag, taste, and add seasoning if needed. Serve with sautéed zucchini and mashed potatoes.

These rounds of pork are stuffed with a delicate mix of celery, pecan nuts, and sage, then cooked in white wine and stock. It would be delicious served with applesauce or cranberry sauce.

Stuffed pork chops

SERVES 4

¼ cup butter
1 large onion, finely chopped
1 celery stalk, finely chopped
4 sage leaves, finely chopped
¾ cup pecan nut halves, finely chopped
salt and freshly ground black pepper

2¼lb (1kg) boneless pork tenderloin, excess fat trimmed and cut across into four 1½in (4cm) chops
2 tbsp olive oil
1 cup white wine
about 1 cup hot vegetable stock for the slow cooker (about 1¼ cups for the traditional method)

in the slow cooker   **PREP** 20 MINS   **COOK** 20 MINS PRECOOKING; **AUTO/LOW** 6–8 HRS OR **HIGH** 3–4 HRS

1 Preheat the slow cooker, if required. To make the stuffing, heat half the butter in a large Dutch oven over medium heat, add the onion, celery, and sage and cook for 5–7 minutes until soft. Remove from the heat, add three-quarters of the pecan nuts, season with salt and pepper, and stir to combine. Remove and set aside to cool.

2 Using a boning knife, make a deep slit in the side of each pork chop to form a pocket. Season the chops inside and out, then spoon the stuffing into each pocket, packing it in well. Secure the opening in each chop with a toothpick. Heat the oil and remaining butter in the pot over medium-high heat, then add the chops, stuffed-side up, and brown thoroughly for 3–5 minutes, without turning and in batches, if necessary. Pour in the wine and bring to a boil. Transfer everything to the slow cooker and pour in enough stock to come halfway up the chops. Cover with the lid and cook on auto/low for 6–8 hours or on high for 3–4 hours. Remove the toothpick before serving, sprinkle the remaining chopped nuts over the dish, and serve with some Savoy cabbage and roasted potatoes.

traditional method   **PREP** 20 MINS   **COOK** 2 HRS

1 Preheat the oven to 350°F (180°C). To make the stuffing, heat half the butter in a large Dutch oven over medium heat, add the onion, celery, and sage and cook for 5–7 minutes until soft. Remove from the heat, add three-quarters of the pecan nuts, season with salt and pepper, and stir to combine. Remove and set aside to cool.

2 Using a boning knife, make a deep slit in the side of each pork chop to form a pocket. Season the chops inside and out, then spoon the stuffing into each pocket, packing it in well. Secure the opening in each chop with a toothpick. Heat the oil and remaining butter in the pot over medium-high heat, then add the chops, stuffed-side up and brown thoroughly for 3–5 minutes, without turning and in batches, if necessary. Pour in the wine and bring to a boil, then pour in enough stock to come halfway up the chops. Cover and cook in the oven for 1–1¼ hours, turning once, until the chops are tender. Check occasionally that it's not drying out, topping up with a little hot water if needed. Remove the toothpick before serving, sprinkle the remaining chopped nuts over the dish, and serve with some Savoy cabbage and roasted potatoes.

Warming and satisfying, it's difficult to beat a traditional beef stew. For a tasty twist, Stilton is added to the dumplings, which also melts slightly into the deliciously rich ale and beef sauce.

Beef stew with Stilton dumplings

SERVES 4–6 **FREEZE** UP TO 3 MONTHS

2 tbsp olive oil, plus extra as needed
2½lb (1.1kg) chuck steak, cut into chunky pieces
1 tbsp flour, seasoned with salt and pepper
1 large onion, finely chopped
pinch of sugar
1 tbsp tomato paste
1 tbsp Worcestershire sauce
salt and freshly ground black pepper
3 carrots, peeled and roughly chopped

9oz (250g) button mushrooms
1½ cups light ale
1½ cups hot beef stock for the slow cooker
  (3 cups for the traditional method)
sprig of rosemary
1 cup self-rising flour
½ cup vegetable shortening
5½oz (150g) Stilton cheese, crumbled

in the slow cooker **PREP** 20 MINS **COOK** 15 MINS PRECOOKING;
AUTO/LOW 8 HRS OR **HIGH** 4 HRS

1 Preheat the slow cooker, if required. Heat half the oil in a large Dutch oven over high heat and toss the meat in the flour. Add in batches to the pot and cook for about 10 minutes until browned all over. Remove and set aside. Heat the remaining oil, reduce the heat to medium, and cook the onion for 3–4 minutes until soft. Add the sugar, tomato paste, Worcestershire sauce, and seasoning and cook for 1–2 minutes. Stir in the carrots and mushrooms. Increase the heat, add the ale, and boil for a few minutes for the alcohol to evaporate. Transfer everything to the slow cooker, add the meat with stock to cover, then add the rosemary. Cover and cook on auto/low for 8 hours or on high for 4 hours.

2 Meanwhile, mix together the self-rising flour, shortening, and seasoning. Add in a little water and mix to a soft dough. Add the Stilton and mix with your hands, then roll into small balls. Add to the slow cooker for the last 45 minutes of cooking on auto/low (last 30 minutes if on high) and push them down a little into the liquid. Remove the rosemary and serve in warmed bowls with mashed potatoes.

traditional method **PREP** 20 MINS **COOK** 2¾ HRS

1 Preheat the oven to 325°F (160°C). Heat half the oil in a large Dutch oven over high heat and toss the meat in the flour. Add in batches to the pot and cook for about 10 minutes until browned all over. Remove and set aside. Heat the remaining oil, reduce the heat to medium, and cook the onion for 3–4 minutes until soft. Add the sugar, tomato paste, Worcestershire sauce, and seasoning and cook for 1–2 minutes. Stir in the carrots and mushrooms. Increase the heat, add the ale, and boil for a few minutes for the alcohol to evaporate. Then add the meat and stock and bring back to a boil. Reduce to a simmer, add in the rosemary, cover with the lid and put in the oven for 2 hours. Check occasionally that it's not drying out, topping up with a little hot water if needed.

2 Meanwhile, mix together the self-rising flour, shortening, and seasoning. Add in a little water and mix to a soft dough. Add the Stilton and mix with your hands, then roll into small balls. Add to the stew and push them down a little into the liquid. Cover again and put back in the oven for another 20 minutes, then remove the lid and cook for a further 10 minutes until browned. Remove the rosemary and serve in warmed bowls with mashed potatoes.

Here is a light stew that is best served during the spring when lamb is particularly full of flavor. Fava beans and dill complement each other perfectly—and, of course, the meat.

Lamb with artichokes, fava beans, and dill

SERVES 4–6 ❄ **FREEZE** UP TO 1 MONTH

2¾lb (1.25kg) lamb shoulder, with bones,
  trimmed and cut into bite-sized pieces
salt and freshly ground black pepper
2 tbsp olive oil
2 onions, roughly chopped
3 carrots, peeled and roughly chopped
1 tbsp all-purpose flour
½ cup dry white wine

1¾ cups hot vegetable stock for the slow cooker
  (3 cups for the traditional method)
few sprigs of rosemary
grated zest of ½ lemon and juice of 1 lemon
1½lb (675g) antipasti artichoke hearts, drained
heaping ½ cup frozen or fresh fava beans
bunch of dill, finely chopped

in the slow cooker ⏱ **PREP** 15 MINS **COOK** 20 MINS PRECOOKING; AUTO/LOW 6–8 HRS OR **HIGH** 3–4 HRS

1 Preheat the slow cooker, if required. Season the meat with salt and pepper. Heat half the oil in a large Dutch oven over high heat, add the lamb (in batches, if necessary), and cook for 6–8 minutes until no longer pink. Remove from the pot and set aside.

2 Heat the remaining oil in the pot over medium heat, add the onions, and cook for 3–4 minutes until soft. Season with salt and pepper, add the carrots, and cook for a further 5 minutes. Sprinkle over the flour, stir, and cook for a couple of minutes. Then add the wine, increase the heat, and cook the sauce for a minute.

3 Transfer everything to the slow cooker, including the lamb. Pour in the stock and add the rosemary, lemon juice and zest, artichokes, and fava beans. Cover and cook on auto/low for 6–8 hours or on high for 3–4 hours. Taste and season as required, and add the dill to taste. Serve with crusty bread.

traditional method ⏱ **PREP** 15 MINS **COOK** 1¾ HRS

1 Preheat the oven to 350°F (180°C). Season the meat with salt and pepper. Heat half the oil in a large Dutch oven over high heat, add the lamb (in batches, if necessary), and cook for 6–8 minutes until no longer pink. Remove from the pot and set aside.

2 Heat the remaining oil in the pot over medium heat, add the onions, and cook for 3–4 minutes until soft. Season with salt and pepper, add the carrots, and cook for a further 5 minutes. Sprinkle over the flour, stir, and cook for a couple of minutes. Add the wine, increase the heat, and cook the sauce for a minute.

3 Pour in the stock and add the rosemary, lemon juice and zest, and lamb. Bring to a boil, reduce to a simmer, cover, and put in the oven for 1 hour. Check occasionally that it's not drying out, topping up with a little hot water if needed. Stir in the artichokes and fava beans and cook for a further 30 minutes. Taste and season as required, and add the dill to taste. Serve with crusty bread.

Casseroles, cassoulets, & meatballs

A robust dish that will hit the spot on cold days and fill you up. The lentils become soft and tender and, because they are cooked for so long, they are flavored by the sausages.

Lentil and sausage casserole

SERVES 4–6   ✱ **FREEZE** UP TO 1 MONTH

2 tbsp olive oil
8 Italian sweet sausages, roughly chopped
1 onion, finely chopped
2 carrots, peeled and finely diced
freshly ground black pepper
3 garlic cloves, finely chopped
5oz (140g) dried chorizo, diced
3 sprigs of rosemary

few sprigs of thyme
1 cup Puy lentils or brown lentils, rinsed and
   picked over for any stones
¾ cup red wine
2 cups hot chicken stock for the slow cooker
   (3 cups for the traditional method)
1 red chile, left whole
splash of extra virgin olive oil, to serve

in the slow cooker   🕐 PREP 15 MINS   COOK 15 MINS PRECOOKING; **AUTO/LOW** 6–8 HRS

1 Preheat the slow cooker, if required. Heat half the oil in a large Dutch oven over high heat, add the sausages, and cook for a few minutes until they begin to turn golden. Remove from the pot and set aside.

2 Add the remaining oil, stir in the onion and carrot, and turn to coat. Season with pepper and leave to cook for a few minutes, stirring occasionally. Add the garlic, chorizo, and herbs, give it all a stir, then return the sausages to the pot and stir in the lentils. Add the wine, bring to a boil, and cook for a minute. Transfer everything to the slow cooker, add the chicken stock and chile, cover with the lid, and cook on auto/low for 6–8 hours.

3 Taste and season, if necessary, remove the whole chile, then ladle into warmed bowls and serve with a splash of extra virgin olive oil and some crusty bread.

traditional method   🕐 PREP 15 MINS   COOK 1¾ HRS

1 Preheat the oven to 325°F (160°C). Heat half the oil in a large Dutch oven over high heat, add the sausages, and cook for a few minutes until they begin to turn golden. Remove from the pot and set aside.

2 Add the remaining oil, stir in the onion and carrot, and turn to coat. Season with pepper and leave to cook for a few minutes, stirring occasionally. Add the garlic, chorizo, and herbs, give it all a stir, then return the sausages to the pot and stir in the lentils. Add the wine, bring to a boil, and cook for a minute.

3 Pour in the stock, bring to a boil, then reduce to a simmer. Add the chile, cover with the lid, and put in the oven for 1½ hours. Check occasionally that it's not drying out, topping up with a little hot water if needed. Taste and season, if necessary, remove the whole chile, then ladle into warmed bowls and serve with a splash of extra virgin olive oil and some crusty bread.

Look for ready-diced packs of game meat, which cut down on preparation time. Cider, carrot, and parsnip lend a sweetness to this dish and the fennel seeds add a welcome touch of aniseed.

Autumn game casserole

SERVES 4 **FREEZE** UP TO 3 MONTHS

2 tbsp olive oil
about 1lb (500g) boneless, skinless game,
   such as venison or rabbit, or boneless
   chicken thighs, cut into bite-sized cubes
1 onion, chopped
1 carrot, peeled and chopped
1 parsnip, peeled and chopped
1 fennel bulb, diced, fronds reserved

2 tbsp all-purpose flour
1 cup dry cider or apple juice
1 cup hot chicken stock, for both methods
9oz (250g) cremini mushrooms, thickly sliced
½ tsp fennel seeds
salt and freshly ground black pepper
small handful of flat-leaf parsley, chopped (optional)

in the slow cooker
PREP 20 MINS   **COOK** 15 MINS PRECOOKING;
AUTO/LOW 6–8 HRS OR **HIGH** 2–3 HRS

1 Preheat the slow cooker, if required. Heat the oil in a large Dutch oven over medium-high heat and cook the meat, stirring occasionally, for 3–4 minutes until lightly browned. Remove and set aside.

2 Lower the heat to medium, add the onion, carrot, parsnip, and fennel to the pot and cook, stirring occasionally, for 4–5 minutes until lightly colored. Sprinkle in the flour and gradually stir in the cider and stock. Add the mushrooms and fennel seeds, then bring to a boil. Transfer everything to the slow cooker, including the meat, season well with salt and pepper, and cover with the lid. Cook on auto/low for 6–8 hours or on high for 2–3 hours. Sprinkle the finished dish with the reserved fennel fronds or chopped parsley and serve hot with some creamy mashed potatoes.

traditional method
PREP 20 MINS   **COOK** 1½ HRS

1 Preheat the oven to 325°C (160°C). Heat the oil in a large Dutch oven over medium-high heat and cook the meat, stirring occasionally, for 3–4 minutes until lightly browned. Remove and set aside.

2 Lower the heat to medium, add the onion, carrot, parsnip, and fennel to the pot and cook, stirring occasionally, for 4–5 minutes until lightly colored. Sprinkle in the flour and gradually stir in the cider and stock. Add the mushrooms and fennel seeds, then return the meat, season well with salt and pepper, and bring to a boil. Cover tightly with the lid and put in the oven for about 1¼ hours, or until the meat and vegetables are tender. Sprinkle the finished dish with the reserved fennel fronds or chopped parsley and serve hot with some creamy mashed potatoes.

Try using a Normandy cider for this dish, for an authentic flavor. Crème fraîche can be used in place of the cream. Stir in a handful of walnuts at the end to add flavor.

Pork Normandy

SERVES 4–6

2 tbsp olive oil
pat of butter
2lb (900g) lean pork, cut into bite-sized pieces
2 onions, finely chopped
2 tbsp Dijon mustard
4 garlic cloves, finely chopped
4 celery stalks, finely chopped
3 carrots, peeled and finely chopped

1 tbsp chopped rosemary leaves
2 Granny Smith apples, peeled, cored, and
  roughly chopped
1 cup dry cider
1 cup hot light chicken stock,
  for both methods
1 cup heavy cream
1 tsp black peppercorns

in the slow cooker
PREP 30 MINS **COOK** 25 MINS PRECOOKING;
AUTO/LOW 6–8 HRS OR **HIGH** 3–4 HRS

1 Preheat the slow cooker, if required. Heat the oil and butter in a large Dutch oven over medium heat, add the pork (in batches, if necessary), and cook for about 10 minutes, stirring occasionally, until golden brown on all sides. Remove and set aside.

2 Reduce the heat to low, add the onions, and cook for about 5 minutes until soft. Stir in the mustard, garlic, celery, carrots, and rosemary, and cook, stirring often, for about 10 minutes until tender. Add the apples and cook for a further 5 minutes.

3 Pour in the cider, increase the heat, and boil for a couple of minutes while the alcohol evaporates. Transfer everything to the slow cooker, including the pork, and pour in the stock. Cover with the lid and cook on auto/low for 6–8 hours or on high for 3–4 hours. Add the cream and peppercorns for the last 20 minutes of cooking. Serve with fluffy rice or creamy mashed potatoes.

traditional method
PREP 30 MINS **COOK** 1½ HRS

1 Preheat the oven to 350°F (180°C). Heat the oil and butter in a large Dutch oven over medium heat, add the pork (in batches, if necessary), and cook for about 10 minutes, stirring occasionally, until golden brown on all sides. Remove and set aside.

2 Reduce the heat to low, add the onions, and cook for about 5 minutes until soft. Stir in the mustard, garlic, celery, carrots, and rosemary, and cook, stirring often, for about 10 minutes until tender. Add the apples and cook for a further 5 minutes.

3 Pour in the cider, increase the heat, and boil for a couple of minutes while the alcohol evaporates. Return the pork to the pot and pour in the stock and cream. Stir in the peppercorns, bring to a boil, cover with the lid, and put in the oven for 1 hour, or until the sauce has reduced and the pork is tender. Serve with fluffy rice or creamy mashed potatoes.

In this classic French casserole, long, slow braising ensures the meat becomes tender, cooked as it is in red wine. Traditionally, the French use red Burgundy wine, but it's not obligatory.

Boeuf bourguignon

SERVES 4 · **FREEZE** UP TO 3 MONTHS

6oz (175g) sliced bacon, chopped
1–2 tbsp olive oil
2lb (900g) chuck steak, cut into 1½in (4cm) cubes
12 small shallots, peeled and left whole
1 tbsp all-purpose flour
1¼ cups red wine
1 cup hot beef stock for the slow cooker
  (1¼ cups for the traditional method)

4oz (115g) button mushrooms
1 bay leaf
1 tsp dried herbes de Provence
salt and freshly ground black pepper
¼ cup chopped flat-leaf parsley

in the slow cooker · **PREP** 20 MINS · **COOK** 20 MINS PRECOOKING; **AUTO/LOW** 6–8 HRS

1 Preheat the slow cooker, if required. Fry the bacon in a large Dutch oven over medium heat until lightly browned. Drain on paper towels, then set aside and keep warm. Depending on how much fat is left from the bacon, add a little oil to the pot, if necessary, so you have 2–3 tablespoons, and increase the heat to high. Fry the beef (in batches, if necessary) for 8–10 minutes until browned all over. Remove, set aside, and keep warm. Reduce the heat to medium and fry the shallots for 6–8 minutes and then remove these too, and set aside with the meat.

2 Stir the flour into the remaining fat in the pot. If the pot is quite dry, mix the flour with a little of the wine or stock. Pour the remaining wine and stock into the pot and bring to a boil, stirring, until smooth. Add the mushrooms, bay leaf, and dried herbs. Add seasoning and then transfer everything to the slow cooker, including the bacon, beef, and shallots. Cover with the lid and cook on auto/low for 6–8 hours. Sprinkle with the chopped parsley, remove the bay leaf, and serve with mashed potatoes, baby carrots, and a green vegetable such as broccoli or green beans.

traditional method · **PREP** 25 MINS · **COOK** 2½ HRS

1 Preheat the oven to 325°F (160°C). Fry the bacon in a large Dutch oven over medium heat until lightly browned. Drain on paper towels, then set aside and keep warm. Depending on how much fat is left from the bacon, add a little oil to the pot, if necessary, so you have 2–3 tablespoons, and increase the heat to high. Fry the beef (in batches, if necessary) for 8–10 minutes until browned all over. Remove, set aside, and keep warm. Reduce the heat to medium and fry the shallots for 6–8 minutes and then remove these too, and set aside with the meat.

2 Stir the flour into the remaining fat in the pot. If the pot is quite dry mix, the flour with a little of the wine or stock. Pour the remaining wine and stock into the pot and bring to a boil, stirring, until smooth. Add the mushrooms, bay leaf, and dried herbs. Add seasoning and return the meat and shallots to the pot. Cover and cook in the oven for 2 hours, or until the meat is very tender. Check occasionally that it's not drying out, topping up with a little hot water if needed.

3 Sprinkle with the chopped parsley, remove the bay leaf, and serve with mashed potatoes, baby carrots, and a green vegetable such as broccoli or green beans.

The flavor varies with the wine used: a Rhône wine gives a rich sauce; a Loire wine, a fruitier dish. Start the recipe a day ahead to allow time for marinating. Serve with new potatoes.

Coq au vin

SERVES 4–6

1 onion, thinly sliced
1 celery stalk, thinly sliced
1 carrot, peeled and thinly sliced
2 garlic cloves, 1 peeled and left whole,
  1 finely chopped
6 black peppercorns
1½ cups red wine
4½lb (2kg) chicken, jointed into 8 pieces
2 tbsp olive oil
1 tbsp vegetable oil

1 tbsp butter
4½oz (125g) piece of slab bacon, diced
18–20 baby onions, peeled
3 tbsp flour
2 cups hot chicken stock, for both methods
2 shallots, finely chopped
1 bouquet garni
salt and freshly ground black pepper
9oz (250g) mushrooms, quartered

in the slow cooker   **PREP** 30 MINS,   **COOK** 20 MINS PRECOOKING;
                         PLUS MARINATING   **AUTO/LOW** 6–8 HRS OR **HIGH** 3–4 HRS

1 For the marinade, put the onion, celery, carrot, whole garlic clove, and peppercorns in a pan. Pour in the wine and bring to a boil. Simmer for about 5 minutes, then cool and pour into a non-metallic bowl. Add the chicken and oil, cover, and refrigerate for 12–18 hours, turning the chicken occasionally.

2 Preheat the slow cooker, if required. Remove the chicken from the marinade and dry on paper towels. Strain the marinade and reserve the liquid and vegetables. Heat the vegetable oil and butter in a Dutch oven until foaming. Add the bacon, brown it, remove, and set aside. Add the chicken and cook for 10–15 minutes until brown. Remove and set aside. Discard all but 2 tablespoons of the fat. Reduce the heat to medium and cook the onions for 3–4 minutes until soft. Add the reserved vegetables and cook over a very low heat for 5 minutes until soft. Add the flour and cook for 2 minutes until lightly browned. Stir in the reserved marinade, stock, chopped garlic, shallots, bouquet garni, and seasoning. Bring to a boil, then transfer to the slow cooker, adding the bacon and chicken. Cover with the lid and cook on auto/low for 6–8 hours or on high for 3–4 hours. Add the mushrooms with 15 minutes remaining.

traditional method   **PREP** 30 MINS, PLUS MARINATING   **COOK** 1½–1¾ HRS

1 For the marinade, put the onion, celery, carrot, whole garlic clove, and peppercorns in a pan. Pour in the wine and bring to a boil. Simmer for about 5 minutes, then cool and pour into a non-metallic bowl. Add the chicken and oil, cover, and refrigerate for 12–18 hours, turning the chicken occasionally.

2 Remove the chicken from the marinade and dry on paper towels. Strain the marinade and reserve the liquid and vegetables. Heat the vegetable oil and butter in a Dutch oven until foaming. Add the bacon, brown it, remove, and set aside. Add the chicken and cook for 10–15 minutes until brown. Remove and set aside. Discard all but 2 tablespoons of the fat. Reduce the heat to medium and cook the onions for 3–4 minutes until soft. Add the reserved vegetables and cook over low heat for 5 minutes until soft. Add the flour and cook for 2 minutes until lightly browned. Stir in the reserved marinade, stock, chopped garlic, shallots, bouquet garni, and seasoning. Bring to a boil, then return the chicken, cover, and simmer over low heat for 45–60 minutes until tender. Add the mushrooms with 15 minutes remaining.

This Italian classic is served with a zesty gremolata, and it would be delicious with a saffron and Parmesan risotto. Ask your butcher for a hindleg of veal as they are meatier than the front legs.

Osso bucco

SERVES 4–6

¼ cup all-purpose flour
salt and freshly ground black pepper
4–6 pieces of veal shin with bones (about 4lb/1.8kg)
2 tbsp vegetable oil
2 tbsp butter
1 carrot, peeled and thinly sliced
2 onions, finely chopped
1 cup white wine
14oz (400g) can Italian plum tomatoes, drained
  and coarsely chopped

1 garlic clove, finely chopped
finely grated zest of 1 orange
½ cup hot chicken or veal stock for
  both methods

FOR THE GREMOLATA
small bunch of flat-leaf parsley, leaves
  finely chopped
finely grated zest of 1 lemon
1 garlic clove, finely chopped

in the slow cooker   ⏱ PREP 15 MINS   COOK 15 MINS PRECOOKING;
AUTO/LOW 6–8 HRS OR **HIGH** 4 HRS

1 Preheat the slow cooker, if required. Put the flour on a large plate, season with salt and pepper, and stir to combine. Lightly coat the veal pieces with the seasoned flour. Heat the oil and butter in a large Dutch oven over medium heat, add the veal pieces (in batches and with extra oil, if necessary), and brown thoroughly on all sides. Transfer to a plate with a slotted spoon and set aside.

2 Add the carrot and onions and cook, stirring occasionally, until soft. Add the wine and boil until reduced by half. Stir in the tomatoes, garlic, and orange zest, and add seasoning. Transfer everything to the slow cooker, then lay the veal on top, and pour in the stock. Cover with the lid and cook for 6–8 hours on auto/low or on high for 4 hours.

3 For the gremolata, mix the parsley, lemon, and garlic in a small bowl. Put the veal on warmed plates, spoon the sauce on top and sprinkle with the gremolata.

traditional method   ⏱ PREP 30–35 MINS   COOK 1¾–2¼ HRS

1 Preheat the oven to 350°F (180°C). Put the flour on a large plate, season with salt and pepper, and stir to combine. Lightly coat the veal pieces with the seasoned flour. Heat the oil and butter in a large Dutch oven over medium heat, add the veal pieces (in batches and with extra oil, if necessary), and brown thoroughly on all sides. Transfer to a plate with a slotted spoon and set aside.

2 Add the carrot and onions and cook, stirring occasionally, until soft. Add the wine and boil until reduced by half. Stir in the tomatoes, garlic, and orange zest, and add seasoning. Transfer everything to the slow cooker, then lay the veal on top, and pour in the stock. Cover with the lid and put in the oven for 1½–2 hours until very tender. Check occasionally that it's not drying out, topping up with a little hot water if needed.

3 For the gremolata, mix the parsley, lemon, and garlic in a small bowl. Put the veal on warmed plates, spoon the sauce on top and sprinkle with the gremolata.

The vivid flavors of young lamb and baby vegetables marry perfectly in this springtime stew. Cook the lamb until it is soft enough to fall from a fork, while only lightly cooking the vegetables.

Navarin of lamb

🌀 **SERVES** 6   ❄️ **FREEZE** UP TO 3 MONTHS

2 tbsp vegetable oil
about 1lb (500g) baby onions, peeled and left whole
1lb 10oz (750g) boneless lamb shoulder, cut into
  bite-sized pieces
2 tbsp flour, seasoned with salt and pepper
1 tbsp tomato paste
2 garlic cloves, finely chopped
1 bouquet garni made with 5–6 parsley sprigs,
  2–3 thyme sprigs, and 1 bay leaf
about 2 cups hot chicken or lamb stock for the
  slow cooker (2½ cups for the traditional method)
1lb 10oz (750g) small new potatoes, peeled
  or scrubbed

9oz (250g) turnips, peeled and quartered
13oz (375g) tomatoes, skinned, seeded, and
  coarsely chopped
9oz (250g) baby carrots, topped and small
  ones left whole or halved
1 cup fresh or frozen peas (optional)
9oz (250g) French beans, topped and chopped
  into 1in (2.5cm) pieces
salt and freshly ground black pepper
few sprigs of flat-leaf parsley, leaves chopped

in the slow cooker   🕐 **PREP** 20 MINS   **COOK** 20 MINS PRECOOKING;
AUTO/LOW 6–8 HRS OR **HIGH** 3–4 HRS

1 Preheat the slow cooker, if required. Heat the oil in a large Dutch oven over medium heat, add the baby onions, and cook for 5–7 minutes until golden. Remove and set aside. Toss the lamb in the flour and cook (in batches, if necessary) for 5–8 minutes over high heat until browned. Stir in the tomato paste, garlic, and bouquet garni, pour in enough stock to just cover, and bring to a boil.

2 Transfer to the slow cooker, cover with the lid, and cook on auto/low for 6–8 hours or on high for 3–4 hours. Add the baby onions, potatoes, turnips, tomatoes, and carrots for the last 2 hours of cooking and top up with a small amount of hot water to cover, if needed. Add the peas, if using, and beans for the last 15 minutes of cooking until they are just tender. Taste and season with salt and pepper, if needed. To serve, ladle onto warmed plates and sprinkle over the parsley.

traditional method   🕐 **PREP** 20 MINS   **COOK** 2 HRS

1 Heat the oil in a large Dutch oven over medium heat, add the baby onions, and cook for 5–7 minutes until golden. Remove and set aside. Toss the lamb in the flour and cook (in batches, if necessary) for 5–8 minutes over high heat until browned. Stir in the tomato paste, garlic, and bouquet garni, pour in enough stock to just cover, and bring to a boil. Cover with the lid and simmer for 1 hour.

2 Add the baby onions, potatoes, turnips, tomatoes, and carrots. Pour in more stock to almost cover the meat and vegetables. Cover and simmer for 20–25 minutes until the potatoes are tender to the point of a knife. Add the peas, if using, and beans and simmer until they are just tender. Be sure not to cook the navarin for any longer than necessary to cook the vegetables through; they should retain their fresh crunch and bright colors. Taste and adjust the seasoning, if needed. To serve, ladle onto warmed plates and sprinkle over the parsley.

This is a classic one-pot French dish in which chicken is simmered until the meat falls off the bone. If you can use a fresh chicken stock for this, all the better.

Chicken fricassée

SERVES 4   **FREEZE** UP TO 3 MONTHS   **HEALTHY**

2 tbsp olive oil
4 chicken legs, divided into drumstick and
  thigh joints, skin removed
2 tbsp flour, seasoned with salt and pepper
4 shallots, sliced
2 garlic cloves, crushed
4oz (115g) button mushrooms, sliced

4 waxy potatoes, peeled and chopped into
  small pieces
2 tsp finely chopped rosemary leaves
¾ cup dry white wine
1½ cups hot chicken stock, for both methods
1 bay leaf
salt and freshly ground black pepper

in the slow cooker   **PREP** 15 MINS   **COOK** 15 MINS PRECOOKING; AUTO/LOW 5–6 HRS OR **HIGH** 3–4 HRS

1 Preheat the slow cooker, if required. Heat the oil in a large Dutch oven over medium heat. Toss the chicken pieces in the flour and then cook for 8–10 minutes, turning often, until golden brown. Remove and set aside.

2 Add the shallots to the pot and cook for 2–3 minutes, stirring often. Stir in the garlic, mushrooms, potatoes, and rosemary and also cook for 2 minutes.

3 Pour in the wine and bring to a boil, then allow it to simmer and reduce for 1 minute. Transfer everything to the slow cooker and pour in the stock. Add the chicken and the bay leaf, cover with the lid, and cook on auto/low for 5–6 hours or on high for 3–4 hours. Discard the bay leaf and adjust the seasoning, if needed. Serve hot with zucchini or sautéed cabbage.

traditional method   **PREP** 15 MINS   **COOK** 1 HR

1 Heat the oil in a large Dutch oven over medium heat. Toss the chicken pieces in the flour and then cook for 8–10 minutes, turning often, until golden brown. Remove and set aside.

2 Add the shallots to the pot and cook for 2–3 minutes, stirring often. Stir in the garlic, mushrooms, potatoes, and rosemary and also cook for 2 minutes.

3 Pour in the wine and bring to a boil, then allow it to simmer and reduce for 1 minute. Pour in the stock, and bring to a boil. Return the chicken to the pot, add the bay leaf, and cover tightly. Reduce the heat and cook gently for 45 minutes or until the chicken is very tender. Discard the bay leaf and adjust the seasoning, if needed. Serve hot with zucchini or sautéed cabbage.

This popular Mediterranean dish makes an easy vegetarian supper. Make ahead so the flavors become well acquainted, then reheat to serve. Any leftovers are just as good served cold.

Ratatouille

⊘ **SERVES** 4 ❄ **FREEZE** UP TO 3 MONTHS

¼ cup olive oil
1 small eggplant, about 8oz (225g), chopped into 1in (2.5cm) cubes
1 zucchini, trimmed and sliced
1 onion, chopped
1 garlic clove, chopped

1 red bell pepper, seeded and chopped into 1in (2.5cm) pieces
½ cup hot vegetable stock, for both methods
14oz (400g) can chopped tomatoes
2 tsp chopped oregano, plus 2–3 sprigs to serve
salt and freshly ground black pepper

in the slow cooker ⏱ PREP 15 MINS COOK 30 MINS PRECOOKING; AUTO/LOW 4–5 HRS OR HIGH 2–3 HRS

1 Preheat the slow cooker, if required. Heat half the oil in a large heavy-based saucepan over medium heat, add the eggplant, and cook for about 10 minutes until beginning to color. Remove and set aside. Add the zucchini, with more oil if necessary, and cook for 5–8 minutes until golden. Remove and set aside. Now add the onion together with any remaining oil, and cook for 4–5 minutes until soft. Stir in the garlic and peppers and cook for about 5 minutes to soften.

2 Pour in the stock and tomatoes with their juice, stir in the chopped oregano, and bring to a boil. Transfer to the slow cooker, cover with the lid, and cook on auto/low for 4–5 hours or on high for 2–3 hours. Stir in the eggplant and zucchini for the last 30 minutes of cooking.

3 Taste and add salt and pepper, if needed. Spoon the ratatouille into a warmed serving bowl and top with the oregano sprigs. Serve with rice, bulgur wheat, or couscous, and sprinkle some grated cheese over the ratatouille, if you wish.

traditional method ⏱ PREP 15 MINS COOK 1¼ HRS

1 Heat half the oil in a large heavy-based saucepan over medium heat, add the eggplant, and cook for about 10 minutes until beginning to color. Remove and set aside. Add the zucchini, with more oil if necessary, and cook for 5–8 minutes until golden. Also remove and set aside. Now add the onion together with any remaining oil, and cook for 4–5 minutes until soft. Stir in the garlic and peppers and cook for about 5 minutes to soften.

2 Pour in the stock and tomatoes with their juice, stir in the chopped oregano, and bring to a boil. Reduce the heat to low and partially cover with the lid. Cook, stirring occasionally, for about 40 minutes, topping up with a little hot water if needed. Stir in the eggplant and zucchini, and simmer for 10 minutes more.

3 Taste and add salt and pepper, if needed. Spoon the ratatouille into a warmed serving bowl and top with the oregano sprigs. Serve with rice, bulgur wheat, or couscous, and sprinkle some grated cheese over the ratatouille, if you wish.

This is a hearty bean and meat dish from southwest France. Use dried beans if you prefer, but they will need overnight soaking and boiling for 10 minutes before adding to the casserole.

Cassoulet de Toulouse

SERVES 4 · **FREEZE** UP TO 3 MONTHS

1 tbsp olive oil
2 duck legs
4 Toulouse sausages
5½oz (150g) piece of pancetta or a whole chorizo
 sausage, chopped into small pieces
1 onion, peeled and finely chopped
1 carrot, peeled and chopped
4 garlic cloves, crushed
2 x 14oz (400g) cans navy beans, drained and rinsed

1 sprig of thyme, plus ½ tbsp chopped leaves
1 bay leaf
salt and freshly ground black pepper
2 tbsp tomato paste
14oz (400g) can chopped tomatoes
⅔ cup white wine
½ day-old baguette, crusts removed and torn
 into pieces
1 tbsp chopped parsley

in the slow cooker · **PREP** 30 MINS **COOK** 50 MINS PRECOOKING; **AUTO/LOW** 6–8 HRS

1 Preheat the slow cooker, if required. Heat the oil in a large Dutch oven over medium-high heat and add the duck legs, skin-side down. Cook each side for 3–6 minutes until golden. Remove and reserve the duck fat. Add the sausages, cook for 7–8 minutes until browned, then remove and set aside. Cook the pancetta for 5 minutes and also remove and set aside. Add the onions and carrot, cook over medium heat for 10 minutes until soft, then cook most of the garlic for 1 minute. Layer the ingredients in the slow cooker, beginning with half the beans, then the onion, carrot, sausages, pancetta, and duck legs, followed by the remaining beans, and adding the bay leaf and thyme as you go. Season with salt and pepper. Mix 1½ cups of hot water with the tomato paste, tomatoes, and wine, then add to the slow cooker. Cover with the lid and cook on auto/low for 6–8 hours.

2 Put the baguette in a food processor with the remaining garlic. Process into coarse crumbs. Heat 2 tablespoons of the duck fat in a heavy-based saucepan over medium heat and fry the crumbs for 7–8 minutes until golden. Drain on paper towels and stir in the parsley. Sprinkle over the dish and serve.

traditional method · **PREP** 30 MINS **COOK** 3¾ HRS

1 Preheat the oven to 275°F (140°C). Heat the oil in a large Dutch oven over medium-high heat and add the duck legs, skin-side down. Cook each side for 3–6 minutes until golden. Remove and reserve the duck fat. Add the sausages, cook for 7–8 minutes until browned, then remove and set aside. Cook the pancetta for 5 minutes and also remove and set aside. Add the onions and carrot, cook over medium heat for 10 minutes until soft, then cook most of the garlic for 1 minute. Layer the ingredients in the pot, beginning with half the beans, then onions, carrot, sausages, pancetta, and duck legs, followed by the remaining beans, and adding the bay leaf and thyme as you go. Season with salt and pepper. Mix 3 cups of hot water with the tomato paste, tomatoes, and wine, then add to the pot. Cover and cook in the oven for 3 hours, adding extra water if required.

2 Put the baguette in a food processor with the remaining garlic. Process into coarse crumbs. Heat 2 tablespoons of the duck fat in a heavy-based saucepan over medium heat and fry the crumbs for 7–8 minutes until golden. Drain on paper towels and stir in the parsley. Sprinkle over the dish and serve.

Dumplings are the perfect addition to a casserole or stew as they make the dish a complete meal. For variety, add other herbs, such as thyme or tarragon, to the parsley in the mixture.

Vegetable casserole with dumplings

SERVES 4–6 **FREEZE** UP TO 1 MONTH

1 tbsp olive oil
1 onion, roughly chopped
salt and freshly ground black pepper
3 garlic cloves, finely chopped
pinch of dried chile flakes
2 leeks, trimmed and thickly sliced
3 carrots, peeled and roughly chopped
2 celery stalks, roughly chopped

1 tbsp all-purpose flour
2 cups hot vegetable stock for the slow cooker
 (3 cups for the traditional method)
14oz (400g) can cannellini beans, drained and rinsed
few sprigs of rosemary
2 cups self-rising flour
½ cup shortening
2 tbsp finely chopped flat-leaf parsley

in the slow cooker   PREP 25 MINS   COOK 20 MINS PRECOOKING; AUTO/LOW 6–8 HRS OR HIGH 4 HRS

1 Preheat the slow cooker, if required. Heat the oil in a large heavy-based pan over medium heat, add the onion, and cook for 3–4 minutes until soft. Season with salt and pepper, then stir in the garlic and chile flakes. Add the leeks, carrots, and celery and continue cooking for a further 10 minutes, stirring occasionally, until softened. Stir in the all-purpose flour, then gradually stir in the stock. Add the beans and rosemary, and transfer everything to the slow cooker. Cover with the lid and cook on auto/low for 6–8 hours or on high for 4 hours.

2 About 45 minutes before the end of the cooking time, prepare the dumplings. Mix together the self-rising flour, shortening, and parsley and season well. Add about ½ cup cold water to form a soft, slightly sticky dough, trickling in more water if it seems too dry. Form into 12 balls and drop them into the stew for the last 30 minutes of cooking. Push them down a little so they are just immersed and cover with the lid. Remove the rosemary sprigs, ladle the casserole into warmed bowls, and serve with crusty bread.

traditional method   PREP 25 MINS   COOK 1¼ HRS

1 Preheat the oven to 325°F (160°C). Heat the oil in a large Dutch oven over medium heat, add the onion, and cook for 3–4 minutes until soft. Season with salt and pepper, then stir in the garlic and chile flakes. Add the leek, carrots, and celery and continue cooking for a further 10 minutes, stirring occasionally, until softened. Stir in the all-purpose flour, then gradually stir in the stock. Add the beans and rosemary. Bring to a boil, then reduce to a simmer, cover, and put in the oven for 1 hour, checking on the liquid level as it cooks and topping up with hot stock if needed.

2 While this is cooking, prepare the dumplings. Mix together the self-rising flour, shortening, and parsley and season well. Add about ½ cup cold water to form a soft, slightly sticky dough, trickling in more water if it seems too dry. Form into 12 balls and drop them into the stew for the last 30 minutes of cooking. Push them down a little so they are just immersed and cover with the lid. Remove the lid for the final 10 minutes or until the dumplings are browned. Remove the rosemary sprigs, ladle the casserole into warmed bowls, and serve with crusty bread.

The all-important ingredient in a carbonnade—a classic Belgian casserole—is the beer. Here it is topped with slices of French bread and mustard, which soak into the pot and enhance the gravy.

Beef carbonnade

⊘ **SERVES** 4–6 ❄ **FREEZE** UP TO 3 MONTHS

pat of butter
2 tbsp olive oil
2½lb (1.1kg) beef skirt, cut into chunks
1–2 tbsp flour, seasoned with salt and pepper
12 baby shallots, peeled and left whole
salt and freshly ground black pepper
3 garlic cloves, finely chopped
1 tbsp demerara sugar

1 cup Belgian beer or dark brown ale
pinch of grated nutmeg
1 bouquet garni
2 cups hot beef stock for the slow cooker
  (3 cups for the traditional method)
1 tbsp Dijon mustard
1 small French baugette, cut into slices
handful of flat-leaf parsley, finely chopped

in the slow cooker 🕑 **PREP** 10 MINS **COOK** 25 MINS PRECOOKING; AUTO/LOW 8 HRS OR **HIGH** 4 HRS

1 Preheat the slow cooker, if required. Heat the butter and 1 tablespoon of the oil in a large Dutch oven over medium-high heat. Toss the meat in the flour, and cook in batches for about 10 minutes until golden. Remove and set aside. Reduce the temperature, add the remaining oil, and cook the shallots for 8–10 minutes, stirring so they don't burn. Add seasoning, garlic, and sugar, and cook for a few minutes, adding more oil if needed. Remove and set aside.

2 Increase the heat, add the beer, and let it boil for a few minutes. Transfer the beer to the slow cooker, adding the meat, shallot mixture, nutmeg, and bouquet garni. Pour in the stock so it just covers the meat, cover with the lid, and cook on auto/low for 8 hours or on high for 4 hours.

3 Spread the mustard over the slices of French bread and place on top of the stew halfway through the cooking time. Remove the bouquet garni and sprinkle with parsley. Ladle into warmed large shallow bowls to serve.

traditional method 🕑 **PREP** 10 MINS **COOK** 3¼ HRS

1 Preheat the oven to 325°F (160°C). Heat the butter and 1 tablespoon of the oil in a large Dutch oven over medium-high heat. Toss the meat in the flour, and cook in batches for about 10 minutes until golden. Remove and set aside. Reduce the temperature, add the remaining oil, and cook the shallots for 8–10 minutes, stirring so they don't burn. Add seasoning, garlic, and sugar, and cook for a few minutes, adding more oil if needed. Remove and set aside.

2 Increase the heat, add the beer, and let it boil for a few minutes. Then reduce the heat, return the meat and shallot mixture to the pot, and add the nutmeg and bouquet garni. Pour in the stock, cover with the lid, and put the pot in the oven for 2 hours or until the beef is meltingly tender. Check occasionally that it's not drying out, topping up with a little hot water if needed.

3 Spread the mustard over the slices of French bread and place on top of the stew. Cover with the lid and return to the oven for 30 minutes. Uncover and give the topping about 10 minutes to brown. Remove the bouquet garni and sprinkle with parsley. Ladle into warmed large shallow bowls to serve.

Cooking lamb on the bone in the pot adds lots more flavor to the dish. If you can't get hold of lamb shanks, neck of lamb would be a good alternative, and will take the same length of time to cook.

Lamb shanks with harissa and shallots

🕐 **SERVES** 4 ❄️ **FREEZE** UP TO 3 MONTHS

3–4 tbsp olive oil
2 large lamb shanks
1 tbsp flour, seasoned with salt and pepper
12 shallots, peeled and left whole
salt and freshly ground black pepper
2 garlic cloves, crushed
½ cup red lentils, rinsed and picked
  over for stones

14oz (400g) can chopped tomatoes
1½ cups hot chicken or vegetable stock
  for the slow cooker (2 cups for the
  traditional method)
1 tbsp harissa paste
½ bunch of flat-leaf parsley, finely chopped
handful of mint, roughly chopped

in the slow cooker 🕐 **PREP** 20 MINS **COOK** 20 MINS PRECOOKING; AUTO/LOW 6–8 HRS OR **HIGH** 4–5 HRS

1 Preheat the slow cooker, if required. Heat 1 tablespoon of the oil in a large Dutch oven over medium-high heat, and toss the lamb shanks in the flour. Cook the shanks in the oil for 5–6 minutes, turning so they become golden on all sides. Top up with oil as needed. Remove and set aside.

2 Add the remaining oil and reduce the heat to medium. Season the shallots with salt and pepper and cook, stirring, for 8–10 minutes until they begin to color a little. Stir in the garlic and lentils, and transfer everything to the slow cooker, including the lamb.

3 Stir in the tomatoes and stock and add the harissa paste. Season, cover with the lid, and cook on auto/low for 6–8 hours or on high for 4–5 hours until the meat falls off the bone. Shred the meat off the bone and return to the slow cooker. Add the parsley and mint, and serve with boiled potatoes.

traditional method 🕐 **PREP** 20 MINS **COOK** 2¼–2¾ HRS

1 Preheat the oven to 300°F (150°C). Heat 1 tablespoon of the oil in a large Duch oven over medium-high heat, and toss the lamb shanks in the flour. Cook the shanks in the oil for 5–6 minutes, turning so they become golden on all sides. Top up with oil as needed. Remove and set aside.

2 Add the remaining oil and reduce the heat to medium. Season the shallots with salt and pepper and cook, stirring, for 8–10 minutes until they begin to color a little. Stir in the garlic and lentils, then add in the tomatoes and stock, and bring to a boil. Reduce the heat and stir in the harissa paste, then return the lamb shanks to the pot.

3 Cover the pot with the lid and put in the oven for 2–2½ hours until the lamb is tender and falling off the bone. Check occasionally that it's not drying out, topping up with a little hot water if needed. Shred the meat off the bone and return to the pot. Add the parsley and mint, and serve with boiled potatoes.

This is a lighter, vegetarian version of the traditional meaty cassoulet, featuring creamy navy beans and a crispy, herby breadcrumb and Parmesan cheese topping.

Pumpkin and parsnip cassoulet

⏱ **SERVES** 4–6 ❄ **FREEZE** UP TO 3 MONTHS ♡ **HEALTHY**

2 tbsp olive oil
1 onion, finely chopped
salt and freshly ground black pepper
3 garlic cloves, finely chopped
1 tsp ground cloves
2 carrots, peeled and finely chopped
2 celery stalks, finely chopped
1 bay leaf
1lb (450g) pumpkin (prepared weight), peeled,
  seeded, and chopped into bite-sized pieces
1lb (450g) small parsnips, sliced into rounds

1 cup white wine
few sprigs of thyme
4 tomatoes, chopped, or a 14oz (400g) can tomatoes
14oz (400g) can navy beans, rinsed and drained
1¼ cups hot vegetable stock for the slow cooker
  (3 cups for the traditional method)

FOR THE TOPPING
1 cup breadcrumbs, lightly toasted
¼ cup Parmesan cheese, grated
1 tbsp chopped flat-leaf parsley

in the slow cooker 🕐 **PREP** 15 MINS **COOK** 20 MINS PRECOOKING;
AUTO/LOW 8 HRS OR **HIGH** 4 HRS

1 Preheat the slow cooker, if required. Heat the oil in a large heavy-based pan over medium heat, add the onion, and cook for 3–4 minutes until soft. Season with salt and pepper, then add the garlic, cloves, carrots, celery, and bay leaf and cook, stirring occasionally, on very low heat for 8–10 minutes until it is all soft. Stir in the pumpkin and parsnip and cook for a few minutes more, then pour in the wine. Increase the heat, stir, and let it bubble for a minute or two. Then add the thyme, tomatoes, and beans.

2 Transfer everything to the slow cooker, pour in the stock, season with salt and pepper, and stir. Cover with the lid and cook on auto/low for 8 hours or on high for 4 hours. An hour before the end of the cooking time, mix the topping ingredients together in a bowl, sprinkle over the top of the dish, and replace the lid. Ladle into warmed bowls and serve with crusty bread.

traditional method 🕐 **PREP** 15 MINS **COOK** 1¾ HRS

1 Preheat the oven to 350°F (180°C). Heat the oil in a large Dutch oven over medium heat, add the onion, and cook for 3–4 minutes until soft. Season with salt and pepper, then add the garlic, cloves, carrots, celery, and bay leaf and cook, stirring occasionally, on very low heat for 8–10 minutes until it is all soft. Stir in the pumpkin and parsnip and cook for a few minutes more, then pour in the wine. Increase the heat, stir, and let it bubble for a minute or two. Then add the thyme, tomatoes, beans, and stock, and bring to a boil. Reduce to a simmer, season, cover with the lid, and put in the oven for 40 minutes.

2 Mix together the topping ingredients in a bowl, sprinkle it over the cassoulet and put back in the oven for 30 minutes. Then remove the lid and cook for about 10 minutes until the topping is golden. Ladle into warmed bowls and serve with crusty bread.

This is Brazil's national dish and is made with a variety of meats that mingle together for a delicious taste. Canned beans are used for ease but traditionally dried beans would be used.

Feijoada

SERVES 6

2 pig's feet
9oz (250g) smoked pork ribs
6oz (175g) slab smoked bacon, left in 1 piece
7oz (200g) can chopped tomatoes
1 tbsp tomato paste
1 bay leaf
salt and freshly ground black pepper
28oz (800g) can black-eyed peas, drained and rinsed

2 tbsp olive oil
10oz (300g) lean pork filet, sliced, or steaks
1 small onion, finely chopped
2 garlic cloves, finely chopped
6oz (175g) dried chorizo, chopped into small chunks
1 green chile, seeded
1 orange, cut into wedges, to serve
3 scallions, trimmed and chopped, to serve

in the slow cooker   **PREP** 15 MINS   **COOK** 20 MINS PRECOOKING; **AUTO/LOW** 6–8 HRS OR **HIGH** 3–4 HRS

1 Preheat the slow cooker, if required. Place the pig's feet, pork ribs, and bacon in the slow cooker with the canned tomatoes and their juice, the tomato paste, bay leaf, salt and pepper, and beans. Cover with the lid and cook on auto/low for 6–8 hours or on high for 3–4 hours.

2 Heat 1 tablespoon of the oil in a large skillet over medium-high heat, and brown the pork filet for about 5 minutes on each side. Remove and set aside. Add the remaining oil to the pan and cook the onion and garlic over medium heat for 3–4 minutes until soft. Add the chorizo and chile and cook for a further 2 minutes. Transfer to the slow cooker, together with the pork filet, for the last 45 minutes of cooking. To serve, remove the larger pieces of meat and cut into smaller pieces. Squash some of the beans with the back of a fork and remove the bay leaf. Transfer everything to a serving dish and garnish with orange wedges and scallions. Serve with plain boiled rice, steamed or fried shredded kale, and a tomato salsa.

traditional method   **PREP** 15 MINS   **COOK** 1¾ HRS

1 Place the pig's feet, pork ribs, and bacon in a large Dutch oven with the canned tomatoes and their juice, the tomato paste, bay leaf, and salt and pepper. Add enough cold water to cover, bring to a boil, skim off any scum, cover, reduce the heat, and simmer for 50 minutes. Stir in the beans (reserving 3 tablespoons) and top up with a little hot water, if needed, to just cover. Continue to cook, covered, over a low heat for a further 20 minutes.

2 Heat 1 tablespoon of the oil in a heavy-based skillet over medium-high heat, and brown the pork filet for about 5 minutes on each side. Add to the pot and continue to cook for a further 10 minutes or until the meats are tender. Wipe out the skillet, add the remaining oil, and cook the onion and garlic over medium heat for 3–4 minutes until soft. Add the chorizo and chile and cook for a further 2 minutes, stirring. Add the reserved beans to the skillet and squash them with the back of a fork. Transfer everything to the pot, stir, and cook for a further 10 minutes. To serve, remove the larger pieces of meat and cut into smaller pieces. Remove the bay leaf and transfer everything to a serving dish. Garnish with orange wedges and scallions. Serve with plain boiled rice, steamed or fried shredded kale, and a tomato salsa.

This classic Spanish dish of brown lentils relies on salty bacon, spicy chorizo, and paprika for its flavor. The lentils benefit from slow cooking as they become soft, tender, and don't need soaking.

Spanish lentils

SERVES 4

2½ cups brown lentils, rinsed and picked over
    for any stones
2 bay leaves
3oz (85g) dried chorizo, sliced
2 tbsp olive oil
2 garlic cloves, sliced
1 small slice of bread

salt
1 onion, finely chopped
2½oz (75g) thickly sliced bacon,
    cut into strips
1 tbsp flour
1 tsp sweet paprika
⅓ cup hot vegetable stock, for both methods

in the slow cooker   **PREP** 15 MINS   **COOK** 10 MINS PRECOOKING;
                                          AUTO/LOW 5–6 HRS OR **HIGH** 3–4 HRS

1 Preheat the slow cooker, if required. Put the lentils in the slow cooker with just enough water to cover, plus an extra ½ cup. Stir in the the bay leaves and chorizo, cover with the lid, and cook on auto/low for 5–6 hours or on high for 3–4 hours.

2 Meanwhile, heat 1 tablespoon of the oil in a heavy-based skillet over medium-low heat and cook the garlic, stirring, for about 30 seconds until softened but not browned. Remove and set aside. Add the bread to the pan and cook over medium heat until lightly browned on both sides. Transfer to a food processor with the garlic and season with salt. Process into coarse crumbs, then set aside.

3 Add the remaining oil to the pan together with the onion and bacon. Cook for 3–4 minutes until the onion is soft and the bacon is cooked. Stir in the flour and paprika and cook for 1 minute before adding the stock. Bring to a boil and simmer for 2 minutes, then stir into the lentils for the last 30 minutes of cooking. Stir in the crumb mixture for the last 15 minutes of cooking. Transfer to a warmed serving dish and serve with crusty bread.

traditional method   **PREP** 15 MINS   **COOK** 1 HR

1 Put the lentils into a large saucepan with 3½ cups water, the bay leaves, and chorizo. Bring to a boil, then simmer for 35–40 minutes or until the lentils are tender.

2 Meanwhile, heat 1 tablespoon of the oil in a heavy-based skillet over medium-low heat and cook the garlic, stirring, for about 30 seconds until softened but not browned. Remove and set aside. Add the bread to the pan and cook over medium heat until lightly browned on both sides. Transfer to a food processor with the garlic and season with salt. Process into coarse crumbs, then set aside. When the lentils are cooked, drain, then return to the saucepan. Stir in the crumb mixture until combined.

3 Add the remaining oil to the heavy-based skillet together with the onion and bacon. Cook for 3–4 minutes until the onion is soft and the bacon is cooked. Stir in the flour and paprika and cook for 1 minute before adding the stock. Bring to a boil and simmer for 2 minutes, then stir into the lentils. If necessary, add a little more hot water to moisten the lentils. Transfer to a warmed serving dish and serve with crusty bread.

This is an intensely flavored dish from France that is well worth the effort. The fat that the duck legs are cooked in—and this can be duck or goose fat—can be strained, left to cool, and re-used.

French-style duck and lentils

⊙ **SERVES** 4

4 duck legs
1lb 2oz (500g) duck fat
few sprigs of rosemary
1 tbsp olive oil
1 onion, finely chopped
salt and freshly ground black pepper
2 garlic cloves, finely chopped
few sprigs of thyme, leaves only
2 carrots, peeled and finely diced
1 bay leaf
1 tbsp dry sherry

heaping 1 cup Puy lentils, rinsed and picked over for any stones
1½ cups hot chicken stock, for both methods

FOR THE MARINADE
3 tbsp brandy
1 tbsp black peppercorns, crushed
3 garlic cloves, finely chopped
pinch of ground cinnamon
few sprigs of thyme
1 tbsp sea salt

in the slow cooker ⊙ **PREP** 15 MINS, PLUS MARINATING   **COOK HIGH** 50 MINS, THEN **AUTO/LOW** 3½–4 HRS

1 Put the duck legs in a shallow dish and add all the marinade ingredients. Cover with plastic wrap, sit a weight on top, and put in the fridge overnight. Preheat the slow cooker, if required. Remove the duck from the marinade and set aside. Discard the liquid. Put the duck fat in the slow cooker with the rosemary, cover, and melt on high for about 50 minutes. Add the duck legs, cover with the lid, and cook on auto/low for 3½–4 hours until the meat is fork tender. Remove the legs and drain off excess fat.

2 Meanwhile, heat the oil in a large heavy-based saucepan over medium heat, add the onion, and cook for 3–4 minutes until soft. Season, then stir in the garlic, thyme, carrots, and bay leaf. Cook on low heat for 6–10 minutes, stirring, then increase the heat, add the sherry, and cook for 2 minutes. Stir in the lentils and then the stock. Bring to a boil, reduce to a simmer, and cook for about 40 minutes or until the lentils are tender. Top up with more hot water if the lentils start to dry out. Taste and season as needed, remove the bay leaf and thyme sprigs, and serve with the duck legs.

traditional method ⊙ **PREP** 15 MINS, PLUS MARINATING   **COOK** 3¾ HRS

1 Put the duck legs in a shallow dish and add all the marinade ingredients. Cover with plastic wrap, sit a weight on top, and refrigerate overnight. Preheat the oven to 300°F (150°C), and melt the duck fat in a large Dutch oven. Transfer the legs to the pot (discard the liquid), ensuring they are covered in the fat. Throw in the rosemary, cover, and put in the oven for 3 hours or until the meat is fork tender and the skin crispy. Let the pot cool, remove the legs, and drain off excess fat.

2 Meanwhile, heat the oil in a large heavy-based saucepan over medium heat, add the onion, and cook for 3–4 minutes until soft. Season, then stir in the garlic, thyme, carrots, and bay leaf. Cook on low heat for 6–10 minutes, stirring, then increase the heat, add the sherry, and cook for 2 minutes. Stir in the lentils and then the stock. Bring to a boil, reduce to a simmer, and cook for about 40 minutes or until the lentils are tender. Top up with more hot water if the lentils start to dry out. Taste and season as needed, remove the bay leaf and thyme sprigs, and serve with the duck legs.

This is a comforting dish that can be made with chicken or turkey. The cobbler topping makes it a substantial all-in-one dish that can be served without any other extras if there isn't enough time.

Chicken cobbler

⏱ **SERVES** 4 ❄ **FREEZE** UP TO 3 MONTHS

3 tbsp olive oil
1 onion, finely chopped
salt and freshly ground black pepper
3 garlic cloves, finely chopped
3 parsnips, peeled and sliced
6 boneless chicken thighs, with skin on
1 tbsp flour, seasoned with salt and pepper
½ cup Marsala wine, sherry, or white wine

few tarragon leaves
about 1 cup hot chicken stock for the slow cooker
  (1½ cups for the traditional method)
about 1 cup all-purpose flour, sifted
3 tbsp butter, at room temperature
¼ cup Cheddar cheese, grated
3–4 tbsp buttermilk

in the slow cooker 🕐 **PREP** 20 MINS **COOK** 15 MINS PRECOOKING; AUTO/LOW 6–8 HRS OR **HIGH** 4 HRS

1 Preheat the slow cooker, if required. Heat 1 tablespoon of the oil in a large Dutch oven over medium heat, add the onion, and cook for 3–4 minutes until soft. Season with salt and pepper, then stir in the garlic and parsnips and cook for a few more minutes until the parsnips take on some color. Remove the vegetables and set aside. Heat the remaining oil in the pot over a higher heat. Toss the chicken in the flour and cook, skin-side down, for 8–10 minutes or until golden all over. Pour in the Marsala and bring to a boil, then return the onion and parsnips to the pot, add the tarragon, and transfer everything to the slow cooker. Pour in enough stock to cover, season, and cover with the lid. Cook on auto/low for 6–8 hours or on high for 4 hours.

3 Meanwhile, for the cobblers, put the sifted flour in a bowl, season with salt and pepper, then rub in the butter until it resembles fine breadcrumbs. Stir in the cheese and add the buttermilk to form a dough. Roll out on a lightly floured surface to 1in (2.5cm) thick and cut out about ten 2in (5cm) diameter rounds. For the last hour of cooking, place them around the edge of the stew and re-cover.

traditional method 🕐 **PREP** 20 MINS **COOK** 2¼ HRS

1 Preheat the oven to 300°F (150°C). Heat 1 tablespoon of the oil in a large Dutch oven over medium heat, add the onion, and cook for 3–4 minutes until soft. Season with salt and pepper, then stir in the garlic and parsnips and cook for a few more minutes until the parsnips take on some color. Remove the vegetables and set aside. Heat the remaining oil in the pot over a higher heat.

2 Toss the chicken in the flour and cook, skin-side down, for 8–10 minutes, or until golden all over. Pour in the Marsala and bring to a boil, then return the onion and parsnips to the pot, add the tarragon, and pour in the stock. Bring to a boil, reduce to a simmer, cover with the lid, and put in the oven for 2 hours. Check occasionally that it's not drying out, topping up with a little hot water if needed.

3 Meanwhile, for the cobblers, put the sifted flour into a bowl, season, then rub in the butter until it resembles fine breadcrumbs. Stir in the cheese and add the buttermilk to form a dough. Roll out onto a lightly floured surface to 1in (2.5cm) thick and cut out about ten 2in (5cm) diameter rounds. For the last 30 minutes of cooking, place them around the edge of the stew and return to the oven, uncovered.

Dried fruit works well with a fatty meat such as pork belly, and it creates a delicious, sweet sauce that cuts through the richness. The earthiness of celery root is a great addition.

Belly pork and prunes

SERVES 4–6

1 tbsp olive oil
2½lb (1.1kg) pork belly, cut into bite-sized pieces
salt and freshly ground black pepper
1 onion, finely sliced
3 garlic cloves, finely chopped
1 tbsp sherry vinegar
½ cup white wine

2 cups hot vegetable stock for the slow cooker
 (3 cups for the traditional method)
¾ cup soft prunes, finely chopped
6 sage leaves, finely shredded
1lb 5oz (600g) celery root, peeled and chopped
 into bite-sized pieces

in the slow cooker PREP 15 MINS COOK 30 MINS PRECOOKING; **AUTO/LOW** 8 HRS

1 Preheat the slow cooker, if required. Heat half the oil in a large Dutch oven over high heat and season the pork belly with salt and pepper. Add the pork (in batches, if necessary), skin-side down, and cook until it turns golden and begins to crisp a little. Remove and sit the pork on paper towels to drain.

2 Heat the remaining oil in the pot over medium heat, add the onion, and cook for 3–4 minutes until soft. Then stir in the garlic and cook for a minute more. Increase the heat and add the sherry vinegar, letting it simmer for 2–3 minutes. Pour in the wine and continue to boil for a few more minutes until the alcohol evaporates.

3 Transfer everything to the slow cooker, including the pork. Pour in the stock and stir in the prunes, sage, and celery root. Cover with the lid and cook on auto/low for 8 hours. Taste and season more if needed, and serve with creamy mashed potatoes.

traditional method PREP 15 MINS COOK 3–3½ HRS

1 Preheat the oven to 325°F (160°C). Heat half the oil in a large Dutch oven over high heat and season the pork belly with salt and pepper. Add the pork (in batches, if necessary), skin-side down, and cook until it turns golden and begins to crisp a little. Remove and sit the pork on paper towels to drain.

2 Heat the remaining oil in the pot over medium heat, add the onion, and cook for 3–4 minutes until soft. Then stir in the garlic and cook for a minute more. Increase the heat and add the sherry vinegar, letting it simmer for 2–3 minutes. Pour in the wine and continue to boil for a few more minutes until the alcohol evaporates.

3 Add the stock and stir to scrape up the bits from the bottom of the pot. Return the pork to the pot and stir in the prunes, sage, and celery root. Bring back to a boil, cover, and put in the oven for 2½–3 hours. Check occasionally that it's not drying out, topping up with a little hot water if needed. Taste and season more if needed, and serve with creamy mashed potatoes.

Here are some hot and spicy melt-in-your-mouth meatballs all tumbled together and cooked slowly in a zingy tomato sauce. If you are a fan of spicy food, don't seed the chilies.

Mexican meatballs

SERVES 4–6   **FREEZE** UP TO 3 MONTHS

1lb 9oz (700g) ground beef
1 garlic clove, finely chopped
2 red chilies, seeded and finely chopped
½ tsp ground cumin
salt and freshly ground black pepper
1 large egg, lightly beaten
2 tbsp fresh white breadcrumbs
bunch of cilantro, finely chopped
2–3 tbsp all-purpose flour
3 tbsp olive oil

FOR THE SAUCE
1 large onion, finely chopped
1 garlic clove, finely chopped
1 red bell pepper, seeded and finely chopped
½ tsp ground coriander
1 cinnamon stick, broken
pinch of dried chile flakes
splash of Tabasco sauce
½ tsp superfine sugar
2 x 14oz (400g) cans whole tomatoes
⅔ cup hot vegetable stock, for both methods

in the slow cooker   PREP 20 MINS   COOK 20 MINS PRECOOKING; **AUTO/LOW** 6–8 HRS

1 Preheat the slow cooker, if required. Put the ground beef, garlic, chilies, and cumin into a bowl and season. Combine with your hands, then add the egg, breadcrumbs, and fresh cilantro, and mix well again. Shape the mixture into about 20 small balls and toss lightly in the flour. Heat 1 tablespoon of the oil in a large Dutch oven over medium-high heat and cook half the meatballs (in batches and with extra oil, if necessary) for 6–8 minutes until brown all over. Remove with a slotted spoon and sit on paper towels to drain. Wipe the pot out with paper towels.

2 To make the sauce, heat the remaining 1 tablespoon of oil in the pot over medium heat, add the onion, and cook for 3–4 minutes until soft. Stir in the garlic and red bell pepper, and cook for 3 minutes. Transfer the cooked vegetables to the slow cooker along with the remaining ingredients. Add seasoning, cover with the lid, and cook on auto/low for 6–8 hours. Taste and add more Tabasco sauce, if needed. Serve with rice and a green salad.

traditional method   PREP 20 MINS   COOK 1¾–2¼ HRS

1 Preheat the oven to 350°F (180°C). Put the ground beef, garlic, chilies, and cumin into a bowl and season. Combine with your hands, then add the egg, breadcrumbs, and fresh cilantro, and mix well again. Shape the mixture into about 20 small balls and toss lightly in the flour. Heat 1 tablespoon of the oil in a large Dutch oven over medium-high heat and cook half the meatballs (in batches and with extra oil, if necessary) for 6–8 minutes until brown all over. Remove with a slotted spoon and sit on paper towels to drain. Wipe the pot out with paper towels.

2 To make the sauce, heat the remaining 1 tablespoon of oil in the pot over medium heat, add the onion, and cook for 3–4 minutes until soft. Stir in the garlic and bell pepper and cook for 3 minutes, then add the remaining ingredients and bring to a boil. Reduce to a simmer and add the meatballs and stock, pushing the meatballs down so they are immersed in the liquid. Add seasoning, cover, and put in the oven for 1½–2 hours. Check occasionally that it's not drying out, topping up with a little hot water if needed. Taste and add more Tabasco sauce, if needed. Serve with rice and a green salad.

Legend has it that one of Louis XIV's mistresses created this dish in an attempt to stay in the king's good graces. It is delicious, with its succulent chops between layers of sliced potatoes and onions.

Lamb chops champvallon

SERVES 4

1 tbsp olive oil
6–8 lamb loin chops, each 1in (2.5cm) thick,
  (total weight about 2¼lb/1kg), trimmed
  of any excess fat
4 onions, thinly sliced
2½lb (1.1kg) baking potatoes, peeled and
  very thinly sliced

small bunch of thyme, leaves chopped, plus a few
  sprigs, to serve
salt and freshly ground black pepper
3 garlic cloves, finely chopped
about 2 cups hot vegetable stock for the slow cooker
  (about 4 cups for the traditional method)

in the slow cooker   **PREP** 20 MINS   **COOK** 15 MINS PRECOOKING; **AUTO/LOW** 6–8 HRS

1 Preheat the slow cooker, if required. Heat the oil in a large Dutch oven over high heat. Add the chops and cook for 1–2 minutes on each side, until well browned. Remove from the pot and set aside.

2 Pour off all but about 1 tablespoon of fat from the pot. Add the onions and cook over medium heat for 3–4 minutes until soft. Transfer to a large bowl.

3 Gently stir the potato slices into the softened onions and thyme leaves and season with salt and pepper. Spread half the potato mixture at the bottom of the slow cooker, then sprinkle with the garlic. Arrange the chops on top. Cover with the remaining potato, arranging the slices neatly in rows. Pour in enough stock to come just to the top of the potatoes. Cover with the lid and cook on auto/low for 6–8 hours. Serve the chops, potatoes, and onion with a spoonful of the cooking liquid, garnished with sprigs of thyme.

traditional method   **PREP** 25 MINS   **COOK** 2¼ HRS

1 Preheat the oven to 350°F (180°C). Heat the oil in a large Dutch oven over high heat. Add the chops and cook for 1–2 minutes on each side, until well browned. Remove from the pot and set aside.

2 Pour off all but about 1 tablespoon of fat from the pot. Add the onions and cook over medium heat for 3–4 minutes until soft. Transfer to a large bowl.

3 Gently stir the potato slices into the softened onions and thyme leaves and season with salt and pepper. Brush a 9 x 13in (23 x 32cm) baking dish with oil. Spread half the potato mixture on the dish, then sprinkle with the garlic. Arrange the chops on top. Cover with the remaining potato, arranging the slices neatly in rows. Pour in enough stock to come just to the top of the potatoes. Bake, uncovered, for 2 hours, or until the lamb and potatoes are tender when pierced. Serve the chops, potatoes, and onion with a spoonful of the cooking liquid, garnished with sprigs of thyme.

Full of festive flavors, you could make this stew using leftover turkey meat if you have some. If you can't find fresh or frozen cranberries, use a tablespoon or two of cranberry sauce instead.

Turkey and cranberry casserole

SERVES 4–6 **FREEZE** UP TO 3 MONTHS

2 large skinless turkey breasts
salt and freshly ground black pepper
2–3 tbsp olive oil
4 sausages, sliced
1 red onion, finely sliced
3 garlic cloves, finely chopped
9oz (250g) cremini mushrooms, quartered

few sprigs of rosemary
1 tbsp Dijon mustard
1 cup red wine
1½ cups hot chicken stock for the slow cooker
 (2 cups for the traditional method)
handful of fresh or frozen cranberries
9oz (250g) green beans, trimmed

in the slow cooker PREP 15 MINS COOK 15 MINS PRECOOKING; AUTO/LOW 6–8 HRS OR HIGH 4 HRS

1 Preheat the slow cooker, if required. Season the turkey breasts with salt and pepper, and heat half the oil in a large Dutch oven over medium-high heat. Add the turkey to the pot and cook for 6–8 minutes until golden. Remove and set aside.

2 Heat the remaining oil in the Dutch oven and cook the sausage slices for 3–4 minutes until beginning to color. Push them to one side, add the onion, and cook for 2–3 minutes until soft. Stir in the garlic, mushrooms, rosemary, and mustard and cook for a minute, then increase the heat and add the wine. Let the sauce bubble for a minute, then add the stock and bring to a boil.

3 Transfer everything to the slow cooker, including the turkey and cranberries, followed by seasoning with salt and pepper, and cover with the lid. Cook on auto/low for 6–8 hours or on high for 4 hours. Add the beans for the last 15 minutes of cooking. Remove the rosemary and the turkey breasts with a slotted spoon and shred the meat with a fork. Return the meat to the slow cooker and stir in. Serve with creamy mashed potatoes or boiled potatoes.

traditional method PREP 15 MINS COOK 1¼–1¾ HRS

1 Preheat the oven to 325°F (160°C). Season the turkey breasts with salt and pepper, and heat half the oil in a large Dutch oven over medium-high heat. Add the turkey to the pot and cook for 6–8 minutes until golden. Remove and set aside.

2 Heat the remaining oil in the Dutch oven and cook the sausage slices for 3–4 minutes until beginning to color. Push them to one side, add the onion, and cook for 2–3 minutes until soft. Stir in the garlic, mushrooms, rosemary, and mustard and cook for a minute, then increase the heat and add the wine. Let the sauce bubble for a minute, then add the stock and bring to a boil.

3 Return the turkey to the pot, add salt and pepper, and stir in the cranberries. Cover with the lid and put in the oven for 1–1½ hours. Check occasionally that it's not drying out, topping up with a little hot water if needed. Add the beans for the last 15 minutes of cooking. Remove the rosemary and the turkey breasts with a slotted spoon and shred the meat with a fork. Return the meat to the pot and stir in. Serve with creamy mashed potatoes or boiled potatoes.

Pork teams wonderfully with fruit. Red cabbage can look very bulky when first added to the slow cooker or pot, but it soon reduces and adds a sweet, distinctive flavor to the rest of the dish.

Pork with red cabbage, pears, and ginger

SERVES 6   **HEALTHY**

1 tbsp olive oil
1 onion, sliced
3 garlic cloves, finely chopped
½ tsp caraway seeds
2 tsp paprika
grated zest of 1 lemon
few sprigs of thyme
2½lb (1.1kg) boneless pork leg, cut into chunks
1 tbsp flour, seasoned with salt and pepper

½ red cabbage, cored and shredded
1 cup white wine
1½ cups hot vegetable stock for the slow cooker
   (2 cups for the traditional method)
3 sweet pears, quartered, cored, and peeled
2in (5cm) piece of fresh ginger, peeled and
   finely sliced
salt and freshly ground black pepper

in the slow cooker   **PREP** 20 MINS   **COOK** 15 MINS PRECOOKING;
                                              AUTO/LOW 8 HRS OR **HIGH** 4 HRS

1   Preheat the slow cooker, if required. Heat the oil in a large Dutch oven over medium heat, add the onion, and cook for 3–4 minutes until soft. Stir in the garlic, caraway seeds, paprika, lemon zest, and thyme and cook for a minute more.

2   Toss the pork in the flour and add to the pot. Turn to coat, then increase the heat and cook, stirring occasionally, for 5–8 minutes. Stir in the cabbage, increase the heat, and add the wine, letting it bubble for a minute.

3   Transfer everything to the slow cooker, add the stock, and stir in the pears and ginger. Cover with the lid, and cook on auto/low for 8 hours or on high for 4 hours. Taste and season as needed, remove the thyme, and serve with rice or mashed potatoes.

traditional method   **PREP** 20 MINS   **COOK** 1¾ HRS

1   Preheat the oven to 350°F (180°C). Heat the oil in a large Dutch oven over medium heat, add the onion, and cook for 3–4 minutes until soft. Stir in the garlic, caraway seeds, paprika, lemon zest, and thyme and cook for a minute more.

2   Toss the pork in the flour and add to the pot. Turn to coat, then increase the heat and cook, stirring occasionally, for 5–8 minutes. Stir in the cabbage, increase the heat, and add the wine, letting it bubble for a minute. Add the stock, bring to a boil, then reduce to a simmer and add the pears and ginger to the pot.

3   Cover with the lid and put in the oven for 1½ hours. Check occasionally that it's not drying out, topping up with a little hot water if needed. Taste and season as needed, remove the thyme, and serve with rice or mashed potatoes.

There are numerous versions of the "daube," but all are cooked in red wine. Choose a robust wine that you would happily drink. Throw in a cinnamon stick, if you wish, for a touch of warm spice.

Provençal lamb daube with olives

SERVES 4–6 ✺ **FREEZE** UP TO 3 MONTHS

1 orange, zest peeled in wide strips
2 garlic cloves, finely chopped
2 cups red wine
2 bay leaves
3–4 sprigs each of rosemary, thyme, and parsley
10 peppercorns
2lb (900g) boneless lamb shoulder, cut into cubes
2 tbsp olive oil
salt and freshly ground black pepper
10oz (300g) piece of smoked slab bacon,
    cut into ¼in (5mm) lardons

14oz (400g) can chopped tomatoes
2 onions, sliced
2 carrots, peeled and sliced
2 cups mushrooms, trimmed and sliced
about ½ cup pitted green olives
1 cup hot beef stock for the slow cooker
    (1¼ cups for the traditional method)

in the slow cooker
⏱ PREP 15 MINS, PLUS MARINATING   **COOK** 10 MINS PRECOOKING;
AUTO/LOW 6–8 HRS

1 To make the marinade, combine the orange zest, garlic, wine, bay leaves, herbs, and peppercorns in a bowl. Add the lamb and mix well. Pour the oil on top and add salt and pepper. Cover and refrigerate, turning occasionally, and leave to marinate for 2 hours or up to 12 hours if time permits.

2 Preheat the slow cooker, if required. Put the bacon in a large heavy-based pan of water, bring to a boil, and blanch for 5 minutes. Drain and rinse with cold water. Remove the lamb from the marinade and dry on paper towels. Strain the marinade, reserving the liquid, bay leaf, and zest.

3 Put the bacon on the bottom of the slow cooker and cover with the lamb. Layer the tomatoes and onions on top, then the carrots, mushrooms, and olives. Pour in the strained marinade and stock, season with pepper, and add the bay leaf and zest. Cover with the lid and cook on auto/low for 6–8 hours. Remove the bay leaf and zest, taste, and season if needed. Serve with mashed potatoes.

traditional method
⏱ PREP 45–50 MINS, PLUS MARINATING   **COOK** 3¾–4¼ HRS

1 To make the marinade, combine the orange zest, garlic, wine, bay leaves, herbs, and peppercorns in a bowl. Add the lamb and mix well. Pour the oil on top and add salt and pepper. Cover and refrigerate, turning occasionally, and leave to marinate for 2 hours or up to 12 hours if time permits.

2 Preheat the oven to 300°F (150°C). Put the bacon in a large heavy-based pan of water, bring to a boil, and blanch for 5 minutes. Drain and rinse with cold water. Remove the lamb from the marinade and dry on paper towels. Strain the marinade, reserving the liquid, bay leaf, and zest.

3 Put the bacon on the bottom of a large Dutch oven and cover with the lamb. Layer the tomatoes and onions on top, then the carrots, mushrooms, and olives. Pour in the strained marinade and stock, season with pepper, and add the bay leaf and zest. Bring to a boil, cover with the lid, and put in the oven for 3½–4 hours. Check occasionally that it's not drying out, topping up with a little hot water if needed. Remove the bay leaf and zest, taste, and season if needed. Serve with mashed potatoes.

Sweet Madeira wine adds a wonderful flavor to the sauce in this dish, and wide noodles are the perfect accompaniment. If you don't have any chicken stock to hand, use water instead.

Duck with turnips and apricots

SERVES 4   **FREEZE** UP TO 3 MONTHS

4 duck breasts
salt and freshly ground black pepper
1 tbsp vegetable oil
1 tbsp butter
2 tbsp all-purpose flour
¾ cup dry white wine
2 cups hot chicken stock, plus more
  if needed, for both methods

1 bouquet garni, made with 5–6 parsley sprigs,
  2–3 thyme sprigs, and 1 bay leaf
2 shallots, finely chopped
12–16 pickling onions, peeled and left whole
about 1lb (500g) turnips, peeled and roughly chopped
1 tsp granulated sugar
¼ cup Madeira wine
about ¾ cup ready-to-eat dried apricots

in the slow cooker   **PREP** 20 MINS   **COOK** 30 MINS PRECOOKING;
                                                    AUTO/LOW 6–8 HRS OR **HIGH** 3–4 HRS

1 Preheat the slow cooker, if required. Season the duck. Heat the oil and butter in a large Dutch oven over low heat and add the duck, skin-side down. Cook for 20–25 minutes until browned and the fat has rendered. Turn over and cook for only about 5 minutes until browned. Remove and set aside, draining and reserving the duck fat. Heat 2–3 tablespoons of the duck fat in the pot. Add the flour and cook, stirring constantly, for 1–2 minutes until lightly browned but not burnt. Stir in the white wine, stock, bouquet garni, shallots, and seasoning, and bring to a boil. Transfer everything to the slow cooker, including the duck, cover with the lid, and cook on auto/low for 6–8 hours or on high for 3–4 hours.

2 Meanwhile, heat 1–2 tablespoons duck fat in the pot over medium heat. Add the onions, turnips, sugar, and seasoning and cook, stirring occasionally, for 5–7 minutes, until the vegetables are browned and begin to caramelize. Add to the slow cooker together with the Madeira wine and apricots for the last 1½ hours of cooking. Skim off any fat from the surface, remove the bouquet garni, taste, and add salt and pepper, if needed. Serve on warmed plates on a bed of wide noodles.

traditional method   **PREP** 20 MINS   **COOK** 1½–2 HRS

1 Preheat the oven to 350°F (180°C). Season the duck. Heat the oil and butter in a large Dutch oven over low heat and add the duck, skin-side down. Cook for 20–25 minutes until browned and the fat has rendered. Turn over and cook for only about 5 minutes until browned. Remove and set aside, draining and reserving the duck fat. Heat 2–3 tablespoons of the duck fat in the pot. Add the flour and cook, stirring constantly, for 1–2 minutes until lightly browned but not burnt. Stir in the white wine, stock, bouquet garni, shallots, and salt and pepper, and bring to a boil. Return the duck, cover with the lid, and put in the oven for 40–45 minutes.

2 Meanwhile, heat 1–2 tablespoons duck fat in a heavy-based saucepan over medium heat. Add the onions, turnips, sugar, and salt and pepper and cook, stirring occasionally, for 5–7 minutes, until the vegetables are browned and begin to caramelize. Add to the pot with the Madeira wine and apricots, and top up with hot water if necessary. Cover with the lid and return to the oven for 20–25 minutes, until the duck and vegetables are tender. Skim off any fat from the surface, remove the bouquet garni, taste, and add salt and pepper, if needed. Serve on warmed plates on a bed of wide noodles.

Ordinary ground lamb is transformed into a Middle Eastern favorite, packed with herbs, spices, and zesty flavors and served in a colorful tomato and sweet pepper sauce.

Lebanese meatballs

SERVES 6–8

1½lb (675g) lean ground lamb
2 onions, finely chopped
4 garlic cloves, finely chopped
handful of cilantro, finely chopped
handful of flat-leaf parsley, finely chopped
2 tsp paprika
grated zest and juice of 1 lemon
2 tbsp tomato paste
¼ cup pine nuts

2 eggs
6 tbsp all-purpose flour
salt and freshly ground black pepper
¼ cup olive oil
4 potatoes, peeled and chopped into bite-sized pieces
1 red bell pepper, seeded and sliced
1 yellow bell pepper, seeded and sliced
2 x 14oz (400g) cans chopped tomatoes
1 tsp fennel seeds, crushed

in the slow cooker
PREP 30 MINS **COOK** 30 MINS PRECOOKING; AUTO/LOW 6–8 HRS OR **HIGH** 3–4 HRS

1 Preheat the slow cooker, if required. Put the lamb, onions, garlic, cilantro, parsley, paprika, lemon zest and juice, tomato paste, pine nuts, eggs, and flour in a mixing bowl, and season well with salt and pepper. Mix thoroughly, then mash together with your hands to form a chunky paste. Roughly shape into small balls—you should get about 32 meatballs in all.

2 Heat 3 tablespoons of the oil in a large Dutch oven. Cook the meatballs in batches for 6–8 minutes each, turning frequently to ensure they brown all over. As each batch is cooked, remove and set aside. Wipe out the pot with paper towels, add the potatoes and peppers together with the remaining oil, and cook over high heat, turning frequently, for about 10 minutes until becoming golden brown. Add the tomatoes and fennel seeds, stir to combine, then season as needed. Transfer to the slow cooker, add the meatballs, and turn to coat with the sauce. Cover with the lid and cook on auto/low for 6–8 hours or on high for 3–4 hours. Serve with crusty bread and a green salad.

traditional method
PREP 30 MINS **COOK** 1 HR

1 Preheat the oven to 300°F (150°C). Put the lamb, onions, garlic, cilantro, parsley, paprika, lemon zest and juice, tomato paste, pine nuts, eggs, and flour in a mixing bowl, and season well with salt and pepper. Mix thoroughly, then mash together with your hands to form a chunky paste. Roughly shape into small balls—you should get about 32 meatballs in all.

2 Heat 3 tablespoons of the oil in a large Dutch oven. Cook the meatballs in batches for 6–8 minutes each, turning frequently to ensure they brown all over. As each batch is cooked, remove and set aside. Wipe out the pot with paper towels, add the potatoes and peppers together with the remaining oil, and cook over high heat, turning frequently, for about 10 minutes until becoming golden brown. Add the tomatoes and fennel seeds, stir to combine, then season as needed. Return the meatballs to the pot and stir well to coat with the sauce. Cover with the lid and put in the oven for 1 hour. Check occasionally that it's not drying out, topping up with a little hot water if needed. Serve with crusty bread and a green salad.

The meatballs impart all their wonderful flavors in a tomato sauce made smoky with paprika—use fresh tomatoes if you prefer and roast or grill them, then blend and add to the sauce.

Lamb meatballs in a tomato sauce

SERVES 4–6 **FREEZE** UP TO 3 MONTHS

½ onion, roughly chopped
1 chile, seeded and roughly chopped
2 garlic cloves, peeled and left whole
3½oz (100g) dried chorizo, roughly chopped
about 1lb 2oz (500g) ground lamb
pinch of sweet or hot smoked paprika
salt and freshly ground black pepper
2 tbsp all-purpose flour
¼ cup olive oil

FOR THE TOMATO SAUCE
1 onion, finely chopped
3 garlic cloves, finely chopped
½ cup red wine
2 x 14oz (400g) cans whole tomatoes
1 tsp sweet or hot smoked paprika
1 tbsp chipotle sauce or a splash of
   smoked Tabasco sauce

in the slow cooker   **PREP** 30 MINS   **COOK** 25 MINS PRECOOKING; AUTO/LOW 6–8 HRS OR **HIGH** 3 HRS

1 Preheat the slow cooker, if required. To make the meatballs, put the onion, chile, and garlic into a food processor and pulse until finely chopped. Add the chorizo and pulse until combined. Add the mixture into a bowl, stir in the lamb and paprika, and season with salt and pepper. Mix to a paste with your hands. Roll the mixture into small balls and dust each one with a little flour. Heat some of the oil in a large Dutch oven and cook the meatballs (in batches and with extra oil, if necessary), until brown all over. Remove and set aside. Pour off all but about 2 tablespoons of fat from the pot.

2 To make the sauce, cook the onion in the pot over medium heat for 3–4 minutes until soft. Stir in the garlic and wine, and let the sauce bubble for a minute. Add in the tomatoes, bring to a boil, then reduce to a simmer. Stir in the smoked paprika and chipotle or Tabasco sauce and season. Transfer everything to the slow cooker, including the meatballs. Cover with the lid and cook on auto/low for 6–8 hours or on high for 3 hours. Serve the meatballs and sauce piled over spaghetti.

traditional method   **PREP** 30 MINS   **COOK** 2½ HRS

1 Preheat the oven to 300°F (150°C). To make the meatballs, put the onion, chile, and garlic into a food processor and pulse until finely chopped. Add the chorizo and pulse until combined. Add the mixture into a bowl, stir in the lamb and paprika, and season with salt and pepper. Mix to a paste with your hands. Roll the mixture into small balls and dust each one with a little flour. Heat some of the oil in a large Dutch oven and cook the meatballs (in batches and with extra oil, if necessary), until brown all over. Remove and set aside. Pour off all but about 2 tablespoons of fat from the pot.

2 To make the sauce, cook the onion in the Dutch oven over medium heat for 3–4 minutes until soft. Stir in the garlic and wine, and let the sauce bubble for a minute. Add in the tomatoes, bring to a boil, then reduce to a simmer. Stir in the smoked paprika and chipotle or Tabasco sauce and season. Return the meatballs to the pot and push them so they sit just under the sauce. Cover and put in the oven for 2 hours. Check occasionally that it's not drying out, topping up with a little hot water if needed. Serve the meatballs and sauce piled over spaghetti.

A hotpot is traditionally a filling supper dish that takes minimum preparation and uses foods from the pantry. Any sausages can be used for this dish—and they don't have to be spicy.

Red lentil and spicy sausage hotpot

SERVES 4　❄ **FREEZE** UP TO 1 MONTH

2 tbsp olive oil
8 spicy sausages, halved
1 onion, finely chopped
salt and freshly ground black pepper
1 tbsp paprika
2–3 garlic cloves, finely chopped
pinch of dried chile flakes
few sprigs of rosemary, leaves finely chopped
2 celery stalks, finely chopped

2–3 red peppers, seeded and finely chopped
1 cup red lentils, rinsed and picked over
　for stones
1½ cups hot chicken stock for the slow cooker
　(2½ cups for the traditional method)
handful of flat-leaf parsley, finely chopped
handful of cilantro, finely chopped
chili oil (optional)

in the slow cooker　🕐 **PREP** 35 MINS　**COOK** 20 MINS PRECOOKING; AUTO/LOW 6–8 HRS OR **HIGH** 4 HRS

1 Preheat the slow cooker, if required. Heat half the oil in a large Dutch oven over medium-high heat, add the sausages, and cook for about 8 minutes, turning so they become golden on all sides. Remove and set aside.

2 Add the remaining oil and reduce the heat to medium. Add the onion and cook for 3–4 minutes until soft. Season with salt and pepper, stir in the paprika, garlic, chile flakes, and rosemary, then add the celery and peppers and cook gently for about 5 minutes until softened.

3 Stir in the lentils until they are well coated, then add a little of the stock and increase the heat. Add the remaining stock and bring to a boil, reduce to a simmer, and transfer everything to the slow cooker, including the sausages and the remaining stock. Season, cover with the lid, and cook on auto/low for 6–8 hours or on high for 4 hours. Taste and season as needed, then stir in the herbs and serve with some crusty bread. A drizzle of chili oil is also a tasty addition, if you like it.

traditional method　🕐 **PREP** 35 MINS　**COOK** 1¾ HRS

1 Preheat the oven to 325°F (160°C). Heat half the oil in a large Dutch oven over medium-high heat, add the sausages, and cook for about 8 minutes, turning so they become golden on all sides. Remove and set aside.

2 Add the remaining oil and reduce the heat to medium. Add the onion and cook for 3–4 minutes until soft. Season with salt and pepper, stir in the paprika, garlic, chile flakes, and rosemary, then add the celery and peppers and cook gently for about 5 minutes until softened.

3 Stir in the lentils until they are well coated, then add a little of the stock and increase the heat. Add the remaining stock and bring to a boil, reduce to a simmer, and return the sausages to the pot. Cover and put in the oven for 1½ hours. Check occasionally that it's not drying out, topping up with a little hot water if needed. Taste and season as needed, then stir in the herbs and serve with some crusty bread. A drizzle of chili oil is also a tasty addition, if you like it.

Chicken and mustard is a classic combination—and in this recipe mustard is mixed with honey for a sweet marinade. If you can let the chicken marinate for a few hours, it is even better.

Mustard chicken casserole

SERVES 4–6 ❄️ **FREEZE** UP TO 1 MONTH

2 tbsp whole-grain mustard
1 tbsp English mustard
2 tbsp honey
8 bone-in chicken thighs, skin on
salt and freshly ground black pepper
2 tbsp olive oil
2 onions, roughly chopped

10oz (300g) parsnips, peeled and roughly chopped
few sprigs of thyme
2 cups hot vegetable or chicken stock for the slow cooker (3 cups for the traditional method)
bunch of flat-leaf parsley, finely chopped

in the slow cooker

PREP 10 MINS, PLUS MARINATING   **COOK** 10–15 MINS PRECOOKING; **AUTO/LOW** 6–8 HRS OR **HIGH** 3–4 HRS

1 Mix the mustards together in a bowl and stir in the honey. Season the chicken thighs well with salt and pepper, then smother them with the mustard mixture. Cover and leave to marinate for 30 minutes, if time permits.

2 Preheat the slow cooker, if required. Heat half the oil in a large Dutch oven over medium-high heat and add the chicken pieces, a few at a time. Cook for 6–10 minutes until golden—be careful, because the honey may cause them to blacken quickly. Remove and set aside.

3 Heat the remaining oil in the pot over medium heat, add the onions, and toss them around in the pot to coat in any juices. Stir to scrape up the sticky bits from the bottom, then add the parsnips and thyme. Transfer everything to the slow cooker, pour in the stock, and add the chicken pieces. Season, cover with the lid, and cook on auto/low for 6–8 hours or on high for 3–4 hours. Add the parsley, taste, and season, if necessary. Serve with steamed leeks or greens.

traditional method

PREP 10 MINS, PLUS MARINATING   **COOK** 1¾ HRS

1 Preheat the oven to 325°F (160°C). Mix the mustards together in a bowl and stir in the honey. Season the chicken thighs well with salt and pepper, then smother them with the mustard mixture. Cover and leave to marinate for 30 minutes, if time permits.

2 Heat half the oil in a large Dutch oven over medium-high heat and add the chicken pieces, a few at a time. Cook for 6–10 minutes until golden—be careful, because the honey may cause them to blacken quickly. Remove and set aside.

3 Heat the remaining oil in the pot over medium heat, add the onions, and toss them around the pot to coat in any juices. Stir to scrape up the sticky bits from the bottom, then add the parsnips and thyme. Pour in the stock, bring to a boil, and then reduce to a simmer. Return the chicken to the pot together with any juices, nestling them in between the parsnips and making sure they are covered in liquid. Season, cover with the lid, and put in the oven for 1½ hours. Check occasionally that it's not drying out, topping up with a little hot water if needed. Add the parsley, taste, and season, if necessary. Serve with steamed leeks or greens.

The more mature the chicken, the better this dish will be—French cooks use a boiling fowl or, best of all, the traditional male cock bird. Mashed potatoes and peas are the perfect accompaniment.

Chicken in white wine

SERVES 4–6

1 onion, thinly sliced
1 celery stalk, thinly sliced
1 carrot, peeled and thinly sliced
2 garlic cloves, 1 left whole, 1 chopped
6 black peppercorns
1½ cups medium-dry white wine
4½lb (2kg) chicken, cut into 8 pieces
2 tbsp olive oil
1 tbsp vegetable oil

1 tbsp butter
18–20 baby onions, peeled
3 tbsp all-purpose flour
2 shallots, chopped
2 cups hot chicken stock, for both methods
1 bouquet garni
salt and freshly ground black pepper
9oz (250g) mushrooms, quartered

in the slow cooker   **PREP** 30 MINS, PLUS MARINATING   **COOK** 15 MINS PRECOOKING; **AUTO/LOW** 6–8 HRS OR **HIGH** 3–4 HRS

1 Put the onion, celery, carrot, whole garlic clove, and peppercorns in a pan with the wine and bring to a boil. Simmer for 5 minutes, then allow to cool. Put the chicken in a bowl, pour in the marinade, and add the olive oil. Cover and refrigerate for 8–12 hours, turning the pieces occasionally. Remove the chicken and dry on paper towels. Strain the marinade and reserve the liquid and vegetables.

2 Preheat the slow cooker, if required. Heat the vegetable oil and butter in a large Dutch oven over medium-high heat until foaming. Cook the chicken for about 5 minutes on each side, skin-side first, until brown. Remove and set aside. Cook the baby onions for 6–8 minutes until brown. Discard all but 2 tablespoons of the fat, add the reserved vegetables, and cook for 4–5 minutes to soften. Sprinkle in the flour and cook, stirring, until lightly browned. Stir in the marinade, shallots, chopped garlic, stock, bouquet garni, and salt and pepper. Bring to a boil, then transfer to the slow cooker, add the chicken, cover with the lid, and cook on auto/low for 6–8 hours or on high for 3–4 hours. Stir in the mushrooms for the last 10 minutes of cooking.

traditional method   **PREP** 30 MINS, PLUS MARINATING   **COOK** 1½–1¾ HRS

1 Put the onion, celery, carrot, whole garlic clove, and peppercorns in a pan with the wine and bring to a boil. Simmer for 5 minutes, then allow to cool. Put the chicken in a bowl, pour in the marinade, and add the olive oil. Cover and refrigerate for 8–12 hours, turning the pieces occasionally. Remove the chicken and dry on paper towels. Strain the marinade and reserve the liquid and vegetables.

2 Heat the vegetable oil and butter in a large Dutch oven over medium-high heat until foaming. Cook the chicken for about 5 minutes on each side, skin-side first, until brown. Remove and set aside. Cook the baby onions for 6–8 minutes until brown. Discard all but 2 tablespoons of the fat, add the reserved vegetables, and cook for 4–5 minutes to soften. Sprinkle in the flour and cook, stirring, until lightly browned. Stir in the marinade, shallots, chopped garlic, stock, bouquet garni, and salt and pepper. Bring to a boil, return the chicken pieces, cover, and simmer for 45–60 minutes until the pieces are just tender when pierced with a fork. Stir in the mushrooms for the last 10 minutes of cooking.

Caraway seed dumplings are delicious with the chicken, as well as being an aid to the digestion. Steamed, crisp green beans or sugarsnap peas would provide the ideal crunch alongside.

Chicken paprika with dumplings

⊙ **SERVES** 4 ❄ **FREEZE** UP TO 3 MONTHS ♡ **HEALTHY**

3/4 cup self-rising flour
½ tsp salt
¼ cup shortening
2 tsp caraway seeds
4 chicken breasts on the bone
salt and freshly ground black pepper
2 tbsp vegetable oil
1 large onion, diced

2 garlic cloves, finely chopped
2 tbsp paprika, plus more to taste
1 tbsp all-purpose flour
14oz (400g) can chopped tomatoes
1¼ cups hot chicken stock for the slow cooker
  (2 cups for the traditional method)
½ cup sour cream

in the slow cooker ⏱ **PREP** 30 MINS **COOK** 30 MINS PRECOOKING; AUTO/LOW 6–8 HRS OR **HIGH** 3–4 HRS

1 Sift the flour and salt into a large bowl. Mix in the shortening and caraway seeds and make a well in the center. Add cold water, a little at a time, and draw in the flour, stirring to combine. Add more water until it is all combined; the dough should be moist but not soft or sticky. Roll into ¾in (2cm) balls, cover, and refrigerate.

2 Preheat the slow cooker, if required. Season the chicken. Heat the oil in a large Dutch oven over medium-high heat. Add the chicken skin-side down (in batches, if necessary) and cook for about 5 minutes on each side until brown. Remove and set aside. Add the onion and cook over medium heat for 2–3 minutes until soft. Add the garlic and continue cooking for 3–5 minutes longer. Stir in the paprika. Cook gently, stirring occasionally, for about 5 minutes. Stir in the flour, add the tomatoes, stock, and seasoning, and bring to a boil. Transfer everything to the slow cooker, including the chicken, cover with the lid, and cook on auto/low for 6–8 hours or on high for 3–4 hours. Add the dumplings to the slow cooker for the last 40 minutes, pushing them down into the sauce. Stir in the sour cream to serve.

traditional method ⏱ **PREP** 30 MINS **COOK** 1½ HRS

1 Sift the flour and salt into a large bowl. Mix in the shortening and caraway seeds and make a well in the center. Add cold water, a little at a time, and draw in the flour, stirring to combine. Add more water until it is all combined; the dough should be moist but not soft or sticky. Roll into ¾in (2cm) balls, cover, and refrigerate.

2 Preheat the oven to 350°F (180°C). Season the chicken. Heat the oil in a large Dutch oven over medium-high heat. Add the chicken skin-side down (in batches, if necessary) and cook for about 5 minutes on each side until brown. Remove and set aside. Add the onion and cook over medium heat for 2–3 minutes until soft. Add the garlic and continue cooking for 3–5 minutes longer. Stir in the paprika. Cook gently, stirring occasionally, for about 5 minutes. Stir in the flour, add the tomatoes, stock, and seasoning, and bring to a boil. Return the chicken, cover, and cook in the oven for 45–60 minutes until the pieces are just tender when pierced with a fork. Check occasionally that it's not drying out, topping up with a little hot water if needed. Add the dumplings to the pot for the last 30 minutes, pushing them down into the sauce. Stir in the sour cream to serve.

Tagines

This dish is slow cooked in a Dutch oven, but you could always use a tagine if you have one. Preserved lemons have a subtle and distinctive flavor and are available at specialty supermarkets.

Chicken and green olive tagine

⊚ **SERVES** 4–6 ❄ **FREEZE** UP TO 1 MONTH

4 tbsp olive oil
1 tbsp ground ginger
2 tbsp paprika
pinch of cayenne pepper
1 tsp ground turmeric
salt and freshly ground black pepper
8 chicken drumsticks
4 onions, roughly chopped
4 garlic cloves, finely chopped
pinch of saffron threads
1in (2.5cm) piece of fresh ginger,
  peeled and grated

4 large tomatoes, roughly chopped
juice of ½ lemon for the slow cooker
  (1 lemon for the traditional method)
2 cups hot vegetable stock for the slow cooker
  (3 cups for the traditional method)
about ¾ cup green olives in brine, pitted
  and rinsed
2 preserved lemons, halved, flesh discarded,
  and rind shredded (optional)
handful of cilantro, chopped
handful of flat-leaf parsley, chopped

in the slow cooker 🕐 **PREP** 20 MINS, **COOK** 15 MINS PRECOOKING;
PLUS MARINATING **AUTO/LOW** 6–8 HRS OR **HIGH** 3–4 HRS

1 Preheat the slow cooker, if required. In a bowl, mix half the oil together with the spices and season with salt and pepper. Add the chicken drumsticks and toss until they are really well coated. Cover and leave overnight in the fridge, if time allows, or leave for 30 minutes. Heat a large Dutch oven or tagine, add the chicken drumsticks (in batches and with extra oil, if necessary), and cook for 6–8 minutes until golden. Remove from the pot and set aside.

2 Heat 1 tablespoon of the oil in the pot over medium heat, add the onion, and cook for 3–4 minutes until soft. Then stir in the garlic, saffron, and grated ginger and cook for a minute more. Transfer everything to the slow cooker and add the tomatoes, chicken, lemon juice, stock, olives, and the preserved lemons, if using. Season, cover with the lid, and cook on auto/low for 6–8 hours or on high for 3–4 hours. Sprinkle the herbs over and serve with couscous.

traditional method 🕐 **PREP** 20 MINS, PLUS MARINATING **COOK** 2 HRS

1 In a bowl, mix half the oil together with the spices and season with salt and pepper. Add the chicken drumsticks and toss until they are really well coated. Cover and leave overnight in the fridge, if time allows, or leave for 30 minutes. Preheat the oven to 375°F (190°C). Heat a large Dutch oven or tagine, add the chicken drumsticks (in batches and with extra oil, if necessary), and cook for 6–8 minutes until golden. Remove from the pot and set aside.

2 Heat 1 tablespoon of the oil in the pot, add the onion, and cook for 3–4 minutes until soft. Then stir in the garlic, grated ginger, and saffron and cook for a minute more. Stir in the tomatoes and return the chicken to the pot with any juices and the lemon juice. Season and pour in the stock. Bring to a boil, then reduce to a simmer, cover, and put in the oven for 1 hour. Add the olives and preserved lemons, if using, and cook for 30 minutes more. Check occasionally that it's not drying out, topping up with a little hot water if needed. Sprinkle the herbs over and serve with couscous.

Peppers add a fabulous sweetness to the dish—use a mixture of red, yellow, and orange bell peppers for maximum color impact, and use green olives instead of black, if you prefer.

Chicken with olives and peppers

⊙ **SERVES** 4   ⊙ **HEALTHY**

3 tbsp olive oil
6 small onions, 4 thinly sliced and 2 finely chopped
4 pieces bone-in chicken, skin on
about 1lb (500g) tomatoes, skinned and chopped
3 red bell peppers, seeded and roughly chopped
1 lemon, cut into wedges
1 garlic clove, finely chopped

¼ cup olive oil
2 tsp ground cumin
2 tsp ground coriander
salt and freshly ground black pepper
½ cup whole pitted black olives
3–4 sprigs of fresh cilantro, chopped

in the slow cooker   🕐 **PREP** 20 MINS   **COOK** 10 MINS PRECOOKING; AUTO/LOW 6–8 HRS OR HIGH 3–4 HRS

1 Preheat the slow cooker, if required. Heat the oil in a heavy-based saucepan over medium heat, add the sliced onions, and cook for 5 minutes until soft. Remove and set aside. Put the chicken in the slow cooker and cover with the sliced onions, then with the chopped tomatoes, peppers, and one of the lemon wedges.

2 Put the chopped onions into the pan and cook for 5 minutes to soften. Transfer to a bowl and add the garlic, oil, ground cumin, and ground coriander, and add salt and pepper. Spoon the mixture over the chicken and sprinkle over the olives.

3 Cover with the lid and cook on auto/low for 6–8 hours or on high for 3–4 hours. Stir in the fresh cilantro, taste the sauce for seasoning, and remove the lemon wedge. Serve the chicken with couscous or rice, and with the remaining lemon wedges on the side.

traditional method   🕐 **PREP** 20 MINS   **COOK** 1½ HRS

1 Heat the oven to 350°F (180°C). Heat the oil in a heavy-based saucepan over medium heat, add the sliced onions, and cook for 5 minutes until soft. Put the chicken in a large Dutch oven or tagine and cover with the sliced onions, then with the chopped tomatoes, peppers, and one of the lemon wedges.

2 Put the chopped onions into the pan and cook for 5 minutes to soften. Transfer to a bowl and add the garlic, oil, ground cumin, and ground coriander, and add salt and pepper. Spoon the mixture over the chicken and sprinkle over the olives.

3 Cover with the lid and put in the oven for about 1½ hours until the chicken is tender when pierced with a fork. Stir in the fresh cilantro, taste the sauce for seasoning, and remove the lemon wedge. Serve the chicken with couscous or rice, and with the remaining lemon wedges on the side.

Light, fresh, and zingy, this vegetarian version of a tagine is full of punchy flavors. It is a good dish to prepare ahead because the flavors improve with reheating.

Zucchini, herb, and lemon tagine

SERVES 4 **HEALTHY**

2 tbsp olive oil
1 red onion, finely chopped
salt and freshly ground black pepper
3 garlic cloves, finely chopped
pinch of fennel seeds
pinch of ground cinnamon
1–2 tsp harissa paste, plus extra to serve

2 preserved lemons, quartered and flesh discarded
14oz (400g) can whole tomatoes, chopped
1 head broccoli, broken into florets
3 zucchini, trimmed and sliced
juice of 1 lemon
handful of dill, finely chopped
handful of flat-leaf parsley, finely chopped

in the slow cooker **PREP** 25 MINS **COOK** 15 MINS PRECOOKING; **HIGH** 2–3 HRS

1 Preheat the slow cooker, if required. Heat half the oil in a large heavy-based saucepan or tagine over low heat, add the onions, and cook for 8 minutes until soft and translucent. Season well with salt and pepper, then stir in the garlic, fennel seeds, cinnamon, harissa, and preserved lemons.

2 Add the tomatoes and stir well, crushing them with the back of a wooden spoon. Bring to a boil, then reduce to a simmer and transfer to the slow cooker. Cover with the lid and cook on high for 2–3 hours.

3 Cook the broccoli in a pan of boiling salted water for 3–5 minutes or until tender, then drain and refresh in cold water. Drain again and set aside. Heat the remaining oil in a frying pan over low heat, add the zucchini and seasoning, and cook, stirring frequently, for 5 minutes or until they start to color a little. Stir in the lemon juice and dill and transfer with the broccoli to the slow cooker, for the last 15 minutes of cooking. Taste and season as needed, then stir in the parsley. Serve on warmed plates with couscous, lemon wedges, and a spoonful of harissa on the side.

traditional method **PREP** 25 MINS **COOK** 45–55 MINS

1 Heat half the oil in a large heavy-based saucepan or tagine over low heat, add the onions, and cook for 8 minutes until soft and translucent. Season well with salt and pepper, then stir in the garlic, fennel seeds, cinnamon, harissa, and preserved lemons.

2 Add the tomatoes and stir well, crushing them with the back of a wooden spoon. Bring to a boil, then reduce to a simmer and cook over low heat for 30–40 minutes. If the sauce starts to dry out, top up with a little hot water.

3 Cook the broccoli in a pan of boiling salted water for 3–5 minutes or until tender, then drain and refresh in cold water. Drain again and set aside. Heat the remaining oil in a frying pan over low heat, add the zucchini and seasoning, and cook, stirring frequently, for 5 minutes or until they start to color a little. Add the lemon juice and stir in the dill. Add the broccoli and zucchini to the sauce and stir in the parsley. Serve on warmed plates with couscous, lemon wedges, and a spoonful of harissa on the side.

Chickpeas are a typical Middle Eastern ingredient. If you have the dried type, soak them in water for at least eight hours. Strain through a sieve, then rinse them under cold running water.

Middle Eastern lentils and peppers

SERVES 4–6   **HEALTHY**

½ cup brown or green lentils, rinsed
salt and freshly ground black pepper
1 tbsp olive oil
1 onion, finely chopped
3 garlic cloves, finely chopped
pinch of dried oregano
grated zest and juice of 1 lemon
½ tsp ground allspice

pinch of grated nutmeg
½ tsp ground cumin
2 red peppers, seeded and sliced into strips
heaping 1 cup rice
2 cups hot vegetable stock for the slow cooker
    (3 cups for the traditional method)
14oz (400g) can chickpeas, drained and rinsed
bunch of parsley, finely chopped

in the slow cooker   **PREP** 15 MINS   **COOK** 20 MINS PRECOOKING;
AUTO/LOW 4–6 HRS OR **HIGH** 11/2–2 HRS

1 Put the lentils in a large heavy-based pan or tagine, season with salt and pepper, and cover with water. Bring to a boil, then simmer for about 30 minutes until they are beginning to soften, but don't let them turn mushy. Drain and set aside.

2 Preheat the slow cooker, if required. Heat the oil in the same heavy-based pan over medium heat, add the onion, and cook for 3–4 minutes until soft. Add seasoning, then stir in the garlic, oregano, lemon zest, allspice, nutmeg, and cumin and cook for a minute. Add the peppers and cook for about 5 minutes, stirring to coat with the spices. Cook for 2–3 minutes until soft, then stir in the rice and a little stock and bring to a boil. Transfer everything to the slow cooker with the chickpeas and just enough stock to cover. Add the lid and cook on high for 1½–2 hours.

3 About 5 minutes before the end of the cooking time, stir in the lentils, put the lid back on, and let the lentils warm through. Taste and season, then add the parsley and lemon juice. Serve with yogurt and pita bread.

traditional method   **PREP** 15 MINS   **COOK** 45 MINS

1 Put the lentils in a large heavy-based pan or tagine, season with salt and pepper, and cover with water. Bring to a boil, then simmer for about 30 minutes until they are beginning to soften, but don't let them turn mushy. Drain and set aside.

2 Meanwhile, heat the oil in another heavy-based pan over medium heat, add the onion, and cook for 3–4 minutes until soft. Add seasoning, then stir in the garlic, oregano, lemon zest, allspice, nutmeg, and cumin and cook for a minute.

3 Add the peppers and cook for about 5 minutes, stirring to coat with spices. Cook for 2–3 minutes until soft, then stir in the rice and little stock. Bring to a boil, add most of the stock, and boil for a minute. Reduce to a simmer, add the chickpeas, and cook on very low heat for 15–20 minutes. Check occasionally that it's not drying out, topping up with a little hot stock if needed. Stir in the lentils, taste and season, then add the parsley and lemon juice. Serve with yogurt and pita bread.

This is a version of the classic Moroccan tagine, a mixture of chicken, fruit, and spices baked in a conical earthenware dish. You can buy the chicken in four pieces instead of cutting it yourself.

Moroccan chicken baked with spices

SERVES 4

3–4lb (1.5kg) chicken, quartered
6 onions, 4 finely sliced and 2 finely chopped
about 1lb (500g) tomatoes, skinned and chopped
pinch of saffron threads, soaked in 3–4 tbsp
  boiling water
⅓ cup ready-to-eat dried apricots, chopped

2 tbsp honey
2 tsp ground cinnamon
1 tsp ground ginger
few sprigs of parsley, chopped
salt and freshly ground black pepper
¼ cup olive oil

in the slow cooker   **PREP** 15 MINS   **COOK** AUTO/LOW 5–6 HRS OR **HIGH** 4 HRS

1 Preheat the slow cooker, if required. Put the chicken in the slow cooker, then cover with the sliced onions and chopped tomatoes.

2 Mix together the chopped onions, saffron and its liquid, apricots, honey, cinnamon, ginger, and chopped parsley in a bowl; add salt and pepper and olive oil. Spoon the mixture over the chicken.

3 Cover with the lid and cook on auto/low for 5–6 hours or on high for 4 hours. Taste the sauce and add salt and pepper, if needed. Transfer the chicken and sauce straight from the slow cooker onto warmed plates. Serve with couscous.

traditional method   **PREP** 15 MINS   **COOK** 1½ HRS

1 Preheat the oven to 350°F (180°C). Put the chicken in a large Dutch oven or a tagine. Cover with the sliced onions and chopped tomatoes.

2 Mix together the chopped onions, saffron and its liquid, apricots, honey, cinnamon, ginger, and chopped parsley in a bowl; add salt and pepper and olive oil. Spoon the mixture over the chicken.

3 Cover with the lid and put in the oven for about 1½ hours until the chicken is tender when pierced with a fork. Check occasionally that it's not drying out, topping up with only 1 tablespoon of water at a time to stop it from browning too much. Taste the sauce and add salt and pepper, if needed. Transfer the chicken and sauce straight from the pot onto warmed plates. Serve with couscous.

Dried apricots and chutney give an authentic sweetness to this fragrant tagine. The mint adds a freshness to temper the heat. You could use mutton instead, if your butcher has it.

Fiery lamb and chutney tagine

SERVES 4–6 **FREEZE** UP TO 1 MONTH

1 onion, thinly sliced
1 tsp ground coriander
1 tsp ground cumin
1 tsp ground ginger
1 tsp dried thyme
1–2 tsp cayenne pepper
2 tbsp sunflower oil
2lb (900g) boneless lamb, such as shoulder
  or chump steaks, cut into bite-sized pieces

2 tbsp all-purpose flour
1¼ cups orange juice
1¾ cups hot chicken stock for the slow cooker
  (2 cups for the traditional method)
½ cup ready-to-eat dried apricots
¼ cup peach or apricot chutney, or any sweet
  and spicy fruit chutney
salt and freshly ground black pepper
mint leaves, to serve

in the slow cooker   **PREP** 10 MINS, PLUS MARINATING   **COOK** 10 MINS PRECOOKING; AUTO/LOW 6–8 HRS OR **HIGH** 3–4 HRS

1 Put the onion, coriander, cumin, ginger, thyme, cayenne, and 1 tablespoon of the oil in a large, non-metallic bowl, then mix in the lamb. Cover and refrigerate for at least 3 hours or overnight.

2 Preheat the slow cooker, if required. Put the flour in a small bowl and slowly stir in the orange juice until smooth, then set aside. Heat the remaining oil in a large Dutch oven over high heat. Add the lamb mixture and cook, stirring frequently, for about 5 minutes until browned.

3 Stir the flour mixture into the pot with the stock, then stir in the apricots and chutney. Bring to a boil and transfer everything to the slow cooker. Cover with the lid and cook on auto/low for 6–8 hours or on high for 3–4 hours. Taste and add salt and pepper, if needed. Sprinkle the mint leaves over and serve with couscous.

traditional method   **PREP** 10 MINS, PLUS MARINATING   **COOK** 1½ HRS

1 Put the onion, coriander, cumin, ginger, thyme, cayenne, and 1 tablespoon of the oil in a large, non-metallic bowl, then mix in the lamb. Cover and refrigerate for at least 3 hours or overnight.

2 Preheat the oven to 325°F (160°C). Put the flour in a small bowl and slowly stir in the orange juice until smooth, then set aside. Heat the remaining oil in a large Dutch oven over high heat. Add the lamb mixture and cook, stirring frequently, for about 5 minutes until browned.

3 Stir the flour mixture into the pot with the stock. Bring to a boil, stirring, then remove the pot from the heat, cover, and put in the oven for 1 hour. Remove the pot from the oven, stir in the apricots and chutney, re-cover, and return to the oven. Cook for a further 20 minutes or until the lamb is tender. Taste and add salt and pepper, if needed. Sprinkle the mint leaves over and serve with couscous.

One of the ingredients that gives a Moroccan tagine its unique flavor is preserved lemon. The lemons are pickled in salt water with lemon juice and are available at large supermarkets.

Mixed vegetable tagine

SERVES 4–6   **FREEZE** UP TO 3 MONTHS   **HEALTHY**

1 tbsp olive oil
1 red onion, roughly chopped
salt and freshly ground black pepper
3 garlic cloves, finely chopped
2in (5cm) piece of fresh ginger, peeled
  and grated
1 tsp ground turmeric
pinch of saffron threads
1 tsp coriander seeds, ground
½ tsp cumin seeds
4 large potatoes, peeled and chopped into
  chunky pieces

3 carrots, peeled and chopped into chunky pieces
1 fennel bulb, trimmed and chopped into
  chunky pieces
4 tomatoes, finely chopped
about 2½ cups hot vegetable stock, for both methods
handful of mixed olives, pitted and halved (optional)
2 preserved lemons, halved, flesh discarded and
  peel chopped (optional)
bunch of cilantro leaves, roughly chopped

in the slow cooker   **PREP** 20–25 MINS   **COOK** 15 MINS PRECOOKING; **HIGH** 3 HRS

1 Preheat the slow cooker, if required. Heat the oil in a large heavy-based pan or tagine over medium heat, add the onion, and cook for 3–4 minutes until soft. Season with salt and pepper, stir in the garlic, ginger, turmeric, saffron, coriander seeds, and cumin, and cook for 2 minutes.

2 Add the potatoes and toss to coat, then add the carrots and fennel and stir so everything is well combined. Cook for a few minutes, then add the tomatoes, and transfer everything to the slow cooker.

3 Pour in enough stock to cover the vegetables, season, and cover with the lid. Cook on high for 3 hours. Taste and season, then stir in the olives and lemon, if using, and half the cilantro leaves. Transfer to a serving dish and sprinkle over the remaining cilantro leaves. Serve with couscous.

traditional method   **PREP** 20–25 MINS   **COOK** 50 MINS

1 Heat the oil in a large heavy-based pan or tagine over medium heat, add the onion, and cook for 3–4 minutes until soft. Season with salt and pepper, stir in the garlic, ginger, turmeric, saffron, coriander seeds, and cumin, and cook for a couple of minutes.

2 Add the potatoes and toss to coat, then add the carrots and fennel and stir so everything is well combined. Cook for a few minutes, then add the tomatoes and pour in just enough stock to cover the vegetables.

3 Cover with the lid and simmer very gently for 30–40 minutes until the vegetables are soft and a lot of the liquid has evaporated. Top up with more hot stock if needed. Taste and season, then stir in the olives and lemon, if using, and half the cilantro leaves. Transfer to a serving dish and sprinkle over the remaining cilantro leaves. Serve with couscous.

The flavors of this tagine are a harmonious blend of citrus and spice. If you can't find the spice mix ras-el-hanout, use a pinch each of ground cinnamon and ground nutmeg instead.

Chicken and orange tagine

SERVES 4 · **FREEZE** UP TO 3 MONTHS

8 bone-in chicken thighs, skin on
1 tsp ras-el-hanout spice (optional)
salt and freshly ground black pepper
1–2 tbsp olive oil
1 red onion, finely chopped
2 tsp coriander seeds, half of them crushed
2 green chilies, seeded and finely chopped

3 garlic cloves, finely chopped
2 oranges, segmented and juice reserved
4 large tomatoes, roughly chopped
2 cups hot chicken or vegetable stock
 for the slow cooker (3 cups for
 the traditional method)
handful of cilantro, roughly chopped

in the slow cooker · **PREP** 20 MINS · **COOK** 15 MINS PRECOOKING; AUTO/LOW 6–8 HRS OR HIGH 3–4 HRS

1 Preheat the slow cooker, if required. Smother the chicken with the ras-el-hanout spice mix, if using, and season with salt and pepper. Heat half the oil in a large Dutch oven or tagine over medium-high heat, and cook the chicken (in batches, if necessary) for 6–8 minutes until golden. Remove and set aside. Heat the remaining oil in the pot over medium heat, add the onion, and cook for 3–4 minutes until soft. Season with salt and pepper, stir in the coriander seeds, chilies, and garlic, and cook for a further minute.

2 Add the orange juice, increase the heat, and let the sauce bubble for a minute, then return the chicken to the pot together with its juices. Add the tomatoes and a little of the stock and bring to a boil, then transfer everything to the slow cooker. Pour in the remaining stock, cover with the lid, and cook on auto/low for 6–8 hours or on high for 3–4 hours. Add the orange segments for the last 30 minutes of cooking. Stir in most of the cilantro and serve with couscous, with the remaining cilantro sprinkled over the dish.

traditonal method · **PREP** 20 MINS · **COOK** 1¾ HRS

1 Preheat the oven to 375°F (190°C). Smother the chicken with the ras-el-hanout spice mix, if using, and season well with salt and pepper. Heat half the oil in a large Dutch oven or tagine over medium-high heat, and cook the chicken (in batches, if necessary) for 6–8 minutes until golden. Remove and set aside.

2 Heat the remaining oil in the pot over medium heat, add the onion, and cook for 3–4 minutes until soft. Season with salt and pepper, stir in the coriander seeds, chilies, and garlic, and cook for a further minute. Add the orange juice, increase the heat, and let the sauce bubble for a minute, then return the chicken to the pot together with its juices.

3 Add the tomatoes and a little of the stock and bring to a boil, then pour in the remaining stock and boil for 1–2 minutes. Reduce the heat, cover with the lid, and put in the oven for 1½ hours. Check occasionally that it's not drying out, topping up with a little hot water if needed. Add the orange segments for the last 30 minutes of cooking. Stir in most of the cilantro and serve with couscous, with the remaining cilantro sprinkled over the dish.

Fig adds a sweet stickiness to this tagine and works well with lamb. Swap the walnuts for hazelnuts or pecans, if you prefer, and you could use fresh figs when they are in season.

Lamb tagine with walnuts and figs

SERVES 4–6   **FREEZE** UP TO 3 MONTHS

1–2 tbsp olive oil
2lb (900g) boneless lean lamb, cut into
  bite-sized pieces
salt and freshly ground black pepper
2 onions, sliced
3 garlic cloves, peeled and finely chopped
grated zest and juice of 1 lemon
1 tsp ground cinnamon
½ tsp ground coriander
½ tsp ground ginger

2 tsp paprika
1 tbsp tomato paste
1 tbsp honey
about 12 dried figs, roughly chopped
2 x 14oz (400g) cans chickpeas, drained
about 1 cup hot vegetable stock for the slow cooker
  (3 cups for the traditional method)
½ cup walnut halves, roughly chopped
large handful of flat-leaf parsley, roughly chopped

in the slow cooker   ● PREP 20 MINS   **COOK** 15 MINS PRECOOKING;
AUTO/LOW 6–8 HRS OR **HIGH** 3–4 HRS

1 Preheat the slow cooker, if required. Heat 1 tablespoon of the oil in a large Dutch oven or tagine over medium-high heat, season the lamb with salt and pepper, and cook (in batches, if necessary) for 6–8 minutes until browned all over. Remove and set aside.

2 Cook the onions, garlic, and lemon zest and juice (together with a little more oil, if necessary) in the pot over medium heat for 2 minutes. Add seasoning, then stir in the spices and tomato paste.

3 Transfer everything to the slow cooker, including the lamb, add the honey, figs, and chickpeas, then pour in the stock until it just covers the meat. Season and cover with the lid, and cook on auto/low for 6–8 hours or on high for 3–4 hours. Stir in the walnuts and most of the parsley for the last 30 minutes of cooking. Taste and season, if needed, and sprinkle with the remaining parsley. Serve with couscous.

traditional method   ● PREP 20 MINS   **COOK** 1¾–2¼ HRS

1 Preheat the oven to 300°F (150°C). Heat 1 tablespoon of the oil in a large Dutch oven or tagine over medium-high heat, season the lamb with salt and pepper, and cook (in batches, if necessary) for 6–8 minutes until browned all over. Remove and set aside.

2 Cook the onions, garlic, and lemon zest and juice (together with a little more oil, if necessary) in the pot over medium heat for 2 minutes. Add seasoning, then stir in the spices and tomato paste.

3 Add the honey, figs, chickpeas, and stock. Bring to a boil, then reduce the heat to a simmer, return the meat, and add the walnuts and most of the parsley. Cover with the lid and put in the oven for 1½–2 hours. Check occasionally that it's not drying out, topping up with a little hot water if needed. Taste and season, if needed, and sprinkle with the remaining parsley. Serve with couscous.

Hearty chestnuts give substance to this otherwise traditional combination of lamb and orange. The tagine tastes even better reheated the next day as the flavors have melded together.

Slow-cooked lamb with orange and chestnuts

SERVES 4–6 **FREEZE** UP TO 1 MONTH

½ tsp ground cinnamon
½ tsp ground cumin
½ tsp ground coriander
salt and freshly ground black pepper
2lb (900g) boneless lean leg of lamb, diced
2–3 tbsp olive oil
1 onion, chopped

1 cinnamon stick
about 1 cup jarred or canned cooked chestnuts
½ cup fresh orange juice
2 cups hot lamb stock for the slow cooker
  (3 cups for the traditional method)
2 oranges, peeled and cut into thick slices
bunch of cilantro, roughly chopped

in the slow cooker **PREP** 15 MINS **COOK** 15–25 MINS PRECOOKING; **AUTO/LOW** 6–8 HRS

1 Preheat the slow cooker, if required. In a large bowl, mix the spices together and season with salt and pepper, then toss the meat in the mixture. Heat half the oil in a large Dutch oven or tagine over medium-high heat, add the lamb (in batches and with extra oil, if necessary), and cook for 6–8 minutes or until the lamb is browned on all sides. Remove and put in the slow cooker.

2 Heat the remaining oil in the pot over medium heat. Add the onion and cinnamon stick, and stir so the onion is coated in any residual lamb juices. Cook for 3–4 minutes until the onions are soft. Then stir in the chestnuts and pour in the orange juice. Increase the heat and let it bubble for a minute, stirring. Transfer everything to the slow cooker and pour in the stock. Cover and cook on auto/low for 6–8 hours. Add the orange slices for the last 30 minutes of cooking. Check for seasoning, stir in the cilantro, and serve with couscous.

traditional method **PREP** 15 MINS **COOK** 2¼ HRS

1 Preheat the oven to 325°F (160°C). In a large bowl, mix the spices together and season with salt and pepper, then toss the meat in the mixture. Heat half the oil in a large Dutch oven or tagine over a medium-high heat, add the lamb (in batches and with extra oil, if necessary), and cook for 6–8 minutes or until the lamb is browned on all sides. Remove and set aside.

2 Heat the remaining oil in the pot over medium heat. Add the onion and cinnamon stick, and stir so the onion is coated in any residual lamb juices. Cook for 3–4 minutes until the onions are soft. Then stir in the chestnuts and pour in the orange juice. Increase the heat and let it bubble for a minute, stirring. Reduce the heat and return the lamb to the pot along with any juices from the lamb.

3 Pour in the stock, bring to a boil, then reduce to a simmer, cover, and put in the oven for 2 hours. Check occasionally that it's not drying out, topping up with a little hot water, if needed. Add the orange slices for the last 30 minutes of cooking. Check for seasoning, stir in the cilantro, and serve with couscous.

The beef in this tagine is slowly cooked in spices for maximum flavor. Bottom round is the best cut for slow cooking; but if it isn't available top rump or topside are good alternatives.

Cumin beef tagine

⊘ **SERVES** 4–6 ❋ **FREEZE** UP TO 3 MONTHS

2lb (900g) lean beef, such as bottom round,
  cut into 1in (2.5cm) cubes
2 tsp ground cumin
2 tbsp flour, seasoned with salt and pepper
3 tbsp olive oil
1 large onion, chopped
4 garlic cloves, peeled and crushed
1 tsp ground ginger
1 tsp ground cinnamon

½ tsp cayenne pepper
1¾ cups hot chicken stock for the slow cooker
  (2 cups for the traditional method)
1 small butternut squash, peeled, seeded,
  and diced
3 red bell peppers, seeded and chopped into strips
handful of raisins (optional)
salt and freshly ground black pepper

in the slow cooker ⏱ **PREP** 20 MINS **COOK** 15 MINS PRECOOKING;
AUTO/LOW 6–8 HRS OR **HIGH** 3–4 HRS

1 Preheat the slow cooker, if required. Toss the beef in the cumin so it is evenly coated, then do the same with the flour. Heat the oil in a large Dutch oven or tagine over medium-high heat, and cook the beef in batches for about 10 minutes until evenly browned.

2 Reduce the heat, then add the onion, garlic, and all the spices, stir well to coat, and cook for 2 minutes. Pour in the stock and bring to a boil. Reduce the heat and transfer everything to the slow cooker, season, cover with the lid, and cook on auto/low for 6–8 hours or on high for 3–4 hours.

3 Add the squash, peppers, and raisins, if using, for the last hour of cooking. Taste and season if needed. Serve with baby roasted potatoes and couscous or rice.

traditional method ⏱ **PREP** 20 MINS **COOK** 2½ HRS

1 Preheat the oven to 300°F (150°C). Toss the beef in the cumin so it is evenly coated, then do the same with the flour. Heat the oil in a large Dutch oven or tagine over medium-high heat, and cook the beef in batches for 10 minutes until evenly browned.

2 Reduce the heat, then add the onion, garlic, and all the spices, stir well to coat, and cook for 2 minutes. Pour in the stock and bring to a boil. Reduce the heat once more, season, cover with the lid, and put in the oven for 1½ hours.

3 Add the squash and then 15 minutes later, the peppers and raisins, if using, and cook everything for a further 30 minutes, or until tender. You may need to top up with a little hot water. Taste and season if needed. Serve with baby roasted potatoes and couscous or rice.

This is a light dish of vegetables and fish cooked with a heady mix of herbs and spices. Charmoula is a north African marinade that infuses the fish still further with lemon and cilantro.

Fish tagine

SERVES 4–6　**HEALTHY**

2lb (900g) red snapper filets, or use sea bass,
　cut into chunky pieces
1–2 tbsp olive oil
2 onions, sliced into rings
2 celery stalks, finely chopped
salt and freshly ground black pepper
3 garlic cloves, chopped
1 tsp ground ginger
1 preserved lemon, flesh only, finely chopped
　or use grated zest of ½ lemon
2 carrots, peeled and sliced
2 red bell peppers, seeded and roughly chopped
6 new potatoes, halved
about 1 cup hot fish stock for the slow cooker
　(2 cups for the traditional method)

3 tomatoes, seeded and chopped into thin slices
squeeze of lemon juice
cilantro leaves, to serve (optional)

FOR THE CHARMOULA
1 tsp coriander seeds, crushed in a mortar
1 tsp black peppercorns, crushed in a mortar
1 tsp ground cumin
1 tsp paprika
1 tsp ground turmeric
1 red chile, seeded and roughly chopped
¼ cup extra virgin olive oil
juice of 1 lemon
bunch of cilantro leaves
sea salt and freshly ground black pepper

in the slow cooker　**PREP** 20 MINS　**COOK** 15 MINS PRECOOKING; **AUTO/LOW** 4–5 HRS

1 Preheat the slow cooker, if required. Put the charmoula ingredients in a food processor and blend until smooth. Smother the fish with half the charmoula and set aside to marinate. Heat the oil in a large Dutch oven or tagine over medium heat, add the onions and celery, season, and cook for 5–6 minutes until soft. Stir in the garlic, ginger, lemon flesh or zest, and remaining charmoula and cook for a few minutes, then cook the carrots and peppers for 5 minutes.

2 Transfer everything to the slow cooker, add the potatoes, and pour in the stock so it just covers the mixture. Cover with the lid and cook on auto/low for 4–5 hours. Add the fish and layer the tomatoes over the top for the last 30 minutes of cooking. Taste and season, if needed, add a squeeze of lemon juice, and stir in the cilantro leaves, if using. Serve with fluffy couscous and lemon wedges.

traditional method　**PREP** 20 MINS　**COOK** 1¼–1½ HRS

1 Put the charmoula ingredients in a food processor and blend until smooth. Smother the fish with half the charmoula and set aside to marinate. Heat the oil in a large Dutch oven or tagine over medium heat, add the onions and celery, season, and cook for 5–6 minutes until soft. Stir in the garlic, ginger, lemon flesh or zest, and remaining charmoula and cook for a few minutes, then cook the carrots and peppers for 5 minutes.

2 Add the potatoes and stock, bring to a boil, cover with the lid, and cook at a very low simmer for about 45 minutes, topping up with a little hot water if needed. Add the fish and layer the tomatoes over the top, re-cover, and bring up to a simmer once again. Cook for a further 15–30 minutes until the fish is opaque and cooked through. Taste and season, if needed, add a squeeze of lemon juice, and stir in the cilantro leaves, if using. Serve with fluffy couscous and lemon wedges.

One of the spices in this recipe is sumac, a Middle Eastern spice that is slightly tart in taste. It is found in most major supermarkets. Black olives are suggested, but use green if you prefer.

Red mullet with Middle Eastern spices

⊙ **SERVES** 4–6 ❄ **FREEZE** UP TO 1 MONTH ♡ **HEALTHY**

1 tbsp olive oil
6 shallots, finely chopped
1 fennel bulb, trimmed and finely chopped
1 carrot, peeled and finely chopped
½ tsp ground cumin
1 tsp of sumac or use a preserved lemon, flesh discarded and rind finely chopped (optional)
4 plum tomatoes, roughly chopped
2 cups hot vegetable stock for the slow cooker (3 cups for the traditional method)

salt and freshly ground black pepper
8 black olives, pitted
1½lbs (675g) boneless red mullet filets, cut into chunks
small handful of cilantro, finely chopped
small handful of mint, finely chopped
1 preserved lemon, flesh discarded and rind sliced finely, to serve (optional)

in the slow cooker ⏱ **PREP** 15 MINS **COOK** 10 MINS PRECOOKING; **HIGH** 3–4 HRS

1 Preheat the slow cooker, if required. Heat the oil in a large heavy-based pan or tagine over medium heat, add the shallots, fennel, and carrot, and cook for 5 minutes until soft. Stir in the cumin and sumac or preserved lemon, and cook for a further minute.

2 Transfer everything to the slow cooker, then stir in the tomatoes and just enough stock to cover the vegetables, and season with salt and pepper. Add the olives, cover with the lid, and cook on high for 3–4 hours, adding the fish for the last 30 minutes of cooking.

3 Stir in most of the cilantro and mint, taste and season, if needed. Serve with couscous and scatter the remaining fresh herbs and preserved lemon rind over the dish, if using.

traditional method ⏱ **PREP** 15 MINS **COOK** 1½ HRS

1 Heat the oil in a large heavy-based pan or tagine, add the shallots, fennel, and carrot, and cook for 5 minutes until soft. Stir in the cumin and sumac or preserved lemon, and cook for a further minute. Add the tomatoes and stock, season with salt and pepper, and bring to a boil, then reduce to a simmer.

2 Add the olives, partially cover with a lid, and simmer gently for about 1 hour, stirring occasionally and topping up with hot water, if needed. Sit the fish on top of the tomato mixture, cover with the lid, and cook for a further 10 minutes or until the fish is cooked through.

3 Stir in most of the cilantro and mint, taste and season, if needed. Serve with couscous and scatter the remaining fresh herbs and preserved lemon rind over the dish, if using.

This is a good one-pot to serve in late spring or early summer. Slices of lamb are braised with garlic, lemons, and herbs. The peas add color and freshness—use fresh ones when in season.

Braised lamb with lemon and peas

SERVES 6 **FREEZE** UP TO 3 MONTHS

2¼lb (1kg) boneless leg of lamb, cut into slices
1 tbsp parsley, chopped, plus extra to serve
1 tbsp cilantro, chopped, plus extra to serve
2 onions, finely chopped
3 garlic cloves, chopped
1 tsp grated fresh ginger
½ cup olive oil

1 tbsp lemon juice
1¾ cups hot meat stock for the slow cooker
   (2 cups for the traditional method)
4 preserved lemons, cut into quarters, pulp
   removed and discarded, zest thinly sliced
1lb (450g) frozen peas
salt and freshly ground black pepper

in the slow cooker **PREP** 20 MINS, PLUS MARINATING **COOK** 10 MINS PRECOOKING; **AUTO/LOW** 6–8 HRS OR **HIGH** 3–4 HRS

1 Combine the lamb, parsley, cilantro, onions, garlic, ginger, oil, and lemon juice in a large non-metallic dish, cover, and leave to marinate overnight in the refrigerator.

2 Preheat the slow cooker, if required. Remove the lamb, reserving the marinade, and set aside. Heat a large Dutch oven or tagine over medium-high heat, add the lamb (in batches, if necessary), and cook for 5–6 minutes until browned on all sides. Transfer to the slow cooker, spoon over the reserved marinade, and add the stock. Cover with the lid and cook on auto/low for 6–8 hours or on high for 3–4 hours. Add the preserved lemons for the last 30 minutes of cooking and add the peas for the last 10 minutes. Taste and add salt and pepper, if needed.

3 Sprinkle the chopped parsley and cilantro over the dish and serve with lemon wedges, small cubed roasted potatoes, and some purple sprouting broccoli.

traditional method **PREP** 20 MINS, PLUS MARINATING **COOK** 1¼ HRS

1 Combine the lamb, parsley, cilantro, onions, garlic, ginger, oil, and lemon juice in a large non-metallic dish, cover, and leave to marinate overnight in the refrigerator.

2 Remove the lamb, reserving the marinade, and set aside. Heat a large Dutch oven or tagine over medium-high heat, add the lamb (in batches, if necessary), and cook for 5–6 minutes until browned on all sides. Spoon over the reserved marinade and add the stock. Bring to a boil, then reduce the heat and simmer, covered, for 1 hour. Add the preserved lemons for the last 30 minutes of cooking and add the peas for the last 10 minutes. Taste and add salt and pepper, if needed.

3 Sprinkle the chopped parsley and cilantro over the dish and serve with lemon wedges, small cubed roasted potatoes, and some purple sprouting broccoli.

Slowly cooked, the eggplant becomes a delicious sauce and the chicken fork tender. The preserved lemons, available from most large supermarkets, add a wonderful tang to the dish.

Chicken, eggplant, and tomato tagine

🍲 **SERVES** 6 ❄️ **FREEZE** UP TO 3 MONTHS

3–4 tbsp olive oil
8 chicken pieces (thighs and breasts)
salt and freshly ground black pepper
2 eggplants, chopped into bite-sized cubes
1 tsp ground cinnamon
2 onions, finely chopped
3 red chilies, seeded and finely chopped
2 tsp ground cumin

2 bay leaves
3lb (1.35kg) tomatoes, chopped
1 tbsp tomato paste
1 cup hot chicken stock for the slow cooker
  (1½ cups for the traditional method)
4 preserved lemons, halved and pith discarded
handful of cilantro, finely chopped

in the slow cooker 🕐 **PREP** 20 MINS **COOK** 25 MINS PRECOOKING; AUTO/LOW 6–8 HRS OR **HIGH** 3–4 HRS

1 Preheat the slow cooker, if required. Heat 1 tablespoon of oil in a large Dutch oven or tagine over medium-high heat. Season the chicken with salt and pepper and cook in the pot (in batches, if necessary), stirring occasionally, for about 8 minutes until golden. Remove and set aside. Toss the eggplant in the cinnamon and add to the pot with 1 tablespoon of oil. Cook over medium heat (and with extra oil, if necessary), stirring occasionally, for about 10 minutes until golden.

2 Heat 1 tablespoon of oil in the pot over low heat, then add the onions, chilies, cumin, and bay leaves. Season well and cook for about 10 minutes. Transfer everything to the slow cooker, including the chicken. Stir in the tomatoes, tomato paste, and the stock. Cover with the lid and cook on auto/low for 6–8 hours or on high for 3–4 hours. Stir in the preserved lemons and cilantro, remove the bay leaf, and serve with fluffy couscous and some harissa paste on the side.

traditional method 🕐 **PREP** 20 MINS **COOK** 1¼ HRS

1 Heat 1 tablespoon of oil in a large Dutch oven or tagine over medium-high heat. Season the chicken with salt and pepper and cook in the pot (in batches, if necessary), stirring occasionally, for about 8 minutes until golden. Remove and set aside. Toss the eggplant in the cinnamon and add to the pot with 1 tablespoon of oil. Cook over medium heat (and with extra oil, if necessary), stirring occasionally, for about 10 minutes until golden.

2 Heat 1 tablespoon of oil in the pot over low heat, then add the onions, chilies, cumin, and bay leaves. Season well and cook for about 10 minutes. Return the chicken to the pot along with the tomatoes and tomato paste. Pour in the stock, cover with the lid, and simmer over a low heat for 40–50 minutes, topping up with hot water if it starts to look too dry. Stir in the preserved lemons and cilantro, remove the bay leaf, and serve with fluffy couscous and some harissa paste on the side.

This is a vegetarian dish full of taste and texture with its fleshy eggplant and nutty chickpeas. It is an ideal dish to prepare a day ahead because the flavors become even better with time.

Middle Eastern chickpea stew

◎ **SERVES** 4–6 ❄ **FREEZE** UP TO 3 MONTHS ♡ **HEALTHY**

2 tbsp olive oil
1 red onion, finely chopped
salt and freshly ground black pepper
½ tsp ground cinnamon
½ tsp ground cumin
½ tsp sumac (optional)
4 garlic cloves, finely chopped
1 large eggplant, roughly chopped into
 bite-sized pieces
½ cup white wine
2 x 14oz (400g) cans chickpeas, drained and rinsed

14oz (400g) can chopped tomatoes
1–2 tsp harissa paste, depending on how spicy
 you like it
⅓ cup dried cherries or cranberries or use
 fresh pomegranate seeds
2 preserved lemons, quartered, flesh removed
 and discarded (optional)
2 cups hot vegetable stock for the slow cooker
 (3 cups for the traditional method)
bunch of cilantro leaves, chopped

in the slow cooker 🕐 **PREP** 10 MINS **COOK** 15 MINS PRECOOKING;
AUTO/LOW 6–8 HRS OR **HIGH** 3–4 HRS

1 Preheat the slow cooker, if required. Heat the oil in a large heavy-based pan or tagine over medium heat, add the onion, and cook for 3–4 minutes until soft. Season with salt and pepper, then stir in the spices, garlic, and eggplant, and cook for 5–8 minutes, stirring, so it is all coated and the eggplant starts to turn golden brown.

2 Transfer everything to the slow cooker, then add the wine to the pan and stir to deglaze the residual pan juices before transferring this liquid to the slow cooker. Add the chickpeas, tomatoes, harissa paste, cherries, preserved lemons (if using), and the stock. Season and stir, then cover with the lid, and cook on auto/low for 6–8 hours or on high for 3–4 hours.

3 Taste and season if needed, or stir in more harissa paste if you like it hot. Stir in most of the cilantro and ladle into warmed shallow bowls, then sprinkle with the remaining cilantro. Serve with warm flatbread and a spoonful of plain yogurt on the side.

traditional method 🕐 **PREP** 10 MINS **COOK** 1¼ HRS

1 Heat the oil in a large heavy-based pan or tagine over medium heat, add the onion, and cook for 3–4 minutes until soft. Season with salt and pepper, stir in the spices, garlic, and eggplant, and cook for 5–8 minutes, stirring, so it is all coated and the eggplant starts to turn golden brown.

2 Add the wine and let it bubble for a minute, then add the chickpeas, tomatoes, harissa paste, cherries, and preserved lemons, if using. Stir well and pour in the stock. Bring to a boil, then reduce to a simmer, partially cover with the lid, and cook gently for 1 hour, stirring occasionally.

3 Taste and season if needed, or stir in more harissa paste if you like it hot. Stir in most of the cilantro and ladle into warmed shallow bowls, then sprinkle with the remaining cilantro. Serve with warm flatbread and a spoonful of plain yogurt on the side.

Tender lamb is perfectly suited to oregano and lemon. Add the okra to the slow cooker halfway through the cooking time so that it holds its shape. The dish is topped with pine nuts and parsley.

Turkish lamb and lemon

⊙ **SERVES** 4 ❄ **FREEZE** UP TO 3 MONTHS

8 boneless lamb cutlets, trimmed of any fat
1 tsp paprika
1 tbsp olive oil
2 onions, sliced
salt and freshly ground black pepper
3 garlic cloves, finely chopped
grated zest of 1 lemon and juice of 2 lemons
½ tbsp dried oregano

6 tomatoes, roughly chopped
about 1 cup hot vegetable stock for the slow cooker
 (about 1½ cups for the traditional method)
9oz (250g) okra, trimmed and chopped
heaping ½ cup pine nuts, toasted
handful of flat-leaf parsley, finely chopped

in the slow cooker 🕐 PREP 15 MINS   COOK 15 MINS PRECOOKING;
AUTO/LOW 6–8 HRS OR HIGH 3–4 HRS

1 Preheat the slow cooker, if required. Toss the lamb cutlets in the paprika, then heat a tiny drizzle of the oil in a large Dutch oven or tagine over medium-high heat. Add the cutlets and cook for 2–3 minutes on each side or until golden. Remove and set aside.

2 Add the remaining oil to the pot, if needed, reduce the heat, and cook the onions for 4–6 minutes until soft. Season with salt and pepper, then stir in the garlic, lemon zest, and oregano and cook for a minute.

3 Add the tomatoes and lemon juice, and cook for 5 minutes. Transfer everything to the slow cooker, including the lamb, and pour in the stock so it just covers the mixture. Cook on auto/low for 6–8 hours or on high for 3–4 hours, adding the okra halfway through. Taste and season, if needed, then stir in the pine nuts and parsley and serve with boiled potatoes.

traditional method 🕐 PREP 15 MINS   COOK 1¼–1¾ HRS

1 Preheat the oven to 325°F (160°C). Toss the lamb cutlets in the paprika, then heat a tiny drizzle of the oil in a large Dutch oven or tagine over medium-high heat. Add the cutlets and cook for 2–3 minutes on each side or until golden. Remove and set aside.

2 Add the remaining oil to the pot, if needed, reduce the heat, and cook the onions for 4–6 minutes until soft. Season with salt and pepper, then stir in the garlic, lemon zest, and oregano and cook for a minute.

3 Add the okra and cook for 3–4 minutes, stirring, then add the tomatoes and lemon juice, and cook for a further 5 minutes. Return the meat to the pot, and pour over the stock so it just covers. Cover with the lid and put in the oven for 1–1½ hours. Check occasionally that it's not drying out, topping up with a little hot water if needed. Taste and season, if needed, then stir in the pine nuts and parsley and serve with boiled potatoes.

Here is a full-flavored, delightfully simple vegetarian dish with pulses and nuts added for protein and texture. Serve it with spoonfuls of brown rice or couscous for the complete meal.

Chickpea, tomato, and herb tagine

⊚ SERVES 4–6   **❄ FREEZE** UP TO 3 MONTHS   **◯ HEALTHY**

2 tbsp olive oil
2 large onions, chopped into eighths
salt and freshly ground black pepper
3 garlic cloves, peeled and crushed
1 tbsp paprika
½ tsp dried chile flakes
1 tsp ground cinnamon
1 tsp ground ginger
12 tomatoes, left whole

1¾ cups hot vegetable stock for the slow cooker
  (2½ cups for the traditional method)
2 tbsp honey
½ cup sliced almonds
14oz (400g) can chickpeas, drained
handful of flat-leaf parsley, roughly chopped
handful of cilantro, roughly chopped
2 sprigs of thyme
small handful of oregano (optional)

in the slow cooker   **🕐 PREP** 15 MINS   **COOK** 15 MINS PRECOOKING;
                                                        AUTO/LOW 6–8 HRS OR **HIGH** 3–4 HRS

1 Preheat the slow cooker, if required. Heat the oil in a large Dutch oven or tagine over moderate heat, add the onions, and cook for 4–6 minutes until soft. Add seasoning and the garlic and cook for a further minute.

2 Add the paprika, chile flakes, cinnamon, and ginger, and mix so the onions are coated. Then add the tomatoes, stock, and honey, combine well, and bring to a boil.

3 Transfer everything to the slow cooker, then add the almonds, chickpeas, and herbs. Season and cover with the lid, and cook on auto/low for 6–8 hours or on high for 3–4 hours. Remove the thyme sprigs and serve with couscous or brown rice.

traditional method   **🕐 PREP** 15 MINS   **COOK** 1¼ HRS

1 Preheat the oven to 325°F (160°C). Heat the oil in a large Dutch oven or tagine over moderate heat, add the onions, and cook for 4–6 minutes until soft. Add seasoning and the garlic and cook for a further minute.

2 Add the paprika, chile flakes, cinnamon, and ginger, and mix so the onions are coated. Then add the tomatoes, stock, and honey, combine well, and bring to a boil.

3 Add the almonds, chickpeas, and herbs, then season, cover with the lid, and put in the oven for 1 hour. Remove the thyme sprigs and serve with couscous or brown rice.

Curries

This is a relatively dry curry, although if you like a curry with more sauce, you can top up the stock during cooking. Fresh ginger and bird's eye chilies make the dish more fragrant.

Karahi chicken

SERVES 4   **FREEZE** UP TO 1 MONTH   **HEALTHY**

1 tsp coriander seeds
2 green chilies, seeded
3 garlic cloves, peeled
1 tsp ground turmeric
2 tbsp sunflower oil
8 bone-in chicken thighs, skin on, slashed
  a few times across each thigh
salt and freshly ground black pepper

1 onion, roughly chopped
6 tomatoes, roughly chopped
2 cups hot vegetable stock for the slow cooker
  (3 cups for the traditional method)
2in (5cm) piece of fresh ginger, peeled and
  finely chopped
3–4 green bird's eye chilies, left whole
bunch of cilantro, finely chopped

in the slow cooker   **PREP** 15 MINS   **COOK** 25 MINS PRECOOKING;
AUTO/LOW 6 HRS OR **HIGH** 3 HRS

1 Preheat the slow cooker, if required. Put the coriander seeds, chilies, garlic, turmeric, and half the oil into a food processor and blend until it becomes a paste. Season the chicken with salt and pepper and smother them with the paste, using your hands and pushing it into all the cuts. Heat half the remaining oil in a large Dutch oven over medium-high heat and add the chicken pieces. Cook for 5–6 minutes on each side or until beginning to color, then remove and set aside.

2 Heat the remaining oil in the pot over medium heat, add the onion, and cook for 3–4 minutes until soft. Then add the tomatoes and cook for 5–10 minutes until they too are soft. Transfer everything to the slow cooker. Pour over the stock and add the ginger, bird's eye chilies, and chicken, pushing the chicken under the liquid as much as you can. Cover with the lid and cook on auto/low for 6 hours or on high for 3 hours. Remove the chilies, then taste and season as necessary, stirring in the cilantro. Serve with rice, chapatis, and some minted yogurt on the side.

traditional method   **PREP** 15 MINS   **COOK** 1 HR

1 Put the coriander seeds, chilies, garlic, turmeric, and half the oil into a food processor and blend until it becomes a paste. Season the chicken with salt and pepper and smother them with the paste, using your hands and pushing it into all the cuts. Heat half the remaining oil in a large Dutch oven over medium-high heat and add the chicken pieces. Cook for 5–6 minutes on each side or until beginning to color, then remove and set aside.

2 Heat the remaining oil in the pot over medium heat, add the onion, and cook for 3–4 minutes until soft. Then add the tomatoes and cook for a further 5–10 minutes until they, too, are soft. Pour in the stock and bring to a boil. Reduce to a simmer, stir in the ginger and bird's eye chilies, and return the chicken to the casserole. Cover with the lid and cook gently for 30–40 minutes, keeping an eye on the sauce. You want it to be fairly dry, but if it is sticking, add a little hot water.

3 Remove the chilies, then taste and season, as necessary, stirring in the cilantro. Serve with rice, chapatis, and some minted yogurt on the side.

A classic Cambodian braised curry, this recipe has dominant cardamom and ginger flavors; the addition of peanuts helps to thicken the sauce. Serve with rice and pickled vegetables.

Cardamom and ginger beef curry

SERVES 4

1½lb (675g) boneless beef shin steak or thin flank, cut into 1½in (4cm) cubes
3oz (85g) fresh ginger, finely grated and squeezed to extract the juice (discard the fibers)
3 tbsp vegetable oil
1 tbsp shrimp paste
14oz (400ml) can coconut milk
¼ cup palm sugar or granulated sugar
1 tbsp tamarind paste mixed with ¼ cup water
2 tbsp fish sauce (nam pla)
½ cup unsalted roasted peanut halves
2–4 red Thai chilies, seeded and thinly sliced (optional)

FOR THE CURRY PASTE
2 tbsp sunflower oil
3 dried red chilies, soaked, seeded and halved
4 large garlic cloves, crushed
1 large shallot, coarsely chopped
1 stalk lemongrass, trimmed and sliced
3in (7.5cm) piece cinnamon stick
2 star anise
7 cardamom pods, crushed
1 tsp grated nutmeg
½ tsp ground mace
1½ tbsp finely chopped cilantro
¼ tsp ground turmeric

in the slow cooker
PREP 20 MINS, PLUS MARINATING
COOK 15 MINS PRECOOKING; **AUTO/LOW** 5–6 HRS OR **HIGH** 3–4 HRS

1 In a bowl, combine the beef with the ginger juice, tossing to coat. Leave to marinate for 30 minutes. To make the curry paste, heat the oil in a Dutch oven over moderate heat and stir-fry the chilies, garlic, shallot, and lemongrass until fragrant. Add the spices (except cilantro and turmeric) and stir-fry for 5–7 minutes until toasted. Transfer to a food processor, add the cilantro and turmeric, and blend until smooth, adding a little water (1 tablespoon at a time, as necessary) to ease the process. Set the paste aside.

2 Preheat the slow cooker, if required. Heat the oil in the pot over moderate heat and briefly stir-fry the shrimp paste. Add the curry paste and half the coconut milk. Stir, transfer to the slow cooker, and add the beef. Stir in the remaining coconut milk, sugar, tamarind water, fish sauce, and nuts. Cover and cook on auto/low for 5–6 hours or on high for 3–4 hours. Serve with Thai chilies, if using.

traditional method
PREP 20 MINS, PLUS MARINATING **COOK** 2–2¼ HRS

1 In a bowl, combine the beef with the ginger juice, tossing to coat. Leave to marinate for 30 minutes. To make the curry paste, heat the oil in a Dutch oven over moderate heat and stir-fry the chilies, garlic, shallot, and lemongrass until fragrant. Add the spices (except cilantro and turmeric) and stir-fry for 5–7 minutes until toasted. Transfer to a food processor, add the cilantro and turmeric, and blend until smooth, adding water (1 tablespoon at a time, as necessary) to ease the process. Set the paste aside.

2 Heat the oil in the pot over moderate heat and briefly stir-fry the shrimp paste. Add the curry paste and half the coconut milk. Stir, then add the beef. Cook for 20 minutes, stirring occasionally. Reduce the heat to low and stir in the remaining coconut milk, sugar, tamarind water, fish sauce, and nuts. Season with salt, if needed. Simmer, covered, for 1½–2 hours or until the meat is fork tender, adding more coconut milk if the stew thickens too much. Serve with Thai chilies, if using.

An intensely flavored Indonesian speciality, originally made with water buffalo. It can be made up to 2 days ahead and kept in the refrigerator. Bring to room temperature, then reheat on the stove.

Beef rendang

SERVES 6

2 x 14oz (400ml) cans coconut milk
  (3 x 14oz/400ml cans for the traditional method)
4 bay leaves
3lb (1.35kg) beef chuck steak, cut in 2in (5cm) cubes
salt

FOR THE CURRY PASTE
1in (2.5cm) piece cinnamon stick,
  ground or pounded
12 cloves, ground or pounded
2 stalks lemongrass, trimmed and roughly chopped
6 shallots, quartered
3in (7.5cm) piece fresh ginger, roughly chopped
6 garlic cloves, peeled and left whole
6 red chilies, seeded and roughly chopped
1 tsp ground turmeric

in the slow cooker   **PREP** 15 MINS   **COOK** 10 MINS PRECOOKING; **AUTO/LOW** 6–8 HRS

1 Preheat the slow cooker, if required. Put all the ingredients for the curry paste in a food processor and blend to make a thick paste. If the mixture is very thick, add about ¼ cup of the coconut milk. Transfer the curry paste to a wok or large heavy-based saucepan, add the coconut milk, and stir until well mixed. Add the bay leaves and bring to a boil over high heat, stirring occasionally.

2 Transfer the coconut sauce to the slow cooker together with the beef and season with salt. Cover with the lid and cook on auto/low for 6–8 hours.

3 Taste the curry and add more salt if needed. Spoon the curried beef onto a bed of cooked rice on warmed plates or in shallow bowls.

traditional method   **PREP** 15 MINS   **COOK** 3¾ –4¼ HRS

1 Put all the ingredients for the curry paste in a food processor and blend to make a thick paste. If the mixture is very thick, add about ¼ cup of the coconut milk. Transfer the curry paste to a wok or large heavy-based saucepan, add the coconut milk, and stir until well mixed. Add the bay leaves and bring to a boil over high heat, stirring occasionally.

2 Reduce the heat to medium and cook the sauce, stirring occasionally, for about 15 minutes. Add the beef and salt, stir, and bring to a boil. Reduce the heat to medium and simmer, uncovered, stirring occasionally, for 2 hours.

3 Reduce the heat to very low and continue cooking for 1½–2 hours, partially covered, until the beef is tender and the sauce quite thick. Stir frequently to prevent sticking. Skim off all the fat, taste the curry, and add more salt if needed. It will be very thick and rich. Toward the end of cooking, oil will separate from the sauce and the beef will fry in it. Spoon the curried beef onto a bed of cooked rice on warmed plates or in shallow bowls.

This curry has an intense heat of chili running though it, which cuts through the rich, creamy coconut and sweet pumpkin. Use butternut squash if you can't get ahold of pumpkin.

Sri Lankan coconut pumpkin curry

SERVES 4–6

2 tbsp olive oil
2lb (900g) pumpkin or butternut squash, peeled, seeded, and chopped into bite-sized pieces
2 red chilies, seeded and finely chopped
4 shallots, finely chopped
2in (5cm) piece of fresh ginger, peeled and grated
3 garlic cloves, grated
1 lemongrass stalk, trimmed, woody outer leaves removed, and finely chopped

juice of 1 lime
14oz (400ml) can coconut milk
2 cups hot vegetable stock for the slow cooker (3 cups for the traditional method)
pinch of dried chile flakes
about 6 packed cups spinach leaves
salt and freshly ground black pepper

in the slow cooker ⏱ PREP 20 MINS COOK 15 MINS PRECOOKING; **HIGH** 3–4 HRS

1 Preheat the slow cooker, if required. Heat half the oil in a large heavy Dutch oven over medium heat, add the pumpkin or butternut squash, and cook, stirring, for about 10 minutes until it begins to turn golden. Add the chilies and cook for a minute more.

2 Add the remaining oil and then stir in the shallots, ginger, garlic, and lemongrass. Add the lime juice and stir to scrape up any sticky bits from the bottom of the pan. Add a little coconut milk and let it bubble for a few minutes. Transfer everything to the slow cooker, then pour in the remaining coconut milk and stock together with the chile flakes. Cover with the lid and cook on high for 3–4 hours.

3 Stir in the spinach and leave for a few minutes for it to wilt before serving. Taste and season, as necessary, and serve with rice.

traditional method ⏱ PREP 20 MINS COOK 1¼ HRS

1 Preheat the oven to 350°F (180°C). Heat half the oil in a large Dutch oven over medium heat, add the pumpkin or butternut squash, and cook, stirring, for about 10 minutes until it begins to turn golden. Add the chilies and cook for a minute more.

2 Add the remaining oil and then stir in the shallots, ginger, garlic, and lemongrass. Add the lime juice and stir to scrape up the bits from the bottom of the pot. Add a little coconut milk and let it bubble for a few minutes.

3 Pour in the remaining coconut milk and the stock, and bring to a boil. Then reduce to a simmer, add the chile flakes, cover with the lid, and put in the oven for 1 hour. Check occasionally that it's not drying out, topping up with a little hot water if needed. Remove from the oven and stir in the spinach. It will wilt in the heat. Taste and season, as necessary, and serve with rice.

This is much lighter in flavor than lots of other curries. Plenty of lime, ginger, and cilantro make up its basis, and of course, you could always add some cooked chicken or fish if you wish.

Malaysian mango curry

SERVES 4

2 tsp ground turmeric
2 red chilies, seeded
4 garlic cloves, peeled and left whole
2in (5cm) piece of fresh ginger, peeled and roughly chopped
1 tbsp sunflower oil
8 shallots, very finely chopped
salt and freshly ground black pepper
14oz (400ml) can coconut milk

⅓ cup hot vegetable stock for the slow cooker (½ cup for the traditional method)
juice of 1–2 limes
1 tbsp demerara sugar (optional)
5½ oz (150g) vermicelli noodles, soaked in water and drained
2 ripe mangoes, peeled and cut into bite-sized pieces
bunch of cilantro, finely chopped

in the slow cooker **PREP** 20 MINS **COOK** 10 MINS PRECOOKING; **HIGH** 3–4 HRS

1 Preheat the slow cooker, if required. Put the turmeric, chilies, garlic, and ginger in a food processor, blend with half the oil to make a paste, and set aside. Alternatively, grind the ingredients with a pestle and mortar.

2 Heat the remaining oil in a large, heavy saucepan, add the shallots, and cook for 3–4 minutes until soft. Season with salt and pepper, then add the paste and cook, stirring occasionally, for a few more minutes. Pour in the coconut milk and stock, and bring to a boil. Transfer everything to the slow cooker, cover with the lid, and cook on high for 3–4 hours.

3 Stir in the lime juice, to taste, and adjust the flavor with a little sugar and seasoning if needed. Stir in the noodles, mango, and cilantro.

traditional method **PREP** 20 MINS **COOK** 1 HR

1 Put the turmeric, chiles, garlic, and ginger in a food processor, blend with half the oil to make a paste, and set aside. Alternatively, grind the ingredients with a pestle and mortar.

2 Heat the remaining oil in a large, heavy saucepan over medium heat, add the shallots, and cook for 3–4 minutes until soft. Season with salt and pepper, then add the paste and cook, stirring occasionally, for a few more minutes. Pour in the coconut milk and stock and bring to a boil. Reduce the heat to low, partially cover with the lid, and leave to simmer for about 40 minutes, until the sauce has thickened.

3 Stir in the lime juice, to taste, and adjust the flavor with a little sugar and seasoning, if needed. Stir in the noodles, mango, and cilantro.

This is a great vegetarian dish, with distinctively sweet flavors of cinnamon and cardamom. The peanuts add a contrasting texture to the potatoes and eggplant. Make it as hot and fiery as you wish.

Eggplant massaman curry

SERVES 4–6

2 red chilies, seeded
1 lemongrass stalk, tough outer leaves removed
2in (5cm) piece of fresh ginger, peeled and
  roughly chopped
5 cardamom pods, crushed
1 tbsp sunflower oil
1 onion, finely chopped
salt and freshly ground black pepper
2 cups hot vegetable stock for the slow cooker
  (3 cups for the traditional method)
14oz (400ml) can coconut milk

1 cinnamon stick, broken
splash of dark soy sauce
splash of fish sauce (nam pla)—omit if cooking
  for vegetarians
4 potatoes, peeled and chopped into
  bite-sized pieces
6 baby eggplants, halved lengthwise, or use
  2 large ones, roughly chopped
1 tbsp palm sugar or demerara sugar (optional)
½ cup roasted unsalted peanuts, roughly chopped

in the slow cooker PREP 15 MINS COOK 15 MINS PRECOOKING; AUTO/LOW 8 HRS OR HIGH 3–4 HRS

1 Preheat the slow cooker, if required. Put the chilies, lemongrass, ginger, and cardamom in a food processor and blend with a drop of the sunflower oil to make a paste.

2 Heat the remaining oil in a large heavy-based pan over medium heat, add the onion, and cook for 3–4 minutes until soft. Then add the paste and some salt and pepper and cook for a few minutes more. Stir in the stock and coconut milk and bring to a boil, then add the cinnamon stick, soy sauce, and fish sauce, if using, and stir. Reduce to a simmer and leave uncovered for about 20 minutes, for the sauce to thicken slightly. Transfer everything to the slow cooker and add the potatoes and eggplant. Cover with the lid and cook on auto/low for 8 hours or on high for 3–4 hours.

3 Taste and season with the sugar, if using, and stir in half the peanuts. Ladle into warmed bowls and sprinkle with the remaining peanuts. Serve with rice and lime wedges.

traditional method PREP 15 MINS COOK 1 HR

1 Put the chilies, lemongrass, ginger, and cardamom in a food processor and blend with a drop of the sunflower oil to make a paste.

2 Heat the remaining oil in a large heavy-based pan over medium heat, add the onion, and cook for 3–4 minutes until soft. Then add the paste and some salt and pepper and cook for a few minutes more. Stir in the stock and coconut milk, and bring to a boil, then add the cinnamon stick, soy sauce, and fish sauce, if using, and cook on a low heat for about 20 minutes. Stir in the potatoes and eggplant and cook for a further 20 minutes.

3 Stir in half the peanuts, taste, and adjust the flavor by adding the sugar, if using, and more salt or fish sauce, also if using, as needed. Ladle into warmed bowls and sprinkle with the remaining peanuts. Serve with rice and lime wedges.

Prawns need minimum cooking, so they can simply be stirred through at the end. You could use precooked ones instead, if you prefer, or you could stir though some cooked chicken.

Prawn makhani

SERVES 4–6   **FREEZE** UP TO 3 MONTHS, WITHOUT THE CREAM

3 tbsp vegetable oil
3 garlic cloves, finely chopped
2in (5cm) piece of fresh ginger, peeled and finely chopped
1 cinnamon stick, broken into pieces
2 red chilies, seeded and finely chopped
4 cardamom pods, crushed
about 1lb (500g) tomatoes, chopped

1lb 9oz (700g) (shelled weight) uncooked prawns
salt and freshly ground black pepper
7fl oz (200ml) plain greek yogurt
1–2 tsp medium-hot chili powder
¾ cup cashew nuts, ground, plus a handful, roughly chopped, to serve
1–2 tsp ground fenugreek
½ cup heavy cream

in the slow cooker   **PREP** 20 MINS, PLUS MARINATING   **COOK** 10 MINS PRECOOKING; **AUTO/LOW** 4–5 HRS OR **HIGH** 3–4 HRS

1 Preheat the slow cooker, if required. Heat 2 tablespoons of the oil in a large heavy-based saucepan over low heat, add half the garlic, half the ginger, the cinnamon, chilies, and cardamom pods and cook, stirring occasionally, for 2 minutes. Stir in the tomatoes and ½ cup of water. Transfer everything to the slow cooker, cover with the lid, and cook on auto/low for 4–5 hours or on high for 3–4 hours.

2 At the last hour of cooking, season the prawns with salt and pepper and toss with the rest of the garlic and ginger, the remaining oil, the yogurt, and chili powder. Leave to marinate for 20 minutes. Meanwhile, use an immersion blender to blend the mixture in the slow cooker until smooth, stir in the ground cashews and fenugreek, and continue cooking.

3 Heat the pan over high heat, then add the prawns and yogurt marinade and cook, tossing them all the time, for 5–8 minutes until no longer pink. For the last 5 minutes of cooking, add the prawns and cream to the slow cooker. Season if needed. Garnish with the chopped cashews and serve with rice.

traditional method   **PREP** 20 MINS, PLUS MARINATING   **COOK** 40 MINS

1 Heat 2 tablespoons of the oil in a large heavy-based saucepan over low heat, add half the garlic, half the ginger, the cinnamon, chilies, and cardamom pods and cook, stirring occasionally, for 2 minutes. Stir in the tomatoes and cook for 10 minutes or until they start to reduce. Cover with a little hot water and simmer for a further 10 minutes or until puréed. Push the tomato mixture through a sieve into a food processor and blend until smooth.

2 Season the prawns with salt and pepper and toss with the rest of the garlic and ginger, the remaining oil, the yogurt, and chili powder. Leave to marinate for 20 minutes. Heat the pan over high heat, then add the prawns and yogurt marinade and cook, tossing them all the time, for 5–8 minutes until no longer pink. Remove and set aside.

3 Return the tomatoes to the pan, stir in the ground cashews and fenugreek, and simmer for 10 minutes, adding a little hot water if the sauce looks too thick. For the last 5 minutes of cooking, add the prawns and cream. Season if needed. Garnish with the chopped cashews and serve with rice.

Traditionally, dhansak would be made with three different types of lentils and plenty of vegetables. This version is simpler, but no less tasty for that. It can be made two days ahead and reheated.

Lamb dhansak

SERVES 6 **FREEZE** UP TO 3 MONTHS

¼ cup vegetable oil
1lb 10oz (750g) boned shoulder of lamb, cut
  into bite-sized pieces
salt and freshly ground black pepper
1 large eggplant, chopped into bite-sized pieces
1 large onion, finely chopped
¾in (2cm) piece of fresh ginger, peeled and
  finely chopped

5 garlic cloves, finely chopped
2 tsp ground cumin
2 tsp ground coriander
2 tsp ground turmeric
pinch of cayenne pepper
1 tbsp all-purpose flour
¾ cup green lentils
1 small cauliflower, chopped into florets

in the slow cooker   **PREP** 20 MINS   **COOK** 20 MINS PRECOOKING;
                                                AUTO/LOW 6–8 HRS OR HIGH 3–4 HRS

1 Preheat the slow cooker, if required. Heat two-thirds of the oil in a large Dutch oven over high heat. Season the lamb with salt and pepper and cook (in batches, if necessary), stirring, for 3–5 minutes until brown on all sides. Remove and set aside. Add the remaining oil to the pot, then add the eggplant and cook over medium heat, stirring occasionally, for 5–7 minutes until brown. Also remove and set aside, but in a separate bowl.

2 Add the onion to the pot and cook for 7–10 minutes until golden brown. Stir in the ginger and garlic and cook for 2–3 minutes until softened and fragrant. Add the ground cumin, coriander, turmeric, and cayenne and cook for 1–2 minutes until thoroughly combined. Return the lamb with any juices, sprinkle the flour over, and cook, stirring, for about 1 minute. Stir in 2 cups of water and bring to a boil. Transfer everything to the slow cooker, then stir in the lentils. Cover with the lid and cook on auto/low for 6–8 hours or on high for 3–4 hours. Stir in the eggplant and cauliflower for the last 30 minutes of cooking, topping up with water if necessary. Serve with fluffy rice and a mango chutney.

traditional method   **PREP** 20 MINS   **COOK** 2 HRS

1 Heat two-thirds of the oil in a large Dutch oven over high heat. Season the lamb with salt and pepper and cook (in batches, if necessary), stirring, for 3–5 minutes until brown on all sides. Remove and set aside. Add the remaining oil to the pot, then add the eggplant and cook over medium heat, stirring occasionally, for 5–7 minutes until brown. Remove and set aside, but in a separate bowl.

2 Add the onion to the pot and cook for 7–10 minutes until golden brown. Stir in the ginger and garlic and cook for 2–3 minutes until softened and fragrant. Add the ground cumin, coriander, turmeric, and cayenne and cook for 1–2 minutes until thoroughly combined. Return the lamb with any juices, sprinkle the flour over, and cook, stirring, for about 1 minute. Stir in 3½ cups of water and bring to a boil. Lower the heat, cover, and simmer gently, stirring occasionally, for 30 minutes. Stir in the lentils and cook for 15 minutes longer. Stir in the eggplant, cauliflower, and 2 cups more water; continue simmering, stirring often, for 50–60 minutes until completely tender. Add more water during cooking if the curry seems dry. Serve with fluffy rice and a mango chutney.

Vindaloo originates from Goa on the western coast of India, where the cooking combines Portuguese influences with fiery Indian flavors. This is an elaborate dish, but worth the effort.

Pork vindaloo

⊙ **SERVES** 4   ❄ **FREEZE** UP TO 3 MONTHS   ♡ **HEALTHY**

2lb (900g) boneless pork, cut into 2in (5cm) cubes
¼ cup vegetable oil
5 garlic cloves, finely chopped
2 onions, chopped
1 tsp ground turmeric
1–2 tsp chili powder
½ tsp tomato paste
3 tomatoes, chopped
3 tbsp wine vinegar or cider vinegar
salt
pinch of crushed black peppercorns
1 tbsp chopped cilantro leaves

FOR THE SPICE PASTE
1 tsp cumin seeds
4 cardamom pods
4 cloves
1in (2.5cm) cinnamon stick
5 black peppercorns
1–2 green chilies, chopped
1in (2.5cm) piece fresh ginger, chopped
4 garlic cloves, peeled and left whole
3 tbsp lemon juice

in the slow cooker   🕐 **PREP** 30 MINS, PLUS MARINATING   **COOK** 20 MINS PRECOOKING; AUTO/LOW 6–8 HRS OR **HIGH** 3–4 HRS

1 To make the spice paste, grind the cumin seeds, cardamom pods, cloves, cinnamon stick, and peppercorns in a clean coffee grinder or spice mill, into a fine powder. Then blend the spice powder with the green chilies, ginger, garlic and lemon juice in a food processor to make a paste. Mix the pork with the paste in a large bowl, cover with plastic wrap, and put in the refrigerator for 1½ hours.

2 Preheat the slow cooker, if required. Heat the oil in a large Dutch oven, add the garlic, and cook for 1 minute. Add the onions and cook for about 5 minutes, stirring occasionally, until they are golden. Stir in the turmeric, chili powder, tomato paste, tomatoes, and vinegar. Add the marinated pork and some salt, and cook for 10 minutes, stirring occasionally. Transfer everything to the slow cooker and pour in 1¼ cups hot water. Cover with the lid and cook on auto/low for 6–8 hours or on high for 3–4 hours. Add the crushed black pepper, garnish with the chopped cilantro, and serve immediately.

traditional method   🕐 **PREP** 30 MINS   **COOK** 1 HR

1 To make the spice paste, grind the cumin seeds, cardamom pods, cloves, cinnamon stick, and peppercorns in a clean coffee grinder or spice mill, into a fine powder. Then blend the spice powder with the green chilies, ginger, garlic and lemon juice in a food processor to make a paste. Mix the pork with the paste in a large bowl, cover with plastic wrap, and put in the refrigerator for 1½ hours.

2 Heat the oil in a large Dutch oven add the garlic, and cook for 1 minute. Add the onions and cook for about 5 minutes, stirring occasionally, until they are golden. Stir in the turmeric, chili powder, tomato paste, chopped tomatoes, and vinegar. Add the marinated pork and some salt, and cook for 10 minutes, stirring occasionally. Pour in 1¼ cups water and bring to a boil, then reduce the heat and simmer on a really low heat for about 40 minutes, or until the meat is cooked through and the sauce is thick. Check occasionally that it's not drying out, topping up with a little hot water if needed. Add the crushed black pepper, garnish with the chopped cilantro, and serve immediately.

Don't be shy with the garlic and ginger—this dish is big on bold flavors. For vegetarians, cut a block of paneer or tofu into large cubes and add the pieces to the sauce at the end of cooking.

Chicken tikka masala

🌀 **SERVES** 4 ❄ **FREEZE** UP TO 3 MONTHS, WITHOUT THE CREAM

juice of 2 limes
1 tsp paprika
6 skinless boneless chicken thighs, about 1½lb (675g)
  total weight, cut into bite-sized pieces
2 shallots, roughly chopped
4 large garlic cloves, roughly chopped
2 green chilies, seeded and roughly chopped
3in (7.5cm) piece fresh ginger, roughly chopped
⅔ cup plain Greek-style yogurt
½ tsp garam masala

½ tsp coriander seeds, dry-roasted and ground
1½ tsp cumin seeds, dry-roasted and ground
1 tbsp vegetable oil
14oz (400g) can chopped tomatoes
1 rounded tsp tomato paste
handful of cilantro leaves, roughly chopped
½ tsp sugar
3 tbsp unsalted butter
½ cup half and half

in the slow cooker   🕐 **PREP** 20 MINS, PLUS MARINATING   **COOK** 15 MINS PRECOOKING; AUTO/LOW 4–5 HRS OR **HIGH** 2–3 HRS

1 In a bowl, mix together most of the lime juice, paprika, and chicken. Set aside. Put the shallots, garlic, chilies, and half the ginger into a food processor. Strain the lime juice and paprika from the chicken and add the liquid to the processor. Blend until smooth. Put into a bowl and stir in the yogurt, garam masala, and half the coriander and cumin powder. Pour the yogurt mixture over the chicken and turn to coat. Cover with plastic wrap and refrigerate overnight, if time permits, or cook immediately.

2 Preheat the slow cooker, if required. Heat the oil in a large Dutch oven until hot, add the chicken pieces, and cook for about 10 minutes until golden on each side. Remove and set aside. Combine the tomatoes, tomato paste, cilantro leaves, sugar, and the remaining ginger, lime juice, cumin, and coriander powder in a food processor and blend until smooth. Melt the butter in the pot and stir in the tomato mixture. Pour into the slow cooker, add the chicken, cover, and cook on auto/low for 4–5 hours or on high for 2–3 hours. Stir in the half and half and cook for 10 minutes. Serve with Indian breads.

traditional method   🕐 **PREP** 20 MINS, PLUS MARINATING   **COOK** 50 MINS

1 In a bowl, mix together most of the lime juice, paprika, and chicken. Set aside. Put the shallots, garlic, chilies, and half the ginger into a food processor. Strain the lime juice and paprika from the chicken and add the liquid to the processor. Blend until smooth. Put into a bowl and stir in the yogurt, garam masala, and half the coriander and cumin powder. Pour the spiced yogurt mixture over the chicken and turn to coat. Cover with plastic wrap and refrigerate overnight, if time permits, or cook immediately.

2 Heat the oil in a large Dutch oven until hot, add the chicken pieces, and cook for about 10 minutes until golden on each side. Remove and set aside. Combine the tomatoes, tomato paste, cilantro leaves, sugar, and the remaining ginger, lime juice, cumin, and coriander powder in a food processor and blend until smooth. Melt the butter in the pot and stir in the tomato mixture and chicken. Cover and cook for about 30 minutes, topping up with a little hot water if needed. Stir in the half and half and cook for 10 more minutes. Serve with Indian breads.

Sambar is made in hundreds of ways, using various vegetables and roasted spices. You can buy tamarind paste in most major supermarkets or look for it in an Asian store.

Vegetable sambar

⊙ **SERVES** 4　❄ **FREEZE** UP TO 3 MONTHS　♡ **HEALTHY**

½ cup split yellow lentils
1 tsp ground turmeric
1 tsp chili powder
2 onions, cut into small pieces
2 medium (3½oz/100g) carrots, peeled and chopped
1 cup frozen or fresh green beans, chopped
3 tomatoes, quartered
2 medium (3½oz/100g) potatoes, peeled and cubed
1 tbsp tamarind paste mixed with ¼ cup water
salt

FOR THE SPICE PASTE
1¼ cups dried unsweetened flaked coconut
2 tsp coriander seeds
1 dried red chile

FOR TEMPERING
1 tbsp vegetable oil
1 tsp mustard seeds
10 curry leaves
3 dried red chilies

in the slow cooker　🕐 **PREP** 20 MINS　**COOK** 15 MINS PRECOOKING; AUTO/LOW 4–6 HRS OR **HIGH** 2–3 HRS

1 Preheat the slow cooker, if required. For the spice paste, heat a small frying pan over medium heat, add the coconut and spices, and dry-roast until brown. Leave to cool, then put in a food processor and blend to a paste, gradually adding about 1 cup of water.

2 Bring 1½ cups of water to a boil in a large heavy-based pan and add the lentils, turmeric, chili powder, and onions. Simmer for 10–15 minutes until the lentils soften. Transfer to the slow cooker and stir in the vegetables. Then add the tamarind water and salt, to taste, and stir in the spice paste. Cover with the lid and cook on auto/low for 4–6 hours or on high for 2–3 hours.

3 For tempering, heat the oil in a heavy-based frying pan and add the mustard seeds. As they begin to pop, add the curry leaves and dried red chilies. Pour this over the curry and gently stir in. Serve hot with some lime wedges and rice or dosas.

traditional method　🕐 **PREP** 20 MINS　**COOK** 50 MINS

1 For the spice paste, heat a small frying pan over medium heat, add the coconut and spices, and dry-roast until brown. Leave to cool, then put in a food processor and blend to a paste, gradually adding about 1 cup of water.

2 Bring 1½ cups of water to a boil in a large heavy-based pan and add the lentils, turmeric, chili powder, and onions. Simmer for 10–15 minutes until the lentils soften. Stir in the vegetables. Cover with the lid and cook for about 10 minutes until the vegetables are tender. Add the tamarind water and salt, to taste. Cover and cook for a further 5 minutes. Stir in the spice paste. Bring to a boil, then reduce the heat to moderate and cook, uncovered, for 5 minutes, stirring occasionally.

3 For tempering, heat the oil in a heavy-based frying pan and add the mustard seeds. As they begin to pop, add the curry leaves and dried red chilies. Pour this over the curry and gently stir in. Serve hot with some lime wedges and rice or dosas.

This light, easy recipe features chicken gently simmered in coconut sauce with a simple mixture of mushrooms and scallions. You could make this with shrimp, if you prefer.

Thai green chicken curry

SERVES 4

1 tbsp olive oil
4 skinless boneless chicken thighs, about
   1¼lb (550g) total weight, cut into bite-sized pieces
4 tsp Thai green curry paste (use more paste for a
   spicier sauce)
2 tbsp light soy sauce
14oz (400ml) can coconut milk

1–2 tbsp fish sauce (nam pla)
1 cup hot vegetable stock, for both methods
6oz (175g) shiitake mushrooms, chopped
6 scallions, trimmed and with the green part
   chopped into ¼in (5mm) slices
salt and freshly ground black pepper
chopped cilantro, to serve

in the slow cooker   **PREP** 10 MINS   **COOK** 10 MINS PRECOOKING; AUTO/LOW 6–8 HRS OR **HIGH** 3–4 HRS

1 Preheat the slow cooker, if required. Heat the oil in a large Dutch oven over medium heat, add the chicken (in batches, if necessary), and cook for about 10 minutes until lightly browned. Remove and set aside. Stir in the curry paste and cook for a minute.

2 Pour in the soy sauce, coconut milk, fish sauce, and stock, and bring to a boil, stirring. Transfer to the slow cooker, adding the chicken, mushrooms, and most of the scallions, and season with salt and pepper. Cover with the lid and cook on auto/low for 6–8 hours or on high for 3–4 hours. Taste and adjust seasoning, if needed, or add a little more fish sauce. Garnish with the cilantro and remaining sliced scallions. Serve hot with boiled or steamed long-grain rice or plain noodles.

traditional method   **PREP** 10 MINS   **COOK** 1 HR

1 Heat the oil in a large Dutch oven over medium heat, add the chicken (in batches, if necessary), and cook for about 10 minutes until lightly browned. Remove and set aside. Stir in the curry paste and cook for a minute.

2 Pour in the soy sauce, coconut milk, fish sauce, and stock, and bring to a boil, stirring. Lower the heat, add the chicken, mushrooms, and most of the scallions, and season with salt and pepper. Partially cover with the lid and allow to simmer very gently on low heat for about 50 minutes, until the chicken is cooked through. Taste and adjust seasoning, if needed, or add a little more fish sauce. Garnish with the cilantro and the remaining sliced scallions. Serve hot with boiled or steamed long-grain rice or plain noodles.

Fiery, broth-like curries, enriched with coconut milk, are typical of the dishes from East Africa. The best accompaniment is a generous helping of rice to soak up the delectably soupy broth.

Kenyan fish curry

 SERVES 4–6

juice of 1 lime
1 tsp black peppercorns, crushed
1lb 5oz (600g) haddock filet, skinned and cut
 into 2in (5cm) pieces
⅓ cup vegetable oil
1 red onion, finely chopped
1 red bell pepper, seeded and finely chopped
1 red chile, finely chopped
4 garlic cloves, finely chopped
9oz (250g) plum tomatoes, skinned and
 finely chopped

1 cup coconut milk
1 tbsp tamarind paste

FOR THE SPICE MIXTURE
2 dried red chilies
¾ tsp coriander seeds
¾ tsp cumin seeds
1 tsp mustard seeds
¼ tsp ground turmeric

in the slow cooker   🕐 PREP 20 MINS   COOK 15 MINS PRECOOKING; AUTO/LOW 6–8 HRS OR HIGH 3–4 HRS

1 To make the spice mixture, dry-roast the chilies and seeds, then grind to a powder using a mortar and pestle or a clean coffee grinder. Combine with the turmeric and set aside. Combine the lime juice with the peppercorns and pour over the fish. Heat the oil in a large heavy-based skillet over medium heat. Dry the fish with paper towels and cook for about 1 minute on each side until lightly colored, but not quite cooked through. Remove and set aside.

2 Preheat the slow cooker, if required. Add the red onion to the pan, cover, and cook for about 5 minutes until soft. Add in the red bell pepper, chile, and garlic, and continue cooking, uncovered, for about 10 minutes. Stir in the spice mixture and fry briskly for 1 minute, then stir in the tomatoes, and bring to a boil. Transfer to the slow cooker, pour in ½ cup water, and stir in the coconut milk and tamarind paste. Cover with the lid and cook on auto/low for 6–8 hours or on high for 3–4 hours. Add the fish for the last 10 minutes of cooking. Serve hot with rice.

traditional method   🕐 PREP 20 MINS   COOK 45 MINS

1 To make the spice mixture, dry-roast the chilies and seeds, then grind to a powder using a mortar and pestle or a clean coffee grinder. Combine with the turmeric and set aside. Combine the lime juice with the peppercorns and pour over the fish. Heat the oil in a large heavy-based skillet over medium heat. Dry the fish with paper towels and cook for about 1 minute on each side until lightly colored, but not quite cooked through. Remove and set aside.

2 Add the red onion to the pan, cover, and cook for about 5 minutes until soft. Add in the red bell pepper, chile, and garlic, and continue cooking, uncovered, for about 10 minutes. Stir in the spice mixture and fry briskly for 1 minute, then stir in the tomatoes, and bring to a boil. Pour in 1 cup water and simmer for about 20 minutes or until thickened. Stir in the coconut milk and tamarind paste and simmer for a futher 15 minutes. The curry shouldn't be too thick—aim for something almost broth-like in consistency. Add the fish to the pan and simmer for 5–10 minutes. Serve hot with rice.

For this recipe, potatoes and cauliflower are tumbled in a tikka coconut sauce. This is a simple and economical dish to make, and can easily be made ahead and reheated when required.

Cauliflower curry

 SERVES 4–6

1 tbsp vegetable oil
1 onion, roughly chopped
salt and freshly ground black pepper
2in (5cm) piece of fresh ginger,
   peeled and finely chopped
3 garlic cloves, finely chopped
2 green chilies, seeded and finely chopped

2 tbsp medium-hot tikka curry paste
14oz (400g) can chickpeas, drained and rinsed
14oz (400ml) can coconut milk
1¾ cups hot vegetable stock for the slow cooker
   (2 cups for the traditional method)
3 potatoes, peeled and cut into bite-sized pieces
1 cauliflower, cut into bite-sized florets

in the slow cooker　⏱ **PREP** 15 MINS　**COOK** 5 MINS PRECOOKING;
AUTO/LOW 8 HRS OR **HIGH** 4 HRS

1 Preheat the slow cooker, if required. Heat the oil in a large, heavy Dutch oven over medium heat, add the onion, and cook for 3–4 minutes until soft. Season with salt and pepper, stir in the ginger, garlic, and chilies, and cook for a couple of minutes. Stir in the tikka paste and chickpeas and transfer everything to the slow cooker.

2 Pour in the coconut milk and stock, then add the raw potatoes and cauliflower, and stir. Cover with the lid and cook on auto/low for 8 hours or on high for 4 hours. Serve with some rice and naan bread.

traditional method　⏱ **PREP** 15 MINS　**COOK** 1 HR

1 Heat the oil in a large, heavy Dutch oven over medium heat, add the onion, and cook for 3–4 minutes until soft. Season with salt and pepper, stir in the ginger, garlic, and chilies, and cook for a couple of minutes. Stir in the tikka paste, chickpeas, coconut milk, and stock and bring to a boil. Reduce to a simmer and cook gently, partially covered with the lid and stirring occasionally, for 30 minutes.

2 Meanwhile, bring another large pot of salted water to a boil. Add the potatoes and cook for about 15 minutes or until just beginning to soften. Remove the potatoes with a slotted spoon and set aside. Put the cauliflower in the boiling water and cook for about 5 minutes, then drain well.

3 Add the potato and cauliflower into the sauce and turn so they are well coated, then simmer very gently for a further 15 minutes or so, to allow all the flavors to mingle. Serve with some rice and naan bread.

Cashew nuts and golden raisins enrich this lamb curry. Make it as hot as you desire as the yogurt will mellow it a little. The lamb becomes very tender when slow cooked and isn't at all fatty.

Balti lamb curry

SERVES 4–6 ❄ **FREEZE** UP TO 1 MONTH

1 tbsp vegetable oil
1 onion, finely chopped
salt and freshly ground black pepper
3 garlic cloves, finely chopped
2in (5cm) piece of fresh ginger, peeled and
  finely chopped
1–2 red chilies, depending on your heat
  preference, seeded and finely chopped
1 tbsp balti curry paste (available in Indian markets)

2lb (900g) boneless lamb leg, cut into
  bite-sized pieces
2 cups hot vegetable stock for the slow cooker
  (2½ cups for the traditional method)
1 cup golden raisins
½ cup cashew nuts (half of them ground)
½ cup plain yogurt
small bunch of cilantro, finely chopped
lemon wedges, to serve

in the slow cooker   🕒 **PREP** 15 MINS   **COOK** 20 MINS PRECOOKING;
AUTO/LOW 6–8 HRS OR **HIGH** 3–4 HRS

1 Preheat the slow cooker, if required. Heat the oil in a large, heavy Dutch oven over medium heat, add the onion, and cook for 3–4 minutes until soft. Season well with salt and pepper, stir in the garlic, ginger, and chilies, and cook for a few more minutes.

2 Stir in the curry paste, then add the lamb and toss to coat. Increase the heat a little and cook for 5–8 minutes until the lamb is no longer pink. Pour in a little stock and let it bubble for a few minutes, then transfer everything to the slow cooker.

3 Pour in the remaining stock and add in the raisins and ground cashew nuts. Cover with the lid and cook on auto/low for 6–8 hours or on high for 3–4 hours. Stir in the whole cashew nuts for the last 30 minutes of cooking. Stir in the yogurt and cilantro and serve with rice, naan bread, and some lemon wedges on the side.

traditional method   🕒 **PREP** 15 MINS   **COOK** 1½ HRS

1 Preheat the oven to 350°F (180°C). Heat the oil in a large, heavy Dutch oven over medium heat, add the onion, and cook for 3–4 minutes until soft. Season well with salt and pepper, then stir in the garlic, ginger, and chilies and cook for a few more minutes.

2 Stir in the curry paste, then add the lamb and toss to coat. Increase the heat a little and cook for 5–8 minutes until the lamb is no longer pink. Pour in a little stock and let it bubble for a few minutes, then add the remaining stock, bring back to a boil, and reduce to a simmer.

3 Add in the raisins and cashew nuts, both whole and ground, and stir. Cover with the lid and put in the oven for 1 hour. Check occasionally that it's not drying out, topping up with a little hot water if needed. Stir in the yogurt and cilantro and serve with rice, naan bread, and some lemon wedges on the side.

Duck curry is extremely rich and has a great depth of flavor. If you like your curry hot, use two red chilies rather than the one specified—and leave the seeds in for an even greater kick.

Duck curry

SERVES 4 ❄ **FREEZE** UP TO 1 MONTH

2 whole boneless duck breasts, with skin
1 tbsp sunflower oil
1 onion, finely chopped
2 celery stalks, finely chopped
salt and freshly ground black pepper
3 garlic cloves, finely chopped
1 red chile, seeded and finely chopped
2in (5cm) piece of fresh ginger, peeled
  and finely chopped

2 carrots, peeled and finely chopped
1 tbsp garam masala
1 tsp ground turmeric
1 tsp paprika
1 tbsp tomato paste
2 x 14oz (400g) cans chopped tomatoes
2 cups hot vegetable stock for the slow cooker
  (3 cups for the traditional method)

in the slow cooker ⏱ **PREP** 15 MINS **COOK** 25 MINS PRECOOKING; **AUTO/LOW** 8 HRS

1 Preheat the slow cooker, if required. Heat a heavy-based pan over medium-high heat and add the duck breasts, skin-side down. Cook each side for 3–6 minutes until golden. Remove and set aside. Heat the oil in the pan over medium heat, add the onion and celery, and cook for about 5 minutes until soft. Season with salt and pepper, stir in the garlic, chile, and ginger, and cook for a couple more minutes. Add the carrots, turn to coat, and continue cooking for 5 more minutes, stirring occasionally. Stir in the spices and tomato paste and cook for 1–2 minutes.

2 Transfer everything to the slow cooker and then add the tomatoes and stock. Add the duck breasts and tuck them into the sauce. Cover with the lid and cook on auto/low for 8 hours. Remove the duck breasts, peel off the skin and discard, and then shred the meat. Put the duck meat back into the slow cooker and stir, then taste and season, as required. Serve with rice and chapatis.

traditional method ⏱ **PREP** 15 MINS **COOK** 2 HRS

1 Preheat the oven to 350°F (180°C). Heat a large Dutch oven over medium-high heat and add the duck breasts, skin-side down. Cook each side for 3–6 minutes or until golden. Remove and set aside. Heat the oil in the pot over medium heat, add the onion and celery, and cook for about 5 minutes until soft. Season with salt and pepper, stir in the garlic, chile, and ginger, and cook for a couple more minutes.

2 Add the carrots, turn to coat, and continue cooking for 5 more minutes, stirring occasionally. Stir through the spices and tomato paste and cook for 1–2 minutes, then add in the tomatoes and stock. Bring to a boil, reduce to a simmer, and return the duck breasts to the pot, tucking them into the sauce. Cover with the lid and put in the oven for 1½ hours. Check occasionally that it's not drying out, topping up with a little hot water if needed.

3 Remove from the oven and spoon out the duck breasts. Peel off the skin and discard, then shred the meat. Put the duck meat back into the pot and return it to the oven for another 30 minutes (if the sauce is too thin, remove the lid). Taste and season, if necessary. Serve with rice and chapatis.

This is a hot and sour curry that features chilies and pineapple in a thick sauce of lentils, which successfully temper the heat and add texture to the finished dish.

Shrimp dhansak

⟲ **SERVES** 6 ❄ **FREEZE** UP TO 3 MONTHS

1¼ cups red lentils
salt and freshly ground black pepper
3 tbsp vegetable oil or 2 tbsp ghee
4 cardamom pods, crushed
2 tsp mustard seeds
2 tsp chili powder
2 tsp ground turmeric
2 tsp ground cinnamon
2 onions, finely chopped

4in (10cm) piece fresh ginger, peeled and
  finely chopped
4 garlic cloves, finely chopped
3–4 green chilies, seeded and finely sliced
½ pineapple, peeled and cut into bite-sized pieces
6 tomatoes, skinned and roughly chopped
1lb (450g) (shelled weight) uncooked large shrimp
handful of cilantro, finely chopped

in the slow cooker 🕐 **PREP** 15 MINS **COOK** 10 MINS PRECOOKING; AUTO/LOW 6–8 HRS OR **HIGH** 3–4 HRS

1 Preheat the slow cooker, if required. Put the lentils in the slow cooker, season well with salt and pepper, then pour in enough cold water to cover. Cover with the lid and cook on auto/low for 6–8 hours or on high for 3–4 hours.

2 Meanwhile, as the lentils are starting to cook in the slow cooker, heat 1 tablespoon of the oil or ½ tablespoon of the ghee in a large heavy-based skillet, add the dried spices, and cook, stirring, for 2 minutes or until the seeds pop. Stir in the onions, ginger, garlic, and chilies, and cook for 5 minutes or until soft. Transfer to the slow cooker with the lentils, re-cover with the lid, and continue cooking.

3 Heat 1 tablespoon of the oil or ½ tablespoon of ghee in the pan, stir in the pineapple and tomatoes, then stir these into the lentils for the last 30 minutes of cooking. When ready to serve, heat the remaining oil or ghee, add the shrimp, and cook briefly until pink, then stir them into the lentils. Taste and season with salt and pepper if needed, stir in the cilantro, and serve with rice or naan bread.

traditional method 🕐 **PREP** 15 MINS **COOK** 50 MINS

1 Put the lentils in a large heavy-based saucepan, season well with salt and pepper, then pour in enough cold water to cover. Cover with the lid, bring to a boil, then reduce to a simmer, and cook for 20 minutes or until soft. Top up with hot water if they begin to dry out. Drain and set aside.

2 Meanwhile, heat 1 tablespoon of the oil or ½ tablespoon of the ghee in a large heavy-based skillet, add the dried spices, and cook, stirring, for 2 minutes or until the seeds pop. Stir in the onions, ginger, garlic, and chilies, and cook for 5 minutes or until soft and fragrant.

3 Add 1 tablespoon of the oil or ½ tablespoon of ghee to the pan, stir in the pineapple, add the lentils and tomatoes, and a little hot water so the mixture is slightly sloppy, then simmer on a really low heat for about 15 minutes. Meanwhile, heat the remaining oil or ghee, add the shrimp and cook briefly until pink, then stir them into the lentils. Taste and season with salt and pepper if needed, stir in the cilantro, and serve with rice or naan bread.

This is a mild vegetarian curry and the sweet peppers marry well with the paneer. This is an Indian cheese that won't melt upon cooking; you'll find it with the other cheeses at the supermarket.

Paneer and sweet pepper curry

SERVES 4–6   **HEALTHY**

2 tbsp vegetable oil
1 x 8oz package paneer, cubed
4in (10cm) piece fresh ginger, peeled and sliced
2 red chilies, seeded and finely chopped
2 tbsp dried curry leaves, crushed
2 tsp cumin seeds

4 tsp garam masala
2 tsp ground turmeric
6 red bell peppers, seeded and sliced
6 tomatoes, skinned and roughly chopped
salt and freshly ground black pepper
bunch of fresh cilantro, finely chopped

in the slow cooker   **PREP** 20 MINS   **COOK** 15 MINS PRECOOKING; AUTO/LOW 5–6 HRS OR **HIGH** 3–4 HRS

1 Preheat the slow cooker, if required. Heat half the oil in a heavy-based skillet over medium-high heat, add the paneer, and cook for 5–8 minutes, stirring, until golden all over. Remove and set aside.

2 Heat the remaining oil in the pan, add the ginger, chilies, curry leaves, cumin seeds, garam masala, and turmeric, and stir well to coat with the oil. Then add the peppers, tomatoes, and ½ cup water and bring to a boil.

3 Transfer everything to the slow cooker, including the paneer, and season with salt and pepper. Cover with the lid and cook on auto/low for 5–6 hours or on high for 3–4 hours. Stir in the cilantro and serve with rice, chapatis, or naan bread.

traditional method   **PREP** 20 MINS   **COOK** 1 HR

1 Heat half the oil in a heavy-based skillet over medium-high heat, add the paneer and cook for 5–8 minutes, stirring, until golden all over. Remove and set aside.

2 Heat the remaining oil in the pan, add the ginger, chilies, curry leaves, cumin seeds, garam masala, and turmeric, and stir well to coat with the oil. Then add the peppers and cook over low heat for about 15 minutes until beginning to soften.

3 Add the tomatoes and ½ cup water and cook on low for 15 minutes. Return the paneer to the pan, season with salt and pepper, then simmer gently for 15–20 minutes, topping up with a little hot water if needed. Stir in the cilantro and serve with rice, chapatis, or naan bread.

Lots of spices enliven these red lentils, making them delicious enough to eat on their own with rice. Wash the lentils well before using and pick them over for any stones.

Red lentil dahl

⊚ **SERVES** 4 ❄ **FREEZE** UP TO 3 MONTHS ♡ **HEALTHY**

1 tbsp sunflower oil
1 onion, finely chopped
salt and freshly ground black pepper
3 garlic cloves, finely chopped
1 red chile, seeded and finely chopped
2in (5cm) piece of fresh ginger, peeled
  and grated
1 tsp ground cumin
1 tsp ground coriander
1 tsp ground turmeric

1 tsp paprika
6 curry leaves, crushed
¾ cup red lentils, rinsed and picked over
  for any stones
14oz (400g) can chopped tomatoes
2 cups hot vegetable stock for the slow cooker
  (3 cups for the traditional method)
juice of ½ lemon (optional)
small bunch of cilantro leaves, finely chopped
plain yogurt, to serve

in the slow cooker 🕐 **PREP** 15 MINS **COOK** 10 MINS PRECOOKING;
AUTO/LOW 8 HRS OR **HIGH** 4 HRS

1 Preheat the slow cooker, if required. Heat the oil in a large, heavy Dutch oven over medium heat, add the onion, and cook for 3–4 minutes until soft. Season with salt and pepper, stir in the garlic, chile, and ginger, and cook for a couple more minutes.

2 Add all the spices and curry leaves and stir well, then stir in the lentils so they get well coated with the spices. Add in the tomatoes and transfer everything to the slow cooker. Pour in the stock, cover with the lid, and cook on auto/low for 8 hours or on high for 4 hours.

3 Taste and season as needed, adding the lemon juice, if using, and stir in the cilantro. Serve with rice, chapatis, and a spoonful of yogurt on the side.

traditional method 🕐 **PREP** 15 MINS **COOK** 1¼ HRS

1 Heat the oil in a large, heavy Dutch oven over medium heat, add the onion, and cook for 3–4 minutes until soft. Season with salt and pepper, stir in the garlic, chile, and ginger, and cook for a couple more minutes.

2 Add all the spices and curry leaves and stir well, then stir in the lentils so they are well coated with the spices. Add in the tomatoes and 2 cups of the stock. Bring to a boil, then reduce to a simmer, partially cover with the lid, and cook on low heat for about 1 hour, stirring occasionally and topping up with the reserved stock when needed.

3 Taste and season as needed, adding the lemon juice, if using, and stir in the cilantro. Serve with rice, chapatis, and a spoonful of yogurt on the side.

Okra is becoming more popular, and when chopped and cooked in this way it still remains firm. Lots of ginger is the key to this dish, it works really well with the acidity of the tomatoes.

Ginger and okra curry

SERVES 4   **FREEZE** UP TO 1 MONTH   **HEALTHY**

1 tbsp sunflower oil
6 shallots, finely chopped
salt and freshly ground black pepper
1–2 green chilies, depending on your heat
  preference, seeded and finely chopped
3 garlic cloves, finely chopped
6oz (175g) okra, tops trimmed
4in (10cm) piece of fresh ginger, peeled
  and finely chopped

1 tsp black onion seeds (optional)
4 tomatoes, finely chopped
14oz (400g) can chopped tomatoes
1 cup hot vegetable stock for the slow cooker
  (2 cups for the traditional method)
lemon wedges, for serving

in the slow cooker   **PREP** 15 MINS   **COOK** 15 MINS PRECOOKING;
AUTO/LOW 8 HRS OR **HIGH** 4 HRS

1 Preheat the slow cooker, if required. Heat the oil in a large, heavy-based pan over medium heat, add the shallots, and cook for about 5 minutes until soft. Season with salt and pepper, stir in the chilies and garlic, and cook for a few more minutes.

2 Add the okra, increase the heat a little and fry them, stirring, until they take on some color. Stir in the ginger and onion seeds, turning to coat. Transfer everything to the slow cooker. Stir in the fresh and canned tomatoes and the stock. Cover with the lid and cook on auto/low for 8 hours or on high for 4 hours. Taste and season, as necessary, and serve the curry with rice, chapatis, and lemon wedges on the side.

traditional method   **PREP** 15 MINS   **COOK** 1¼ HRS

1 Heat the oil in a large heavy-based pan over medium heat, add the shallots, and cook for about 5 minutes until soft. Season with salt and pepper, then stir in the chilies and garlic, and cook for a few more minutes.

2 Add the okra, increase the heat a little and fry them, stirring, until they take on some color. Stir in the ginger and onion seeds (if using), turning to coat.

3 Add the fresh and canned tomatoes and bring to a boil, then pour in the stock and let the sauce bubble for a few minutes more. Reduce to a simmer, cover with the lid, and cook on low heat for about 1 hour, stirring occasionally and topping up with hot water if needed. For the last 15 minutes or so, remove the lid and let the sauce simmer to thicken. Taste and season, as necessary, and serve the curry with rice, chapatis, and lemon wedges on the side.

This is a simple vegetarian curry centered on nutty chickpeas and spices. You could stir in some fresh spinach at the end and spice it up with chilies if you wish.

Chickpea curry with cardamom

SERVES 4 ✳ **FREEZE** UP TO 3 MONTHS ♡ **HEALTHY**

1 tbsp vegetable oil
1 onion, finely chopped
salt and freshly ground black pepper
1 tsp cumin seeds
1 tsp ground turmeric
1 tsp ground coriander

6 cardamom pods, lightly crushed
14oz (400g) can chickpeas, drained and rinsed
14oz (400g) can chopped tomatoes
1–2 tsp garam masala
1 tsp chili powder

in the slow cooker   🕑 PREP 10 MINS   COOK 10 MINS PRECOOKING;
AUTO/LOW 4–5 HRS OR HIGH 2–3 HRS

1 Preheat the slow cooker, if required. Heat the oil in a large heavy-based skillet over low heat, add the onion and a pinch of salt, and cook gently for about 5 minutes until soft. Stir in the cumin seeds, turmeric, coriander, and cardamom and continue cooking for about 5 minutes until fragrant.

2 Add the chickpeas to the pan and stir well, crushing them slightly with the back of a wooden spoon. Add in the tomatoes, including any juices, then fill the can with water and add this also. Sprinkle in the garam masala and chili powder and bring to a boil. Transfer everything to the slow cooker, cover with the lid, and cook on auto/low for 4–5 hours or on high for 2–3 hours. Taste and season with salt and pepper if needed. Serve hot with a squeeze of lemon and topped with a spoonful of yogurt, together with naan bread and basmati rice.

traditional method   🕑 PREP 10 MINS   COOK 50 MINS

1 Heat the oil in a large heavy-based skillet over low heat, add the onion and a pinch of salt, and cook gently for about 5 minutes until soft. Stir in the cumin seeds, turmeric, coriander, and cardamom and continue cooking for about 5 minutes until fragrant.

2 Add the chickpeas to the pan and stir well, crushing them slightly with the back of a wooden spoon. Add in the tomatoes, including any juices, then fill the can with water and add this also. Sprinkle in the garam masala and chili powder and bring to a boil.

3 Reduce the heat to low and simmer gently for about 40 minutes, until the sauce begins to thicken slightly, and topping up with a little hot water if needed. Taste and season if needed. Serve hot with a squeeze of lemon and topped with a spoonful of yogurt, together with naan bread and basmati rice.

Korma refers to a fragrant Indian dish in which meat is gently cooked with spices and plain yogurt. Here, the korma is made with lamb, but you could also use chicken and shrimp.

Lamb korma

SERVES 6 | **FREEZE** UP TO 3 MONTHS

½ cup vegetable oil
6 onions, total weight about 1lb 10oz (750g), sliced
1in (2.5cm) piece of fresh ginger, peeled and grated
2 garlic cloves, finely chopped
3lb (1.4kg) boned lamb shoulder, excess fat trimmed, and cut into bite-sized pieces
1 cup plain yogurt
salt
1 cup heavy cream
3–5 sprigs of cilantro, leaves chopped

FOR THE SPICE MIXTURE
2 dried red chilies, seeded
5 cardamom pods, seeds extracted
1 cinnamon stick, crushed, or 2 tsp ground cinnamon
5 whole cloves
7 black peppercorns
2 tsp ground cumin
1 tsp ground mace
1 tsp paprika

in the slow cooker
PREP 25 MINS | **COOK** 25 MINS PRECOOKING; **AUTO/LOW** 5–6 HRS OR **HIGH** 3–4 HRS

1 Preheat the slow cooker, if required. To make the spice mixture, put the chilies, cardamom seeds, crushed cinnamon, cloves, and peppercorns in a mortar or clean coffee grinder and grind them as finely as possible. Stir in the cumin, mace, paprika, and ground cinnamon, if using.

2 Heat the oil in a large Dutch oven over low heat, add the onions, and cook for about 20 minutes until soft and golden brown. Stir in the ginger and garlic and cook for about 2 minutes until soft and fragrant. Stir in the spice mixture and cook for 1–2 minutes until thoroughly combined. Add the lamb and cook for about 5 minutes, stirring and tossing constantly, so it absorbs the flavor of the spices. Then add the yogurt and a little salt, and transfer everything to the slow cooker. Cover with the lid and cook on auto/low for 5–6 hours or on high for 3–4 hours. Stir in the cream for the last 20 minutes of cooking. Taste and season with salt and pepper if needed, garnish with the cilantro, and serve with rice.

traditional method
PREP 25 MINS | **COOK** 2½–3 HRS

1 To make the spice mixture, put the chilies, cardamom seeds, crushed cinnamon, cloves, and peppercorns in a mortar or clean coffee grinder and grind them as finely as possible. Stir in the cumin, mace, paprika, and ground cinnamon, if using.

2 Heat the oil in a large Dutch oven over low heat, add the onions, and cook for about 20 minutes until soft and golden brown. Stir in the ginger and garlic and cook for about 2 minutes until soft and fragrant. Stir in the spice mixture and cook for 1–2 minutes until thoroughly combined. Add the lamb and cook for about 5 minutes, stirring and tossing constantly, so it absorbs the flavor of the spices. Then add the yogurt and a little salt, and bring almost to a boil. Reduce the heat to very low, cover, and cook for 2–2½ hours until the lamb is tender enough to crush with your fingers. Stir occasionally during cooking so the meat does not stick. If the liquid evaporates too quickly, add a little hot water. Stir the cream into the lamb. Taste and season with salt and pepper if needed, garnish with the cilantro, and serve with rice.

Chilis & gumbos

A blend of hot spices and dark chocolate combine in this famous Mexican dish. Turkey is a good lean meat, but use chicken if you prefer. Make sure you use the best quality dark chocolate.

Turkey mole

SERVES 4–6   HEALTHY

2lb (900g) boneless turkey thighs
salt and freshly ground black pepper
3 tbsp vegetable oil
1½oz (45g) dark chocolate (70 percent cocoa),
  broken into pieces

FOR THE MOLE MIXTURE
14oz (400g) can chopped tomatoes
½ onion, quartered
3 garlic cloves, peeled and left whole

1 slice of stale white bread, torn into pieces
1 stale corn tortilla, torn into pieces
1 cup blanched almonds
½ cup raisins
1oz (30g) chili powder
1 tsp each of ground cloves, coriander, and cumin
¼ tsp ground aniseed
2 tsp ground cinnamon
2 tbsp sesame seeds

in the slow cooker   PREP 20 MINS   COOK 15 MINS PRECOOKING;
AUTO/LOW 6–8 HRS OR HIGH 3–4 HRS

1 Preheat the slow cooker, if required. Season the turkey and heat half the oil in a large Dutch oven over medium heat. Add the turkey pieces, skin-side down, and cook for 10–15 minutes until browned all over. Set aside. For the mole mixture, put all the ingredients, except for half the sesame seeds, in a food processor and blend to a smooth paste.

2 Heat the remaining oil in the pot over moderate heat, add the mole mixture, and cook, stirring, for about 5 minutes, until it is thick. Add the chocolate and stir until it has melted, then slowly add 1 cup of hot water, stirring. Season with salt and bring to a boil. Transfer everything to the slow cooker, including the turkey. Cover with the lid and cook on auto/low for 6–8 hours or on high for 3–4 hours Remove the turkey and set aside until cool enough to handle. Remove the skin and any fat, and shred the meat with your fingers. Return to the sauce and stir. Taste for seasoning. Toast the remaining sesame seeds for 2–3 minutes in a dry frying pan until lightly golden. Serve with white rice and sprinkle with the sesame seeds.

traditional method   PREP 45–50 MINS   COOK 1¼–1¾ HRS

1 Season the turkey and heat half the oil in a large Dutch oven over medium heat. Add the turkey pieces, skin-side down, and cook for 10–15 minutes until browned all over. Add 3 cups water, bring to a boil, and cover. Simmer for 45–60 minutes, until the turkey is very tender when pierced with a fork. Set aside. Strain the cooking liquid into a bowl. For the mole mixture, put all the ingredients, except for half the sesame seeds, in a food processor and blend to a smooth paste.

2 Heat the remaining oil in the Dutch oven over moderate heat, add the mole mixture, and cook, stirring, for about 5 minutes, until it is thick. Add the chocolate and stir until it has melted. Pour in the cooking liquid, season with salt, and stir. Simmer for 25–30 minutes, to thicken. Toast the remaining sesame seeds for 2–3 minutes in a dry frying pan until lightly golden. Remove the skin and any fat from the turkey and shred the meat with your fingers. Return the turkey to the pot and simmer for 10–15 minutes. Taste for seasoning. Serve with white rice and sprinkle with the sesame seeds.

In Texas, you will never find red beans in a chili; they are served on the side, as in this authentic recipe. Do mix them in with the meat, if you prefer. For a real Texan touch, serve it with cornbread.

Chili con carne

SERVES 6 **FREEZE** UP TO 3 MONTHS **HEALTHY**

3 tbsp vegetable oil, plus more if needed
3lb (1.35kg) chuck steak, cut into bite-sized pieces
3 onions, chopped
3 garlic cloves, finely chopped
2 x 14oz (400g) cans chopped tomatoes
2–4 dried red chilies, seeded and finely chopped
  or crumbled
5–6 sprigs of oregano, leaves chopped or
  1 tbsp dried oregano

2 tbsp chili powder
1 tbsp paprika
2 tsp ground cumin
1–2 tsp Tabasco sauce
salt and freshly ground black pepper
1 tbsp fine cornmeal (polenta)

in the slow cooker **PREP** 35 MINS **COOK** 20 MINS PRECOOKING;
AUTO/LOW 6–8 HRS OR **HIGH** 3–4 HRS

1 Preheat the slow cooker, if required. Heat half the oil in a large Dutch oven over high heat, add the beef (in batches and with extra oil, if necessary), and cook, stirring, until browned. If the meat has been cooked in batches return it all to the pot, then add the onions, garlic, and tomatoes, and cook, stirring, for 8–10 minutes until the onions are just soft.

2 Transfer everything to the slow cooker and pour in 1¼ cups water. Stir, then add the chilies, oregano, chili powder, paprika, cumin, Tabasco sauce, and salt and pepper. Cover with the lid and cook on auto/low for 6–8 hours or on high for 3–4 hours. Stir in the cornmeal for the last hour of cooking. At the end of cooking, the chili should be thick and rich. Taste for seasoning, and serve it with boiled, white long-grain rice and bowls of warmed red kidney beans.

traditional method **PREP** 35 MINS **COOK** 2¼–2¾ HRS

1 Heat half the oil in a large Dutch oven over high heat, add the beef (in batches and with extra oil, if necessary), and cook, stirring, until browned. If the meat has been cooked in batches return it all to the pot, then add the onions, garlic, and tomatoes, and cook, stirring, for 8–10 minutes until the onions are just soft.

2 Pour in 2 cups water and stir into the pot with the chilies, oregano, chili powder, paprika, cumin, Tabasco sauce, and salt and pepper. Bring just to a boil, cover, and simmer over low heat, stirring occasionally, for about 2–2½ hours until the meat is very tender. About 30 minutes before the end of cooking, stir in the cornmeal. At the end of cooking, the chili should be thick and rich. Taste for seasoning, and serve it with boiled, white long-grain rice and bowls of warmed red kidney beans.

In Louisiana, gumbo can be made from any number of ingredients. Best of all is shrimp gumbo bolstered, as here, with oysters. It is thickened with a dark roux of flour toasted slowly in oil.

Shrimp and okra gumbo

SERVES 4–6

1 bay leaf
3–5 sprigs of thyme
1½ tsp berries allspice
1 tsp crushed chilies
¼ cup vegetable oil
½ cup all-purpose flour
1 large onion, finely chopped
3 garlic cloves, finely chopped
2 green bell peppers, seeded and diced
salt and freshly ground black pepper
12oz (350g) tomatoes, skinned and coarsely chopped

5½oz (150g) smoked sausage, such as kielbasa, outer casing removed, if necessary, and cut into ½in (1cm) slices
9oz (250g) okra, chopped into ½in (1cm) slices
1lb (450g) raw medium shrimp, peeled and deveined
12 shelled oysters
small bunch of scallions, trimmed and sliced diagonally
small bunch of parsley, leaves finely chopped
½ tsp Tabasco sauce, plus more to taste

in the slow cooker   **PREP** 45 MINS **COOK** 25 MINS PRECOOKING; AUTO/LOW 6–8 HRS OR **HIGH** 3–4 HRS

1 Preheat the slow cooker, if required. Put the bay leaf, thyme, allspice, and crushed chilies in a cheesecloth bag and tie the top. To make a roux, heat the oil in a large Dutch oven over low heat, stir in the flour, and cook for about 5 minutes, stirring constantly, until the roux is medium brown. Stir the onion, garlic, peppers, and salt and pepper into the roux and cook for 7–10 minutes, stirring, until they are softened and lightly browned. Add the tomatoes and sausage and cook, stirring occasionally, for a further 10–12 minutes. Add the okra, spice bag, and 2 cups water.

2 Transfer everything to the slow cooker, cover with the lid, and cook on auto/low for 6–8 hours or on high for 3–4 hours. Add the shrimp for the last 10 minutes of cooking or until they start to turn pink. Add the oysters and scallions for the last 5 minutes of cooking or until the edges of the oysters start to curl. Discard the spice bag. Stir in the parsley and Tabasco sauce. Taste for seasoning, adding more Tabasco sauce, if you like. To serve, spoon the gumbo into warmed soup bowls.

traditional method   **PREP** 45 MINS **COOK** 1¼ HRS

1 Put the bay leaf, thyme, allspice, and crushed chilies in a cheesecloth bag and tie the top. To make a roux, heat the oil in a large Dutch oven over low heat, stir in the flour, and cook for about 5 minutes, stirring constantly, until the roux is medium brown. Stir the onion, garlic, peppers, and salt and pepper into the roux and cook for 7–10 minutes, stirring, until they are softened and lightly browned. Add the tomatoes and sausage and cook, stirring occasionally, for a further 10–12 minutes. Add the okra, spice bag, and 2 cups water. Partially cover the pot and let it simmer for 40–50 minutes until the okra is very tender and the gumbo is thick and rich.

2 Just before serving, add the shrimp to the gumbo and simmer gently for 3–5 minutes until they begin to turn pink. Add the oysters and scallions and cook for 1–2 minutes, until the edges of the oysters start to curl. Discard the spice bag. Stir in the parsley and Tabasco sauce. Taste for seasoning, adding more Tabasco sauce, if you like. To serve, spoon the gumbo into warmed soup bowls.

Pinto beans are creamy pink and, when mashed, are the common base filling of burritos. If you can't find them, use the same amount of black or kidney beans instead. They will taste just as good.

Pinto bean chili

🍥 **SERVES** 4–6 ❄ **FREEZE** UP TO 3 MONTHS ♡ **HEALTHY**

1 tbsp olive oil
2 red onions, finely chopped
salt and freshly ground black pepper
3 garlic cloves, finely chopped
2–3 red chilies, depending on your heat
   preference, seeded and finely chopped
1 tsp ground allspice
pinch of ground cumin
1 large cinnamon stick
1 tsp dried oregano

2 bay leaves
1 tbsp cider vinegar
2 x 14oz (400g) cans chopped tomatoes
1 tbsp tomato paste
1 tbsp dark brown sugar
2 x 14oz (400g) cans pinto beans, drained and rinsed
1½ cups hot vegetable stock for the slow cooker
   (3 cups for the traditional method)

in the slow cooker 🕐 **PREP** 15 MINS **COOK** 5 MINS PRECOOKING;
                                          AUTO/LOW 6–8 HRS OR **HIGH** 4–5 HRS

1 Preheat the slow cooker, if required. Heat the oil in a large heavy-based pan over medium heat, add the onions, and cook for 3–4 minutes until soft. Season with salt and pepper, stir in the garlic, chilies, ground spices, and herbs, and cook for 2 minutes.

2 Transfer everything to the slow cooker, then stir in the vinegar, tomatoes, tomato paste, sugar, beans, and stock. Cover with the lid and cook on auto/low for 6–8 hours or on high for 4–5 hours.

3 Taste and season as needed, removing the bay leaves and cinnamon stick, and serve with bowls of grated cheese and sour cream, if you like.

traditional method 🕐 **PREP** 15 MINS **COOK** 1½ HRS

1 Heat the oil in a large heavy-based pan over medium heat, add the onions, and cook for 3–4 minutes until soft. Season with salt and pepper, stir in the garlic, chilies, ground spices, and herbs, and cook for 2 minutes.

2 Add the vinegar, tomatoes, tomato paste, sugar, beans, and stock and bring to a boil. Reduce to a simmer, partially cover with the lid, and cook gently for 1–1½ hours until thickened.

3 Taste and season as needed, removing the bay leaves and cinnamon stick, and serve with bowls of grated cheese and sour cream, if you like.

A much-loved favorite with plenty of chile heat, this particular version is cooked in beer. You might want to add a few more bird's eye chilies to the dish depending on how hot you like it.

Hot and fiery chili with beer

SERVES 4–6   **FREEZE** UP TO 3 MONTHS

2½lb (1.1kg) beef skirt, braising steak,
   or lean ground beef
1 tbsp olive oil
1 onion, finely chopped
salt and freshly ground black pepper
3 garlic cloves, finely chopped
1 tsp ground cumin
1 tsp dried chile flakes
1 cup light ale
1 tsp English mustard

2 tbsp tomato paste
14oz (400g) can chopped tomatoes
14oz (400g) can red kidney beans, drained
4–6 red bird's eye chilies, left whole
about 1 cup hot vegetable stock for the slow cooker
   (2 cups for the traditional method)
splash of Tabasco sauce
handful of cilantro, finely chopped

in the slow cooker   PREP 15 MINS   COOK 15 MINS PRECOOKING;
AUTO/LOW 6–8 HRS OR **HIGH** 3–4 HRS

1 Preheat the slow cooker, if required. If using the beef skirt or braising steak rather than the lean ground beef, put the meat in the food processor and pulse until ground. Heat the oil in a large Dutch oven over medium heat, add the onion, and cook for 3–4 minutes until soft. Season with salt and pepper, stir in the garlic, cumin, and chile flakes, and cook for a minute more. Add the beef, increase the heat a little, and stir. Cook for about 8 minutes or until it is all browned, then increase the heat further, add the beer, and let it bubble for a few minutes. Reduce the heat and add the mustard, tomato paste, and tomatoes.

2 Transfer everything to the slow cooker. Add the beans and chilies and pour over the stock just to cover. Season, cover with the lid, and cook on auto/low for 6–8 hours or on high for 3–4 hours. Taste and season, if necessary, then stir in the Tabasco sauce and cilantro, and remove the whole chilies. Serve with fluffy rice, topped with chopped avocado and sour cream, if you like.

traditional method   PREP 15 MINS   COOK 1¾ HRS

1 Preheat the oven to 350°F (180°C). If using the beef skirt or braising steak rather than the lean ground beef, put the meat in the food processor and pulse until ground. Heat the oil in a large Dutch oven over medium heat, add the onion, and cook for 3–4 minutes until soft. Season with salt and pepper, stir in the garlic, cumin, and chile flakes, and cook for a minute more. Add the beef, increase the heat a little, and stir. Cook for about 8 minutes or until it is all browned, then increase the heat further, add the beer, and let it bubble for a few minutes. Reduce the heat, stir in the mustard and tomato paste, and add in the tomatoes and stock. Bring to a boil, then reduce to a simmer, add the kidney beans, and throw in the chilies.

2 Season and cover with the lid and put in the oven for 1½ hours. Check occasionally that it's not drying out, topping up with a little hot water if needed. Taste and season, if necessary, then stir in the Tabasco sauce and cilantro and remove the whole chilies. Serve with fluffy rice, topped with chopped avocado and sour cream, if you like.

This Cajun-style gumbo is a mixture of vegetables, sausages, and chicken. You could also add some shellfish to the dish at the end of cooking for extra variety. Enjoy it spooned over some rice.

Sausage and chicken gumbo

SERVES 4–6 **FREEZE** UP TO 1 MONTH

1 tbsp olive oil
1 onion, finely chopped
salt and freshly ground black pepper
3 celery stalks, finely diced
2 red bell peppers, seeded and finely chopped
2 garlic cloves, finely chopped

14oz (400g) pork sausages, each sliced into 3 pieces
2 tbsp all-purpose flour
2–3 tsp Cajun seasoning
14oz (400g) chicken breast, cut into bite-sized pieces
2 cups hot chicken stock for the slow cooker
    (3 cups for the traditional method)

in the slow cooker **PREP** 20 MINS **COOK** 30 MINS PRECOOKING; AUTO/LOW 6–8 HRS OR **HIGH** 3–4 HRS

1 Preheat the slow cooker, if required. Heat the oil in a large Dutch oven over medium heat, add the onion, and cook for 3–4 minutes until soft. Season with salt and pepper, stir in the celery, peppers, and garlic, and cook for a further 5–8 minutes until very soft. Add the sausages to the pot and cook for 5–8 minutes until no longer pink.

2 Mix the flour and Cajun seasoning on a plate and toss the chicken in the spicy flour. Add to the pot and cook, stirring, for 5–8 minutes, then add a little stock and bring to a boil.

3 Transfer everything to the slow cooker and pour in the remaining stock. Season, cover with the lid, and cook on auto/low for 6–8 hours or on high for 3–4 hours. Taste and season, if necessary, then ladle out over warmed bowls of rice.

traditional method **PREP** 20 MINS **COOK** 2 HRS

1 Preheat the oven to 325°F (160°C). Heat the oil in a large Dutch oven over medium heat, add the onion, and cook for 3–4 minutes until soft. Season with salt and pepper, stir in the celery, peppers, and garlic, and cook for a further 5–8 minutes until very soft. Add the sausages to the pot and cook for 5–8 minutes until no longer pink.

2 Mix the flour and Cajun seasoning on a plate and toss the chicken in the spicy flour. Add to the pot and cook, stirring, for 5–8 minutes, then add a little stock and bring to a boil. Pour in the remaining stock and continue boiling for a minute. Reduce to a simmer and add the seasoning.

3 Cover the pot with the lid and put in the oven for 1½ hours. Check occasionally that it's not drying out, topping up with a little hot water if needed. Taste and season, if necessary, then ladle out over warmed bowls of rice.

Lamb with sweet squash is the perfect combination and the ground meat benefits from long, slow cooking. Stirring mint and oregano leaves into the dish adds a distinct freshness.

Lamb and squash with green chilies

SERVES 4–6 **FREEZE** UP TO 1 MONTH

2 tbsp olive oil
1 butternut squash, peeled, seeded,
  and chopped into bite-sized pieces
salt and freshly ground black pepper
1 onion, finely chopped
handful of fresh oregano, leaves only,
  or 1 tsp dried oregano
handful of thyme, leaves only
3 garlic cloves, finely chopped

1 green chile, seeded and finely chopped
1lb (450g) ground lamb
2 cups hot vegetable stock for the slow cooker
  (3 cups for the traditional method)
14oz (400g) can chopped tomatoes
½ cup golden raisins
bunch of mint leaves, finely chopped
1–2 tsp harissa paste, depending on how spicy
  you like it

in the slow cooker   PREP 25 MINS   COOK 25 MINS PRECOOKING; AUTO/LOW 8 HRS

1 Preheat the slow cooker, if required. Heat half the oil in a large Dutch oven over medium heat and add the squash. Season with salt and pepper and cook for 5–8 minutes, stirring, until it starts to turn golden. Remove the squash from the pot and set aside.

2 Heat the remaining oil in the pot, add the onion, and cook for 3–4 minutes until soft. Stir in the oregano, thyme, garlic, and chile and cook for a few more minutes. Add the lamb, increase the heat a little, and cook, stirring, for 5–8 minutes until it is no longer pink. Reduce the heat, return the squash to the pot, add the stock and tomatoes, and bring to a boil. Transfer everything to the slow cooker and stir in the raisins. Cover with the lid and cook on auto/low for 8 hours.

3 Taste and season, if necessary, then stir in the mint and harissa paste. Serve with rice or warmed pita bread and a lightly dressed crisp green salad.

traditional method   PREP 25 MINS   COOK 1½–2 HRS

1 Preheat the oven to 350°F (180°C). Heat half the oil in a large Dutch oven over medium heat and add the squash. Season with salt and pepper and cook for 5–8 minutes, stirring, until it starts to turn golden. Remove the squash from the pot and set aside.

2 Heat the remaining oil in the pot, add the onion, and cook for 3–4 minutes until soft. Stir in the oregano, thyme, garlic, and chile and cook for a few more minutes. Add the lamb, increase the heat a little, and cook, stirring, for 5–8 minutes until it is no longer pink. Reduce the heat, return the squash to the pot, add the stock and tomatoes, and bring to a boil. Reduce to a simmer, stir in the raisins, cover with the lid, and put in the oven for 1–1½ hours. Check occasionally that it's not drying out, topping up with a little hot water if needed.

3 Taste and season, if necessary, then stir in the mint and harissa paste. Serve with rice or warmed pita bread and a lightly dressed crisp green salad.

The black beans in this recipe become fabulously tender when cooked in the coconut milk. Add lots of chile and garlic and the result is a tasty vegetarian dish.

Spicy black beans and coconut

SERVES 4–6

6oz (175g) black beans, soaked overnight
  and drained
1 tbsp olive oil
1 onion, very finely chopped
salt and freshly ground black pepper

5 garlic cloves, finely chopped
2 red chilies, seeded and finely chopped
2 x 14oz (400ml) cans coconut milk
2 cups hot vegetable stock, for
  both methods

in the slow cooker   **PREP** 10 MINS, PLUS SOAKING   **COOK** 20 MINS PRECOOKING; **AUTO/LOW** 8 HRS

1 Preheat the slow cooker, if required. Put the black beans in a large heavy-based saucepan and cover with plenty of water. Bring to a boil, cover with the lid, and cook for 10 minutes. Drain and set the beans aside in a bowl. Heat the oil in the pan over medium heat, add the onion, and cook for 3–4 minutes until soft. Season with salt and pepper, then stir in the garlic and chilies. Return the beans to the pan and turn until well coated.

2 Add in the coconut milk and stock, season again, and bring the sauce to a boil. Transfer everything to the slow cooker, cover with the lid, and cook on auto/low for 8 hours. Taste and season as required and serve with warm bowls of rice.

traditional method   **PREP** 10 MINS, PLUS SOAKING   **COOK** 1¾–2¼ HRS

1 Preheat the oven to 325°F (160°C). Put the black beans in a large heavy-based saucepan and cover with plenty of water. Bring to a boil, cover with the lid, and cook for 10 minutes. Drain and set the beans aside in a bowl. Heat the oil in the pan over medium heat, add the onion, and cook for 3–4 minutes until soft. Season with salt and pepper, then stir in the garlic and chilies. Return the beans to the pan and stir until well coated.

2 Add in the coconut milk and stock, season again, and bring the sauce to a boil. Cover with the lid and put in the oven for 1½–2 hours or until the beans are soft. Check occasionally that it's not drying out, topping up with a little hot water if needed. Taste and season as required and serve with warm bowls of rice.

This highly flavored, gutsy dish is guaranteed to make the taste buds tingle. To make the most of its flavors, enjoy the jambalaya on its own with a simple salad and crusty bread.

Sausage and shrimp jambalaya

🍲 **SERVES** 6 ❄️ **FREEZE** UP TO 3 MONTHS

1–2 tbsp olive oil
9oz (250g) smoked sausage, cut into bite-sized pieces
9oz (250g) dried chorizo, chopped into thick slices
2 onions, diced
1 green bell pepper, seeded and diced
1 red bell pepper, seeded and diced
salt and freshly ground black pepper
3 garlic cloves, peeled and finely chopped
2 tsp Cajun seasoning

1 tbsp all-purpose flour
about 2 cups hot chicken stock for the slow cooker
  (3 cups for the traditional method)
2 tbsp Worcestershire sauce
1½ cups quick-cook rice
2 bay leaves
9oz (250g) shrimp
9oz (250g) okra, sliced
handful of flat-leaf parsley, finely chopped

in the slow cooker 🕐 **PREP** 15 MINS **COOK** 15 MINS PRECOOKING; AUTO/LOW 3–4 HRS OR **HIGH** 1–2 HRS

1 Preheat the slow cooker, if required. Heat the oil in a large Dutch oven over medium-high heat, add the sausage and chorizo, and cook for 5–8 minutes until golden. Remove and set aside.

2 Reduce the heat to medium, add the onions, and cook for 3–4 minutes until soft. Then stir in the peppers and cook for a few more minutes, until beginning to soften. Add seasoning, stir in the garlic and Cajun seasoning, and cook for 1 minute. Stir in the flour to combine and ladle in a little stock. Return the sausages and chorizo, and add the Worcestershire sauce.

3 Transfer everything to the slow cooker, stir in the rice and bay leaves, then pour over just enough stock to cover the mixure. Cover with the lid and cook on auto/low for 3–4 hours or on high for 1–2 hours. Add the shrimp and okra for the last hour of cooking. Remove the bay leaves, taste and season if needed, then stir in the parsley. Serve with a salad and some crusty bread.

traditional method 🕐 **PREP** 15 MINS **COOK** 2¼ HRS

1 Preheat the oven to 300°F (150°C). Heat the oil in a large Dutch oven over medium-high heat, add the sausage and chorizo, and cook for 5–8 minutes until golden. Remove and set aside.

2 Reduce the heat to medium, add the onions, and cook for 3–4 minutes until soft. Then stir in the pepper and cook for a few more minutes, until beginning to soften. Add seasoning, stir in the garlic and Cajun seasoning, and cook for 1 minute. Stir in the flour to combine and ladle in a little stock. Return the sausages, chorizo, and peppers, and add the Worcestershire sauce.

3 Stir in the rice and bay leaves, then pour in the stock. Mix well, cover with the lid, and put in the oven for 1½ hours. Check occasionally that it's not drying out, topping up with a little hot water if needed. Stir in the shrimp and okra, re-cover, and cook for a further 30 minutes. Remove the bay leaves, taste and season if needed, then stir in the parsley. Serve with a salad and some crusty bread.

This is a Mexican-inspired dish with lots of gutsy heat provided by the chipotle sauce, a key ingredient in many Mexican recipes. You could use pork in place of the beef, cooking until tender.

Beef chili mole

🌀 **SERVES** 4　❄ **FREEZE** UP TO 3 MONTHS

1lb 9oz (700g) beef chuck, cut into bite-sized pieces
1 tbsp chipotle sauce or salsa
3 tbsp olive oil
2 tbsp sesame seeds, toasted
⅓ cup almonds, skin on, toasted
1 red bell pepper, seeded and roughly chopped
4 tomatoes, roughly chopped
2 flour tortillas, roughly torn

1¾ cups hot vegetable stock for the slow cooker
  (2 cups for the traditional method)
3 garlic cloves, finely chopped
1 red chile, seeded and finely chopped
1 green chile, seeded and finely chopped
salt and freshly ground black pepper
small bunch of cilantro leaves, chopped
1 red onion, finely chopped

in the slow cooker　🕒 PREP 15 MINS　COOK 15 MINS PRECOOKING; **AUTO/LOW** 6–8 HRS

1 Preheat the slow cooker, if required. Toss the beef in the chipotle sauce. Heat 1 tablespoon of the oil in a large Dutch oven over high heat and cook the beef for 5–8 minutes (in batches, if necessary), turning it until browned all over. Remove and set aside.

2 Put the sesame seeds and almonds in a food processor and pulse until ground. Leave in the food processor and set aside. Heat 1 tablespoon of the oil in the pot over medium heat, add the bell pepper and tomatoes, and cook for 2–3 minutes until soft. Add to the food processor and blend to a paste. Add the tortillas and some of the stock and blend until it is a saucelike consistency. Set aside.

3 Heat the remaining oil, add the garlic and chilies, and cook for 1 minute, taking care not to burn them. Add the tomato and pepper sauce, the remaining stock, and season well. Bring to a boil, then reduce to a simmer, add the beef, and transfer everything to the slow cooker. Cover with the lid and cook on auto/low for 6–8 hours. Stir in the cilantro and serve scattered with the red onion and some warmed tortillas on the side.

traditional method　🕒 PREP 15 MINS　COOK 2¼–2¾ HRS

1 Preheat the oven to 325°F (160°C). Toss the beef in the chipotle sauce. Heat 1 tablespoon of the oil in a large Dutch oven over high heat and cook the beef for 5–8 minutes (in batches, if necessary), turning it until browned all over. Remove and set aside.

2 Put the sesame seeds and almonds in a food processor and pulse until ground. Leave in the food processor and set aside. Heat 1 tablespoon of the oil in the pot over medium heat, add the bell pepper and tomatoes, and cook for 2–3 minutes until soft. Add to the food processor and blend to a paste. Add the tortillas and some of the stock and blend until it is a saucelike consistency. Set aside.

3 Heat the remaining oil, add the garlic and chilies, and cook for 1 minute, taking care not to burn them. Add the tomato and pepper sauce, the remaining stock, and season well. Bring to a boil, then reduce to a simmer, add the beef, cover with the lid, and put in the oven for 2–2½ hours. Check occasionally that it's not drying out, topping up with a little hot water if needed. Stir in the cilantro and serve with the red onion and some warmed tortillas on the side.

Kidney beans become very tender and soft when they are gently cooked for a long time. Swap the sweet potatoes for squash, if you wish, and add some chopped yam if it is available.

Chilean pork and beans

⊘ **SERVES** 6 ❄ **FREEZE** UP TO 3 MONTHS ♡ **HEALTHY**

2 cups dried red kidney beans, soaked in
   cold water overnight, drained, and rinsed
2 tbsp olive oil
2lb (900g) boned loin of pork, cut into
   bite-sized pieces
1 large onion, finely sliced
2 garlic cloves, finely chopped
salt and freshly ground black pepper
14oz (400g) can chopped tomatoes

1 tbsp tomato paste
few sprigs each of parsley, cilantro, and
   oregano, leaves stripped and chopped
1 green chile, seeded and diced
2 green bell peppers, seeded and diced
about 1lb (500g) sweet potatoes, peeled
   and chopped into 1in (2.5cm) cubes
2 tbsp red wine vinegar

in the slow cooker 🕐 **PREP** 20 MINS, PLUS SOAKING **COOK** 30 MINS PRECOOKING; AUTO/LOW 6–8 HRS

1 Preheat the slow cooker, if required. Put the beans in a saucepan, cover with fresh water, and boil for 10 minutes, then drain and set aside.

2 Heat the oil in a large Dutch oven over medium-high heat, add the pork and cook for about 10 minutes (in batches, if necessary) until brown on all sides. Remove and set aside. Reduce the heat and add the onion, garlic and salt and pepper. Cover with the lid and cook very gently for about 15 minutes until the onion is very soft and brown.

3 Return the pork to the pot, stir in the tomatoes, tomato paste, and herbs, and bring to a boil. Transfer everything to the slow cooker and add the beans, vegetables, and red wine vinegar, together with 2 cups of water to cover. Cover with the lid and cook on auto/low for 6–8 hours. Taste and add seasoning, if needed. Serve with rice or flour tortillas.

traditional method 🕐 **PREP** 20 MINS, PLUS SOAKING **COOK** 3–3½ HRS

1 Put the beans in a saucepan, cover with fresh water, and boil for 10 minutes. Reduce the heat, cover, and simmer for 1 hour or until almost tender but still slightly firm. Drain well.

2 Preheat the oven to 350°F (180°C). Heat the oil in a large Dutch oven over medium-high heat, add the pork, and cook for about 10 minutes (in batches, if necessary) until brown on all sides. Remove and set aside. Reduce the heat and add the onion, garlic, and salt and pepper. Cover with the lid and cook very gently for about 15 minutes until the onion is very soft and brown. Return the pork to the pot and add the tomatoes, tomato paste, and herbs, together with 2 cups of hot water. Cover and put in the oven for 1¼–1½ hours until the pork is just tender.

3 Add the beans and vegetables and top up with enough water to cover. Put back in the oven and cook for a further 45–60 minutes, then remove and sit on the stove. Stir in the red wine vinegar and simmer, uncovered, for 5 minutes. Taste and add seasoning, if needed. Serve with rice or flour tortillas.

Jambalaya is a traditional southern American dish from Louisiana. Variations include spiced sausages in place of the chicken, and shrimp, which are added toward the end of the cooking time.

Chicken jambalaya

SERVES 4–6

2 tbsp olive oil
6 boneless chicken pieces (thigh and breast),
   cut into large chunky pieces
salt and freshly ground black pepper
2 tsp dried oregano
2 tsp cayenne pepper
1 red onion, finely chopped
3 garlic cloves, finely chopped
1 green pepper, seeded and finely chopped

1 red pepper, seeded and finely chopped
7oz (200g) thick slices pre-cooked ham,
   roughly chopped
2 cups hot chicken stock for the slow cooker (3 cups
   for the traditional method), plus extra if necessary
1¾ cups quick-cooking long-grain rice
1 cup frozen or fresh peas
small handful of cilantro, finely chopped (optional)

in the slow cooker   **PREP** 15–20 MINS   **COOK** 20 MINS PRECOOKING; **AUTO/LOW** 2–3 HRS

1 Preheat the slow cooker, if required. Heat half the oil in a large Dutch oven over medium-high heat. Season the chicken pieces with salt and pepper, toss in the oregano and cayenne pepper, then add to the pot (in batches, if necessary) and cook for 6–10 minutes until golden brown. Remove and set aside.

2 Heat the remaining oil in the pot over medium heat, add the onion, garlic, and peppers, and cook for 5–8 minutes, stirring. Transfer everything to the slow cooker, including the chicken. Add the ham and pour in enough stock to just cover the meat. Stir in the rice and peas, then season with salt and pepper, cover with the lid, and cook on auto/low for 2–3 hours or until all the liquid has been absorbed, stirring after an hour of cooking.

3 Taste and add seasoning, if needed, and stir in the cilantro, if using. Try serving with a green salad, green beans, plain yogurt or sour cream, and some crusty bread.

traditional method   **PREP** 15–20 MINS   **COOK** 1½ HRS

1 Heat half the oil in a large Dutch oven over medium-high heat. Season the chicken pieces with salt and pepper, toss in the oregano and cayenne pepper, then add to the pot (in batches, if necessary) and cook for 6–10 minutes until golden brown. Remove and set aside.

2 Heat the remaining oil in the pot over medium heat, add the onion, garlic, and peppers and cook for 5–8 minutes, stirring. Return the chicken to the pot and stir in the ham. Pour in the stock and bring to a boil, then reduce to a simmer, season well, partially cover with the lid, and cook gently for about 40 minutes. Check occasionally that it's not drying out, topping up with a little hot water if needed. Stir in the rice, turning so it absorbs all the stock, and cook for about 15 minutes or until the rice is cooked, topping up with more stock if necessary. Add the peas for the last 5 minutes.

3 Taste and add seasoning, if needed, and stir in the cilantro, if using. Try serving with a green salad, green beans, plain yogurt or sour cream, and some crusty bread.

This easy one-pot dish is so versatile you can make it with pork, beef, or even wild boar sausages. If you can't find jalapeños, add 1–2 teaspoons of crushed dried chilies.

Sausage chili pot

SERVES 4–6 ❄ **FREEZE** UP TO 3 MONTHS

1 tbsp olive oil
1¾lb (800g) fresh pork sausages, skinned
1 onion, finely chopped
salt and freshly ground black pepper
2 red bell peppers, seeded and diced
½ x 10½oz (300g) jar jalapeño peppers, drained
4 garlic cloves, finely chopped

2 x 14oz (400g) cans chopped tomatoes
14oz (400g) can black eye peas, drained and rinsed
1 cup hot chicken or vegetable stock for the slow cooker (2 cups for the traditional method)
pinch of cayenne pepper

in the slow cooker ⏱ PREP 20 MINS   COOK 15 MINS PRECOOKING;
AUTO/LOW 6–8 HRS OR HIGH 3–4 HRS

1 Preheat the slow cooker, if required. Heat the oil in a large Dutch oven over medium-high heat, add the sausage meat, and break it up with the back of a wooden spoon. Cook for about 5 minutes, or until no longer pink, then add the onion, season with salt and pepper, and cook for 2 minutes.

2 Stir in the red peppers and cook for another couple of minutes, then add the jalapeño peppers and garlic and cook for a minute. Transfer everything to the slow cooker and add in the tomatoes, beans, stock, and cayenne pepper. Combine well and add seasoning, then cover with the lid and cook on auto/low for 6–8 hours or on high for 3–4 hours. Serve with fluffy rice or baked potatoes.

traditional method ⏱ PREP 20 MINS   COOK 1¾ HRS

1 Preheat the oven to 300°F (150°C). Heat the oil in a large Dutch oven over medium-high heat, add the sausage meat, and break it up with the back of a wooden spoon. Cook for about 5 minutes, or until no longer pink, then add the onion, season with salt and pepper, and cook for 2 minutes.

2 Stir in the red peppers and cook for another couple of minutes, then add the jalapeño peppers and garlic and cook for a minute. Add in the tomatoes, beans, stock, and cayenne pepper. Combine well and add seasoning, then cover with the lid and put in the oven for 1½ hours. Serve with fluffy rice or baked potatoes.

Hot and spicy with the flavors of Mexico—add some seeded and finely chopped chipotle chilies if you like it really hot. Serve with plain boiled rice, some sour cream, and tortillas.

Chipotle chicken

⚙ **SERVES** 4–6 ❄ **FREEZE** UP TO 3 MONTHS

1 tbsp olive oil
8 chicken thighs, skin on
salt and freshly ground black pepper
1 onion, finely chopped
3 garlic cloves, finely chopped
½ tsp cumin seeds
2 red bell peppers, seeded and roughly chopped
4 tbsp chipotle paste or salsa
grated zest of ½ lime and juice of 1 lime
1 tbsp white wine vinegar

2 x 14oz (400g) cans whole tomatoes
1 cup hot chicken stock for the slow cooker
  (2 cups for the traditional method)
14oz (400g) can black beans, drained and rinsed
1 cinnamon stick
handful of cilantro, leaves roughly chopped
1 avocado, halved, pitted, peeled, and chopped
  into bite-sized pieces (toss in lime juice to avoid
  discoloring) (optional)

in the slow cooker   🕐 **PREP** 15 MINS   **COOK** 15 MINS PRECOOKING;
AUTO/LOW 6–8 HRS OR HIGH 3–4 HRS

1 Preheat the slow cooker, if required. Heat the oil in a large Dutch oven over medium-high heat. Season the chicken with salt and pepper and cook (in batches, if necessary) for 6–8 minutes until golden all over. Remove and set aside. Lower the heat to medium, add the onion, garlic, and cumin seeds, and cook for a minute. Add the peppers and cook for about 5 minutes more, until they begin to soften. Return the chicken to the pot and stir in the chipotle paste, turning to coat. Add the lime zest and juice and vinegar, increase the heat, and let the sauce bubble for a few minutes.

2 Add the tomatoes and a little stock and bring to a boil, then transfer everything to the slow cooker. Add the remaining stock, beans, cinnamon stick, and some pepper, cover with the lid, and cook on auto/low for 6–8 hours or on high for 3–4 hours. Remove the cinnamon stick, taste and season if needed, then stir in most of the cilantro and top with the avocado, if using. Sprinkle over the remaining cilantro leaves. Serve with rice, sour cream, and tortillas.

traditional method   🕐 **PREP** 15 MINS   **COOK** 1¾ HRS

1 Preheat the oven to 350°F (180°C). Heat the oil in a large Dutch oven over medium-high heat. Season the chicken with salt and pepper and cook (in batches, if necessary) for 6–8 minutes until golden all over. Remove and set aside. Lower the heat to medium, add the onion, garlic, and cumin seeds, and cook for a minute. Add the peppers and cook for about 5 minutes more, until they begin to soften. Return the chicken to the pot and stir in the chipotle paste, turning to coat. Add the lime zest and juice and vinegar, increase the heat, and let the sauce bubble for a few minutes.

2 Add the tomatoes and a little stock and bring to a boil. Pour in the remaining stock and add the beans. Continue boiling for a few minutes then reduce to a simmer. Add the cinnamon stick and some pepper, cover with the lid, and put in the oven for 1½ hours. Check occasionally that it's not drying out, topping up with a little hot water if needed. Remove the cinnamon stick, taste and season if needed, then stir in most of the cilantro and top with the avocado, if using. Sprinkle over the remaining cilantro leaves. Serve with rice, sour cream, and tortillas.

The addition of a red chile (and chile flakes, too, if you like) to the turkey breasts gives a real boost to this dish. The sweetness of the corn and squash complement it perfectly.

Spicy turkey and corn

SERVES 4–6 **FREEZE** UP TO 3 MONTHS **HEALTHY**

1 tbsp olive oil
1 onion, finely chopped
salt and freshly ground black pepper
3 garlic cloves, finely chopped
1 red chile, seeded and finely chopped
1 butternut squash, peeled, seeded and diced
pinch of dried chile flakes (optional)
½ cup white wine

14oz (400g) can tomatoes
14.5oz (425g) can corn, drained
1½ cups hot chicken stock for the slow cooker
   (2 cups for the traditional method)
2–3 turkey breasts
splash of Tabasco sauce
grated Parmesan cheese, to serve (optional)

in the slow cooker **PREP** 20 MINS **COOK** 15 MINS PRECOOKING; **AUTO/LOW** 6–8 HRS

1 Preheat the slow cooker, if required. Heat the oil in a large heavy-based pan over medium heat, add the onion, and cook for 3–4 minutes until soft. Season with salt and pepper, stir in the garlic and chile, and cook for a few more minutes.

2 Add the squash and chile flakes, if using, and cook for about 5 minutes, stirring so it doesn't burn. Pour in the wine, increase the heat, and cook for a couple of minutes until the alcohol evaporates.

3 Transfer everything to the slow cooker, then add the tomatoes, corn, stock, and turkey and season well. Cover with the lid and cook on auto/low for 6–8 hours. Remove the turkey breasts, shred, and stir into the pot along with the Tabasco sauce, to taste. Serve with a sprinkling of Parmesan cheese, if you like, and some crusty bread.

traditional method **PREP** 20 MINS **COOK** 1¼ HRS

1 Heat the oil in a large Dutch oven over medium heat, add the onion, and cook for 3–4 minutes until soft. Season with salt and pepper, stir in the garlic and chile, and cook for a few more minutes.

2 Add the squash and chile flakes, if using, and cook for about 5 minutes, stirring so it doesn't burn. Pour in the wine, increase the heat, and cook for a couple of minutes until the alcohol evaporates.

3 Add in the tomatoes, corn, and stock and season with salt and pepper. Add the turkey breasts and bring to a boil, then reduce to a low simmer, partially cover with the lid, and put in the oven for about 1 hour. Check occasionally that it's not drying out, topping up with a little hot water if needed. Remove the turkey breasts, shred, and stir into the Dutch oven together with the Tabasco sauce, to taste. Serve with a sprinkling of Parmesan cheese, if you like, and some crusty bread.

Hot chipotle sauce added to this slow-cooked bean mixture makes for a fabulous vegetarian dish—the sauce is so rich and tasty that you don't even notice there isn't any meat in it.

Hot chili and beans

SERVES 4   **FREEZE** UP TO 3 MONTHS   **HEALTHY**

1 tbsp olive oil
1 onion, finely chopped
salt and freshly ground black pepper
1 red chile, seeded and finely chopped
1 tsp coriander seeds, crushed
handful of thyme sprigs, leaves only
3 garlic cloves, finely chopped
3 celery stalks, finely chopped
3 carrots, peeled and finely chopped
1 star anise

1 tbsp white wine vinegar
14oz (400g) can kidney beans, drained and rinsed
14oz (400g) can mixed beans in chili sauce
14oz (400g) can adzuki beans, drained and rinsed
1 tbsp chipotle sauce or salsa, or splash of
   Tabasco chipotle sauce
1½ cups hot vegetable stock for the slow cooker
   (2 cups for the traditional method)
lime wedges, to serve
sour cream, to serve (optional)

in the slow cooker   **PREP** 30 MINS   **COOK** 20 MINS PRECOOKING;
           AUTO/LOW 8 HRS OR **HIGH** 4 HRS

1 Preheat the slow cooker, if required. Heat the oil in a large, heavy Dutch oven over medium heat, add the onion, and cook for 3–4 minutes until soft. Season with salt and pepper, then stir in the chile, coriander seeds, thyme, and garlic and cook for a few more minutes.

2 Add the celery, carrots, and star anise and cook on very low heat for about 15 minutes, stirring occasionally, until the mixture becomes soft and juicy. Increase the heat a little, pour in the vinegar, and stir to scrape up the bits from the bottom of the pan. Stir in the beans and the chipotle sauce or salsa, add a little of the stock, and let it simmer.

3 Transfer everything to the slow cooker and pour over the remaining stock. Cover with the lid and cook on auto/low for 8 hours or on high for 4 hours. Remove the star anise, taste the sauce, and season as required. Serve with lime wedges, sour cream, if you wish, and hot corn tortillas.

traditional method   **PREP** 30 MINS   **COOK** 1 HR

1 Heat the oil in a large, heavy Dutch oven over medium heat, add the onion, and cook for 3–4 minutes until soft. Season with salt and pepper, then stir in the chile, coriander seeds, thyme, and garlic and cook for a few more minutes.

2 Add the celery, carrots, and star anise and cook on very low heat for about 15 minutes, stirring occasionally, until the mixture becomes soft and juicy. Increase the heat a little, pour in the vinegar, and stir to scrape up the bits from the bottom of the pan. Stir in the beans and the chipotle sauce or salsa, add a little of the stock, and let it simmer.

3 Add the remaining stock, bring to a boil, then reduce to a simmer and cook, partially covered, for about 40 minutes. Stir occasionally and top up with hot water if needed. Remove the star anise, taste, and season as required. Serve with lime wedges, sour cream, if you wish, and hot corn tortillas.

The basis of this tasty stew is corn. If you can't get hold of creamed corn, use a can of regular corn and blend it in the food processor. Omit the fish if you are cooking for vegetarians.

Creole fish and corn stew

 SERVES 4–6 **FREEZE** UP TO 1 MONTH **HEALTHY**

2 tbsp olive oil
1 onion, finely chopped
3 garlic cloves, finely chopped
3 celery stalks, finely chopped
3 carrots, peeled and finely chopped
1 tsp dried oregano
few sprigs of thyme, leaves only
1 tsp cayenne pepper (use less if you
  don't like it too hot)
14oz (400g) can creamed corn

14oz (400g) can corn, drained
2 cups hot vegetable stock for the slow cooker
  (3 cups for the traditional method)
salt and freshly ground black pepper
2 potatoes, peeled and diced into bite-sized pieces
7oz (200g) precooked shrimp, chopped
10oz (300g) white fish such as catfish or cod,
  skinned and cut into chunky pieces
splash of Tabasco sauce (optional)

in the slow cooker **PREP** 15 MINS   **COOK** 10 MINS PRECOOKING; **HIGH** 3–4 HRS

1 Preheat the slow cooker, if required. Heat the oil in a large Dutch oven over medium heat, add the onion, and cook for 3–4 minutes until soft. Then stir in the garlic, celery, and carrot and cook on a gentle heat for a further 5 minutes, or until the carrot is soft.

2 Stir in the herbs and cayenne pepper, then add both the cans of corn. Transfer everything to the slow cooker, pour in the stock, season with salt and pepper, and then add the potatoes.

3 Cover with the lid and cook on high for 3–4 hours. For the last 15 minutes of cooking, add the shrimp and fish and cook until the fish is opaque and cooked through. Taste and season further, if necessary, and stir in the Tabasco sauce, if using. Ladle into warmed bowls and serve with crusty bread.

traditional method **PREP** 15 MINS   **COOK** 1¼ HRS

1 Heat the oil in a large Dutch oven over medium heat, add the onion, and cook for 3–4 minutes until soft. Then stir in the garlic, celery, and carrot and cook on a gentle heat for a further 5 minutes or until the carrot is soft.

2 Stir in the herbs and cayenne pepper, then add both the cans of corn and the stock. Season well with salt and pepper, bring to a boil, reduce to a simmer and cook gently, partially covered, for 30–40 minutes. Add the potatoes and cook for a further 15 minutes.

3 Add the shrimp and fish to the pot and simmer gently for 6–10 minutes, until the fish is opaque and cooked through. Taste and season further, if necessary, and stir in the Tabasco sauce, if using. Ladle into warmed bowls and serve with crusty bread.

This is a rich ragu-type dish using stewing beef, cooked slowly with tomatoes. Try it spooned over some rich, comforting polenta made with butter and Parmesan cheese, or with pasta.

Slow-cooked beef

SERVES 4–6 **FREEZE** UP TO 3 MONTHS

1 tbsp olive oil
2lb (900g) chuck steak, cut into bite-sized pieces
salt and freshly ground black pepper
1 onion, finely chopped
3 garlic cloves, finely chopped
3 carrots, peeled and finely chopped
3 celery stalks, finely chopped

1 red pepper, seeded and roughly chopped
pinch of dried oregano
pinch of paprika
6 anchovies, chopped
grated zest of 1 orange
2 x 14oz (400g) cans chopped tomatoes
grated Parmesan cheese, to serve (optional)

in the slow cooker **PREP** 20 MINS **COOK** 20 MINS PRECOOKING; **AUTO/LOW** 6–8 HRS

1 Preheat the slow cooker, if required. Heat half the oil in a large Dutch oven over medium heat, add the steak (in batches, if necessary), season with salt and pepper, and cook for about 5 minutes, until browned. Remove and set aside.

2 Heat the remaining oil over medium heat, add the onion, and cook for a few minutes. Stir in the garlic, carrots, and celery and cook on low heat, stirring occasionally for 5–8 minutes, until soft. Add the pepper, oregano, paprika, anchovies, and orange zest. Return the meat to the pan and stir to coat, then add in the tomatoes, season with salt and pepper, and bring to a boil. Transfer everything to the slow cooker, cover with the lid, and cook on auto/low for 6–8 hours.

3 Taste and season some more, if needed. Serve piled onto polenta or pasta, with a sprinkling of Parmesan cheese, if you like.

traditional method **PREP** 20 MINS **COOK** 2¼ HRS

1 Preheat the oven to 325°F (160°C). Heat half the oil in a large Dutch oven over medium heat, add the steak (in batches, if necessary), season with salt and pepper, and cook for about 5 minutes until browned. Remove and set aside.

2 Heat the remaining oil over medium heat, add the onion and cook for a few minutes. Stir in the garlic, carrots, and celery and cook on low heat, stirring occasionally for 5–8 minutes, until soft. Add the pepper, oregano, paprika, anchovies, and orange zest. Return the meat to the pan and stir to coat, then add in the tomatoes, season with salt and pepper, and bring to a boil.

3 Cover with the lid and put in the oven for 2 hours. Check occasionally that it's not drying out, topping up with a little hot water if needed. You want it fairly thick, so don't dilute it too much and shred the meat a little, if you wish.

4 Taste and season some more, if needed. Serve piled onto polenta or pasta, with a sprinkling of Parmesan cheese, if you like.

Far removed from canned baked beans, these haricot beans benefit from being cooked for a long time. They become rich and satisfying as they absorb so much flavor from the bacon pieces.

New England beans

⊘ **SERVES** 4   ❄ **FREEZE** UP TO 3 MONTHS

1lb 2oz (500g) dried haricot or navy beans,
  soaked overnight and drained
1 tbsp olive oil
14oz (400g) thick-sliced smoked bacon, chopped
3 tbsp light soft brown sugar
2 tbsp molasses

1 tbsp English mustard
1 tbsp tomato purée
1½ cups hot vegetable stock for the slow cooker
  (2 cups for the traditional method)
freshly ground black pepper

in the slow cooker   ⏱ **PREP** 10 MINS, PLUS SOAKING   **COOK** 10 MINS PRECOOKING; AUTO/LOW 8 HRS

1 Preheat the slow cooker, if required. Put the beans in a large Dutch oven, cover with water, and bring to a vigorous boil for 10 minutes. Drain and return to the pan.

2 Meanwhile, in a separate large heavy-based pan, heat the oil over medium heat and cook the bacon for a few minutes until soft, then stir it into the beans together with the brown sugar, molasses, mustard, and tomato purée. Pour in the stock and season with pepper.

3 Transfer everything to the slow cooker, pour in the stock, and season well with pepper. Cover with the lid and cook on auto/low for 8 hours. Serve the beans with some chunky pieces of toast and plenty of pepper.

traditional method   ⏱ **PREP** 10 MINS, PLUS SOAKING   **COOK** 3¼–3¾ HRS

1 Preheat the oven to 275°F (140°C). Put the beans in a large Dutch oven, cover with water and bring to a vigorous boil for 10 minutes. Reduce to a gentle simmer, partially cover with the lid, and simmer for about 1 hour until the beans are just tender. Drain and set aside.

2 Heat the oil in the pot over medium heat, add the bacon, and cook for a few minutes until soft. Then add the cooked beans together with the brown sugar, molasses, mustard, and tomato purée. Pour in the stock and season with pepper.

3 Cover with the lid and put in the oven for 2–2½ hours. Check occasionally that it's not drying out, topping up with a little hot water if needed. Serve the beans with some chunky pieces of toast and plenty of pepper.

A good barbecue sauce adds flavor and moisture to the meat. This one features tangy tomato spiked with vinegar, orange juice, and cloves to add a spicy-sweet twist to a classic sauce.

Shredded beef in barbecue sauce

SERVES 4–6 **FREEZE** UP TO 3 MONTHS

1 tbsp olive oil
2½lb (1.1kg) beef brisket

FOR THE BARBECUE SAUCE
1 onion, very finely chopped
3 garlic cloves, finely chopped
1 red chile, seeded and finely chopped
1 tbsp tomato paste
½ cup white wine vinegar

juice of 1 orange
pinch of ground cloves
1 tbsp demerara sugar
1 tbsp honey
1 cup tomato purèe
½ cup hot vegetable stock for the slow cooker
  (1 cup for the traditional method)
salt and freshly ground black pepper

in the slow cooker **PREP** 15 MINS **COOK** 15 MINS PRECOOKING; **AUTO/LOW** 8 HRS

1 Preheat the slow cooker, if required. In a bowl, mix together all the barbecue sauce ingredients and season well with salt and pepper.

2 Heat the oil in a large Dutch oven over medium-high heat. Season the beef with salt and pepper and cook in the pot for 4–6 minutes on each side, including on its edge, until the meat is browned evenly all over. Add the barbecue sauce and bring to a boil, then transfer everything to the slow cooker. Cover with the lid and cook on auto/low for 8 hours.

3 Remove the brisket from the slow cooker, shred it with two forks, and stir it into the sauce. Serve with hot crusty rolls or pita bread and some crisp green salad leaves.

traditional method **PREP** 15 MINS **COOK** 3¼ HRS

1 Preheat the oven to 325°F (160°C). In a bowl, mix together all the barbecue sauce ingredients and season well with salt and pepper.

2 Heat the oil in a large Dutch oven over medium-high heat. Season the beef with salt and pepper and cook in the pot for 4–6 minutes on each side, including on its edge, until the meat is browned evenly all over. Add the barbecue sauce and let it bubble for a minute, then cover and put in the oven for 3 hours. Check regularly that it's not drying out, topping up with a little hot water if needed. Don't add too much water, though, or it will dilute the taste—reduce the oven temperature a little instead.

3 Remove from the oven, shred the brisket with two forks, and stir it into the sauce. Serve with hot crusty rolls or pita bread and some crisp green salad leaves.

Pot roasts
& ribs

This beef is slow cooked in sweet Madeira for maximum flavor. Buy the meat in one piece from your butcher and don't forget to soak the dried porcini mushrooms in water for 20 minutes.

Beef pot roast

SERVES 4–6   **FREEZE** UP TO 1 MONTH

2 tbsp olive oil
2lb (900g) piece of beef chuck roast
salt and freshly ground black pepper
1 large onion, chopped into eighths
1 tbsp whole-grain mustard
⅔ cup Madeira wine

about 1 cup dried porcini mushrooms, soaked
  in ½ cup warm water for 20 mins, strained,
  and liquid reserved
2 cups hot beef stock for the slow cooker
  (3 cups for the traditional method)
handful of flat-leaf parsley, finely chopped

in the slow cooker
PREP 10 MINS, PLUS SOAKING   **COOK** 25 MINS PRECOOKING;
AUTO/LOW 8 HRS

1 Preheat the slow cooker, if required. Heat half the oil in a large Dutch oven over medium-high heat. Season the beef with salt and pepper, add it to the pot, and cook for 6–8 minutes on each side until golden. It is ready when it lifts away from the bottom of the pot easily. Remove and set aside.

2 Heat the remaining oil in the pot over medium heat, add the onion, and cook for 3–4 minutes until soft. Stir in the mustard, increase the heat, and add the Madeira wine. Cook for a minute, then add the drained mushrooms.

3 Transfer everything to the slow cooker, including the beef. Add the stock and the strained mushroom liquid. Cover with the lid and cook on auto/low for 8 hours. Taste and season as necessary. Sprinkle with parsley and serve with mashed potatoes or baby cubed roasted potatoes.

traditional method
PREP 10 MINS, PLUS SOAKING   **COOK** 2½ HRS

1 Preheat the oven to 325°F (160°C). Heat half the oil in a large Dutch oven over medium-high heat. Season the beef with salt and pepper, add it to the pot, and cook for 6–8 minutes on each side until golden. It is ready when it lifts away from the bottom of the pot easily. Remove and set aside.

2 Heat the remaining oil in the pot over medium heat, add the onion, and cook for 3–4 minutes until soft. Stir in the mustard, increase the heat, and add the Madeira wine. Cook for a minute, then add the drained mushrooms, beef stock, and the strained mushroom liquid. Bring to a boil and stir, then reduce to a simmer and return the beef to the pot.

3 Cover with the lid and put in the oven for 2 hours. Check occasionally that it's not drying out, topping up with a little hot water if needed. Be careful not to add too much, however, or this will dilute the flavor. Taste and season as necessary. Sprinkle with parsley and serve with mashed potatoes or baby cubed roasted potatoes.

Chicken wings are cheap to buy and have lots of succulent meat on them. Serve these moreish, sticky charred chicken wings with a fiery hot dip or with something cool, such as a blue cheese dip.

Buffalo chicken wings

SERVES 4

2 tbsp olive oil, plus extra for oiling
1 shallot, finely chopped
1 garlic clove, crushed
2 tbsp tomato paste
1 tbsp dried oregano

few drops of Tabasco sauce
2 tsp light soft brown sugar
salt and freshly ground black pepper
12 chicken wings, tips removed

in the slow cooker   **PREP** 20 MINS, PLUS MARINATING   **COOK** AUTO/LOW 5–6 HRS

1 Preheat the slow cooker, if required. Place the oil, shallot, garlic, tomato paste, oregano, Tabasco, and sugar in a food processor, season with salt and pepper, and blend to a paste. Spoon into a large food bag and add the chicken wings. Shake the bag until the meat is well coated with the marinade, then chill in the refrigerator for at least 30 minutes to marinate.

2 Put the chicken wings and marinade into the slow cooker, spreading them evenly across the bottom. Cover with the lid and cook on auto/low for 5–6 hours, turning them halfway through the cooking time, if you wish. Serve with a spicy salsa or a blue cheese dip and some salad.

traditional method   **PREP** 20 MINS, PLUS MARINATING   **COOK** 40 MINS

1 Place the oil, shallot, garlic, tomato paste, oregano, Tabasco, and sugar in a food processor, season with salt and pepper, and blend to a paste. Spoon into a large food bag and add the chicken wings. Shake the bag until the meat is well coated with the marinade, then chill in the refrigerator for at least 30 minutes to marinate.

2 Preheat the oven to 325°F (160°C). Remove the chicken wings from the bag and lay them, skin-side down, on 2 lightly oiled baking trays. Put in the oven for 20 minutes. Turn the chicken wings over and cook for a further 20 minutes or until cooked through. Serve with a spicy salsa or a blue cheese dip and some salad.

Gherkins, sea salt, and mustard are the classic accompaniments to a pot au feu. It can be served as two courses—first, the rich cooking broth, then the meat and vegetables to follow.

Pot au feu

SERVES 4–6

2¼lb (1kg) boneless beef shin, tied with string lengthwise at 1in (2.5cm) intervals
1½lb (675g) beef blade steak
2 cups hot chicken stock for the slow cooker (14 cups for the traditional method)
1 onion, peeled and studded with 2 cloves
1 large bouquet garni, made with 12–15 sprigs of parsley, 4–5 sprigs of thyme, and 2 bay leaves
salt

10 peppercorns
8 carrots, chopped into 3in (7.5cm) lengths
1 small head of celery, chopped into 3in (7.5cm) lengths
4 leeks, chopped into 3in (7.5cm) lengths
about 2¼lb (1kg) marrow bones (optional)
½ French loaf, sliced diagonally and toasted

in the slow cooker   **PREP** 40 MINS   **COOK** 10 MINS PRECOOKING; **AUTO/LOW** 6–8 HRS

1 Preheat the slow cooker, if required. Put the shin, blade steak, and stock in the slow cooker and add the onion, bouquet garni, a pinch of salt, and the peppercorns. Cover with the lid and cook on auto/low for 6–8 hours. Tie the carrots, celery, leeks, and marrow bones, if using, each in a separate bundle of cheesecloth and add to the slow cooker for the last 2 hours of cooking, along with salt for seasoning.

2 Remove the meat and marrow bones from the broth. Discard the strings from the beef shin and cut it into slices, then cut the blade steak into pieces, discarding any bones. Remove the vegetable bundles, unwrap, and arrange them on a serving platter with the meat. Cover with foil and keep warm.

3 Strain the broth into a clean saucepan and taste, add salt and pepper if needed. If necessary, boil it until reduced and well flavored. If using the marrow bones, scoop out the marrow with a teaspoon and spread it on the toasts. Discard the bones. Place the toasts in warmed bowls, pour over the hot broth, and serve immediately with the meat and vegetables.

traditional method   **PREP** 40 MINS   **COOK** 3½–4 HRS

1 Put the shin, blade steak, and stock in a large Dutch oven. Bring to a boil, skimming. Add the onion, bouquet garni, a pinch of salt, and the peppercorns. Simmer gently, uncovered, for 2 hours, skimming occasionally. Tie the carrots, celery, leeks, and marrow bones, if using, each in a separate bundle of cheesecloth and add to the casserole. Season with salt. Simmer for 1½–2 hours until the meat and vegetables are very tender. Add more hot water if needed to ensure everything is always covered.

2 Remove the meat and marrow bones from the broth. Discard the strings from the beef shin and cut it into slices, then cut the blade steak into pieces, discarding any bones. Remove the vegetable bundles, unwrap, and arrange them on a serving platter with the meat. Cover with foil and keep warm.

3 Strain the broth into a clean saucepan and taste, add salt and pepper if needed. If necessary, boil it until reduced and well flavored. If using the marrow bones, scoop out the marrow with a teaspoon and spread it on the toasts. Discard the bones. Place the toasts in warmed bowls, pour over the hot broth, and serve immediately with the meat and vegetables.

Knuckle or ham hock is amazing value, and tasty, too.
The Jerusalem artichokes add a nutty, creamy texture,
but if they're not available you can use parsnips instead.

Pot roast smoked ham

⚙ **SERVES** 4–6 ❄ **FREEZE** UP TO 1 MONTH

2 smoked ham hocks (knuckles),
  about 3lb (1.35kg) each
1 bay leaf
1 tbsp olive oil
1 onion, finely chopped
salt and freshly ground black pepper
3 garlic cloves, finely chopped

few sprigs of thyme
3 carrots, peeled and chopped
8oz (225g) Jerusalem artichokes, peeled and sliced
½ cup yellow split peas
½ cup dry cider
2 cups hot vegetable stock for the slow cooker
  (3 cups for the traditional method)

in the slow cooker 🕐 **PREP** 25 MINS   **COOK** 15 MINS PRECOOKING; **AUTO/LOW** 8 HRS OR
HIGH 4 HRS, THEN **AUTO/LOW** 8 HRS OR **HIGH** 4 HRS

1 Preheat the slow cooker, if required. Put the ham hocks and bay leaf in the slow cooker and pour
in 6 cups of water. Cook on auto/low for 8 hours or on high for 4 hours. Remove the hams and,
when cool enough to handle, peel away the skins and discard. Set the hams aside. (You can reserve
the stock and use it if you wish, but it can be salty.)

2 Heat the oil in a large Dutch oven over medium heat, add the onion, and cook for 3–4 minutes
until soft. Season with salt and pepper, stir in the garlic, thyme, carrots, and artichokes, and cook
for a few more minutes. Stir in the split peas to coat. Increase the heat and pour in the cider, let it bubble
for a minute, then add the stock. Transfer everything to the slow cooker, including the hams, tucking
them down as much as possible. Cover with the lid and cook on auto/low for 8 hours or on high for
4 hours. The ham meat should now slide off the bone, so remove it with a fork and stir into the slow
cooker. Taste and season, if necessary, and serve with some crusty bread.

traditional method 🕐 **PREP** 25 MINS   **COOK** 3¼ HRS

1 Put the ham hocks and bay leaf in a large Dutch oven, cover with water, and cook for about 2 hours,
skimming away any scum that comes to the top of the pan. Remove the hams and, when cool
enough to handle, peel away the skins and discard. Set the hams aside. (You can reserve the stock and
use it if you wish, but it can be salty.)

2 Preheat the oven to 350°F (180°C). Heat the oil in a large Dutch oven over medium heat, add the
onion, and cook for 3–4 minutes until soft. Season with salt and pepper, stir in the garlic, thyme,
carrots, and artichokes, and cook for a few more minutes. Stir in the split peas to coat. Increase the
heat and pour in the cider, let it bubble for a minute, then add the stock and bring to a boil. Reduce to
a simmer and return the hams, tucking them down as much as possible.

3 Cover and put in the oven for about 1 hour or until the split peas are soft. Check that it's not
drying out too much, topping up with hot water if needed. The ham meat should now slide off
the bone, so remove it with a fork and stir into the pot. Taste and season, if necessary, and serve with
some crusty bread.

This slow-cooked whole chicken becomes meltingly tender and also results in no waste, as the chicken bones can be used to make stock for a soup. Swap the vegetables to match the seasons.

Pot roast chicken with turnips and fennel

SERVES 4–6

2 tbsp olive oil
1 whole chicken, weighing about 3lb (1.35kg)
salt and freshly ground black pepper
6 pork sausages, roughly chopped
1 fennel, roughly chopped
1 bay leaf

2 sprigs of rosemary
1 cup white wine
9oz (250g) turnips, peeled and roughly chopped
2 cups hot chicken stock for the slow cooker
 (3 cups for the traditional method)

in the slow cooker   **PREP** 15 MINS   **COOK** 30 MINS PRECOOKING; AUTO/LOW 8 HRS OR **HIGH** 4 HRS

1 Preheat the slow cooker, if required. Heat half the oil in a large Dutch oven, season the chicken with salt and pepper, then add it to the pot, breast-side down. Cook for about 10 minutes, then turn and cook the other side for about the same time. Remove and set aside.

2 Heat the remaining oil in the pot on high heat, add the sausages, and cook for 6–8 minutes until browned. Then reduce the heat, add the fennel, bay leaf, and rosemary, and cook for a further 5 minutes. Increase the heat, add the wine, and let it bubble for a minute, then add the turnips.

3 Transfer everything to the slow cooker. Add the chicken, breast-side down, and shuffle the vegetables around it. Pour in the stock, cover with the lid, and cook on auto/low for 8 hours or on high for 4 hours. Carefully remove the chicken from the pot (together with the bay leaf and rosemary), peel off the skin, and pull off the meat, putting it back into the slow cooker. Serve immediately with steamed Savoy cabbage.

traditional method   **PREP** 15 MINS   **COOK** 2–2½ HRS

1 Preheat the oven to 350°F (180°C). Heat half the oil in a large Dutch oven, season the chicken with salt and pepper, then add it to the pot, breast-side down. Cook for about 10 minutes, then turn and cook the other side for about the same time. Remove and set aside.

2 Heat the remaining oil in the pot on high heat, add the sausages, and cook for 6–8 minutes until browned. Then reduce the heat, add the fennel, bay leaf, and rosemary, and cook for a further 5 minutes. Increase the heat, add the wine, and let it bubble for a minute, then add the turnips.

3 Return the chicken to the pot, breast-side down, and shuffle the vegetables around it. Pour in the stock, bring to a boil, then cover with the lid and put in the oven for 1½–2 hours. Check occasionally that it's not drying out, topping up with a little hot water if needed. Carefully remove the chicken from the pot (together with the bay leaf and rosemary), peel off the skin, and pull off the meat, putting it back into the pot. Serve immediately with steamed Savoy cabbage.

The rich tomato sauce on these ribs is made with fresh tomatoes and spiced with lots of fresh ginger. There's no need to seed the red chilies, if you like really spicy food.

Ribs in a chile and ginger tomato sauce

SERVES 4–6

rack of pork ribs, about 12 ribs (about 2¾lb/1.25kg)
salt and freshly ground black pepper
1 tsp black peppercorns
1 tbsp olive oil
1 onion, finely chopped
4 garlic cloves, finely chopped
2in (5cm) piece of fresh ginger, peeled and
  finely chopped

2 red chilies, seeded and finely chopped
grated zest and juice of 1 lime
2¼lb (1kg) tomatoes, roughly chopped
1 tsp ground cinnamon
1 tbsp tomato paste
1 tbsp demerara sugar

in the slow cooker ⏱ PREP 15 MINS COOK 15 MINS PRECOOKING; **AUTO/LOW** 6–8 HRS

1 Preheat the slow cooker, if required. Chop the rack into individual ribs and put in a bowl. Season with salt, add the peppercorns, cover, and set aside.

2 To make the tomato sauce, heat the oil in a large heavy-based saucepan over medium heat, add the onion, garlic, ginger, chilies, and lime zest, and season well with salt and pepper. Cook for about 5 minutes until the vegetables begin to soften, then add the tomatoes, cinnamon, tomato paste, sugar, and lime juice, and cook on a very low heat, stirring occasionally, for about 10 minutes.

3 Transfer everything to the slow cooker, including the ribs, turning so they are coated. Cover with the lid and cook on auto/low for 6–8 hours. Serve with fluffy rice.

traditional method ⏱ PREP 15 MINS COOK 2–3 HRS

1 Preheat the oven to 325°F (160°C). Put the rack of ribs in a large pan and cover with water. Season with salt and add the peppercorns. Bring to a boil, then reduce to a simmer, partially cover with the lid, and cook for 1–1½ hours until the meat starts to come away from the bone. Remove and set aside until cool enough to handle.

2 To make the tomato sauce, heat the oil in a large heavy-based saucepan over medium heat, add the onion, garlic, ginger, chilies, and lime zest, and season well with salt and pepper. Cook for about 5 minutes until the vegetables begin to soften, then add the tomatoes, cinnamon, tomato paste, sugar, and lime juice, and cook on a very low heat, stirring occasionally, for about 10 minutes.

3 Slice the rack into individual ribs and nestle them into the sauce in the pot. Cover with the lid and put in the oven for 1–1½ hours. Check occasionally that it's not drying out, topping up with a little hot water if needed—the sauce should be fairly thick though. Serve with fluffy rice.

This dish can be made a day ahead and kept, covered, in the refrigerator. Reheat the birds with the cabbage, add the remaining plums, and thicken the sauce just before serving.

Poussins with plums and cabbage

⊚ **SERVES** 4 ♡ **HEALTHY**

2–3 poussins, each weighing about 1lb (500g), trussed with string so wings and legs are neatly tucked in (your butcher can do this)
salt and freshly ground black pepper
2 tbsp vegetable oil
9oz (250g) sliced bacon

½ Savoy cabbage, cored and coarsely shredded
4 purple plums, halved and pitted
1 onion, peeled and studded with 1 clove
1 bouquet garni
1 cup dry white wine
2 cups hot chicken stock, for both methods

in the slow cooker ⏱ **PREP** 15 MINS **COOK** 30 MINS PRECOOKING; **AUTO/LOW** 6–8 HRS

1 Preheat the slow cooker, if required. Season the poussins inside and out. Heat the oil in a large Dutch oven, add the birds, one or two at a time, and cook for 5–10 minutes until browned all over. Remove and set aside. Reduce the heat and cook the bacon, stirring, for 3–5 minutes until the fat has rendered. Spoon off all but 2 tablespoons of fat and stir in the cabbage, then add half of this mixture to the slow cooker and set the rest aside. Top with the poussins and two-thirds of the plums. Add the clove-studded onion and bouquet garni. Pour in the wine and stock. Cover with the lid and cook on auto/low for 6–8 hours. Add the remaining cabbage and bacon for the last 30 minutes of cooking and the plums for the last 20 minutes of cooking.

2 Discard the onion and bouquet garni. Transfer the birds to a chopping board; remove the strings. Taste the cabbage for seasoning, then transfer the cabbage and plums to a serving dish. Set the birds on top, cover with foil, and keep warm. Strain the cooking liquid into a pan and boil for 10–15 minutes until reduced by about half. Taste, and season if needed. Serve the sauce with the poussins.

traditional method 🕐 **PREP** 15 MINS **COOK** 1¾ HRS

1 Preheat the oven to 350°F (180°C). Season the poussins inside and out. Set aside. Put the cabbage in a pan of salted boiling water and cook for 2 minutes until beginning to soften. Drain and set aside. Heat the oil in a large Dutch oven, add the birds, one or two at a time, and cook for 5–10 minutes until browned all over. Remove and set aside. Reduce the heat and cook the bacon, stirring, for 3–5 minutes until the fat has rendered. Spoon off all but 2 tablespoons of fat and spread half the cabbage across the base of the pot. Add the poussins and two-thirds of the plums. Add the clove-studded onion and bouquet garni. Cover with the remaining cabbage and pour in the wine and stock. Cover with the lid and put in the oven for 45–55 minutes, until the birds are cooked and the juices run clear when the thighs are pierced with a sharp knife.

2 Discard the onion and bouquet garni. Transfer the birds to a chopping board; remove the strings. Taste the cabbage for seasoning, then transfer to a serving dish. Set the birds on top, cover with foil, and keep warm. Add the remaining plums to the cooking liquid and simmer for 5–8 minutes until tender, then remove them and transfer to the serving dish. Boil the sauce for 10–15 minutes until reduced by about half. Taste, and season if needed. Serve the sauce with the poussins.

This simple recipe leaves the chicken incredibly moist and fragrant with lemon and fennel. It is served with a rich cheese and cream sauce. Good with crisply cooked vegetables.

Chicken en cocotte with Parmesan

SERVES 4

1 chicken, trussed with string so wings and legs
   are neatly tucked in (your butcher can do this)
salt and freshly ground black pepper
3 tbsp butter
1 onion, roughly chopped
1 fennel bulb, trimmed and roughly chopped
1 cup white wine
2 lemons, peeled, pith removed and zest cut
   into fine slices
handful of flat-leaf parsley, chopped

FOR THE CHEESE SAUCE
½ cup chicken stock
½ cup heavy cream
1 tsp cornstarch
¼ cup Parmesan cheese, grated

in the slow cooker   ⏱ **PREP** 15 MINS   **COOK** 10 MINS PRECOOKING; **AUTO/LOW** 6–8 HRS

1 Preheat the slow cooker, if required. Season the chicken with salt and pepper inside and out. Melt the butter in a large Dutch oven. Add the chicken and cook for about 10 minutes until browned all over. Put the onion and fennel in the slow cooker and sit the chicken on top. Pour in the wine, then add the lemon zest. Cover with the lid and cook on auto/low for 6–8 hours. Transfer the bird to a board, cover with foil, and keep warm. Discard the onion and fennel.

2 Meanwhile, make the sauce. Remove any excess fat from the pot and add the stock. Bring to a boil, stirring to dissolve the pan juices. Boil for about 5 minutes, until well reduced, then strain it into a saucepan. Whisk in the cream and bring just to a boil. Mix the cornstarch and 1 tablespoon water together in a small bowl to form a smooth paste. Whisk in enough of the paste to thicken the sauce. It should lightly coat the back of a spoon. Take the sauce from the heat and whisk in the Parmesan cheese. Taste and add seasoning if needed. Set aside and reheat when required. Discard the trussing strings from the chicken, carve, and serve with the sauce and a scattering of chopped parsley.

traditional method   ⏱ **PREP** 15 MINS   **COOK** 45 MINS

1 Preheat the oven to 375°F (190°C). Season the chicken inside and out with salt and pepper. Melt the butter in a large Dutch oven. Add the chicken and cook it for about 10 minutes until browned all over. Add the onion, fennel, wine, and lemon zest and cover. Cook in the oven for 30–40 minutes, turning occasionally, so it cooks evenly. The juices should run clear when pierced with a sharp knife. Transfer the bird to a board, cover with foil, and keep it warm. Discard the onion and fennel.

2 To make the sauce, remove any excess fat from the pot and add the stock. Bring to a boil, stirring to dissolve the pan juices. Boil for about 5 minutes, until well reduced, then strain it into a saucepan. Whisk in the cream and bring just to a boil. Mix the cornstarch and 1 tablespoon water together in a small bowl to form a smooth paste. Whisk in enough of the paste to thicken the sauce. It should lightly coat the back of a spoon. Take the sauce from the heat and whisk in the Parmesan cheese. Taste and add salt and pepper if needed. Keep warm. Discard the trussing strings from the chicken, carve, and serve with the sauce and a scattering of chopped parsley.

Instead of a traditional Sunday dinner, try this lamb recipe that renders the meat meltingly tender and boasts a delicious coating that mixes with the sauce as it cooks.

Lamb with parsley, tomato, and bread crumbs

SERVES 4–6

4½lb (2kg) boneless leg of lamb
1 tbsp olive oil
3 large onions, sliced
handful of rosemary
about 2 cups white wine, for both methods

FOR THE RUB
bunch of flat-leaf parsley
¼ cup sun-dried tomatoes
2 garlic cloves, peeled
⅓ cup fine bread crumbs, toasted
2 tbsp olive oil
salt and freshly ground black pepper

in the slow cooker   **PREP** 20 MINS   **COOK** 10 MINS PRECOOKING; **AUTO/LOW** 8 HRS

1 Preheat the slow cooker, if required. First make the rub by putting the ingredients into a food processor and pulsing until blended. Set aside.

2 Wipe the meat, season it well, then stab it all over with a sharp knife. Heat the oil in a large Dutch oven over medium-high heat, add the lamb, and fry for about 8 minutes, turning until it is evenly browned. Remove the meat from the pot and rub the parsley mixture all over it and into all the cuts. Put it in the slow cooker together with the onions and rosemary and pour over enough wine to cover the meat. Cover with the lid and cook on auto/low for 8 hours.

3 Remove the lamb from the slow cooker, discard the rosemary, loosely cover the meat with foil, and leave it to rest for about 15 minutes. Serve with minted peas and new potatoes.

traditional method   **PREP** 20 MINS   **COOK** 3¼ HRS

1 Preheat the oven to 325°F (160°C). First make the rub by putting the ingredients into a food processor and pulsing until blended. Set aside.

2 Wipe the meat, season it well, then stab it all over with a sharp knife. Heat the oil in a large Dutch oven over medium-high heat, add the lamb, and fry for about 8 minutes, turning until it is evenly browned. Remove the meat from the pot and rub the parsley mixture all over it and into all the cuts. Set aside.

3 Add the onions to the pot, reduce the heat to medium, and cook for about 10 minutes, until softened. Season with salt and pepper, then sit the lamb on top of the onions, add the rosemary, and pour in the wine. Cover with the lid and put in the oven for 3 hours. Check occasionally that it's not drying out, topping up with a little hot water if needed. Remove from the oven, discard the rosemary, loosely cover the meat with foil, and leave it to rest for about 15 minutes. Serve with minted peas and new potatoes.

Pot-roasting a pheasant retains all its flavor and moistness. Choose a plump bird, it should be meaty enough for four. Otherwise, if your slow cooker will accommodate it, use two pheasants.

Pot-roast pheasant

SERVES 4

2 tbsp olive oil
¼ cup butter, chilled
1 prepared pheasant, about 2¼lb (1kg)
salt and freshly ground black pepper
9oz (250g) cremini mushrooms

2 tbsp chopped thyme
1 large onion, finely chopped
3½oz (100g) sliced bacon, chopped
2½ cups red wine, for both methods

in the slow cooker   **PREP** 40 MINS   **COOK** 20 MINS PRECOOKING; **AUTO/LOW** 6–8 HRS

1 Preheat the slow cooker, if required. Heat half the oil and half the butter in a large Dutch oven. Brown the pheasant evenly for 6–8 minutes and season with salt and pepper. Remove and set aside. Add the mushrooms and thyme to the pot and cook for 5 minutes, or until colored. Also remove and set aside.

2 Heat the remaining oil in the pot, add the onion and bacon, and cook for 4–5 minutes until the onion softens. Transfer to the slow cooker, together with the pheasant and mushrooms, and add the wine. Cover with the lid and cook on auto/low for 6–8 hours. Transfer the pheasant to a serving platter, cover with foil, and keep warm.

3 Strain the liquid from the slow cooker into a heavy-based saucepan. Skim away any fat, then bring to a boil and simmer briskly for about 10 minutes until reduced by a third. Whisk in the remaining butter to make the sauce glossy. Carve the pheasant and serve with the hot gravy and some carrots, mashed rutabagas, and French beans.

traditional method   **PREP** 40 MINS   **COOK** 1¾ HRS

1 Preheat the oven to 375°F (190°C). Heat half the oil and half the butter in a large Dutch oven. Brown the pheasant evenly for 6–8 minutes and season with salt and pepper. Remove and set aside. Add the mushrooms and thyme to the pot and cook for 5 minutes, or until colored. Also remove and set aside.

2 Heat the remaining oil in the pot, add the onion and bacon, and cook for 4–5 minutes until the onion softens. Add the pheasant and mushrooms and then the wine. Cover and put in the oven for 1½ hours, or until the pheasant is cooked and a leg pulls away from the bird easily. Transfer the pheasant to a serving platter, cover with foil, and keep warm.

3 Strain the liquid from the pot into a heavy-based saucepan. Skim away any fat, then bring to a boil and simmer briskly for about 10 minutes until reduced by a third. Whisk in the remaining butter to make the sauce glossy. Carve the pheasant and serve with the hot gravy and some carrots, mashed rutabagas, and French beans.

Pork belly is an ideal cut for slow cooking and it's great value, too. The pairing with cabbage is perfect for this dish and some mashed potatoes would be an excellent accompaniment.

Spicy pork with cabbage and caraway seeds

SERVES 4–6

handful of thyme leaves
4 garlic cloves, roughly chopped
2 tbsp olive oil
2 tsp dried chile flakes
2¼lb (1kg) piece pork belly, skin scored
2 tsp salt and freshly ground black pepper

1¼ cups dry cider for the slow cooker
 (2 cups for the traditional method)
1 Savoy cabbage, halved, cored, and shredded
1 tsp caraway seeds
pat of butter

in the slow cooker   PREP 10 MINS   COOK 15 MINS PRECOOKING; AUTO/LOW 6–8 HRS

1 Preheat the slow cooker, if required. Put the thyme, garlic, half the oil, and chile flakes in a food processor and blend to a paste, then rub this all over the flesh of the pork. Rub the salt all over the skin-side of the pork, getting it into all the cracks.

2 Add the remaining oil to a large Dutch oven, add the pork, skin-side down, and cook for about 15 minutes until golden and the skin is crispy. Add the cider and bring to a boil. Transfer everything to the slow cooker, cover with the lid, and cook on auto/low for 6–8 hours. Add the cabbage and caraway seeds for the last 30–40 minutes of cooking.

3 Transfer the cabbage to a warmed serving bowl and top with the butter and a pinch of pepper. Slice or cut the pork into bite-sized pieces and arrange on top of the cabbage along with the juices. Serve with creamy mashed potatoes and a spoonful of chili jelly on the side.

traditional method   PREP 10 MINS   COOK 2½ HRS

1 Preheat the oven to 425°F (220°C). Put the thyme, garlic, half the oil, and chile flakes in a food processor and blend to a paste, then rub this all over the flesh of the pork. Sit the pork in a roasting pan, skin-side up, and rub with the salt, getting it into all the cracks. Cook in the oven for about 30 minutes or until the skin is golden.

2 Reduce the oven to 350°F (180°C). Pour the cider around the pork, cover with foil, securing it around the edges of the pan, and cook for 2 hours.

3 Just before the 2 hours are up, put the cabbage in a pan of boiling salted water and cook for 4–6 minutes until soft. Drain, then toss with the caraway seeds, butter, and a pinch of pepper. Transfer to a warmed serving bowl. Slice or cut the pork into bite-sized pieces and arrange on top of the cabbage along with the juices. Serve with mashed potatoes and a spoonful of chili jelly on the side.

No meat performs better when it is slow cooked than pork belly, as it becomes meltingly tender. It's a really economical cut, too. Use pumpkin instead of squash when it's in season.

Belly pork and squash

SERVES 4–6

1 tbsp olive oil
1lb 9oz (700g) pork belly
salt and freshly ground black pepper
1 onion, finely chopped
3 garlic cloves, finely chopped
3 sage leaves, finely chopped

1 sprig of rosemary
1 butternut squash, peeled, seeded, and cut
   into cubes
½ cup dry sherry
6 cups hot vegetable stock for the slow cooker
   (1 quart for the traditional method)

in the slow cooker **PREP** 30 MINS **COOK** 15 MINS PRECOOKING; **AUTO/LOW** 8 HRS

1 Preheat the slow cooker, if required. Heat half the oil in a large Dutch oven over medium-high heat. Season the pork belly with salt and pepper and add it, skin-side down, to the pot. Cook for about 10 minutes or until it begins to color and become crispy. Remove from the pot and set aside.

2 Heat the remaining oil in the pot over medium heat, add the onion, and cook for 3–4 minutes until soft. Then stir in the garlic, sage, and rosemary, followed by the squash and turn to coat. Pour in the sherry, increase the heat, and let it bubble for a minute.

3 Transfer everything to the slow cooker, including the pork. Pour in the stock, cover with the lid, and cook on auto/low for 8 hours. Slice or cut the pork into bite-sized pieces and serve in warmed shallow bowls together with the squash and its juices. Serve with crusty bread.

traditional method **PREP** 30 MINS **COOK** 2¼–2¾ HRS

1 Preheat the oven to 325°F (160°C). Heat half the oil in a large Dutch oven over medium-high heat. Season the pork belly with salt and pepper and add it, skin-side down, to the pot. Cook for about 10 minutes or until it begins to color and become crispy. Remove from the pot and set aside.

2 Heat the remaining oil in the pot over medium heat, add the onion, and cook for 3–4 minutes, until soft. Then stir in the garlic, sage, and rosemary, followed by the squash and turn to coat. Pour in the sherry, increase the heat, and let it bubble for a minute.

3 Return the pork belly to the pot, add the stock, and bring to a boil. Reduce to a simmer, cover with the lid and put in the oven for 2–2½ hours. Check occasionally that it's not drying out, topping up with a little hot water if needed. Slice or cut the pork into bite-sized pieces and serve in warmed shallow bowls together with the squash and its juices. Serve with crusty bread.

Slow cooking is the best way to transform brisket into tender, succulent meat that just falls into the sauce. The red onion adds a sweetness to balance the bitter Guinness in this dish.

Beef brisket and baby onions

SERVES 4–6

1 tbsp olive oil
2½lb (1.1kg) beef brisket
salt and freshly ground black pepper
2 red onions, roughly chopped
12 baby onions, peeled and left whole
2 celery stalks, roughly chopped
3 garlic cloves, finely chopped

1 bay leaf
6 juniper berries
¾ cup Guinness
1½ cups hot beef stock for the slow cooker
  (3 cups for the traditional method)
3 carrots, peeled and roughly sliced
2 sprigs of rosemary

in the slow cooker   **PREP** 20 MINS   **COOK** 15 MINS PRECOOKING; **AUTO/LOW** 8 HRS

1 Preheat the slow cooker, if required. Heat the oil in a large Dutch oven over medium-high heat, season the brisket with salt and pepper, and add to the pot. Cook for 6–8 minutes on each side, using tongs to turn it. It is ready when it comes away from the bottom of the pot easily. Remove from the pot and set aside.

2 Add the red onions to the pot and cook in the meat fat for about 10 minutes until they begin to soften. Add seasoning, then stir in the baby onions, pushing the red ones to one side a little so they get some color. Cook for about 5 minutes, then add the celery and garlic, bay leaf, and juniper berries and cook for a further 5 minutes.

3 Pour in the Guinness and a little stock, and bring to a boil. Add the carrots, rosemary, and the remaining stock and bring to a boil. Transfer everything to the slow cooker, including the brisket, cover with the lid, and cook on auto/low for 8 hours. To serve, slice or shred the brisket and spoon over the juices and vegetables, removing the rosemary sprigs. Serve with mashed potatoes.

traditional method   **PREP** 20 MINS   **COOK** 2–2½ HRS

1 Preheat the oven to 350°F (180°C). Heat the oil in a large Dutch oven over medium-high heat, season the brisket with salt and pepper, and add to the pot. Cook for 6–8 minutes on each side, using tongs to turn it. It is ready when it comes away from the bottom of the pan easily. Remove and set aside.

2 Add the red onions to the pot and cook in the meat fat for about 10 minutes until they begin to soften. Add seasoning, then stir in the baby onions, pushing the red ones to one side a little so they get some color. Cook for about 5 minutes, then add the celery and garlic, bay leaf, and juniper berries and cook for a further 5 minutes.

3 Pour in the Guinness and a little stock, increase the heat, and let it bubble for few minutes. Add the carrots, rosemary, and the remaining stock and bring to a boil. Reduce to a simmer, return the brisket to the pot, cover with the lid, and put in the oven for 1½–2 hours. Spoon in the juices halfway through to keep it moist. To serve, slice or shred the brisket and spoon over the juices and vegetables, removing the rosemary sprigs. Serve with creamy mashed potatoes.

Pork ribs are cheap, full of succulent meat, and extremely filling. You can buy them in packs or, for the best value, get them as a rack of ribs from your butcher and chop them up yourself.

Asian pork ribs

SERVES 4

1 rack of pork ribs, about 12 ribs
  (about 1lb 9oz/700g)
salt
2 tsp black peppercorns
1–2 scallions, green parts
  finely sliced, to serve

FOR THE MARINADE
2 tbsp sesame oil
½ cup dark soy sauce
½ cup honey
6 tbsp teriyaki sauce
1 tsp five-spice powder
juice of 2 limes
pinch of dried chile flakes

in the slow cooker   **PREP** 5 MINS   **COOK** AUTO/LOW 8 HRS

1 Preheat the slow cooker, if required. Chop the rack into ribs and put them in the slow cooker. Season with salt and add the peppercorns. In a bowl, mix together all the marinade ingredients, add to the slow cooker, and turn the ribs to coat.

2 Cover the slow cooker with the lid and cook on auto/low for 8 hours. Remove the ribs from the slow cooker and serve with rice or on their own while piping hot. Garnish with the scallions.

traditional method   **PREP** 5 MINS   **COOK** 2–2½ HRS

1 Put the rack of ribs in a large heavy-based pan and cover with water. Season with salt and add the peppercorns. Bring to a boil, then reduce to a simmer, partially cover with the lid, and cook for 1–1½ hours until the meat starts to come away from the bone. Remove the ribs from the pan with tongs and set aside in a baking pan until they are cool enough to handle.

2 Preheat the oven to 325°F (160°C). In a bowl, mix together all the marinade ingredients. Chop the rack into ribs and put them in a large Dutch oven. Pour the marinade over the ribs, turning them to coat. Cover with the lid and put in the oven for about 1 hour, keeping an eye on them to check they don't dry out completely—they may need turning in the marinade. Remove and serve with rice or on their own while piping hot. Garnish with the scallions.

Rather than using ground pepper to season the ribs, use black peppercorns to give it more of a spicy hit. The marinade cooks to a lovely, thick, sticky coating—you'll need napkins to hand.

Spicy deviled pork ribs

SERVES 4

rack of pork ribs, about 12 ribs
  (about 1lb 9oz/700g)
salt
2 tsp black peppercorns

FOR THE MARINADE
2 tbsp tomato ketchup
1 tbsp English mustard
1 tbsp Worcestershire sauce
3 garlic cloves, finely chopped
2 tbsp honey
2 tbsp soy sauce
splash of smoked Tabasco sauce

in the slow cooker **PREP** 5 MINS **COOK** AUTO/LOW 6–8 HRS

1 Preheat the slow cooker, if required. Chop the rack into ribs and put in the slow cooker. Season with salt and add the peppercorns. Mix all the marinade ingredients together in a bowl, add to the slow cooker, and turn the ribs to coat. Cover with the lid and cook on auto/low for 6–8 hours, turning them halfway through the cooking time. Remove from the slow cooker and serve while piping hot.

traditional method **PREP** 5 MINS **COOK** 2–2½ HRS

1 Put the rack of ribs in a large heavy-based saucepan and cover with water. Season with salt and add the peppercorns. Bring to a boil, then reduce to a simmer, partially cover with the lid, and cook for 1–1½ hours until the meat starts to come away from the bone. Remove from the pan and set aside until cool enough to handle.

2 Preheat the oven to 325°F (160°C). Mix all the marinade ingredients together in a bowl. Chop the rack into ribs, then sit them in a large Dutch oven. Pour over the marinade and turn the ribs to coat. Cover with the lid and put in the oven for about 1 hour, keeping an eye on them so they don't dry out; they may need turning in the marinade to prevent this from happening. Remove from the pot and serve while piping hot.

Shanks are ideal for slow cooking because the meat melts off the bone into the sauce to create the most delicious dish. Tart vinegar and tomato paste counteract the fattiness of the lamb.

Sweet and sour lamb

SERVES 4–6

4–6 lamb shanks (allow 1 per person)
salt and freshly ground black pepper
1–2 tbsp olive oil
1 onion, cut into eighths
2 tbsp tomato paste
¼ cup red wine vinegar

2 tbsp demerara brown sugar
1 cup hot vegetable stock for the slow cooker
 (1½ cups for the traditional method)
1 cinnamon stick
1 small Savoy cabbage, trimmed and shredded

in the slow cooker   **PREP** 15 MINS   **COOK** 20 MINS PRECOOKING; **AUTO/LOW** 6–8 HRS

1 Preheat the slow cooker, if required. Season the lamb with salt and pepper. Heat the oil in a large Dutch oven over medium-high heat, add the meat, and cook (in batches, if necessary) for 10–15 minutes, turning several times, until browned all over. Reduce the heat to medium, add the onion, and cook for 3–4 minutes, until soft.

2 Add the tomato paste, vinegar, and sugar and pour over 1 cup of water. Bring to a boil, then transfer everything to the slow cooker. Add the stock and cinnamon stick, cover with the lid, and cook on auto/low for 6–8 hours. Add the cabbage for the last 30 minutes of cooking. Taste and season as required and serve on a bed of fluffy rice.

traditional method   **PREP** 15 MINS   **COOK** 2 HRS

1 Preheat the oven to 325°F (160°C). Season the lamb with salt and pepper. Heat the oil in a large Dutch oven over medium-high heat, add the meat, and cook (in batches, if necessary) for 10–15 minutes, turning several times, until browned all over. Reduce the heat to medium, add the onion, and cook for 3–4 minutes, until soft.

2 Add the tomato paste, vinegar, and sugar and pour in 1 cup of water. Bring to a boil, then add the stock and cinnamon stick, cover with the lid, and put in the oven for about 1½ hours. Check occasionally that it's not drying out, topping up with a little hot water if needed. Add the cabbage for the last 20 minutes of cooking. Taste and season as required and serve on a bed of fluffy rice.

This is a substantial vegetarian dish. The artichokes and butter beans give it a wonderful creamy finish and breadcrumbs are stirred in at the last minute to add some texture.

Artichokes, butter beans, and peas

SERVES 4–6   **FREEZE** UP TO 3 MONTHS   **HEALTHY**

1 tbsp olive oil
1 onion, finely chopped
3 garlic cloves, finely chopped
1½ cups small button mushrooms,
  larger ones halved
1 cup dried butter beans, soaked overnight
  and drained, or use 2 x 14oz (400g) cans
  butter beans, drained and rinsed
pinch of ground nutmeg

juice of ½ lemon
salt and freshly ground black pepper
2 cups hot vegetable stock for the slow cooker
  (3 cups for the traditional method)
1 cup frozen or fresh garden peas
1½lb (675g) antipasti artichoke hearts, drained
⅓ cup breadcrumbs, toasted
few sprigs of flat-leaf parsley, finely chopped,
  to serve

in the slow cooker   **PREP** 15 MINS   **COOK** 20 MINS PRECOOKING; AUTO/LOW 4–6 HRS OR **HIGH** 2–3 HRS

1 Preheat the slow cooker, if required. Heat the oil in a large Dutch oven over medium heat, add the onion, and cook for 3–4 minutes until soft. Then stir in the garlic and mushrooms and cook for about 5 minutes until the mushrooms are tender. Meanwhile, if using the dried butter beans rather than canned beans, put them in a pan, cover with water, and boil on high for 10 minutes. Drain and set aside.

2 Transfer the mushroom mixture to the slow cooker, then stir in the butter beans, add the nutmeg and lemon juice, and season with salt and pepper. Pour in the stock, add the peas and artichokes, cover with the lid, and cook on auto/low for 4–6 hours or on high for 2–3 hours.

3 Spoon over the breadcrumbs and carefully fold some in, then top with the parsley. Serve with some freshly baked crusty bread.

traditional method   **PREP** 15 MINS   **COOK** 1½ HRS

1 Heat the oil in a large Dutch oven over medium heat, add the onion, and cook for 3–4 minutes until soft. Then stir in the garlic and mushrooms and cook for about 5 minutes until the mushrooms are tender.

2 Stir in the butter beans, add the nutmeg and lemon juice, and season with salt and pepper. Pour in the stock and bring to a boil. Boil for about 10 minutes, then reduce to a simmer, partially cover with the lid, and cook for 45 minutes. Check occasionally that it's not drying out, topping up with a little hot water if needed.

3 Stir in the peas and artichokes and cook gently for a further 15–20 minutes or until the butter beans are completely soft. Spoon over the breadcrumbs and carefully fold some in, then top with the parsley. Serve with some freshly baked crusty bread.

Risottos, pilafs, & paellas

Full of spring flavors—you can mix and match vegetables, such as French beans or broccoli, depending on what you have on hand. You could use chicken stock, if you aren't cooking for vegetarians.

Risotto primavera

SERVES 4–6

2 tbsp olive oil
3 tbsp butter
1 onion, finely chopped
salt and freshly ground black pepper
3 garlic cloves, finely chopped
1½ cups arborio rice or carnaroli rice
1 cup white wine
2 cups hot vegetable stock for the slow cooker
   (3 cups for the traditional method)

½ cup fresh or frozen fava or lima beans
bunch of asparagus spears, trimmed and
   chopped into bite-sized pieces
2 small zucchini, diced
½ cup grated Parmesan cheese, plus extra
   for serving

in the slow cooker   **PREP** 15 MINS   **COOK** 10 MINS PRECOOKING; **AUTO/LOW** 1½–2 HRS

1 Preheat the slow cooker, if required. Heat the oil and half the butter in a large Dutch oven over medium heat, add the onion, and cook for 3–4 minutes until soft. Season with salt and pepper, add the garlic, and cook for a minute.

2 Stir in the rice and turn it in the oily butter so all the grains are coated. Cook for a few seconds. Increase the heat, add the wine, and let it bubble for 1–2 minutes until it has been absorbed. Transfer everything to the slow cooker, then pour in the stock and add the fava beans, asparagus, and zucchini. Cover with the lid and cook on auto/low for 1½–2 hours.

3 Stir in the remaining butter together with the Parmesan cheese, taste, and season if needed. Serve with more Parmesan and a lightly dressed wild arugula and tomato salad on the side.

traditional method   **PREP** 15 MINS   **COOK** 1 HR

1 Heat the oil and half the butter in a large Dutch oven over medium heat, add the onion, and cook for 3–4 minutes until soft. Season with salt and pepper, add the garlic, and cook for a minute.

2 Stir in the rice and turn it in the oily butter so all the grains are coated. Cook for a few seconds. Increase the heat, add the wine, and let it bubble for 1–2 minutes until it has been absorbed. Then add a ladleful of the hot stock at a time (keeping the rest simmering in a saucepan) and stir, cooking until it has been absorbed. Continue doing this for 30–40 minutes or until the rice is cooked to al dente and is creamy. You may not use all the stock or you may need a little more.

3 While that's cooking, add the fava beans to a large pan of boiling salted water, and cook for 3–4 minutes, then drain well and set aside. Heat the remaining oil in another frying pan over medium heat, add the asparagus and zucchini, and cook for a few minutes until they just begin to color. Stir all the vegetables into the risotto, dot the remaining butter all over, and stir it in. Then stir in the Parmesan cheese, taste and season, if needed. Serve with more Parmesan and a lightly dressed wild arugula and tomato salad on the side.

Eggplant and paprika work together really well, as the eggplant absorbs the flavor of this pungent spice. The chickpeas make this a substantial supper dish. Serve it alone or with lamb cutlets.

Paprika rice and eggplant

⊚ **SERVES** 4–6 ◌ **HEALTHY**

3–4 tbsp olive oil
2 eggplants, chopped into bite-sized pieces
1 tbsp paprika
1 onion, finely chopped
1 tsp dried mint
salt and freshly ground black pepper
3 garlic cloves, finely chopped
2 green chilies, seeded and finely chopped

grated zest of 1 lemon and juice of 2 lemons
1¾ cups quick-cooking basmati rice
14oz (400g) can chickpeas, drained
about 2 cups hot vegetable stock for the slow cooker
  (3 cups for the traditional method)
small bunch of cilantro leaves, roughly chopped
small bunch of flat-leaf parsley, roughly chopped

in the slow cooker ⏱ **PREP** 20 MINS **COOK** 15 MINS PRECOOKING; **AUTO/LOW** 3 HRS

1 Preheat the slow cooker, if required. Heat half the oil in a large heavy-based saucepan over medium heat. Toss the eggplant in the paprika, add to the pan, and cook for 6–8 minutes, adding more oil if needed. Remove and set aside.

2 Heat the remaining oil, if necessary, and reduce the heat to low. Add the onion and mint, season with salt and pepper, and cook for 3–4 minutes until soft. Stir in the garlic, chilies, and lemon zest and cook for a further 2 minutes.

3 Stir in the rice and mix it in the oil, so all the grains are coated, and cook for a few seconds. Add the lemon juice and chickpeas, and return the eggplant to the pan. Transfer everything to the slow cooker, pour over the stock to just cover, season again, then cover with the lid and cook on auto/low for 3 hours. Stir in the herbs. Serve with a spoonful of Greek-style yogurt on top, a lightly dressed leaf and tomato salad, and some lamb cutlets.

traditional method ⏱ **PREP** 20 MINS **COOK** 45–55 MINS

1 Heat half the oil in a large heavy-based saucepan over medium heat. Toss the eggplant in the paprika, add to the pan, and cook for 6–8 minutes, adding more oil if needed. Remove and set aside.

2 Heat the remaining oil, if necessary, and reduce the heat to low. Add the onion and mint, season with salt and pepper, add cook for 3–4 minutes until soft. Stir in the garlic, chilies, and lemon zest and cook for a further 2 minutes.

3 Stir in the rice and turn it in the oil, so all the grains are coated, and cook for a few seconds. Add the lemon juice and chickpeas, and return the eggplant to the pan. Pour in the stock, season again, then partially cover with the lid and leave to cook for 30–40 minutes, topping up with a little hot water if needed, and stirring occasionally so it doesn't stick. Stir in the herbs. Serve with a spoonful of Greek-style yogurt on top, a lightly dressed leaf and tomato salad, and some lamb cutlets.

In this recipe, the rice slowly steams on top of the meat and yogurt mixture. The cardamom pods also release their aromatic flavor during the long cooking time—but don't eat them!

Saffron and lamb biryani

SERVES 4–6

1 tsp saffron threads, ground with a pestle and mortar
½ cup hot milk
½ cup unsalted butter
1 tsp ground cinnamon
10 cardamom pods, split
10 whole cloves
20 black peppercorns
3 bay leaves
2 large onions, diced

8 garlic cloves, peeled and chopped
1 tsp ground ginger
1 tsp ground cumin
2 tsp medium hot chili powder
2 tsp ground coriander
1½ cups plain yogurt
2¼lb (1kg) boneless lean lamb, cut into small pieces
2¼ cups quick-cooking basmati rice
1 cup toasted sliced almonds

in the slow cooker   🕐 **PREP** 20 MINS   **COOK** 15 MINS PRECOOKING;
AUTO/LOW 6–8 HRS OR **HIGH** 3–4 HRS

1 Preheat the slow cooker, if required. Put the saffron into the hot milk and set aside. Melt the butter in a large Dutch oven, then stir in the cinnamon, cardamom, cloves, and peppercorns and cook for 5 minutes. Add the bay leaves and onions and cook for 2–3 minutes until soft.

2 Add the garlic, ginger, cumin, chili powder, coriander, and yogurt and stir to combine, then add the lamb and half the saffron milk. Mix thoroughly and turn off the heat.

3 Bring a large pan of salted water to a boil and add the rice. Cook for about 2 minutes and drain well. Add the lamb mixture to the slow cooker and top with the rice and the remaining saffron milk. Cover with the lid and cook on auto/low for 6–8 hours or on high for 3–4 hours until the rice is tender and the lamb is cooked. Discard the cardamom pods. Stir in the toasted almonds, combine gently with a fork, and serve with chutney and chapatis.

traditional method   🕐 **PREP** 20 MINS   **COOK** 1¾ HRS, PLUS STEAMING

1 Put the saffron into the hot milk and set aside. Melt the butter in a large Dutch oven, then stir in the cinnamon, cardamom, cloves, and peppercorns and cook for 5 minutes. Add the bay leaves and onions and cook for 2–3 minutes until soft.

2 Add the garlic, ginger, cumin, chili powder, coriander, and yogurt and stir to combine, then add the lamb and half the saffron milk. Mix thoroughly and turn off the heat.

3 Bring a large pan of salted water to the boil and add the rice. Cook for about 2 minutes and drain well, then add the rice on top of the lamb mixture and pour over the remaining saffron milk. Cover the pot tightly with foil to create a good seal, then cover it with the lid. Cook over very low heat for 1½ hours until the rice is tender and the lamb is cooked. Check occasionally that it's not drying out, topping up with a little hot water if needed. Remove from the heat and stand for 15 minutes without opening. Uncover and discard the cardamom pods, then add the toasted almonds, combine gently with a fork, and serve with chutney and chapatis.

This delightfully simple dish is made extra tasty with a blend of parsley, thyme, and sage, which would be extra flavorful if picked freshly from the garden or pots on the windowsills.

Pork with rice and tomatoes

SERVES 4–6 ❄ **FREEZE** UP TO 3 MONTHS ♡ **HEALTHY**

¼ cup olive oil
2 onions, diced
2lb (900g) lean pork, cut into 2in (5cm) chunks
3 garlic cloves, finely chopped
handful of flat-leaf parsley, chopped
1 tbsp thyme leaves

1 tbsp chopped sage leaves
1 tsp paprika
½ cup dry white wine
heaping 1 cup long-grain rice
2 x 14oz (400g) cans chopped tomatoes
salt and freshly ground black pepper

in the slow cooker ⏱ **PREP** 30 MINS **COOK** 15 MINS PRECOOKING; **AUTO/LOW** 1–1½ HRS

1 Preheat the slow cooker, if required. Heat the oil in a large Dutch oven over medium heat, add the onions, and cook for 4–5 minutes until soft. Add the pork and cook, stirring occasionally, for about 5 minutes until no longer pink. Add the garlic, parsley, thyme, sage, and paprika and combine well, then add the wine and cook for 5 minutes. Add the rice and tomatoes, stir to combine, then season well with salt and black pepper.

2 Transfer everything to the slow cooker, cover with the lid, and cook on auto/low for 1–1½ hours. Stir halfway through, if you wish. Serve with a lightly dressed salad and crusty bread.

traditional method ⏱ **PREP** 30 MINS **COOK** 1 HR

1 Preheat the oven to 300°F (150°C). Heat the oil in a large Dutch oven over medium heat, add the onions, and cook for 4–5 minutes until soft. Add the pork and cook, stirring occasionally, for about 5 minutes until no longer pink. Add the garlic, parsley, thyme, sage, and paprika and combine well, then add the wine and cook for 5 minutes. Add the rice and tomatoes, stir to combine, then season well with salt and black pepper.

2 Cover with the lid and put in the oven for 1 hour. Check occasionally that it's not drying out, topping up with a little hot water if needed. Remove from the oven and allow to stand for 10 minutes with the lid on before serving. Serve with a lightly dressed salad and crusty bread.

Choose an authentic Italian short-grain rice, such as arborio or carnaroli, to ensure the risotto has a creamy consistency. Shape any leftovers into patties, coat with bread crumbs, and pan-fry.

Mushroom risotto

SERVES 6   **HEALTHY**

3 tbsp sunflower oil
1 onion, chopped
1¾ cups arborio rice or carnaroli rice
about 2 cups hot vegetable stock for the slow cooker
  (5½ cups for the traditional method)

¼ cup butter, diced
1lb (450g) cremini mushrooms, sliced
⅓ cup Parmesan cheese, grated, plus
  extra shavings to serve

in the slow cooker   **PREP** 10 MINS   **COOK** 20 MINS PRECOOKING; **AUTO/LOW** 2–3 HRS

1 Preheat the slow cooker, if required. Heat the oil in a large heavy-based skillet over medium heat, add the onion, and cook for 4–5 minutes until soft. Add the rice and stir in so all the grains are well coated and cook for 2 minutes. Transfer to the slow cooker and pour in just enough stock to cover. Cover with the lid and cook on auto/low for 2–3 hours, giving it a stir halfway through.

2 Meanwhile, melt the butter in the pan over medium heat. Add the mushrooms and cook for about 10 minutes, stirring frequently, until the mushrooms have browned and their liquid evaporates. Stir into the rice and continue cooking for the full length of time. Stir in the Parmesan cheese, then leave to rest, covered, for 5 minutes. Serve in warmed serving bowls with the Parmesan shavings on top.

traditional method   **PREP** 10 MINS   **COOK** 40 MINS

1 Heat the oil in a large heavy-based skillet over medium heat, add the onion, and cook for 4–5 minutes until soft. Add the rice and stir in so all the grains are well coated and cook for 2 minutes. Slowly add a ladleful of the hot stock at a time (keeping the rest simmering in a saucepan) and stir, cooking, until it has been absorbed. Continue doing this for about 20 minutes until the rice is cooked to al dente.

2 Meanwhile, melt the butter in another pan over medium heat. Add the mushrooms and cook for about 10 minutes, stirring frequently, until the mushrooms have browned and their liquid evaporates. Stir the mushrooms into the rice and turn off the heat. Stir in the Parmesan cheese, then leave to rest, covered, for 5 minutes. Serve in warmed serving bowls with the Parmesan shavings on top.

Fragrant and full of color, this pilaf has lots of layers of flavor. Swap in different dried fruits and nuts for variety. Dates and apricots are often used in Turkish dishes, as are almonds.

Turkish lamb and pomegranate pilaf

SERVES 4–6

2 tbsp olive oil, plus extra for drizzling
1½lb (675g) lamb leg, cut into bite-sized pieces
1 onion, finely chopped
salt and freshly ground black pepper
3 garlic cloves, finely chopped
1 green chile, seeded and finely sliced
1 tsp dried mint
1 tsp ground cinnamon
½ cup golden raisins

1¾ cups quick-cooking basmati rice
2 cups hot lamb stock for the slow cooker
 (3 cups for the traditional method)
⅓ cup hazelnuts, toasted and roughly chopped
small handful of dill, finely chopped
½ cup pomegranate seeds (about 1 pomegranate)
½ cup feta cheese, crumbled (optional)

in the slow cooker   PREP 15 MINS   COOK 15–20 MINS PRECOOKING; AUTO/LOW 2–3 HRS

1 Preheat the slow cooker, if required. Heat the oil in a large Dutch oven over medium-high heat, add the lamb (in batches, if necessary), and cook for 6–8 minutes until browned on all sides. Remove and set aside. Add the onion to the pot and cook over medium heat for 3–4 minutes until soft. Season with salt and pepper, then stir in the garlic, chile, mint, and cinnamon and cook for another 2 minutes. Stir in the raisins.

2 Stir in the rice and turn it, so all the grains are coated and the juices soaked up. Return the lamb to the pot, pour in the stock, and bring to a boil. Transfer everything to the slow cooker, cover with the lid, and cook on auto/low for 2–3 hours, stirring halfway through, or until the rice is tender and the liquid has been absorbed. Taste and season, then stir in the hazelnuts and dill, and scatter with the pomegranate seeds. Top with crumbled feta, if using, and serve with warm pita bread and a lightly dressed crisp green salad.

traditional method   PREP 15 MINS   COOK 1 HR

1 Heat the oil in a large Dutch oven over medium-high heat, add the lamb (in batches, if necessary) and cook for 6–8 minutes until browned on all sides. Remove and set aside.

2 Add the onion to the pot and cook over medium heat for 3–4 minutes until soft. Season with salt and pepper, then stir in the garlic, chile, mint, and cinnamon, and cook for another 2 minutes. Stir in the raisins.

3 Stir in the rice and turn it, so all the grains are coated and the juices soaked up. Return the lamb to the pot, pour in the stock, and reduce to a simmer. Partially cover and cook for 30–40 minutes, topping up with a little more hot stock if it begins to dry out. Taste and season, then stir in the hazelnuts and dill, and scatter with the pomegranate seeds. Top with crumbled feta, if using, and serve with warm pita bread and a lightly dressed crisp green salad.

This is a traditional dish from the American South. You could cook the ham a day in advance, then chill the meat until ready to use. Dark cabbage or kale would make an ideal accompaniment.

Hoppin' John

SERVES 4–6

1 smoked ham hock, weighing about 2½lb (1.1kg)
1 bouquet garni, made with celery, thyme sprigs,
 and 1 bay leaf
2 large onions, chopped
1 dried red chile, chopped (optional)

1 tbsp groundnut oil or sunflower oil
1 cup long-grain rice
2 x 14oz (400g) cans black-eyed peas,
 drained and rinsed
salt and freshly ground black pepper

in the slow cooker   ● PREP 15 MINS   COOK 5 MINS PRECOOKING; **AUTO/LOW** 4–6 HRS, THEN **AUTO/LOW** 2 HRS

1 Preheat the slow cooker, if required. Sit the ham hock in the slow cooker and pour in enough cold water to cover. Add the bouquet garni, half the onions, and the chile, if using, then cover with the lid and cook on auto/low for 4–6 hours until you can pierce the ham easily with a knife. Remove the ham and set aside. Turn off the slow cooker and strain and reserve the stock. Discard the bouquet garni, onions, and chile. Turn the slow cooker back on to auto/low.

2 Heat the oil in a heavy-based skillet over medium heat, add the remaining onion, and cook for 4–5 minutes until soft. Add the rice and stir, then transfer to the slow cooker. Add the black-eyed peas and pour in enough of the reserved stock to cover, adding a little hot water if needed. Return the ham to the slow cooker, cover with the lid, and continue cooking on auto/low for 2 hours. Stir the rice halfway through the cooking time.

3 Lift out the ham, then remove the meat from the bone and cut it into large chunks. Return the meat back to the slow cooker and stir in. Serve with steamed dark cabbage or kale and a splash of Tabasco sauce.

traditional method   ● PREP 15 MINS   COOK 3–3½ HRS

1 Put the ham hock in a heavy-based saucepan, pour in enough cold water to cover, and set over high heat. Slowly bring to a boil, skimming the surface as necessary. Reduce the heat to low, add the bouquet garni, half the onions, and the chile, if using, then re-cover the pan and leave to simmer for 2½–3 hours or until the meat is very tender when pierced with a knife. Remove the ham and set aside. Strain the stock and reserve.

2 Heat the oil in the pan over medium heat, add the remaining onion, and cook for 4–5 minutes until soft. Add the rice and stir. Stir in 2 cups of the reserved stock and the black-eyed peas. Taste and add salt and pepper if needed. Bring to a boil, then reduce the heat to low, cover tightly, and simmer for 20 minutes without lifting the lid.

3 Meanwhile, remove the meat from the bone and cut it into large chunks. Remove the pan from the heat and leave to stand for 5 minutes without lifting the lid. Using a fork, stir in the ham. Serve with steamed dark cabbage or kale and a splash of Tabasco sauce.

You could swap the chicken in this one-pot dish for pre-cooked shrimp, stirring them in at the end of cooking. Apricots, dates, or figs would be worthy replacements for the golden raisins.

Chicken and chickpea pilaf

SERVES 4   **HEALTHY**

2 tsp vegetable oil
6 skinless boneless chicken thighs, cut
  into bite-sized pieces
2 tsp ground coriander
1 tsp ground cumin
1 onion, sliced
1 red bell pepper, seeded and chopped
2 garlic cloves, crushed
heaping 1 cup long-grain rice

1¾ cups hot chicken stock for the slow cooker
  (2½ cups for the traditional method)
2 bay leaves
pinch of saffron threads, soaked in ½ cup hot
  water for 10 minutes
14oz (400g) can chickpeas, drained and rinsed
½ cup golden raisins
½ cup sliced almonds or pine nuts, toasted
3 tbsp chopped flat-leaf parsley

in the slow cooker   **PREP** 20 MINS   **COOK** 20 MINS PRECOOKING; **AUTO/LOW** 2–3 HRS

1 Preheat the slow cooker, if required. Heat half the oil in a large Dutch oven over medium heat, add the chicken, coriander, and cumin, and cook for about 10 minutes, stirring frequently. Remove and set aside. Reduce the heat, add the rest of the oil together with the onion, red bell pepper, and garlic, and cook for about 10 minutes until soft.

2 Stir in the rice so all the grains are coated, then transfer everything to the slow cooker, including the chicken. Pour in the stock, or just enough to cover, and add the bay leaves and saffron with its soaking water. Stir in the chickpeas, cover with the lid, and cook on auto/low for 2–3 hours, giving it a stir halfway though. Add the raisins for the last 30 minutes of cooking. Transfer to a warmed platter and serve hot, sprinkled with the toasted nuts and chopped parsley.

traditional method   **PREP** 20 MINS   **COOK** 45 MINS

1 Heat half the oil in a large Dutch oven over medium heat, add the chicken, coriander, and cumin, and cook for about 10 minutes, stirring often. Remove and set aside. Reduce the heat, add the rest of the oil together with the onion, red bell pepper, and garlic, and cook for about 10 minutes until soft.

2 Stir in the rice so all the grains are coated, return the chicken to the pot, and pour in about three-quarters of the stock (keeping the rest simmering in a saucepan). Add the bay leaves and saffron with its soaking water, and bring to a boil. Simmer for about 20 minutes or until the rice is almost cooked, adding more stock as needed. Stir in the chickpeas and raisins and continue cooking the pilaf on a gentle heat for about 15 minutes, stirring occasionally so it doesn't stick. Transfer to a warmed platter and serve hot, sprinkled with the toasted nuts and chopped parsley.

Vibrant and robust, this is a simple supper dish that will satisfy the hungriest diners and requires little more than a simple tomato salad and some fresh crusty bread to accompany it.

Sausage and mixed pepper savory rice

SERVES 4–6

2 tbsp olive oil
1 large onion, finely chopped
salt and freshly ground black pepper
14oz (400g) fresh pork sausages, skinned
 and mashed with a fork
2 green bell peppers, seeded and diced
2 red bell peppers, seeded and diced
2 yellow bell peppers, seeded and diced

4 garlic cloves, finely chopped
1–2 tsp smoked paprika
1 tsp coriander seeds, crushed
1½ cups long-grain rice
about 1¾ cups hot chicken stock for the slow cooker
 (2½ cups for the traditional method)
handful of flat-leaf parsley, finely chopped
small handful of cilantro, finely chopped

in the slow cooker ⏱ **PREP** 20 MINS **COOK** 15 MINS PRECOOKING; **AUTO/LOW** 2–3 HRS

1 Preheat the slow cooker, if required. Heat the oil in a large Dutch oven over medium heat, add the onion, and cook for 3–4 minutes until soft. Season with salt and pepper, add the sausage meat, and cook for 5–8 minutes until it is no longer pink.

2 Add the peppers and garlic and cook for a further 3 minutes, stirring so it all combines, then stir in the paprika, coriander seeds, and rice. Transfer everything to the slow cooker, then pour in enough stock to cover the contents. Season, cover with the lid, and cook on auto/low for 2–3 hours, stirring halfway through to prevent the rice from sticking. Stir in the herbs and serve with a lettuce and tomato salad and some crusty bread.

traditional method ⏱ **PREP** 20 MINS **COOK** 1 HR

1 Preheat the oven to 325°F (160°C). Heat the oil in a large Dutch oven over medium heat, add the onion, and cook for 3–4 minutes until soft. Season with salt and pepper, then add the sausage meat and cook for 5–8 minutes until it is no longer pink.

2 Add the peppers and garlic and cook for a further 3 minutes, stirring so it all combines, then stir in the paprika, coriander seeds, and rice. Pour in the stock and stir well, let it bubble for a minute, then season, cover with the lid, and put in the oven for about 40 minutes until cooked and the stock has been absorbed. Stir halfway through to prevent the rice from sticking. Stir in the herbs and serve with a lettuce and tomato salad and some crusty bread.

This is a fragrant mix of pantry staples—rice and lentils. Dukkah is an Egyptian mix of spices, roasted nuts, and ground sesame seeds. Add toasted almonds or hazelnuts, if you wish.

Egyptian rice

SERVES 4 **HEALTHY**

2 tbsp olive oil
2 large onions, sliced
salt and freshly ground black pepper
3 garlic cloves, grated
1 tsp cumin
3 tsp Dukkah spice (optional)
1 cup quick-cooking basmati rice
2 cups hot vegetable stock for the slow cooker
  (3 cups for the traditional method)

1 cup Puy lentils, rinsed and picked over for
  any stones
1 bay leaf
juice of 1 lemon
small handful of flat-leaf parsley, finely chopped
small handful of mint leaves, finely chopped
small handful of cilantro, finely chopped
7oz (200g) feta cheese, crumbled

in the slow cooker   **PREP** 15 MINS   **COOK** 10 MINS PRECOOKING; **AUTO/LOW** 2–2½ HRS

1 Preheat the slow cooker, if required. Heat the oil in a large heavy-based saucepan over medium heat, add the onions, and cook for 8–10 minutes until they just begin to crisp slightly. Add seasoning, stir in the garlic, cumin, and dukkah spice, if using, and cook for a minute.

2 Add the rice and stir well so all the grains are coated, then transfer everything to the slow cooker. Pour the stock over the rice and stir in the lentils and bay leaf. Cover with the lid and cook on auto/low for 2–2½ hours, stirring the rice halfway through. Add the lemon juice and most of the herbs, remembering to remove the bay leaf. Serve topped with the feta or spoon over a tomato-based sauce or plain yogurt. Sprinkle over the remaining fresh herbs to garnish.

traditional method   **PREP** 15 MINS   **COOK** 1¼ HRS

1 Put the lentils and bay leaf in a heavy-based saucepan and pour in the stock. Season with salt and pepper, then bring to a boil, reduce the heat to a simmer, cover with the lid, and cook for about 20 minutes (depending on the package's instructions). Remove the lid and cook for a further 10 minutes or so until the lentils are beginning to soften. Turn off the heat, put the lid back on, and set aside.

2 Put the rice in a separate pan, cover with water so it just skims the top of the rice, and bring to a boil. Reduce to a simmer and cook gently, partially covered with the lid, for about 10 minutes or until the rice is cooked through—you may need to top up the hot water if it the rice is becoming dry. Turn off the heat, cover with the lid, and set aside—the rice will continue to steam.

3 Heat the oil in a large Dutch oven over medium heat, add the onions, and cook for 8–10 minutes until they just begin to crisp slightly. Add seasoning, stir in the garlic, cumin, and dukkah spice, if using, and cook for a minute. Drain the lentils, then add to the rice, stirring well so all the grains and lentils are coated and everything is heated through. Add the lemon juice and most of the herbs, remembering to remove the bay leaf. Serve topped with the feta or spoon over a tomato-based sauce or plain yogurt. Sprinkle over the remaining fresh herbs to garnish.

This light and delicately flavored pilaf requires gentle cooking, with fresh, fragrant ingredients added just before serving. It makes a perfect summer dish—just right for outdoor dining.

Coconut, mango, and lime pilaf

SERVES 4–6

1 tbsp olive oil
1 onion, finely chopped
3 garlic cloves, finely chopped
2 red chilies, finely chopped
grated zest of 1 lime and juice of 2 limes
pinch of ground allspice
salt and freshly ground black pepper
1¾ cups quick-cooking basmati rice

¾ cup dried unsweetened coconut flakes
3 cups hot vegetable stock for the slow cooker
 (1 quart for the traditional method)
1 mango, pitted, peeled, and chopped into
 bite-sized pieces
small bunch of cilantro, leaves roughly chopped

in the slow cooker   **PREP** 15 MINS   **COOK** 10 MINS PRECOOKING; **AUTO/LOW** 2–3 HRS

1 Preheat the slow cooker, if required. Heat the oil in a large Dutch oven over medium heat, add the onion, and cook on low heat for 3–4 minutes until soft. Season with salt and pepper, stir in the garlic, chilies, lime zest, and allspice, and cook for a further 2 minutes.

2 Stir in the rice, turning it until the grains are thoroughly coated, then stir in half the lime juice and the coconut. Pour in the stock, season again, and bring to a boil.

3 Transfer everything to the slow cooker, cover with the lid, and cook on auto/low for 2–3 hours or until the rice is tender and the liquid has all been absorbed. Stir in the mango and cilantro and add the remaining lime juice. Serve with a crisp green salad.

traditional method   **PREP** 15 MINS   **COOK** 45 MINS

1 Heat the oil in a large Dutch oven over medium heat, add the onion, and cook on low heat for 3–4 minutes until soft. Season with salt and pepper, stir in the garlic, chilies, lime zest, and allspice, and cook for a further 2 minutes.

2 Stir in the rice, turning it until the grains are thoroughly coated, then stir in half the lime juice and the coconut. Pour in the stock, season again, and bring to a simmer. Partially cover with the lid and leave to cook for 30–40 minutes, stirring occasionally, and topping up with hot stock if needed. Stir in the mango and cilantro and add the remaining lime juice. Serve with a crisp green salad.

This Spanish recipe of saffron-flavored rice with chicken, shrimp, mussels, and chorizo is named after the paellera in which it is traditionally cooked. It remains a firm favorite across the world.

Paella

⊚ **SERVES** 4–6   ⬤ **HEALTHY**

3 tbsp olive oil
14oz (400g) skinless boneless chicken thighs, cut into bite-sized pieces
salt and freshly ground black pepper
5½oz (150g) dried chorizo, sliced
1 large onion, diced
1 large red bell pepper, seeded and sliced
2 cups paella rice or other short-grain rice
3 garlic cloves, finely chopped

2 large pinches of saffron threads, soaked in ½ cup hot water for 10 minutes
14oz (400g) can chopped tomatoes
4½oz (125g) French beans, cut into ½in (1cm) slices
10oz (300g) small mussels, scrubbed and debearded (discard any that do not close when tapped)
10oz (300g) raw, unpeeled large shrimp, deveined and legs removed
1–2 tbsp chopped flat-leaf parsley

in the slow cooker   ⬤ **PREP** 20 MINS   **COOK** 20 MINS PRECOOKING; AUTO/LOW 2 HRS, THEN **HIGH** 40 MINS

1 Preheat the slow cooker, if required. Heat the oil in a wide heavy-based frying pan over medium heat, add the chicken and seasoning, and cook for 10–12 minutes until browned all over. Remove and set aside. Cook the chorizo for 1–2 minutes on each side until browned. Also remove and set aside. Add the onion and red bell pepper to the pan and cook for 5–7 minutes until soft. Add the rice and stir, so all the grains are coated, and cook for 2–3 minutes. Transfer the rice to the slow cooker, add the chicken and chorizo, then add the garlic, saffron with its soaking liquid, and seasoning. Push the chicken down into the rice, add the tomatoes, and pour over 1 cup water or just enough to cover.

2 Cover with the lid and cook on auto/low for 2 hours, adding the beans after 1 hour of cooking. Then turn the slow cooker to high, pour in ½ cup boiling water, add the mussels and shrimp, and continue cooking for 40 minutes. Remove the lid, cover with a dish towel, and let it stand for 5 minutes. Discard any mussels that haven't opened. Garnish with the parsley and serve.

traditional method   ⬤ **PREP** 20 MINS   **COOK** 1 HR

1 Heat the oil in a wide heavy-based frying pan over medium heat, add the chicken and seasoning, and cook for 10–12 minutes until browned all over. Remove and set aside. Cook the chorizo for 1–2 minutes on each side until browned. Also remove and set aside. Add the onion and red bell pepper to the pan and cook for 5–7 minutes until soft. Add the rice and stir, so all the grains are coated, and cook for 2–3 minutes. Stir in 3 cups water, then the garlic, saffron with its soaking liquid, and plenty of salt and pepper. Push the chicken pieces down into the rice. Scatter the chorizo slices over, followed by the tomatoes and beans, and bring to a boil.

2 Simmer on low heat, uncovered, for about 30 minutes until all the liquid has evaporated and the rice is al dente. Do not stir or the rice will become sticky. If the rice is undercooked or starts to stick to the pan, add a little more hot water and simmer for a few minutes longer. Add the mussels and shrimp to the pan for the last 15 minutes of cooking, cover, and cook until the mussels open and the shrimp turn pink. Remove from the heat and discard any mussels that have not opened. Cover with a dish towel and let it stand for 5 minutes. Garnish with the parsley and serve.

Vary this colorful dish to suit your mood or your pantry—use chili powder instead of paprika, or carrots instead of peas. Stir in herbs, such as parsley or cilantro, at the end.

Arroz con pollo

⊚ **SERVES** 4   ◍ **HEALTHY**

2 tbsp olive oil
8 chicken thighs with bones in
1 Spanish onion or large onion, finely sliced
1 green bell pepper, seeded and chopped
1 red bell pepper, seeded and chopped
2 garlic cloves, finely chopped
1 tsp smoked paprika
1 bay leaf
7oz (200g) can chopped tomatoes
1 tsp thyme leaves

1 tsp dried oregano
1 cup long-grain rice
pinch of saffron threads, soaked in ½ cup hot
 water for 10 minutes
1½ cups hot chicken stock for the slow cooker
 (2½ cups for the traditional method)
2 tbsp tomato paste
juice of ½ lemon
salt and freshly ground black pepper
1 cup frozen peas

in the slow cooker   🕑 **PREP** 20 MINS   **COOK** 20 MINS PRECOOKING; **AUTO/LOW** 3–3½ HRS

1 Preheat the slow cooker, if required. Heat half the oil in a large Dutch oven over high heat, add the chicken thighs (in batches, if necessary), and cook for about 15 minutes until browned all over. Remove and set aside.

2 Add the remaining oil, reduce the heat, and cook the onion for 4–5 minutes until soft. Add the peppers and garlic and cook for about 5 minutes until they start to soften. Add the paprika, bay leaf, tomatoes, thyme, and oregano, and stir in the rice. Fry for 1–2 minutes, stirring constantly. Transfer to the slow cooker and add the saffron with its soaking liquid, stock to cover, tomato paste, lemon juice, and salt and pepper.

3 Add the chicken thighs, pushing them down into the rice, cover with the lid, and cook on auto/low for 3–3½ hours. Add the peas for the last 10 minutes of cooking. Remove the bay leaf and serve hot.

traditional method   🕑 **PREP** 20 MINS   **COOK** 45 MINS

1 Preheat the oven to 350°F (180°C). Heat half the oil in a large Dutch oven over high heat, add the chicken thighs (in batches, if necessary), and cook for about 15 minutes until browned all over. Remove and set aside.

2 Add the remaining oil, reduce the heat, and cook the onion for 4–5 minutes until soft. Add the peppers and garlic and cook for about 5 minutes until they start to soften. Add the paprika, bay leaf, tomatoes, thyme, and oregano, and stir in the rice. Fry for 1–2 minutes, stirring constantly. Add the saffron with its soaking liquid, stock, tomato paste, lemon juice, and salt and pepper.

3 Return the chicken thighs to the pot, pushing them down into the rice, cover with the lid, and put in the oven for 15 minutes. Add the peas and return to the oven for a further 10 minutes, or until the rice is tender and has absorbed the cooking liquid. Remove the bay leaf and serve hot.

Sweet squash combines with salty pecorino in this delicious, creamy risotto. For vegetarian fare, you could omit the sausage. Use Parmesan cheese rather than the pecorino if it's easier to find.

Squash, sausage, and pecorino risotto

SERVES 4–6

2 tbsp olive oil
2 tbsp butter
1 large onion, finely chopped
salt and freshly ground black pepper
3 garlic cloves, finely chopped
2–3 sprigs of thyme
14oz (400g) fresh pork sausages, skinned

1 cup white wine
1 butternut squash, peeled, seeded,
 and chopped into ½in (1cm) cubes
1 cup arborio rice or carnaroli rice
about 2 cups hot chicken stock,
 for both methods
1½ cups pecorino cheese, grated

in the slow cooker   **PREP** 20 MINS   **COOK** 15 MINS PRECOOKING; **AUTO/LOW** 1½–2 HRS

1 Preheat the slow cooker, if required. Heat the oil and butter in a large Dutch oven, add the onion, and cook for 3–4 minutes until soft. Season with salt and pepper and stir in the garlic and thyme. Add the sausage meat and cook for 3–5 minutes until no longer pink, mashing them with the back of a wooden spoon to break it up. Add the wine and cook for a couple more minutes, then stir in the squash and combine so everything is coated.

2 Stir in the rice and turn it in the juices so all the grains are coated, and cook for a few seconds. Transfer everything to the slow cooker and pour in the stock so it just covers the contents. Cover with the lid and cook on auto/low for 1½–2 hours. You may need to stir it halfway through. Stir in the pecorino (removing the thyme at the same time), taste, and add some pepper if needed. Serve with a crisp green salad.

traditional method   **PREP** 20 MINS   **COOK** 50–60 MINS

1 Heat the oil and butter in a large Dutch oven, add the onion, and cook for 3–4 minutes until soft. Season with salt and pepper and stir in the garlic and thyme.

2 Add the sausage meat and cook for 3–5 minutes until no longer pink, mashing them with the back of a wooden spoon to break it up. Add the wine and cook for a couple more minutes, then stir in the squash and combine so everything is coated. Cook on low heat for 5–10 minutes for the squash to soften slightly.

3 Stir in the rice and turn it in the juices so all the grains are coated, and cook for a few seconds. Increase the heat, add a ladleful of the hot stock at a time (keeping the rest simmering in a saucepan) and stir, cooking, until it has been absorbed. Continue doing this for 30–35 minutes until the rice is cooked to al dente and is creamy. You may not need all the stock or you may need a little more. Stir in the pecorino (removing the thyme at the same time), taste, and add some pepper if needed. Serve with a crisp green salad.

Creamy and light, this is a perfect dinner for vegetarians, although you could stir in some pancetta, for something a little more substantial, and fresh herbs at the end of cooking.

Artichoke risotto

SERVES 4

1 tbsp olive oil
2 tbsp butter
1 onion, finely chopped
salt and freshly ground black pepper
3 garlic cloves, finely chopped
1½ cups arborio rice or carnaroli rice
1 cup white wine

about 2½ cups hot chicken stock
  for the slow cooker (about 3½ cups
  for the traditional method)
2 x 10oz (280g) jars antipasti artichokes,
  drained and large ones halved
1/4 cup Parmesan cheese, grated, plus
  extra to serve

in the slow cooker **PREP** 20 MINS **COOK** 15 MINS PRECOOKING; **AUTO/LOW** 1–1¼ HRS

1 Preheat the slow cooker, if required. Heat the oil and half the butter in a large heavy-based saucepan over medium heat, add the onion, and cook for 3–4 minutes until soft. Season with salt and pepper, stir in the garlic, and cook for about a minute.

2 Stir in the rice and turn it in the oily butter so all the grains are coated, and cook for a few seconds. Increase the heat, add the wine, and let it bubble for 1–2 minutes or until it has been absorbed. Then pour in the stock, bring to a boil, and transfer everything to the slow cooker. Add the artichokes, cover with the lid, and cook on auto/low for 1–1¼ hours.

3 Stir in the remaining butter and Parmesan cheese, taste, and season, if needed. Serve with more Parmesan and some lightly dressed wild arugula and tomato salad on the side.

traditional method **PREP** 20 MINS **COOK** 45–50 MINS

1 Heat the oil and half the butter in a large heavy-based saucepan over medium heat, add the onion, and cook for 3–4 minutes until soft. Season with salt and pepper, stir in the garlic, and cook for about a minute.

2 Stir in the rice and turn it in the oily butter so all the grains are coated, and cook for a few seconds. Increase the heat, add the wine, and let it bubble for 1–2 minutes or until it has been absorbed. Then add a ladleful of the hot stock at a time (keeping the rest simmering in a saucepan) and stir, cooking, until it has been absorbed. Continue doing this for 30–35 minutes until the rice is cooked to al dente and is creamy. You may not need all the stock or you may need a little more.

3 Add the artichokes to the risotto for the last 10 minutes of cooking and carefully stir them in. Dot with the remaining butter and stir it in together with the Parmesan cheese, taste, and season, if needed. Serve with more Parmesan and some lightly dressed wild arugula and tomato salad on the side.

You can serve this nutty, gingery pilaf on its own or with grilled lamb or fish. Grated ginger freezes well, so wrap small quantities in plastic wrap and you'll always have some on hand.

Cashew and zucchini rice

 **SERVES** 4　 **HEALTHY**

1–2 tbsp olive oil
1 onion, finely chopped
salt and freshly ground black pepper
4in (10cm) piece of fresh ginger, peeled
  and grated
4 zucchini, sliced into quarters lengthwise
  and chopped into bite-sized pieces
3 garlic cloves, finely chopped
1 tbsp cider vinegar

pinch of cayenne pepper
1 cup quick-cooking basmati rice
1 cup hot vegetable stock for the slow cooker
  (about 3 cups for the traditional method)
¼ cup cashew nuts, roughly chopped
bunch of scallions, green part only, thinly sliced
bunch of cilantro, leaves only, chopped

in the slow cooker　 **PREP** 15 MINS　 **COOK** 10 MINS PRECOOKING; **HIGH** 2–2½ HRS

1 Preheat the slow cooker, if required. Heat 1 tablespoon of oil in a large Dutch oven over medium heat, add the onion, and cook for 3–4 minutes until soft. Season with salt and pepper, increase the heat, and stir in the ginger and zucchini. Cook for 2–5 minutes until the zucchini is lightly golden (adding more oil, if necessary), and then add the garlic and cook for a further 3 minutes.

2 Increase the heat, add the vinegar, and let it cook for a minute, then stir in the cayenne pepper and rice. Add a little stock and turn it so all the grains are coated. Transfer to the slow cooker, pour in enough stock just to cover, then cover with the lid, and cook on high for 2–2½ hours, stirring halfway through.

3 Stir in the cashew nuts, scallions, and half the cilantro, taste, and season as needed. Sprinkle with the remaining cilantro to serve.

traditional method　 **PREP** 15 MINS　 **COOK** 40 MINS

1 Heat 1 tablespoon of oil in a large Dutch oven over medium heat, add the onion, and cook for 3–4 minutes until soft. Season with salt and pepper, increase the heat, and stir in the ginger and zucchini. Cook for 2–5 minutes until the zucchini is lightly golden (adding more oil, if necessary), and then add the garlic and cook for a further 3 minutes.

2 Increase the heat, add the vinegar, and let it cook for a minute, then stir in the cayenne pepper and rice. Add a little stock and turn it so all the grains are coated. Bring to a boil, add enough stock to cover, cover with a lid, and simmer gently for about 20 minutes or until the rice is tender. Top it up with more stock when needed.

3 Stir in the cashew nuts, scallions, and half the cilantro, taste, and season as needed. Sprinkle with the remaining cilantro to serve.

Taleggio is a mellow Italian cheese with a slight tang that melts into the rice, making it deliciously creamy. Pair it with asparagus when in season, or try broccoli or peas when not available.

Asparagus and Taleggio risotto

SERVES 4

1 tbsp olive oil
2 tbsp butter
1 onion, finely chopped
3 garlic cloves, finely chopped
salt and freshly ground black pepper
1½ cups arborio rice or carnaroli rice

1 cup white wine
2 cups hot chicken stock for the slow cooker
  (about 3 cups for the traditional method)
bunch of asparagus, trimmed
2½oz (75g) Taleggio cheese, roughly sliced

in the slow cooker   **PREP** 20 MINS   **COOK** 15 MINS PRECOOKING; **AUTO/LOW** 1–1¼ HRS

1 Preheat the slow cooker, if required. Heat the oil and butter in a large heavy-based saucepan over medium heat, add the onion, and cook for 3–4 minutes until soft, then stir in the garlic and cook for a further minute. Season with salt and pepper.

2 Stir in the rice and turn it in the oily butter so all the grains are coated, and cook for a few seconds. Increase the heat, add the wine, and let it bubble for 1–2 minutes or until it has been absorbed. Then pour in the stock and bring to a boil. Transfer everything to the slow cooker, cover with the lid, and cook on auto/low for 1–1¼ hours.

3 Meanwhile, add the asparagus to a pan of boiling salted water and cook for 4–6 minutes, then drain, slice each spear into three and add to the rice along with the Taleggio cheese. Taste and season, if needed, and serve with a tomato and red onion salad.

traditional method   **PREP** 20 MINS   **COOK** 45–55 MINS

1 Heat the oil and butter in a large heavy-based saucepan over medium heat, add the onion, and cook for 3–4 minutes until soft, then stir in the garlic and cook for a further minute. Season with salt and pepper.

2 Stir in the rice and turn it in the oily butter so all the grains are coated, and cook for a few seconds. Increase the heat, add the wine, and let it bubble for 1–2 minutes or until it has been absorbed. Then add a ladleful of the hot stock at a time (keeping the rest simmering in a saucepan) and stir, cooking, until it has been absorbed. Continue doing this for 30–40 minutes until the rice is cooked to al dente and is creamy. You may not need all the stock or you may need a little more.

3 Meanwhile, add the asparagus to a pan of boiling salted water and cook for 4–6 minutes, then drain, slice each spear into three and add to the rice along with the Taleggio cheese. Taste and season, if needed, and serve with a tomato and red onion salad.

This is a rich seafood rice dish with lots of flavor. For even more variety, add a handful of shrimp and clams toward the end of the cooking time, together with the mussels.

Risotto with mussels

SERVES 4–6

1 tbsp olive oil
2 tbsp butter
1 onion, finely chopped
salt and freshly ground black pepper
3 garlic cloves, finely chopped
pinch of chile flakes
1 fennel bulb, trimmed and finely chopped
1½ cups arborio rice or carnaroli rice
½ cup white wine

2 cups hot vegetable stock for the slow cooker
   (about 3 cups for the traditional method)
2lb (900g) mussels, scrubbed and debearded
   (discard any that do not close when tapped)
bunch of flat-leaf parsley, finely chopped
few sprigs of dill, finely chopped
juice of 1 lemon, to serve (optional)

in the slow cooker   🕐 PREP 20 MINS   COOK 15 MINS PRECOOKING; AUTO/LOW 1 HR

1 Preheat the slow cooker, if required. Heat the oil and butter in a large heavy-based saucepan over medium heat, add the onion, and cook for 3–4 minutes until soft. Season with salt and pepper, stir in the garlic and chile flakes, and cook for 1 minute.

2 Add the fennel and cook for about 5 minutes until soft, then stir in the rice, turning well so the grains are coated. Increase the heat, add the wine, and let it bubble for 1–2 minutes until it has been absorbed. Then add the hot stock and bring to a boil.

3 Transfer everything to the slow cooker, season, and cover with the lid. Cook on auto/low for 1 hour or until the rice is cooked and the liquid has been absorbed. Add the mussels for the last 10 minutes of cooking, then stir in the parsley and dill, and add a squeeze of lemon juice, if using. Taste and season with some pepper if needed. Serve immediately, discarding any mussels that haven't opened when cooked.

traditional method   🕐 PREP 20 MINS   COOK 45–55 MINS

1 Heat the oil and butter in a large heavy-based saucepan over medium heat, add the onion, and cook for 3–4 minutes until soft. Season with salt and pepper, stir in the garlic and chile flakes, and cook for 1 minute.

2 Add the fennel and cook for about 5 minutes until soft, then stir in the rice, turning well so the grains are coated. Increase the heat, add the wine, and let it bubble for 1–2 minutes until it has been absorbed. Then add a ladleful of the hot stock at a time (keeping the rest simmering in a saucepan) and stir, cooking, until it has been absorbed. Continue doing this for 30–40 minutes or until the rice is cooked to al dente and is creamy. You may not need all the stock or you may need a little more.

3 Stir in the mussels, cover with the lid, and leave for a few minutes until all the mussels have opened (discard any that do not open). Stir in the parsley and dill, and add a squeeze of lemon juice, if using. Taste and season with some pepper if needed. Serve immediately.

For a successful risotto, keep checking the rice—it should be creamy but still have some bite. Stirring risotto rice releases starch from its grains, giving it its smooth texture.

Shrimp risotto

SERVES 6   **HEALTHY**

⅓ cup olive oil
about 1lb (500g) small or medium raw shrimp
2 garlic cloves, finely chopped
small bunch of flat-leaf parsley, leaves chopped
salt and freshly ground black pepper

¼ cup dry white wine
2 cups hot fish or chicken stock for the slow cooker
 (3½ cups for the traditional method)
1 onion, finely chopped
2 cups arborio rice or carnaroli rice

in the slow cooker   **PREP** 15 MINS   **COOK** 10 MINS PRECOOKING; **AUTO/LOW** 2–3 HRS

1 Preheat the slow cooker, if required. Heat a third of the oil in a large heavy-based skillet over medium heat, add the shrimp, garlic, parsley, and salt and pepper, and cook for 1–2 minutes, stirring, until the shrimp turn pink. Pour in the wine and stir thoroughly. Transfer the shrimp to a bowl, set aside, and when cool, cover and chill. Simmer the liquid in the pan for 2–3 minutes until reduced by three-quarters. Add the stock, bring to a boil, and then reduce to a simmer.

2 Heat half the remaining oil in a second heavy-based skillet over medium heat, add the onion, and cook for 3–4 minutes until soft. Add the rice and stir until all the grains are coated with oil. Transfer to the slow cooker and pour in the simmering liquid or just enough to cover the rice. Cover with the lid and cook on auto/low for 2–3 hours or until the rice is cooked to al dente, giving it a stir halfway through. About an hour before the end of the cooking time, stir in the cooked shrimp and the remaining olive oil. Taste and add seasoning if needed (you may not need much salt). Spoon the risotto into warmed bowls and serve immediately.

traditional method   **PREP** 15 MINS   **COOK** 50 MINS

1 Heat a third of the oil in a large heavy-based saucepan over medium heat, add the shrimp, garlic, parsley, and salt and pepper, and cook for 1–2 minutes, stirring, until the shrimp turn pink. Pour in the wine and stir thoroughly. Transfer the shrimp to a bowl and set aside. Simmer the liquid in the pan for 2–3 minutes until reduced by three-quarters. Add the stock and 1 cup water and bring to a boil, then reduce to a simmer.

2 Heat half the remaining oil in a second heavy-based saucepan over medium heat, add the onion, and cook for 3–4 minutes until soft. Add the rice and stir until all the grains are coated with oil. Then add a ladleful of the hot stock at a time, stirring constantly, until all the liquid is absorbed. Continue doing this for 30–40 minutes until the rice is cooked to al dente and creamy.

3 At the end of the cooking time, stir in the shrimp and the remaining olive oil and cook until pink. Taste and add seasoning if needed (you may not need much salt). Spoon the risotto into warmed bowls and serve immediately.

In this dish, the rice is cooked first and then is gently steamed in the spiced vegetable mixture. Adjust the vegetable list according to what is in your refrigerator, adding more or less as you wish.

Vegetable biryani

SERVES 6   **HEALTHY**

1½ cups basmati rice
1 large carrot, peeled and sliced
2 potatoes, peeled and chopped into small pieces
½ cauliflower, chopped into small florets
3 tbsp vegetable oil
1 red onion, chopped
1 red bell pepper, seeded and chopped
1 green bell pepper, seeded and chopped
1 zucchini, chopped

½ cup frozen peas
1 tsp ground turmeric
1 tsp mild chili powder
2 tsp ground coriander
2 tsp mild curry paste
1 tsp cumin seeds
¾ cup hot vegetable stock, for both methods
60g (2oz) cashew nuts, lightly toasted

in the slow cooker   **PREP** 30 MINS   **COOK** 30 MINS PRECOOKING; **AUTO/LOW** 2–3 HRS

1 Preheat the slow cooker, if required. In a pan of simmering water, cook the rice for 10 minutes or until just tender. Drain and set aside. Cook the carrot and potatoes in a pan of boiling water for about 5 minutes until almost tender. Then add the cauliflower and cook for a further 6–8 minutes until all the vegetables are tender. Drain and set aside.

2 Heat the oil in a large heavy-based saucepan over medium heat, add the onion, and cook for 4–5 minutes until soft. Add the red and green bell peppers and the zucchini, and cook for 5 minutes, stirring occasionally. Add the boiled vegetables and frozen peas, then stir in the turmeric, chili powder, coriander, curry paste, and cumin seeds. Cook for a further 5 minutes, then transfer half the rice to the slow cooker and top with the vegetable mixture. Pour over the stock and top with the remaining rice. Cover with the lid and cook on auto/low for 2–3 hours, stirring halfway through. Scatter over the cashews and serve with naan bread, mango chutney, lime pickle, or raita.

traditional method   **PREP** 30 MINS   **COOK** 1¼ HRS

1 Preheat the oven to 350°F (180°C). In a pan of simmering water, cook the rice for 10 minutes or until just tender. Drain and set aside. Cook the carrot and potatoes in a pan of boiling water for about 5 minutes until almost tender. Then add the cauliflower and cook for a further 6–8 minutes until all the vegetables are tender. Drain and set aside.

2 Heat the oil in a large heavy-based saucepan over medium heat, add the onion, and cook for 4–5 minutes until soft. Add the red and green bell peppers and the zucchini, and cook for 5 minutes, stirring occasionally. Add the boiled vegetables and frozen peas, then stir in the turmeric, chili powder, coriander, curry paste, and cumin seeds. Cook for a further 5 minutes, then stir in the stock.

3 Spoon half the rice into an ovenproof dish and top with the vegetable mixture. Top with the remaining rice, cover with foil, and bake for about 30 minutes until hot. Scatter over the cashews and serve with naan bread, mango chutney, lime pickle, or raita.

In this Caribbean dish, the "peas" are known as gungo peas in Jamaica and pigeon peas in Trinidad. It would be particularly good served with grilled or roasted meat and poultry or fried fish.

Rice and peas

SERVES 4   **HEALTHY**

14oz (400g) can gungo peas or black-eyed peas, drained and rinsed
14oz (400ml) can coconut milk
1 large onion, finely chopped

1 green bell pepper, seeded and chopped
⅔ cup long-grain rice
salt and freshly ground black pepper
chili powder, to serve

in the slow cooker   **PREP** 10 MINS   **COOK** AUTO/LOW 2–3 HRS

1 Preheat the slow cooker, if required. Put the peas, coconut milk, onion, green bell pepper, and rice in the slow cooker. Season with salt and pepper. Cover with the lid and cook on auto/low for 2–3 hours. Serve garnished with chili powder.

traditional method   **PREP** 10 MINS   **COOK** 45 MINS

1 Put the peas, coconut milk, onion, and bell pepper in a large heavy-based saucepan, and simmer over low heat for 5 minutes. Stir in the rice and season with salt and pepper. Cover with the lid and cook for 35 minutes, or until the rice is tender, stirring occasionally. Serve garnished with chili powder.

Traditional flavorings of coconut and kaffir lime leaves are used in this popular Asian dish. It's an easy dish to put together as most of the ingredients will be in the pantry or fridge.

Thai coconut rice

SERVES 4–6

2 tbsp olive oil
2 tbsp butter
1 red chile, seeded and chopped
2 shallots, finely chopped
¼ cup Thai red curry paste
grated zest of 1 lime
1 tsp chopped cilantro stems

1¾ cups Thai jasmine rice
1 tsp salt
14oz (400ml) can coconut milk
large pinch of shredded kaffir lime leaves
2 scallions, trimmed and thinly sliced
1 tsp chopped cilantro leaves

in the slow cooker   **PREP** 10 MINS   **COOK** 10 MINS PRECOOKING; **AUTO/LOW** 2½–3 HRS

1 Preheat the slow cooker, if required. Heat the oil and butter in a large heavy-based skillet over low heat, add the chile and shallots, and cook, stirring, for about 5 minutes until it starts to turn golden. Stir in the curry paste and cook for 30 seconds. Add the lime zest, cilantro stems, rice, and salt, and stir until the grains of rice are coated in the curry paste.

2 Transfer everything to the slow cooker, then pour in the coconut milk and 1 cup water. Scatter in the lime leaves, cover with the lid, and cook on auto/low for 2½–3 hours. Stir the rice halfway through.

3 When ready to serve, stir in the scallions and sprinkle the cilantro leaves over. Serve on its own or with some soy-marinated roasted fish or stir-fried chicken.

traditional method   **PREP** 10 MINS   **COOK** 40 MINS

1 Heat the oil and butter in a large heavy-based skillet over low heat, add the chile and shallots, and cook, stirring, for about 5 minutes until it starts to turn golden. Stir in the curry paste and cook for 30 seconds. Add the lime zest, cilantro stems, rice, and salt, and stir until the grains of rice are coated in the curry paste.

2 Pour in the coconut milk and 1¾ cups water and stir well. Bring to simmering point over medium heat, stirring occasionally, so the rice doesn't stick. Scatter in the lime leaves and simmer, uncovered, for 5 minutes.

3 Give the rice a thorough stir, cover, and leave over a very low heat for 15 minutes or until the rice is tender. If the liquid has been absorbed but the rice is still not ready, add a little extra hot water. When ready to serve, stir in the scallions and sprinkle the cilantro leaves over. Serve on its own or with some soy-marinated roasted fish or stir-fried chicken.

Desserts

Rich and decadent, these mini cakes are delicious served hot with some vanilla ice cream. To cook the puddings in one batch, use a slow cooker that is a minimum of 5 quarts (4.5 liters) in size.

Chocolate and prune sponge puddings

MAKES 6

½ cup butter, at room temperature
½ cup superfine sugar
2 eggs, beaten

1 cup self-rising flour, sifted
¼ cup cocoa powder, mixed with 2 tbsp milk
½ cup prunes, pitted and chopped

in the slow cooker PREP 30–40 MINS COOK HIGH 45 MINS

1 Preheat the slow cooker, if required. Grease six 5fl oz (150ml) metal pudding molds. Put the butter and sugar into a mixing bowl and beat together until creamy and pale. Add the eggs slowly, beating as you go and adding a little flour to prevent any curdling. Then fold in the remaining flour until it is thoroughly combined, and stir in the cocoa mixture and prunes.

2 Divide the mixture between the molds and cover each one with a pleated piece of greased parchment paper and a sheet of foil kept in place with string.

3 Sit the pudding molds in the slow cooker and pour in enough boiling water to come halfway up the sides of the pudding molds. Cover with the lid and cook on high for 45 minutes. Carefully lift the molds out of the slow cooker, remove the string, foil, and paper, and turn out onto warmed plates. Serve hot with ice cream, cream, custard, or chocolate sauce.

traditional method PREP 30–40 MINS COOK 45 MINS

1 Grease six 5fl oz (150ml) metal pudding molds. Put the butter and sugar into a mixing bowl and beat together until creamy and pale. Add the eggs slowly, beating as you go and adding a little flour to prevent any curdling. Then fold in the remaining flour until it is thoroughly combined, and stir through the cocoa mixture and prunes.

2 Divide the mixture between the molds and cover each one with a pleated piece of greased parchment paper and a sheet of foil kept in place with string.

3 Sit the molds in a large heavy-based pan and pour in enough boiling water to come halfway up the sides of the pudding molds. Cover with the lid and leave to simmer gently for about 45 minutes, topping up with more boiling water as and when needed. Carefully lift the molds out of the pan, remove the string, foil, and paper, and turn out onto warmed plates. Serve hot with ice cream, cream, custard, or chocolate sauce.

Also known as *Arroz doce*, this is a traditional Portuguese dessert. Use whole milk because it will work far better. The eggs will cook in the residual heat. Try it sprinkled with ground cinnamon.

Chocolate rice pudding

SERVES 4–6

2½ cups short-grain rice
1 tsp salt
1 quart whole milk
1 tbsp cocoa powder
1 cup superfine sugar
6 egg yolks
¼ cup grated dark chocolate

in the slow cooker 🕐 **PREP** 10 MINS **COOK** AUTO/LOW 2½–3 HRS

1 Preheat the slow cooker, if required. Put the rice and salt into the slow cooker. Stir in the milk and cocoa powder, then add sugar, and stir again. Cover with the lid and cook on auto/low for 2½–3 hours. Turn off the slow cooker, beat in the eggs yolks, and leave to sit, unheated, for a few minutes.

2 Divide the rice between individual serving dishes, level the tops, and sprinkle with grated chocolate. Leave to cool, then serve.

traditional method 🕐 **PREP** 10 MINS **COOK** 40 MINS

1 Bring 7 cups of water to a boil in a large saucepan. Add the rice and salt and bring back to a boil. Reduce the heat, cover, and cook for 10 minutes, then drain.

2 Pour the milk into a saucepan and add the cocoa. Bring to a boil, then add the rice. Reduce the heat and cook, uncovered, for 30 minutes or until the rice is soft. Add the sugar and stir until dissolved, then remove from the heat, and quickly beat in the egg yolks.

3 Divide the rice between individual serving dishes, level the tops, and sprinkle with grated chocolate. Leave to cool, then serve.

This sweet, creamy, and very rich dessert is a popular party dish in Brazil where it is known as *Quindim*. It needs to be made ahead so it has plenty of time to chill in the fridge.

Brazilian baked custards with coconut

SERVES 4

½ cup superfine sugar
4 egg yolks
2 tbsp grated fresh coconut or dried coconut, plus
  extra, toasted, to serve
¼ cup coconut milk

in the slow cooker   **PREP** 15 MINS, PLUS CHILLING   **COOK** AUTO/LOW 1–2 HRS

1 Preheat the slow cooker, if required. Whisk the sugar and egg yolks in a bowl until light and creamy. Add the grated or dried coconut and coconut milk and stir until evenly combined. Spoon into four 5fl oz (150ml) ramekins and cover each one with foil.

2 Stand the ramekins in the slow cooker, stacking if necessary (but not directly on top of each other), and pour in enough warm water to come halfway up the sides of the ramekins on the bottom.

3 Cover with the lid and cook on auto/low for 1–2 hours until the custards are set. Carefully lift the ramekins out of the slow cooker, leave to cool, and then chill for at least 3–4 hours. Serve with the toasted coconut sprinkled on top.

traditional method   **PREP** 15 MINS, PLUS CHILLING   **COOK** 25–30 MINS

1 Preheat the oven to 350°F (180°C). Whisk the sugar and egg yolks in a bowl until light and creamy. Add the grated or dried coconut and coconut milk and stir until evenly combined. Spoon into four 5fl oz (150ml) ramekins and cover each one with foil.

2 Stand the ramekins in a roasting pan and pour in enough warm water to come halfway up the sides of the dishes. Put in the oven for 25–30 minutes until the custards are set. Carefully lift the dishes out of the pan, leave to cool, and then chill for at least 3–4 hours. Serve with the toasted coconut sprinkled on top.

Here is a light citrussy pudding that is best enjoyed with plenty of custard. You could add a small handful of chopped almonds to the mixture for added texture.

Lemon sponge pudding

SERVES 4–6

grated zest and juice of 2 lemons
juice of ½ large orange
packed ¼ cup light soft brown sugar
½ cup unsalted butter, at room temperature

¼ cup superfine sugar
1 tbsp light corn syrup
2 eggs
1½ cups self-rising flour, sifted

in the slow cooker   **PREP** 30–40 MINS   **COOK** HIGH 2–3 HRS

1 Preheat the slow cooker, if required. Grease a 3½ cup (1-liter) pudding basin. Stir together the juice of 1 lemon with the orange juice and brown sugar in a bowl, and pour this into the pudding basin. Put the butter, sugar, and corn syrup into a mixing bowl along with the lemon zest and beat together until creamy and pale. Add the eggs slowly, beating as you go and adding a little flour to prevent any curdling. Then fold in the remaining flour until it is thoroughly combined and stir in the remaining lemon juice.

2 Pour the mixture into the basin and cover with a pleated piece of greased parchment paper and a sheet of foil. Secure with string, looping it around the basin to form a handle.

3 Sit the pudding in the slow cooker and pour in enough boiling water to come halfway up the side of the basin. Cover with the lid and cook on high for 2–3 hours. Carefully lift the basin out of the slow cooker, remove the string, foil, and paper, and turn the pudding out onto a plate. Serve piping hot with custard or cream.

traditional method   **PREP** 30–40 MINS   **COOK** 1½ HRS

1 Grease a 3½ cup (1-liter) pudding basin. Stir together the juice of 1 lemon with the orange juice and brown sugar in a bowl, and pour this into the pudding basin. Put the butter, sugar, and corn syrup into a mixing bowl along with the lemon zest and beat together until creamy and pale. Add the eggs slowly, beating as you go and adding a little flour to prevent any curdling. Then fold in the remaining flour until it is thoroughly combined, and stir in the remaining lemon juice.

2 Pour the mixture into the basin and cover with a pleated piece of greased parchment paper and a sheet of foil. Secure with string, looping it around the basin to form a handle.

3 Sit the pudding bowl in a large heavy-based pan and pour in enough boiling water to come halfway up the side of the basin. Cover with the lid and leave to simmer gently for about 1½ hours, topping up with more boiling water as and when needed. Carefully lift the basin out of the pan, remove the string, foil, and paper, and turn the pudding out onto a plate. Serve piping hot with custard or cream.

Steamed puddings do not have to be stodgy—this light version is a case in point and it's full of dried fruit and spices. For something a little simpler, use golden raisins in place of the mixed dried fruit.

Mixed fruit pudding

SERVES 4–6   **FREEZE** UP TO 3 MONTHS

½ cup butter, at room temperature
¼ cup superfine sugar
2 eggs, lightly beaten
¾ cup self-rising flour, sifted
about ¾ cup mixed dried fruit

pinch of ground cinnamon
pinch of pie spice
1 tbsp milk
1–2 tbsp honey or golden syrup

in the slow cooker   **PREP** 15 MINS   **COOK** 10 MINS PRECOOKING; **HIGH** 3–4 HRS

1 Preheat the slow cooker, if required, and lightly grease a 2 cup pudding basin. Put the butter and sugar in a standing mixer and beat until pale and creamy, or use a hand-held electric mixer.

2 Add the eggs, a little at a time, with a little of the flour, beating gently as you go. Then add the remaining flour together with the fruit and spices and beat lightly. Finally, add the milk and stir until everything is combined.

3 Put 1–2 tablespoons of the honey (depending on how sweet you like it) in the bottom of the pudding basin, then spoon the mixture into the basin. Cover with a pleated piece of parchment paper and a sheet of foil. Secure with string, looping it around the basin to form a handle. Sit the pudding basin in the slow cooker and pour in enough boiling water to come halfway up the sides of the basin. Cover with the lid and cook on high for 3–4 hours. Carefully remove the basin from the slow cooker, remove the string, foil, and paper, and turn the pudding out onto a plate. Serve with ice cream or custard.

traditional method   **PREP** 15 MINS   **COOK** 1¾ HRS

1 Lightly grease a 2 cup pudding basin. Put the butter and sugar in a standing mixer and beat until pale and creamy, or use a hand-held electric mixer.

2 Add the eggs, a little at a time, with a little of the flour, beating gently as you go. Then add the remaining flour together with the fruit and spices and beat lightly. Finally, add the milk and stir until everything is combined.

3 Put 1–2 tablespoons of the honey (depending on how sweet you like it) in the bottom of the pudding basin, then spoon the mixture into the basin. Cover with a pleated piece of parchment paper and a sheet of foil. Secure with string, looping it around the basin to form a handle. Sit the pudding basin in a large heavy-based saucepan and pour in enough boiling water to come halfway up the side of the basin. Cover with the lid and simmer gently for about 1½ hours, topping up with more boiling water if needed. Carefully remove the basin from the pan, remove the string, foil, and paper, and turn the pudding out onto a plate. Serve with ice cream or custard.

For an even richer experience, consider using flavored mint, ginger, or coffee chocolate. To cook the mousses in one batch, use a slow cooker that is a minimum of 5 quarts (4.5 liters) in size.

Chocolate mousses

MAKES 6

2 eggs
3 egg yolks
½ cup superfine sugar

3½oz (100g) dark chocolate (70 percent
  cocoa solids), broken into pieces
1 cup heavy cream

in the slow cooker
PREP 20 MINS, PLUS CHILLING   **COOK** 10 MINS PRECOOKING; **AUTO/LOW** 2½–3 HRS

1 Preheat the slow cooker, if required, and grease six 3½fl oz (100ml) ramekins or metal pudding basins. Put the eggs, egg yolks, and sugar in a mixing bowl and whisk until creamy. Set aside.

2 Put the chocolate in a heatproof bowl and sit it over a pan of barely simmering water. Stir occasionally until melted, remove from the heat, and set aside. Heat the cream in a pan so it is warm, but do not boil, then slowly add the egg mixture, whisking as you go. Stir in the chocolate until it is very well combined.

3 Pour the mixture into the prepared ramekins or basins and cover each one with foil. Pour 1¼in (3cm) hot water into the slow cooker and carefully place the mousses in the slow cooker, stacking them, if necessary, to fit (but not sitting directly on top of each other). Cover with the lid and cook on auto/low for 2½–3 hours; they should still have a wobble in them when they are ready. Remove the ramekins or basins from the slow cooker and leave to cool, then transfer to the refrigerator for a couple of hours to chill. Turn out each mousse onto a bowl and serve with ice cream or shortbread cookies.

traditional method
PREP 20 MINS **COOK** 30 MINS

1 Preheat the oven to 325°F (160°C) and grease six 3½fl oz (100ml) ramekins or metal pudding basins. Put the eggs, egg yolks, and sugar in a mixing bowl and whisk until creamy. Set aside.

2 Put the chocolate in a heatproof bowl and sit it over a pan of barely simmering water. Stir occasionally until melted, remove from the heat, and set aside. Heat the cream in a pan so it is warm, but do not boil, then slowly add the egg mixture, whisking as you go. Stir in the chocolate until it is very well combined.

3 Pour the mixture into the prepared ramekins or basins, then sit them in a roasting pan and carefully pour hot water into the pan so it comes halfway up the sides of the ramekins. Sit in the oven and cook for 15–20 minutes; they should still have a wobble in them when they are ready. Remove from the oven and leave to cool, then transfer to the refrigerator for a couple of hours to chill. Turn out each mousse onto a bowl and serve with ice cream or shortbread cookies.

This is a delicious classic infused with the taste of vanilla. In this recipe, the seeds are discarded, but for something more aromatic, seed the pod and add the seeds to the milk at the same time.

Classic crème caramel

MAKES 6

2 cups whole milk
1 vanilla pod, split lengthwise and seeded
1 cup superfine sugar

2 whole eggs
4 egg yolks

in the slow cooker　**PREP** 15 MINS, PLUS INFUSING AND CHILLING　**COOK** 25 MINS PRECOOKING; **AUTO/LOW** 3–4 HRS

1 Preheat the slow cooker, if required. Pour the milk into a heavy-based pan, add the vanilla pod, and very gently bring almost to a boil. Turn off the heat, cover the pan with the lid, and leave for 20 minutes. This is to give the vanilla pod time to infuse the milk while it cools.

2 Add half of the sugar to another heavy-based pan, then pour in 5 tablespoons of cold water. Slowly bring to a boil, swirling it around the pan occasionally to ensure all the sugar has dissolved, then boil for about 15 minutes, until the liquid turns a dark golden caramel. Pour this into six 5fl oz (150ml) ramekins, or use larger ones if making fewer crème caramels.

3 Put the remaining sugar with the eggs and egg yolks into a bowl and whisk until well combined and the sugar has dissolved. Discard the vanilla pod and pour the cooled milk into the egg mixture, then briefly whisk again and pour through a sieve into the ramekins. Cover each ramekin with foil and sit them in the slow cooker. Pour in enough boiling water to come halfway up the sides of the ramekins. Cover with the lid and cook on low for 3–4 hours. Lift the slow cooker dish out and leave them to cool in it, then remove the ramekins and chill them overnight in the fridge. Turn out to serve.

traditional method　**PREP** 15 MINS, PLUS INFUSING AND CHILLING　**COOK** 1½ HRS

1 Preheat the oven to 300°F (150°C). Pour the milk into a heavy-based pan, add the vanilla pod, and very gently bring almost to a boil. Turn off the heat, cover the pan with the lid, and leave for 20 minutes. This is to give the vanilla pod time to infuse the milk while it cools.

2 Add half of the sugar to another heavy-based pan, then pour in 5 tablespoons of cold water. Slowly bring to a boil, swirling it around the pan occasionally to ensure the sugar has dissolved, then boil for about 15 minutes, until the liquid turns a dark golden caramel. Pour this into six 5fl oz (150ml) ramekins, or use larger ones if making fewer crème caramels.

3 Put the remaining sugar with the eggs and egg yolks into a bowl and whisk until well combined and the sugar has dissolved. Discard the vanilla pod and pour the cooled milk into the egg mixture, then briefly whisk again and pour through a sieve into the ramekins. Sit the ramekins in a deep ovenproof dish, pour in boiling water to come two-thirds of the way up the sides of the ramekins, and cook for 1 hour. Remove the dish from the oven, leaving the ramekins in the hot water for 30 minutes to continue setting. Then leave to cool and chill overnight in the fridge. Turn out to serve.

Careful cooking at a low temperature will produce a pudding with a smooth, velvety texture—a perfect use for leftover white bread. For extra decadence, you could use brioche or croissants.

Bread and butter pudding

SERVES 4

2 tbsp butter, plus extra to grease
5–6 slices of day-old bread, crusts removed,
  about 6oz (175g) weight total
½ cup raisins
3 eggs
1¼ cups whole milk

¾ cup heavy cream
¼ cup superfine sugar
1 tsp pure vanilla extract
¼ cup apricot jam
2–3 tsp lemon juice

in the slow cooker   ⏱ **PREP** 15 MINS, PLUS SOAKING   **COOK** AUTO/LOW 4–5 HRS

1 Lightly grease an ovenproof dish with a little butter (one that will fit in the slow cooker, a soufflé dish would be good). Spread the remaining butter on the slices of bread. Cut each slice in half diagonally, then in half again to form 4 triangles.

2 Place the raisins in the bottom of the dish and arrange overlapping slices of bread across the top. Beat together the eggs, milk, cream, sugar, and vanilla extract in a bowl. Carefully pour the mixture over the bread, cover with foil, and leave to soak for at least 30 minutes.

3 Preheat the slow cooker, if required. Place the dish in the slow cooker and pour in enough boiling water to come halfway up the side of the dish. Cover with the lid and cook on auto/low for 4–5 hours or until still slightly moist in the center, but not runny.

4 Meanwhile, put the jam in a small pan with the lemon juice and 1 tablespoon water. Bring to a boil, then push the melted jam through a fine strainer. Carefully brush or spoon the sieved jam over the surface of the hot pudding to glaze. Serve with cream or custard.

traditional method   ⏱ **PREP** 15 MINS, PLUS SOAKING   **COOK** 40 MINS

1 Lightly grease an ovenproof dish with a little butter. Spread the remaining butter on the slices of bread. Cut each slice in half diagonally, then in half again to form 4 triangles.

2 Place the raisins in the bottom of the dish and arrange overlapping slices of bread across the top. Beat together the eggs, milk, cream, sugar, and vanilla extract in a bowl. Carefully pour the mixture over the bread, cover with foil, and leave to soak for at least 30 minutes.

3 Preheat the oven to 350°F (180°C). Place the dish in a deep roasting pan and pour boiling water into the pan to a depth of 1in (2.5cm). Bake in the oven for 30–40 minutes, until still slightly moist in the center, but not runny.

4 Meanwhile, put the jam in a small pan with the lemon juice and 1 tablespoon water. Bring to a boil, then push the melted jam through a fine strainer. Carefully brush or spoon the sieved jam over the surface of the hot pudding to glaze. Serve with cream or custard.

Both the rice and the peaches can be prepared one day ahead and kept covered in the refrigerator. Let the rice come to room temperature, or warm it in a low oven, before serving.

Creamy rice pudding with peaches

SERVES 4–6

½ cup short-grain rice
3½ cups milk, plus more if needed
2in (5cm) cinnamon stick
¼ cup superfine sugar
salt

FOR THE PEACHES
4 ripe peaches, peeled, halved, pitted, and
  cut into wedges
¼ cup superfine sugar, plus more if needed
1 cup dry red wine, plus more if needed

in the slow cooker   **PREP** 15–20 MINS, PLUS MACERATING AND STANDING   **COOK** HIGH 3–4 HRS

1 To prepare the peaches, put them in a non-metallic bowl and sprinkle with sugar; they may need more or less sugar than specified, depending on their sweetness. Pour over enough red wine to cover the fruit completely. Set a plate on top and leave to macerate in the refrigerator for at least 2 hours and up to 24 hours. Strain the liquid into a saucepan, bring to a boil, and simmer for 2 minutes until syrupy. Stir it back into the peaches.

2 Preheat the slow cooker, if required. Put the rice, milk, cinnamon stick, sugar, and a pinch of salt into the slow cooker and stir. Cover with the lid and cook on high for 3–4 hours, giving it a stir halfway through if needed. Let it stand for 1 hour. Discard the cinnamon stick, ladle into serving bowls, and serve with the peaches and wine syrup, which can be either warmed or cold.

traditional method   **PREP** 15–20 MINS, PLUS MACERATING AND STANDING   **COOK** 3 HRS

1 To prepare the peaches, put them in a non-metallic bowl and sprinkle with sugar; they may need more or less sugar than specified, depending on their sweetness. Pour over enough red wine to cover the fruit completely. Set a plate on top and leave to macerate in the refrigerator for at least 2 hours and up to 24 hours. Strain the liquid into a saucepan, bring to a boil, and simmer for 2 minutes until syrupy. Stir it back into the peaches.

2 Preheat the oven to 300°F (150°C). Put the rice, milk, cinnamon stick, sugar, and a pinch of salt into an ovenproof dish and stir. Put it in the oven for 3 hours, uncovered, and stirring gently every 30 minutes until the pudding is thick and creamy. Cover the dish with foil if it starts to brown too much.

3 Remove the pudding from the oven. Carefully slip a spoon down the side and stir from the bottom. Let it stand for 1 hour. Discard the cinnamon stick, ladle into serving bowls, and serve with the peaches and wine syrup, which can be either warmed or cold.

You could change the cinnamon in these dumplings for grated nutmeg or pie spice, and use orange zest instead of lemon for a slightly sweeter finish.

Apple dumplings

SERVES 4

scant 2 cups self-rising flour, sifted
½ cup vegetable shortening
1 tsp ground cinnamon, plus extra to serve
grated zest of 1 lemon

4 cooking apples, peeled and cored but left whole
1 tbsp demerara sugar
½ cup golden raisins
confectioner's sugar, to serve

in the slow cooker   ⏱ PREP 20 MINS   COOK HIGH 3–4 HRS

1 Preheat the slow cooker, if required. To make the pastry, put the flour, shortening, cinnamon, and lemon zest into a bowl. Then slowly trickle in about ½ cup of cold water and mix together until it forms a dough.

2 Roll out the pastry and cut out 4 circles, large enough for each apple. Sit an apple on each round, sprinkle the demerara sugar into the apple holes, and add the raisins to each. Brush the edges of the pastry with water and bring them together at the top, pinching to secure.

3 Turn the apples over so the sealed side is face down. If you have any pastry left over, you could fashion leaves and stalks for the dumplings. Loosely wrap foil around each, and seal. Sit the dumplings in the slow cooker and add boiling water so it is about 1in (2.5cm) deep. Cover with the lid and cook on high for 3–4 hours. Lift the dumplings out of the slow cooker and remove the foil—be careful because they will be very hot. Sprinkle the dumplings with confectioner's sugar and ground cinnamon and serve with cream, custard, or ice cream.

traditional method   ⏱ PREP 20 MINS   COOK 30–40 MINS

1 Preheat the oven to 350°F (180°C) and lightly grease a baking sheet. To make the pastry, put the flour, shortening, cinnamon, and lemon zest into a bowl. Then slowly trickle in about ½ cup of cold water and mix together until it forms a dough.

2 Roll out the pastry and cut out 4 circles, large enough for each apple. Sit an apple on each round, sprinkle the demerara sugar into the apple holes, and add the raisins to each. Brush the edges of the pastry with water and bring them together at the top, pinching to secure.

3 Turn the apples over so the sealed side is face down. If you have any pastry left over, you could fashion leaves and stalks for the dumplings. Sit them on the baking sheet. Cook in the oven for 30–40 minutes until golden. Sprinkle the dumplings with confectioner's sugar and ground cinnamon and serve with cream, custard, or ice cream.

Tapioca is a starchy substance derived from the cassava plant. It is usually simmered in milk or coconut milk, but here fruit juice is used, which turns this dish into something far more lively.

Tapioca pudding

SERVES 4–6

10oz (300g) can mandarin oranges in natural juice
7oz (220g) can pineapple slices in natural juice
1¾–2 cups orange juice
½ cup tapioca
¼ cup superfine sugar, or to taste

½ cup plain Greek-style yogurt or lightly
   whipped cream (optional)
freshly grated nutmeg or ground
   cinnamon (optional)

in the slow cooker   **PREP** 10 MINS   **COOK** HIGH 1½–2 HRS

1 Preheat the slow cooker, if required. Strain the juice from the oranges and pineapple into a large measuring cup and add orange juice to equal 1¾ cups. Set aside. Chop the pineapple into small pieces and set aside with the mandarin segments.

2 Put the tapioca in the slow cooker and stir in the juice. Cover with the lid and cook on high for 1½–2 hours until the tapioca "pearls" become translucent and the mixture is thick and glossy.

3 Stir in sugar to taste, then stir the fruit into the pudding and serve hot. Top with a spoonful of plain yogurt or whipped cream, if desired, and sprinkle with a little nutmeg or cinnamon, if using.

traditional method   **PREP** 10 MINS   **COOK** 50 MINS

1 Strain the juice from the oranges and pineapple into a large measuring cup and add orange juice to equal 2 cups. Set aside. Chop the pineapple into small pieces and set aside with the mandarin segments.

2 Put the tapioca and juice in a heavy-based saucepan over high heat and bring to a boil, stirring. The liquid will be very cloudy as it comes up to a boil, but will then clear. Boil gently for 30–50 minutes (or as directed on the package), stirring often, and brushing down the side of the pan with a pastry brush, until the small "pearls" become translucent and the mixture is thick and glossy.

3 Remove the pan from the heat and stir in sugar to taste, then stir the fruit into the pudding and serve hot. Top with a spoonful of plain yogurt or whipped cream, if desired, and sprinkle with a little nutmeg or cinnamon, if using.

This traditional English pudding was originally steamed in a cloth or shirt sleeve. Here it is cooked as a roll with a layer of jam running through it. Raspberry jam works particularly well.

Hot jam roll

SERVES 4

2 cups self-rising flour, sifted
½ cup shortening
4–5 tbsp jam

in the slow cooker   **PREP** 15 MINS   **COOK** HIGH 3–4 HRS

1 Preheat the slow cooker, if required. Put the flour and shortening into a mixing bowl and add ½ cup water. Using a round-bladed knife, mix to a soft, but not wet dough. Add more water, if necessary. Put the dough onto a floured work surface and roll it out to a rectangle measuring about 7 x 10in (18 x 25cm), ensuring it is no wider than the dimension of the slow cooker.

2 Gently warm the jam in a small pan, but do not allow it to get too hot or it will burn. Spread the jam over the pastry, ensuring there is a narrow border of pastry around the edge so the jam doesn't ooze out when the pastry is rolled up. Roll it up loosely and wrap in parchment paper and foil, making a pleat in each to allow for the pudding to expand. Pinch the foil at the edges to secure it tightly so no moisture can get in. Secure with string, looping it around the pudding to form a handle.

3 Sit the pudding in the slow cooker, seam-side up, and pour in just enough hot water to come halfway up the side of the pudding, cover with the lid, and cook on high for 3–4 hours. Remove and leave for 10 minutes, then carefully remove the string, foil, and parchment paper, being careful as it will be incredibly hot. Serve sliced with custard or cream.

traditional method   **PREP** 15 MINS   **COOK** 30–40 MINS

1 Put the flour and shortening into a mixing bowl and add ½ cup water. Using a round-bladed knife, mix to a soft, but not wet dough. Add more water, if necessary. Put the dough onto a floured work surface and roll it out to a rectangle measuring about 7 x 10in (18 x 25cm), ensuring it is no wider than the dimension of a steaming pan.

2 Gently warm the jam in a small pan, but do not allow it to get too hot or it will burn. Spread the jam over the pastry, ensuring there is a narrow border of pastry around the edge so the jam doesn't ooze out when the pastry is rolled up. Roll it up loosely and wrap in parchment paper and foil, making a pleat in each to allow for the pudding to expand. Pinch the foil at the edges to secure it tightly so no moisture can get in.

3 Put the roll in the steaming pan and place it over a pan three-quarters filled with simmering water. Cover and steam for 1½–2 hours or until firm to the touch. Top up with water if it gets too low. Rest for 10 minutes then unwrap. Serve sliced with custard or cream.

Index

Entries in *italics* indicate references
to techniques.

Author

Heather Whinney is an experienced food writer and home economist. She has been the food editor of *Family Circle* and *Prima* magazines and freelance food editor at *BBC Good Food* magazine, as well as working freelance for several publications such as *Good Housekeeping* and *Woman and Home*. She is now the contributing food editor for *Prima*. As a working mother bringing up a family, she understands the issues families and busy households face when it comes to putting good food on the table. Her style and food philosophy has always remained constant—to keep it simple, and write easy recipes for the everyday cook. She is the author of *Cook Express* (2009) and co-author of *The Diabetes Cooking Book* (2010).

Acknowledgments

Heather Whinney would like to thank:

Emma Callery for excellent recipe editing and Tia Sarkar at DK for sterling hard work—what a good team we've made. Thanks to my husband Jos who is my ever-reliable recipe taster and critic and to my daughters Kim and Lorna for having healthy appetites!

Dorling Kindersley would like to thank:

Photography art direction: Luis Peral, Sara Robin
Food stylists: Katie Giovanni, Bridget Sargeson
Prop stylist: Rob Merret
Recipe testers: Jane Bamforth, Rebecca Blackstone, Louisa Carter, Sonja Edridge, Jan Fullwood, Katy Greenwood, Sylvain Jamois, Ann Reynolds, Natalie Seldon
Image retouching: Steve Crozier
Indexer: Hilary Bird

Thanks also to Kajal Mistry and David Fentiman for editorial assistance; and to Danaya Bunnag for design assistance.